Dictionary of
Literary Terms

Dictionary of Literary Terms

Harry Shaw

McGRAW-HILL BOOK COMPANY

New York   St. Louis   San Francisco
Düsseldorf / Johannesburg / Kuala Lumpur / London
Mexico / Montreal / New Delhi / Panama
Rio de Janeiro / Singapore / Sydney / Toronto

Dictionary of Literary Terms

Library of Congress Cataloging in Publication Data

Shaw, Harry, 1905-
    Dictionary of literary terms.

    1. Literature-Terminology.   I. Title.
PN44.5.S46   803   72-179884
ISBN 0-07-056490-6   JUL 13 72

Preface

This book defines, explains, and, where feasible, illustrates all literary terms, references, and allusions that today's general reader and student are likely to encounter. And its scope is broad, taking literature to include magazines and newspapers as well as books, and reaching out to encompass the works that often are not even printed: films, plays, television programs, and speeches.

The information is aimed at the ordinary reader, the student, and the aspiring poet, novelist, and dramatist. Because the aim is to communicate, the information provided is spelled out in simple, easy-to-understand language. Further, the descriptions are full and normally include illustrations of the term "in action." Dictionaries have improved since the days of Samuel Johnson, but they can still perplex the neophyte with an array of alternative definitions, each of them terse, technical, and requiring further interpretation.

Preface

That the facts of a definition are indispensable but not always fully revealing is indicated by this passage from Charles Dickens's *Hard Times:*

> "Bitzer," said Thomas Gradgrind. "Your definition of a horse."
>
> "Quadruped. Graminivorous. Forty teeth, namely twenty-four grinders, four eyeteeth, and twelve incisive. Sheds coat in the spring; in marshy countries sheds hoofs, too. Hoofs hard, but requiring to be shod with iron. Age known by marks in mouth." Thus (and much more) Bitzer.
>
> "Now, girl number twenty," said Mr. Gradgrind. "You know what a horse is."

No one can deny that Bitzer unfolded factual details, but it is doubtful that he or anyone else would recognize a horse encountered in real life if this definition (not greatly unlike a modern dictionary entry) provided the only facts available.

Anyone who thinks of an *apostrophe* as an upended comma is not entirely mistaken, but he should know that the apostrophe is also an important literary device which contains some of the most telling and profound thoughts in world literature. In this work, an apostrophe is defined, explained, and illustrated in such a way that a reader will understand the term in the context in which he finds it and will instantly recognize this conventional device whenever and wherever he encounters it thereafter.

Preface

If a reader owns and uses a good dictionary, he can learn that *graffiti* has nothing to do with either "graphs" or "graft." He will discover that he has his own *idiolect*, regardless of his "ideas" or lack of them or his opinion of "idols" and "idleness." He can find out that a *homily* is not a cereal, that *parallelism* is unrelated to a contraption in a gymnasium, and that *paronomasia* is not some kind of disease. But unless these (and hundreds of other terms) are explained and illustrated, his newfound knowledge is likely to vanish quickly.

These and approximately 2,000 additional terms in this book come from a variety of separate and interrelated disciplines. There are terms originating in the elements of the language itself, like *homophone* and *sibilant*. There are those that come from the way elements are employed or are connected, like *intonation, inversion,* or *combining form.* There are terms that come from rhetoric; they describe the devices writers use to convey more meaning than would seem to reside in the bare bones of their words, like *allusion, hyperbole, irony.*

There are also terms that denote form and structure, many of which are essential tools of literary classification: *anapest, epigram, catachresis, profile, short story, rondel.* Finally, there are terms taken from the varied mechanical processes of setting type, reading proof, and printing and binding books. Harry Shaw

Preface

has worked on the assumption that no term in reasonably general use that describes the production of literature is outside his scope, because all these terms are relevant to the interests of the student, the practitioner, and the serious reader.

Professor Shaw comes by his interest in this subject honestly; in the words of the citation read when Davidson College named him Doctor of Letters, his scholarship, teaching, editing, and writing serve "all who read and write the English language." In his books and in his work, he has championed clarity, simplicity, and grace. Anyone who has been subjected to the influence of this master teacher—as this writer was—knows that he feels strongly that although the art of writing cannot always be taught, reading appreciatively can be—and readers and writers alike need some understanding of the tools of the writer's trade. To the extent that this work makes a mastery of these tools possible, it will have served its purpose.

Daniel N. Fischel

Dictionary of Literary Terms

A

Abecedarian

A member of a sixteenth-century religious sect that despised learning because its followers believed all that was needed to interpret divine revelations was the guidance of a Holy Spirit. The lowercase term *abecedarian* is occasionally applied to (1) anyone who scorns formal learning, (2) one learning the alphabet, and (3) one who teaches the rudiments of learning. As an adjective, *abecedarian* means "primary," "elementary," "rudimentary."

abecedarium

An alphabet book, a *primer.

abecedarius

A composition in verse in which the *stanzas or *lines begin with the letters of the alphabet in regular order. The first stanza of Chaucer's *A B C* begins with the word *Almighty,* the second with *Bountee,* the third with *Comfort,* etc. A more rigid kind of abecedarius is that in which every word in a line begins with the same letter, progressing through the alphabet from line to line:

>An Austrian army, awfully array'd,
>Boldly by battery besieged Belgrade.

ab initio

This Latin term means "from the beginning," "from the very outset."

ab ovo

A Latin term meaning "from the egg," that is, "from the beginning," "from the start."

abracadabra

A word now used to mean "nonsense," "gibberish," or "jargon," *abracadabra* originally was the name of a mystical charm worn about the neck or spoken aloud to ward off evil spirits, misfortune, or death.

abridged

Abridged means "shortened by condensation or omission." *Unabridged* means "complete," "not cut down." Many works of literature have been abridged with the aim of making them more easily and quickly read. Publishers of books in paperback form usually announce that their versions are "complete and unabridged," that is, copies of the original works.

abridgment

The noun form of *abridged* is *abridgment* (from Latin *ad,* meaning "toward," and *breviare,* meaning "to shorten"), a condensed version intended to retain the principal ideas and basic form of the original. Terms related to *abridgment* are *abstract, *aperçu, *brief, *condensation, *conspectus, *epitome, *précis, *redaction, *résumé, *summary, and *synopsis.

abstract

This term, derived from a Latin word meaning "to pull or draw away," is applied to a *summary of a document, speech, or statement. *Abstract* is usually applied to nonfictional types of writing; it presents the main points of the original in the order of their first appearance; it neither possesses nor claims independent literary worth of its own.

abstract diction

A word or phrase is abstract when it is not specific and definite in meaning.

Abstract words vary in their degree of indefiniteness. Such words as *nation, crime,* and *taxation* are not really specific, but they have more tangible meanings than *beauty, culture,* and *honor.* The word *housing* is somewhat abstract, but the idea can be made less so by substituting terms like *apartment house, mansion, bungalow, cabin, shanty,* and *lean-to.*

Abstract nouns, especially prevalent in philosophical essays, are less exact and less forceful (because less understood) than concrete words. Consequently, a writer may use an abstract term but immediately make it more communicative by providing concrete examples of what is meant or by translating its meaning into other terms. In Robert Louis Stevenson's *An Apology for Idlers* appears this sentence: " . . . The services of no single individual are indispensable." Despite the partial abstraction of "services," "individual," and "indispensable," the statement is seemingly clear. Yet Stevenson follows it with a concrete *figure of speech which reinforces his idea: "Atlas was just a gentleman with a protracted nightmare." The concept is now unmistakable.

An effective writer, Stuart Chase, once used the abstract term * *laissez faire* and several allied ones but made his meanings clear by equating governmental "laissez faire" with a city that had "no traffic system"; by referring to "enforced competition" as a system in which "traffic cops protect little cars"; by referring to "government regulation" as being similar to "traffic cops advising how to drive"; and by referring to "government ownership" as a procedure according to which "a traffic officer throws the driver out and gets behind the wheel himself."

Abstract diction appears often in literature and cannot be avoided. But many writers unfailingly remember the adage that "all we know gets into our heads as itemized bits of experience" and thus employ concrete diction or else attempt to make abstract diction more specific and meaningful.

For instance, in *The Eve of St. Agnes,* John Keats wished in the first stanza to make as concrete and specific as possible the somewhat abstract idea of "coldness." Not a single word in the stanza is abstract:

> St. Agnes' Eve—Ah, bitter chill it was!
> The owl, for all his feathers, was a-cold;
> The hare limped trembling through the frozen
>   grass,
> And silent was the flock in woolly fold:
> Numb were the Beadsman's fingers, while he told
> His rosary, and while his frosted breath,
> Like pious incense from a censer old,
> Seemed taking flight for heaven, without a death,
> Past the sweet Virgin's picture, while his prayer
>   he saith.

abstraction

The act of considering or evaluating something in terms of general characteristics or qualities apart from specific objects and concrete realities. For example, Robert Burns stated that his love was like "a red, red rose." From the actual qualities of a rose he abstracted the ideas of beauty, freshness, and fragrance and omitted the realities of thorns and decay.

This process of thought has led to the further meaning of *abstraction* as something considered visionary and unrealistic.

Absurd, Theater of the

See THEATER OF THE ABSURD.

academic

This term is derived from the name of the olive grove where Plato had his "classroom" in fourth-century-B.C. Athens. *Academic* is now applied to the nature and functions of schools and colleges, particularly to studies that are not directly vocational or applied. Hence come the meanings of *academic* as "theoretical," "unrealistic," "not useful," and "impractical."

Academic drama is a name given to plays written, studied, and produced by students in continental Europe and in Great Britain during the *Renaissance. *Academy* is a name for a body of established opinion, such as the French Academy established in the seventeenth century to compile a dictionary and to set authoritative standards for the French language.

academician

A member of an association or institution for the advancement of learning; a follower of artistic or philosophical traditions and movements.

acatalectic

This is a term applied to a line of poetry that carries out the full basic metrical pattern of the poem in which it appears; a verse complete in the number of syllables called for by a metrical scheme. A *catalectic line is one that is incomplete at the end, that is, not containing the full number of syllables called for by a set metrical pattern. Of these lines from a poem by John Keats, the first is acatalectic (full), whereas the second line is catalectic (lacking the final syllable):

And this / is why / I so/journ here
Alone / and pale/ly loit/ering.

accent

Several meanings of *accent* apply particularly to writing and speech.

1. Accent is the *emphasis or *stress placed on a certain *syllable in a foot of poetry. Three types of accent appear in English: *word* accent, *rhetorical* accent (in which the placement of stress determines meaning), and *metrical* accent. English verse consists of a series of stressed and unstressed syllables. For details on this meaning of accent, see FOOT, METRICS, SCANSION.

2. When some person or some character in a literary selection has an accent, he reveals his distinguishing regional or national manner of pronouncing or the tone of his voice ("a Boston accent," "a Southern accent," "a hillbilly accent," "a Scottish accent"). In literature, such accents are indicated largely or entirely by the dialogue of the various characters.

3. *Accent* may refer to emphasis placed upon some part

of an entire artistic design or composition. In most of Thomas Hardy's novels, the role of Egdon Heath is accented (played up, made dominant); the accent in Poe's *The Fall of the House of Usher* is on foreboding, decay, and impending doom; in *Othello,* the theme and role of jealousy are accented.

accidence

The Latin word from which *accidence* is derived means "that which befalls" and is closely related to *accident.* Accidence deals with the *inflections of words, the changes they undergo as a result of *declension, *conjugation, and *comparison (the accidents or nonessentials of words). The changes from *boy* to *boy's, swim* to *swam,* and *good* to *better* constitute accidence (but do not fundamentally change basic meanings).

accismus

From a Greek word meaning "demure" or "coy," accismus is an insincere refusal of something offered with the hope that the offer will be renewed forcefully. In Shakespeare's *Richard III,* the title character, desperately plotting to be crowned, protests that he is "unfit for state and majesty."

acronym

A *coined word, a *neologism, formed with the initial letters or syllables of successive words in a phrase: *loran* ("long-range navigation"), *radar* ("radio detecting and ranging"), *pluto* ("pipeline under the ocean").

acrostic

A composition of some sort (puzzle, poem, series of lines) in which the first, last, or other particular letters form a word, phrase, or sentence. If written on successive lines, the words *heart, ember, abuse, resin,* and *trend* read the same from left to right and top to bottom. The first letters of the surnames of five ministers of Charles II of England (Clifford, Arlington, Buckingham, Ashley, and Lauderdale) formed an *acronym reputed to have given added meaning to the word *cabal* (clique, coterie). See ABECEDARIUS, ACRONYM.

act

One of the principal divisions of a play or opera. In classical drama, such major divisions were indicated by appearances of a *chorus, thus usually resulting in plays of five acts. Many Roman tragedies, following this division observed by Aristotle, also appeared in five acts. These divisions in tragic drama generally indicated action as follows: (1) preliminary and background information, details about characters and prior situations; (2) *complication, *rising action, increasing *conflict; (3) the *climax, or *crisis, a turning point in action involving the highest emotional response from spectator or reader; (4) *falling action; (5) final *catastrophe.

Elizabethan and other "modern" playwrights likewise tended to present tragic drama in five acts, but in the nineteenth century, certain dramatists, including Ibsen, began to write in four acts. Most modern full-length plays appear in three acts, although some have only two, like most comic *operas and *musical comedies. Some modern plays eliminate act structure entirely and appear as scenes or episodes. See ONE-ACTER.

action

Action means an event or series of real or imagined happenings forming the subject of a novel, story, play, or narrative poem. Such an unfolding of events in drama or a work of fiction supplies an answer to the question "What happens?" What characters say, do, and think and what results from their saying, doing, and thinking constitute the action of all narrative literature. A *planned* series of related and interrelated actions, which may be physical or mental or both, is said to make up the *plot of a work of fiction or drama.

acyrologia

This word, from a Greek term meaning "improper word choice," refers to a *euphemism, a supposedly delicate way of expressing an idea thought to be uncouth. Example: *mortal remains* for *corpse* or *cadaver.*

adage

A traditional saying expressing a universal observation or experience, such as "It never rains but it pours" and "It is always darkest before the dawn." *Adage,* a statement given credit by general acceptance and long usage, is related to other terms that denote expressions of general truth: *aphorism, *apothegm, *axiom, *gnomic, *maxim, *motto, *proverb, *saw, and *saying.

adaptation

The recasting of a work to fit another medium while retaining the *action, *characters, and as much as possible of the language and *tone of the original. *Novels are frequently adapted for films, the stage, or television; a play may reappear as an adaptation in novel form or as a radio presentation, etc. Stephen Vincent Benét's short story *The Devil and Daniel Webster* was adapted for films and radio.

ad astra

A Latin phrase meaning "to the stars." The term sometimes appears in literature as *ad astra per aspera* ("to the stars through difficulties") and is often used to characterize the laborious efforts of writers as well as the struggles of some characters appearing in literary works.

ad captandum

This phrase means "for pleasing," "designed to attract or captivate." The term is used in *argumentation, where it frequently appears as *ad captandum vulgus* ("courting the crowd," "in order to please the mob"). Ad captandum argument tries to arouse the sympathy or emotion of uninformed readers and listeners.

addendum

An addition, something added, such as the *appendix to a *book. The plural, *addenda,* is used by some writers with a singular verb with the understanding that added materials combine to form one "supplement" or "one group of explanations."

ad hominem

Literally meaning "to the man," *ad hominem* is a term applied to statements or arguments that appeal to one's emotions, prejudices, or special interests rather than to one's reason or intellect. The phrase is used in *argumentation to signify remarks attacking an opponent's character and personality rather than answering his contentions and beliefs.

ad ignorantiam

A term applied to *argument that challenges one's opponent to disprove rather than seriously attempting to prove. An argument "to ignorance" consists of maintaining that one is right because no one can prove him wrong. A character in Mark Twain's *Roughing It*, contending that a buffalo can climb a tree, argues that no one has ever seen a buffalo fail to perform this feat.

ad infinitum

Literally "to the endless," *ad infinitum* is used to mean "without limit," "endlessly."

ad libitum

This Latin phrase means "at one's pleasure." In music, it means "not obligatory," "not so important that it cannot be omitted" (as contrasted with *obbligato*). In the abbreviated form *ad lib,* the meaning is "makeshift," "impromptu," "acting or speaking without preparation."

adventure story

In the sense that all *fiction and much *nonfiction deal with events and with undertakings of man's mind and body, nearly every work of literature can be called an adventure story. The term is usually applied to literary material in which the reader's primary attention is focused upon "What happens next?" to the exclusion of such questions as "Why?" and "How?" Well-known types of adventure stories are *science fiction, *Western stories, *mystery stories, and all writing in which *action seems more important than *characterization, *theme, or *setting. However, a reader might consider *Hamlet, War and Peace,* and *Moby Dick* as adventure stories (which they are); more skilled readers understand them to be adventure stories plus.

Aeolic

Also spelled *Eolic, Aeolic* refers to the Greek *dialect of ancient Aeolis and Thessaly, coastal regions of Greece. The term is applied also to a style of architecture used in Greek territories of the Aegean Sea in the seventh and sixth centuries B.C. Specifically, *Aeolic* is applied to the dialect in which certain ancient Greek poets, including Alcaeus and Sappho, wrote their lyric poems. See ALCAICS, SAPPHIC.

A related but different term, *Aeolian,* refers to Aeolus, who in classical mythology was the ruler of the winds and the legendary founder of the Aeolian (Greek) nation.

aesthetic distance

This term from criticism, and especially *New Criticism, means detachment from, and nonidentification with, the circumstances or characters of a work of art. It involves a kind of *objectivity which permits an author to present imagined characters or events without expressing his own views or revealing his own judgments and personality. Aesthetic distance also represents the degree of detachment and objectivity that a critical reader maintains if he wishes fully to understand and evaluate what he is reading. In short, aesthetic distance rules out personal involvement with subject matter on the part of both writer and reader, lest art become confused with reality. According to the theory of aesthetic distance, Hawthorne, for example, was not personally involved with the characters and episodes in *The Scarlet Letter;* a reader of this novel should form his opinions of it without regard to his own feelings about Puritanism, adultery, or hypocrisy. See CRITICISM, OBJECTIVE CORRELATIVE.

aesthetics

A study of the emotions and the mind in relation to their sense of beauty in literature (and all the fine arts) as distinguished from moral, social, political, practical, or economic considerations. Aesthetics is concerned with concepts of what is beautiful or ugly, sublime or comic, and has no direct concern for usefulness or morality. Aestheticism, a movement that followed "art for art's sake" (*ars gratia artis), has been influential in French, English, and American literature for the past century. The supreme statement on

the subject is John Keats's lines in his *Ode on a Grecian Urn:*
"Beauty is truth, truth beauty,"—that is all
Ye know on earth, and all ye need to know.

affaire d'honneur

A French term meaning "affair of honor" and, in literature, usually applied to a duel. Other somewhat related terms from French are *affaire d'amour* and *affaire de coeur* ("love affair").

affectation

Artificial behavior or manners intended to impress others, mannerisms for effect involving some kind of show or pretense. Characters in novels or plays who exhibit qualities or provide appearances not really possessed are usually considered by both author and readers to be artificial, pompous, and pitiable.

affective fallacy

The "error" of judging a literary work by its emotional effects upon readers; a confusion between the work itself and its results ("what it *is* and what it *does*"). This term is related to *intentional fallacy, the error (if such it be) of analyzing a literary work in terms of its author's expressed aim and biographical background. (See EXPLICATION, NEW CRITICISM.) Those critics who claim that these attitudes toward a work are genuine fallacies insist that Mark Twain's *Huckleberry Finn,* for example, should be judged for what it is and not for its effects upon readers' opinion of slavery or Twain's disclaimer of motives and plot. Perhaps most readers would agree with Alexander Pope:
In every work regard the writer's End,
Since none can compass more than they intend.
It should be noted that Aristotle's theory of *catharsis is a notable example of the affective fallacy.

affix

An element added to the *base, *stem, or *root of a word to form a fresh word or stem. The principal kinds of affix are *prefixes and *suffixes. The prefix *un-* is an affix which, added to *balanced,* makes *unbalanced.* The suffix *-ed* is an affix which, added to *wish,* makes *wished.* See COMBINING FORM.

afflatus

An impelling force acting from within a person. *Afflatus* is synonymous with *inspiration.* Many writers have claimed that they received *divine afflatus in the conception and execution of a given work, meaning that they experienced communication to their inner beings of knowledge and insight from some outside source. See DIVINE AFFLATUS.

aficionado

A term from Spanish meaning "affectionate." In literary circles, one may be referred to as an aficionado (devotee, lover, admirer) of the *mystery story, or *drama, or any other *genre or even individual author.

a fortiori

A Latin term meaning "all the more," "even more certain," "for a still stronger reason." The term is used in such expressions as *a fortiori proof* and *a fortiori argument.*

agape

This is a term from Greek meaning the unselfish love of one person for another. Agape is not related to filial or parental love, which may be thought to be obligatory, nor does it have sexual implications. "Brotherly and sisterly love" is the closest English *synonym for this term.

agenda

A list, outline, or plan of things to be done, items to be considered, and matters to be discussed or voted upon. The singular of this term, which is derived from a Latin word meaning "to do," is the rarely used *agendum.*

agent provocateur

A French term for a secret operative hired to entice or trap suspected persons into performing illegal acts that will make them liable to arrest and punishment.

Age of Reason

Any period in history noted for its critical approach to social, religious, and philosophical concerns; an age which tends to deny beliefs or systems not based upon, or justified by, reason. It is especially a term applied to the seventeenth- and eighteenth-century philosophical trend in Europe and Great Britain that emphasized the importance of scientific methods and discoveries and that tried to overthrow entrenched superstitions and tyrannies of all kinds, social, religious, and political. A French writer, Diderot, summed up the extreme aims of "enlightened" thought when he wrote, "Man will never be free until the last king is strangled with the entrails of the last priest." Less radical advocates of the philosophy of the *Enlightenment were Benjamin Franklin and Thomas Jefferson. See DEISM.

agitprop

A coinage from abbreviations of *agitation* and *propaganda.* A Russian term in origin, *agitprop* refers to a governmental agency that directs agitation and propaganda and to a person trained to take part in such activities.

Agnus Dei

A Latin term meaning "lamb of God," emblematic of Jesus Christ. The phrase refers to any representation of the figure of Christ, to a wax medallion stamped with this image, to a *chant preceding a Roman Catholic mass, and to certain music used in connection with still other ecclesiastical services.

agon

A Greek term meaning "a contest." In ancient Greek drama, *agon* was the name of a debate or argument between two characters, each of whom was supported by a *chorus. In every kind of literature, *agon* refers to *conflict and is a *root appearing in such words as *antagonist, *deuteragonist, *protagonist, and *tritagonist.

agrarianism

A word of several meanings; in literature, a term referring to a way of life associated with a farm economy and with a country habitation, villages, and hamlets as contrasted with urban and industrial society. The term *agrarian* has often been applied to a group of early twentieth-century American writers who opposed industrial capitalism and urged "a return to the land." See PASTORAL, REGIONALISM.

airbrushing

The use of an airbrush to produce an art object or to improve the appearance of one. Airbrushes, often used in preparing photographs and *line drawings for reproduction in *periodicals and *books, are atomizers which, through the use of compressed air, discharge sprays of paint or watercolor pigment.

alarum

An archaic form of *alarm*. In early drama, *alarum* was used in *stage directions to signify a call to battle, one heard offstage, indicated by the sound of trumpets, drums, and clashing weapons. The phrase is sometimes written "alarums and excursions," especially when the alarum involves a brief appearance of soldiers running on and off stage.

alazon

A stock character, the braggart of Greek comedy. Under one name or another, such a type appears as the *miles gloriosus of Plautus, in Shakespeare's *The Comedy of Errors,* and in Molière's *Tartuffe.*

alba

A French lyric, usually involved with the parting of lovers at sunrise. (The word *alba* is a Provençal term for dawn.)

alcaics

Verses written in the manner of Alcaeus, a sixth-century-B.C. Greek poet. Alcaics are poems of four stanzas of four lines each, each line having four stresses (accents). No true alcaics exist in the English language; the closest approximation is Tennyson's *Milton,* which begins:

O mighty-mouthed inventor of harmonies,
O skilled to sing of Time or Eternity,
God-gifted organ-voice of England,
Milton, a name to resound for ages.

alexandrine

A verse line with six *iambic *feet (iambic *hexameter) that derives its name from French romances about Alexander the Great. It was used in the early English sonnets of Wyatt and Surrey and appears in all *Spenserian stanzas. An *alexandrine* and its effect are illustrated in Alexander Pope's *Essay on Criticism:*

A need/less Al/exan/drine ends / the song
That, like / a wound/ed snake, / drags its /
slow length / along.

alias

An assumed name; another name. See ALLONYM.

alienation

Withdrawal or detachment from one's fellows or from society. A sense of alienation is dominant in much literature of the past half century, especially in the *Theater of the Absurd, in the doctrine of *existentialism, and in the beliefs of the *beat generation.

✗allegory

A method of representation in which a person, abstract idea, or event stands for itself *and* for something else. *Allegory* may be defined as extended *metaphor: the term is often applied to a work of fiction in which the author intends characters and their actions to be understood in terms other than their surface appearances and meanings. These subsurface or extended meanings involve moral or spiritual concepts more significant than the actual narrative itself.

The most famous and most obvious of such two-level narratives in English is Bunyan's *Pilgrim's Progress;* in this religious allegory, Christian, Faithful, Mr. Worldly Wiseman, and Despair are real people who are also symbols of mankind, personifications of abstract ideas applicable to everyone. In Spenser's *Faerie Queene,* figures are actual characters and also abstract qualities. Parts of Dante's *Divine Comedy* and Tennyson's *Idylls of the King* are allegorical in that action is revealed not so much for the story as for the purpose of presenting moral or spiritual truth.

Forms of allegory are the *parable, in which a story is told primarily to express a religious truth, and the *fable, in which animals by their speech and actions reveal supposed truths about mankind. *Satire can be a form of allegory, as in Swift's *Gulliver's Travels,* where the adventures of Lemuel Gulliver, surgeon, sea captain, and traveler, are intended as satiric comment on man's foibles and weaknesses. Aside from literature, a great painting or statue also suggests or implies far more than meets the eye.

allegro

A term derived from a Latin word meaning "lively, brisk, spirited" and closely related in origin and meaning to the word *alacrity.* In music and literature, *allegro* indicates rapid movement and brisk style. The best-known use of this word in literature, illustrating its basic meaning, is in Milton's *L'Allegro.*

alliteration

A device commonly used in poetry and occasionally in prose: the repetition of an initial sound in two or more words of a phrase, line of poetry, or sentence ("Cupid and my Campaspe played / At cards for kisses"). Alliteration is considered ornament or decoration to appeal to the ear, a device to create an effect such as *onomatopoeia. Shakespeare clearly made fun of alliteration in *A Midsummer Night's Dream:* "Whereat, with blade, with bloody blameful blade, / He bravely broach'd his boiling bloody breast." An American poet, Vachel Lindsay, created a similar effect in "Booth led boldly with his big bass drum," but his intent was not to mock the device. Coleridge's line "The fair breeze blew, the white foam flew" and Tennyson's "The moan of doves in immemorial elms / And murmuring of innumerable bees" illustrate the appealing effects of alliteration and closely related methods of ornamentation.

allonym

The name of another person assumed by an author as a *pen name; also, a work published under a name that is not that of the author. The signature "Publius" masked the collaboration of Alexander Hamilton, John Jay, and James Madison in *The Federalist,* a series of papers influential in the ratification of the United States Constitution. *Allonym* is closely related to the general term *pseudonym,* a fictitious name used by an author to conceal his identity. Synonyms for *pseudonym* are *nom de plume and *alias.

allophone

A speech sound constituting one of the variants of a *phoneme (a basic unit of sound in any language). The short *a* in *bat* and the long *a* in *rate* are allophones.

allusion

A reference, usually brief, often casual, occasionally indirect, to a person, event, or condition presumably familiar but sometimes obscure or unknown to the reader. In *The Merchant of Venice,* Shakespeare used a Biblical allusion when he referred to a "Daniel come to judgment." Complex allusions abound in the work of such modern writers as T. S. Eliot; one cannot understand *The Love Song of J. Alfred Prufrock* without digging into its classical and Shakespearean allusions. The purpose of allusion is to bring in a wealth of experience and knowledge beyond the limits of plain statement.

almanac

In current use, an almanac is an annual publication containing a calendar, tables of phenomena, and much other statistical and general information on a variety of topics of widespread interest. This name for a *compendium of useful and interesting facts appears in Spenser's *Shepheardes Calender* (1579), a series of twelve poems under the subtitles of the twelve months. During the eighteenth century, almanacs began to contain humor and bits of homely wisdom, as in Franklin's *Poor Richard's Almanac* (1732–1758). The *Almanacs* of Davy Crockett in the middle of the nineteenth century contained *tall tales and other revelations and aspects of American frontier *culture.

alphabet verse

Whimsical, contrived *doggerel that employs all the letters of the alphabet. (See ACROSTIC, LIPOGRAM, PANGRAM.) Alphabet verse is a stunt without literary merit.

alter ego

A second self; a substitute or deputy. In Stevenson's famous story, Mr. Hyde is the alter ego of Dr. Jekyll. One's closest friend is often referred to in literature as one's alter ego.

altruism

Unselfish concern for, and devotion to, the welfare of others. The *antonym of *egoism, altruism has motivated much great literature of the past and present, expecially *problem novels and plays. An outstanding example of altruism at work is *Uncle Tom's Cabin,* an antislavery novel written without thought of fame or personal enrichment for the author.

ambience

The *mood, quality, *tone, character, or *atmosphere of an environment or *milieu. For example, it has been said that the company of actors to which Shakespeare belonged had a hard-working, professional ambience and that the ambience surrounding Hawthorne was one of guilt, gloom, and foreboding.

ambiguity

Doubtfulness or uncertainty of intention or meaning. Derived from a Latin word meaning "to wander about," "to waver," *ambiguity* refers to a statement that is subject to more than one interpretation. Some ambiguity is due to carelessness, but the term is applied in genuine literature to words that suggest two or more appropriate meanings or that convey both a basic meaning and overtones that are rich and complex. The difficulty in understanding some literature stems from a deliberate choice of words that simultaneously causes several different streams of thought in the reader's mind. See PLURISIGNATION.

ambivalence

Uncertainty; having opposed attitudes toward the same person or object; a capacity to see two or more sides of an issue or a personality. For example, some historians have claimed that Lincoln was ambivalent in his attitude toward the Civil War because his hatred of slavery conflicted with his overriding desire to save the Union.

ambrosia

In classical mythology, the food, drink, or perfume of the gods. In literature, *ambrosia* is used to refer to anything providing a sense of divinity, such as *afflatus, and to something delightful to touch, smell, or taste.

American Dream

This often-used term can have no clear and fixed definition because it means whatever its user has in mind at a particular time and has whatever interpretation the reader chooses to give it. Perhaps to most authors and readers, the phrase has *connotations of "life, liberty, and the pursuit of happiness." The American Dream, like all dreams, is a succession of images, emotions, and thoughts passing through the mind when one is either asleep or awake.

Americanism

A word, phrase, or other expression that is especially characteristic of the English language as spoken and written in the United States.

Amerind

This combination of *American* and *Indian* is the name of an individual of one of the native peoples of America, an Indian or Eskimo. *Amerind literature* refers to that body of writing and oral tradition developed by these aboriginal tribes: narrative accounts of heroes and gods, tribal traditions, and the rituals of seasonal and annual festivals.

amicus curiae

This Latin term meaning "friend of the court" refers to a by-stander (an individual or corporation) who suggests a matter of law designed to assist a court of law. More specifically, an amicus curiae is a lawyer who files a *brief or makes an oral argument before a court on behalf of a person or institution that is not actually a party to a pending case but is interested in it.

amorality

State of being outside the bounds of considerations to which moral standards apply. Some writers have insisted that their works are neither *moral* nor *immoral* and should not be judged by any known criteria of *morality.

amour propre

Literally meaning "love of oneself," this French term implies "self-esteem," "self-love," "self-respect."

ampersand

A character, or symbol (&), for *and.* The word is a contraction of *and per se and.* See PER SE.

amphibology

*Ambiguity in language; a statement susceptible of more than one interpretation. The prophecies made by the witches in Shakespeare's *Macbeth* are amphibologies.

amphibrach

A metrical *foot consisting of three *syllables, the second accented, the first and third unaccented:

    The old oak/en bucket, / the iron-/bound bucket.

amphigory

Nonsense verse; lines that sound all right but contain little sense or meaning. Swinburne mocked himself in a poem that begins with amphigory: "From the depth of the dreamy decline of the dawn through a notable nimbus of nebulous moonshine." See DOUBLE TALK.

amphimacer

A metrical *foot consisting of three *syllables, the first and last accented, the second unaccented: man-at-arms, three fif-teen. Tennyson's poem *The Oak* contains these lines: "Live thy life, / Young and old, / Like yon oak, / Bright in spring, / Living gold."

anabasis

A term from Greek meaning a "stepping up" or "going up." In literature, *anabasis* refers to a military expedition. The term was first applied in Xenophon's historical work the *Anabasis,* which narrates a march from the coast into the interior made by Cyrus the Younger against Artaxerxes.

anachronism

From a Greek word meaning "to be late," an anachronism is an error in chronology: placing an event, person, item, or language expression in the wrong period. For example, an absolute monarchy is an anachronism in the twentieth century. It is apparently difficult to avoid anachronisms when writing about an earlier time: Shakespeare referred to cannon in *King John,* a play set in time long before cannon were used in England; Shakespeare also placed a clock in *Julius Caesar.*

In a serious or realistic work of literature, an anachronism can destroy an effect and damage a reader's confidence in the author. Realizing this, motion-picture and television producers maintain staffs to avoid such mistakes as having Cleopatra wear a wristwatch. In romantic writing, not always to be taken seriously, an anachronism may seem amusing to an alert and knowing reader. Mark Twain deliberately used a series of anachronisms to achieve his satirically humorous purposes in *A Connecticut Yankee in King Arthur's Court.* And Edwin Arlington Robinson's Miniver Cheevy was a human anachronism ("born too late") who longed for earlier times in which he thought he might have been happier.

anacoluthon

Failure to complete a sentence according to the structural plan on which it was begun. From the Greek term meaning "out of sequence," anacoluthon may result from ignorance or carelessness, but it is also a recognized figure of speech used for emotional and rhetorical effects. The term is applied to units of writing greater than sentences, especially in talks where the speaker judges that a sudden shift in subject matter will regain the interest of his audience. See APOSIOPESIS.

anacreontics

Verse characterized by an erotic, passionate, and bacchanalian spirit resembling the mood and manner of poems by the Greek poet Anacreon (570–480 B.C.), famed for his drinking songs and love poems. An anacreontic stanza consists of four lines rhyming *abab* or *aabb;* each line has three *trochaic feet with one long syllable added at the end.

anacrusis

An unstressed syllable or group of syllables that begins a line of verse but is not considered a part of the first foot. The word *anacrusis* literally means an upward or back beat; in music, *anacrusis* refers to the note or notes preceding a downbeat. The word *from* in this line from Shelley's *To a Skylark* is an anacrusis: "From / rainbow / clouds there / flow not."

anadiplosis

Repetition in the first part of a clause or sentence of a distinctive word from the latter part of a preceding clause or sentence, sometimes with a change or extension of meaning. Such repetition is a device frequently used in political speeches and in literature of *persuasion.

anagnorisis

A term applied to ancient Greek tragedy signifying the critical moment of recognition or discovery preceding the reversal of fortune for the *protagonist. In comedy, anagnorisis leads to his success; in tragedy, it leads to his fall. See CLIMAX, CRISIS.

anagoge

A spiritual or mystical interpretation or application of words, especially of words considered to be of divine origin, such as those of the Bible. For example, Jerusalem is actually a city in ancient Palestine (Israel), but it is also an anagoge for "the heavenly city of God."

anagram

A word or phrase formed by the transposition of letters in another word. Samuel Butler's novel *Erewhon* derives its title from the word *nowhere.* A tribe in *Erewhon* is called the Sumarongi, which is *ignoramus* spelled backward. See ACRONYM, PALINDROME.

analects

Selected passages from the writings of an author or of different authors. The *Analects of Confucius* is a compilation of the *aphorisms and *maxims of this Chinese philosopher. See ANTHOLOGY, CHRESTOMATHY.

analogue

Something having analogy (similarity) to something else; for example, Racine has been called a French analogue of Shakespeare. In word study, related words from different languages are called analogues (*father, pater, padre,* etc.). In literature, two versions of the same story are called analogues; for example, many *Western stories are analogues of the *Robin Hood theme, in that the poor are defended against the rich and justice triumphs over might. *Romeo and Juliet* and *West Side Story* are analogues.

analogy

A partial similarity of features on which a comparison may be based: an analogy between the heart and a pump. In *argumentation and *persuasion, analogy is often employed as a form of reasoning in which one thing is compared to or contrasted with another in a certain respect on the basis of known similarity or dissimilarity in other respects. *Metaphors, *similes, and *antonomasia are forms of analogy. This simile from Pope's *An Essay on Criticism* is a kind of analogy:

'Tis with our judgments as our watches, none
Go just alike, yet each believes his own.

The implied comparison is always an analogy buried in a literary work, awaiting discovery by a reader. Much of *Gulliver's Travels* implies lessons the reader should draw (infer) from Swift's comparison of human life and a society of pygmies. Again, an entire literary selection may be based upon an extended analogy as, for example, Thomas Huxley's *A Liberal Education,* in which life is explained as analogous to a game of chess, or another essay by the same author in which the method of scientific investigation is compared with the customary workings of the human mind.

analysis

The separation or breaking up of a whole into its component parts and fundamental elements. Analysis involves a detailed examination of anything complex: a watch, an automobile, a chemical compound, a dynamo, a novel, essay, play, or poem. In literature, the term is applied to criticism and evaluation which view a work of art as an entity, an autonomous whole, and implies that the meaning, significance, and artistic worth of a selection can be unearthed by applying careful and logical systems of study to its individual parts and their organization.

Analysis is sometimes considered a more productive approach to the study of literature than any other means of attack. It outranks consideration of a literary work in relation to its author (the biographical approach) and in relation to its readers and backgrounds (the historical or social or philosophical approach). In analysis, focus is kept steadily and intently upon the work itself; "start with the text and stay with it" is an all-important maxim to analytical students of literature.

But if one does "start and stay with" the text itself, what is he expected to receive from his study? First, he looks for feelings, attitudes, and ideas as they are unfolded directly in essays and books of nonfiction and more often indirectly (by implication, to be inferred) in novels, stories, poems, and plays. The stuff of literature is human experience, and analytical reading will increase acquaintanceship with mankind's emotional, intellectual, moral, and spiritual experiences. And yet analysis involves more than *what* a work says; even more important is *how* the work says what it does. The technique of an author is not a series of devices superimposed upon his writing but a real part of what is said.

Various literary types require analytical study. Each requires its own method of approach, but all analytical consideration of literature focuses upon the selection itself

and bears upon the questions of *what* and *how*. In studying
an essay, an analytical reader is as much concerned with
*point of view, *purpose, *structure, and *theme as he is
when studying a novel or short story. In reading *fiction
and *drama, he directs attention to *plot, *characterization,
*motivation, and *setting. In studying poetry, a reader may
consider many of these matters as well as *meter, *rhyme,
*stanzaic structure, and the like.

anapest

A trisyllabic metrical foot consisting of two unstressed syllables
followed by a stressed syllable: *condéscend.*

> Oh he flies / through the air / with the great/est
> of ease.

anaphora

Also called *epanaphora,* anaphora is the repetition of a word
or words at the beginning of two or more successive lines
of verse, sentences, etc. A well-known example is the Beati-
tudes in the Bible, nine successive statements that begin
with "Blessed are." ("Blessed are the poor in spirit, for
theirs is the kingdom of heaven. Blessed are they that
mourn, for they shall be comforted," etc.)

anarchy

A state of society without law or firm government; social
and political disorder caused by the absence of regulating
controls. Some writers indirectly or directly have regarded a
cooperative and voluntary association of individuals and
groups as a political ideal superior to any possible form of
government.

anastrophe

Reversal of the usual, logical, or normal order of the parts
of a sentence. The second and third lines of this *quatrain
from Lewis Carroll's *Jabberwocky* exhibit anastrophe; the
first and fourth lines are in normal word order:

> He took his vorpal sword in hand;
> Long time the manxome foe he sought.
> So rested he by the Tumtum tree,
> And stood awhile in thought.

anathema

A curse or imprecation. The term also refers to a person or
thing accursed and assigned to damnation or destruction,
such as the fallen angels in Milton's *Paradise Lost.*

ancien régime

A French term meaning "old system" and referring particularly to the political and social regime in France before the

revolution of 1789. In literature, *ancien régime* is used to refer to any system or culture no longer prevailing.

anecdote

A short narrative account of an amusing, curious, revealing, or otherwise interesting event. Anecdotes present individuals in actions that illustrate or reinforce specific ideas and illuminate certain aspects of character or personality. Every effective anecdote has a single, definite point; in each, *dialogue, *setting, and *characters are subordinate to the main point. Except in poolrooms or behind closed doors, the anecdote never stands alone. But such short narratives abound in *exposition because of their effectiveness in making instantly clear otherwise possibly difficult ideas. Anecdotes "humanize" individuals and turn abstract concepts into concrete ones. The effectiveness of anecdotes is obvious: probably most of what is remembered about Washington or Lincoln or Churchill, for example, is recalled as stories (anecdotes) about them and their characteristics.

Anglicism

A word, idiomatic expression, or characteristic feature of the English language occurring in or borrowed by another language. The term is also applied to any word or expression used in England but not in general use in the United States. Examples of Anglicisms, also known as Briticisms, are *accumulator* for *storage battery, gaol* for *jail,* and *croft* for *small enclosed field.*

Anglo-Saxon

The name of a Teutonic tribal group which invaded what is now England in the fifth and sixth centuries. Comprised in the group were Angles, Saxons, and Jutes, who came from the northern shores of the Continent. The Angles gave their name (Angle-land) to England. The term *Anglo-Saxon* is now used to distinguish "English" peoples resident in Great Britain, the United States, Canada, and certain other dominions and territories. *Anglo-Saxon* is also a name given to the language known as *Old English. See SASSENACH.

angst

A feeling of anxiety, dread, or anguish. Angst is especially notable in the work of such writers as Jean-Paul Sartre and Albert Camus. See EXISTENTIALISM, THEATER OF THE ABSURD.

animadversion

Censure, criticism, adverse comment. Animadversion can be direct, as in Thomas Paine's pamphlet *Common Sense,* setting forth arguments for American independence from England, or indirect, as in Jonathan Swift's *A Modest Proposal,* a *satiric commentary on the plight of Ireland and the unfeelingness of the British government.

animation

A synonym for *liveliness* and *vivacity, animation* generally refers to the lifelikeness of characters in literature. In motion pictures (especially *cartoons) and in commercial advertisements for *television, *animation* refers to various mechanical devices that impart movement to inanimate objects.

animism

A belief that all natural objects and phenomena, as well as the universe itself, possess souls which exist apart from their material bodies. In line with this belief is the conviction that the soul, not the body, is the fundamental principle of life, health, and well-being.

anisometric

A term meaning "of unequal measurement," "not isometric," *anisometric* is applied to *stanzas composed of lines of unequal length. See SYMMETRY.

annalist

A recorder and chronicler of yearly events. A compiler of an *almanac is an annalist.

annals

Historical records, especially those of yearly events arranged in chronological order. *Annals* is also applied to periodical publications containing formal reports of scientific, political, literary, and other organizations.

anno Domini

A Latin phrase meaning "in the year of our Lord" and referring to time since the birth of Jesus Christ.

annotation

A note, or notes, supplied to explain, comment upon, or criticize literary or other written material. An annotated edition is one printed with comments by the author or by someone else. An outstanding example of annotation is the *variorum editions of the plays of Shakespeare.

annuals

Books or reports issued annually. Annuals usually review the events of the year just passed within specified fields of interest, such as college annuals. In the nineteenth century, the term was used for compilations of poems, essays, and stories issued in time for Christmas sale. Annuals are important in American literary history because in them first appeared the work of such writers as Poe, Hawthorne, and Emerson.

annus mirabilis

A Latin term meaning "wonderful year" and often applied to any period notable for its exciting, dramatic, or important events

anonymous

Without any name acknowledged as author; of unknown name. *Anonymous* is also applied to persons or places lacking unique character or distinction (a long row of anonymous buildings). As applied to unknown authors, the term is usually shortened to *anon; anon* is also an archaic adverb meaning "soon," "in a short time," or "immediately." The phrase "ever and anon" means "now and then."

antagonist

One who contends with, or opposes, another in a fight, conflict, or battle of wills. In literature, such an adversary is the principal opponent, or *foil, of the main character and is thus often called, sometimes loosely and incorrectly, the *villain. If the dominant plot centers in the career or exploits of a *hero who overcomes an opponent trying to thwart him, the latter is the antagonist, the hero a *protagonist. If main interest centers upon the career of a villain whose plans are overcome by a hero, the latter is the antagonist, the former a protagonist.

In *Hamlet,* Laertes and the King (Claudius) are among the antagonists; Hamlet is himself the protagonist. In Melville's *Billy Budd,* the young British sailor is the protagonist opposed by the master-at-arms of the *Indomitable,* the antagonist Claggart. See AGON, DEUTERAGONIST, PROTAGONIST, TRITAGONIST.

antecedent

An adjective meaning "preceding" and "existing, being, or going before." As a noun, *antecedent* refers to a prior event, circumstance, object, or the like. *Antecedents* is a noun meaning "ancestors" and also the history of one's earlier life. In grammar, an antecedent is a word or phrase which is replaced in a sentence by a pronoun or other substitute.

antecedent action

Events that took place before the beginning of action in a novel, play, story, or narrative poem. When it is necessary for the viewer or reader to understand what has happened in the past, this antecedent action is revealed in *dialogue or by direct *exposition. See FLASHBACK, IN MEDIAS RES.

antediluvian

The literal meaning of this adjective is "before the flood," meaning the flood that is recorded in the Bible (Genesis

7–8). The term means "antiquated" or "primitive" and, as a noun, names a person who is old or old-fashioned.

anthem

A *hymn of praise, patriotism, or devotion. In literature, *anthem* is sometimes used to refer to a *psalm or hymn chanted responsively (that is, in alternate parts).

anthology

A book or other collection of selected writings by various authors; sometimes, a gathering of works by one author. (The origin of *anthology* is revealing: it comes from two Greek words meaning "flower" and "to gather." *The Greek Anthology,* a grouping of early poems, was "a collection of flowers.") See CHRESTOMATHY.

anthropomorphism

Ascribing human form or characteristics to animals or inanimate objects. The mythological concept that the gods have human form and attributes is a form of anthropomorphism. Most *fables illustrate this belief. See BESTIARY.

antibacchius

A rare trisyllabic foot in which the accent falls on the first two syllables: *five dozen.*

anticlimax

A drop, often sudden and unexpected, from a dignified or important idea or situation to a trivial one, a descent from something sublime to something ridiculous. In fiction and drama, anticlimax involves action which is in disappointing contrast to a previous moment of intense interest; in a story or play anything which follows the *climax (the decisive, culminating struggle and resolution of *conflict) is called an anticlimax. Some popular novels devote a final chapter to comment on the futures of prominent characters whose actual story has already ended. Such an anticlimax satisfies the interest and curiosity of readers but frequently weakens narrative effect as a whole.

George Bernard Shaw had afterthoughts about his play *Pygmalion.* But even this talkative playwright ended his play at its climax, or nearly so, and added anticlimactic comments in a *sequel, a separate essay which begins, "The rest of the story need not be shown in action, and indeed, would hardly need telling if our imaginations were not so enfeebled by their lazy dependence on the ready-mades and reach-me-downs of the ragshop in which Romance keeps its stock of 'happy endings' to misfit all stories."

Pope effectively used anticlimax for humorous purposes in his line "Men, monkeys, lap-dogs, parrots, perish all," and so did E. E. Cummings in " 'Then shall the voices of liberty be mute?' / He spoke. And drank rapidly a glass of water."

antihero

A character who lacks the qualities needed for heroism; an antihero does not possess nobility of life or mind and does not have an attitude marked by high purpose and lofty aim. King Claudius in *Hamlet* is an antihero.

antimasque

A grotesque or comic performance, such as a dance or *mummery, presented before or between acts of a *masque (a pageant of music, drama, and dance). The purpose of an antimasque (or comic mask, as it is sometimes called) is to prevent the masque itself from becoming overly serious, meaningful, or disturbing. See COMIC RELIEF.

antiphon

Like an *anthem, an antiphon is a verse or song rendered responsively (in separate parts). The term is usually applied to church music; see LITURGY.

antiphrasis

The use of a word which conveys a sense opposite to its usual meaning. Antiphrasis can be a form of *irony, *sarcasm, or *satire. For instance, Shakespeare's Othello refers to "honest" Iago, when of course he is characterizing Iago as anything but honest.

antiquarianism

Interest in the customs, art, social structure, and history of earlier peoples and civilizations. Antiquarianism is a feature of *historical plays, *chronicles, and *epics (such as Spenser's *Faerie Queene*). The study of former times through literary and other artistic relics is an important part of *romanticism.

antistrophe

One of the three *stanzaic forms of the Greek choral *ode, the other two forms being *strophe and the *epode. In early Greek plays the chorus sang (chanted) an antistrophe while returning from left to right of the stage as an answer to a previous strophe (stanza).

antithesis

A *figure of speech in which contrary ideas are expressed in a *balanced sentence. The second part of "Man proposes, God disposes" is antithetically parallel to the first part. When asked where Polonius's corpse is secreted, Hamlet responds "At supper . . . not where he eats, but where he is eaten." Later in the same reply, Hamlet remarks, "We fat all creatures else to fat us, and we fat ourselves for maggots." See OXYMORON.

Outright assertion and flat denial are the clearest forms of antithesis, but a part of the word is *thesis, meaning a statement or proposal itself positive and thus more than merely "against" (*anti-*). Consequently, in a larger structural concept, the term *antithesis* may apply to a writer's entire contribution, an evaluation of what he was for and what he opposed. For example, with Shakespeare or Faulkner, formal religion may be a minor consideration, but it is a major one in the works of Dante and Milton. Whitman's insistence upon the brotherhood of man may or may not imply his opposition to an antithetical force or opinion. Discovering the pro and con of a writer's work is a valuable part of literary study.

antonomasia

The identification of a person by an *epithet or other term that is not his name; the use of a proper name for a common noun. Thus a great lover may be termed a Don Juan or an evil woman may be called a Jezebel. The device of antonomasia is shown in these lines from Gray's *Elegy:*

Some mute inglorious Milton here may rest,
Some Cromwell guiltless of his country's blood.

antonym

A word opposite in meaning to that of another word. All effective *dictionaries provide antonyms for selected entries; books of *synonyms and *thesauruses provide lists of antonyms.

aperçu

A French word literally meaning "perceived" and used in English to mean "a hasty glance," "a glimpse." In criticism, *aperçu* means an *outline or brief *summary.

aphaeresis

The loss of a letter or syllable at the beginning of a word, as in *count* from *account, cute* from *acute,* and *squire* from *esquire.*

aphorism

A brief, pithy, unusually concise statement of a principle, truth, or sentiment. Notable more for its thought and wisdom than its wit, an aphorism is closely related in meaning to such terms as *maxim, *saw, *adage, *proverb, and *epigram, all of which agree in denoting a sententious expression of a general truth or belief. Examples of aphorisms: Mark Twain, in commenting on his own preferences about afterlife, wrote, "Heaven for climate, hell for society," and Pope wrote, "The proper study of mankind is man."

apocalyptic

Characteristic of literature that provides a prophecy or revelation. The term is derived from the Apocalypse, or Revelation of Saint John the Divine, the last book in the

Bible. *Apocalyptic* is now used to refer to any literary selection that reveals and predicts the future.

apocope

Loss or omission of the last letter or syllable of a word. *Curio,* from *curiosity,* is an example of apocope.

apocryphal

This adjective means "of doubtful authenticity," "spurious," "mythical," or "untrustworthy." The term implies a mysterious or dubious source of origin and consequently suggests sham or fakery. It is derived from the noun *apocrypha,* a general term first and most prominently applied to writings not admitted by Protestants into the *canons of the Old and New Testaments (the Bible). In literary study, *apocryphal* refers to any piece of writing of unknown or uncertain authorship. For example, a few Elizabethan plays of doubtful origin, attributed to Shakespeare, are considered apocryphal and not in the Shakespearean canon. *Apocryphal* has been further extended in meaning so that it is now used to refer to a story *about* an individual which may or may not be authentic. Many *anecdotes about Shakespeare, Washington, Jefferson, Winston Churchill, and Joseph Stalin are considered apocryphal.

apodosis

In a conditional sentence, an apodosis is the clause expressing the consequence: "If you decide to leave, *then I will, too.*"

⳹Apollonian

An adjective referring to Apollo, the ancient Greek and Roman god of light, music, healing, prophecy, and poetry. *Apollonian* is used to describe writing and authors who are serene, calm, poised, disciplined, and well balanced. The cult of Apollo is often contrasted with that of Dionysus (which represented the frenzied and undisciplined in life and literature). See DIONYSIA.

apologue

A moral *fable or didactic narrative. As a form of *allegory, an apologue is represented by most of the *parables in the Bible, by some of Aesop's fables, and by James Thurber's collection of pithy tales entitled *Fables for Our Time.*

apology

An expression of regret, sorrow, or remorse; a defense and justification for some doctrine, piece of writing, cause, or action. The most famous apology of all time is Plato's dialogue in defense of Socrates before the tribunal that sentenced Socrates to death. At the end of *The Canterbury Tales,* Chaucer wrote what he called a "retractation," an apology for his work which is both an explanation and an expression of regret. One of Cardinal Newman's most famous writings is entitled *Apologia pro Vita Sua,* a spiritual autobiography. One of the most charming essays in English is Stevenson's *An Apology for Idlers.*

apophasis

Denial of one's intention to speak or write of a subject which is simultaneously named or suggested. Marcus Antonius (Mark Antony) illustrates apophasis in Shakespeare's *Julius Caesar:*

I come not, friends, to steal away your hearts.
I am no orator, as Brutus is;
But, as you know me all, a plain blunt man . . .
For I have neither wit, nor words, nor worth,
Action, nor utterance, nor the power of speech
To stir men's blood; I only speak right on.

aporia

The expression of a doubt, real or feigned, as to where to begin or what to do or say. At the beginning of *Paradise Lost,* Milton invokes aid for his "adventrous song . . . while it pursues / Things unattempted yet in prose or rime" and asks help for "what in me is dark."

aposiopesis

A sudden breaking off in the middle of a sentence, resulting from unwillingness or inability to proceed. In discussing his mother's hasty remarriage, Hamlet says:

Like Niobe, all tears—why, she, even she—
O God! a beast that wants discourse of reason
Would have mourned longer.

apostasy

Desertion of or departure from one's principles, religion, cause, or party. In a poem called *The Lost Leader,* Browning accused Wordsworth of apostasy when the latter changed his views from liberal to conservative:

He alone breaks from the van and the freemen—
He alone sinks to the rear and the slaves.

a posteriori

Latin for "from the one behind," this phrase means (1) from effect to cause and (2) based upon experimental data or actual observation. A posteriori argument is especially persuasive because it seems to be based on *objectivity. Many of the writings of Newton, Darwin, Huxley, and Einstein are built upon a posteriori argument. See A PRIORI.

apostrophe

A figure of speech in which a person not present or a *personified nonhuman object is addressed (spoken to). Characteristic instances of apostrophe in poetry are *invocations to the

*Muses and in *oratory to the shades of men such as Julius Caesar, Oliver Cromwell, and Thomas Jefferson. Wordsworth's *London, 1802* begins "Milton! Thou shouldst be living at this hour." (Milton died in 1674.) Writers of *whimsy and *humor occasionally employ the device: in 1942, E. B. White wrote an essay in letter form addressed to a man who had been dead for eighty years. The essay begins: "Miss Nims, take a letter to Henry David Thoreau. Dear Henry...." Inspired by Lord Byron's "Roll on, thou deep and dark blue ocean, roll," W. S. Gilbert wrote *To the Terrestrial Globe,* beginning "Roll on, thou ball, roll on!"

apothegm
A terse remark, pithy comment, instructive saying. An apothegm is a pointed, often startling *aphorism, such as Dr. Johnson's remark "Patriotism is the last refuge of a scoundrel."

apparition
A phantom or specter, a ghostly appearance. The meaning of *apparition* as "a wraith" has been extended to include any event or circumstance that appears remarkable. Washington Irving's "headless horseman" of Sleepy Hollow is an apparition.

appendix
Material added at the end of a *book or *article. An appendix is not part of the text but illustrates, expands, or illuminates it. An appendix provides useful information but is not essential to the work it follows. A *bibliography is an example of appendix material. See BACK MATTER.

appropriateness
The quality or state of being suitable, fitting, and proper. Applied to concerns of dress, behavior, manners, and morals, any comment on appropriateness involves taste and judgment. In a sense, literature always involves direct and basic considerations of appropriateness, of suitability, of fittingness.

One should and does ask such questions as "Are the *diction, *tone, and *style of this selection appropriate to its message?" "Is this an appropriate subject for treatment by this particular writer?" "Are conclusions drawn appropriate to facts and ideas presented?" "Is the *form (type) of this selection appropriate to the particular thesis involved?"

All selections of good literature are appropriate, although not necessarily appropriate for every reader at a given age level or in a given time or place. Seeking the appeals and levels of literature appropriate now, and seeking to elevate these levels and appeals during months and years and decades of reading, are primary purposes in studying literature. It is also true that a specific literary work may be appropriate on one level for a reader now and, after he has read widely and matured steadily, may be even more appropriate at a later time. Shakespeare's *Julius Caesar* is suitable in one sense for reading in the eighth grade and even more fitting for study in adult life.

approximate rhyme

A term suggesting that *rhyme (repetition of the same or similar sounds) need not always be entirely accurate and that it can merely approach a standard. Approximate rhyme may also be called *near rhyme, *half rhyme, *imperfect rhyme, and *slant rhyme. An approach to rhyme, but not its full attainment, can be observed in these lines from Emily Dickinson:

> The Brain, within its Groove
> Runs evenly—and true—
> But let a Splinter swerve—
> 'Twere easier for you—

a priori

This term has basic meanings resembling those of *a posteriori.* It means "from cause to effect" and "from a general law to a particular instance." (See DEDUCTION.) It also means "nonanalytic" in the sense of "not being based on prior study or examination." The distinction is that one usually refers to "a posteriori argument" and to "a priori judgment (or belief)."

apron

The edge of a stage in front of the *proscenium arch. The Elizabethan theater, for which Shakespeare designed his plays, was built around such an apron stage.

aquatint

A process of producing tones in an engraving by etching with acid on copperplate intended for printing. Etching in aquatint is a standard engraving process.

aqua vitae

Literally meaning "water of life," *aqua vitae* applies to spirituous liquor but is occasionally used to refer to *euphoria or to any state or condition of happiness and well-being or to a cause for such emotions.

Arcadia

A mountainous region of ancient Greece, famed for the pastoral and contented innocence of its inhabitants, an ideal rustic paradise. *Arcadian* is applied to any region and period where life is considered idyllic, such as the imagined golden age described by Virgil or Shakespeare's Forest of Arden. See PASTORAL.

arcane

Secret, obscure, mysterious. Literature which appears to have secret meanings or to imply hidden mysteries is often referred to as arcane. Contemporary works by John Barth and Samuel Beckett have been so characterized.

archaism

A word or phrase no longer in actual use, such as *enow* for *enough* and *gramercy* for *thank you.* Two archaic words appear in these lines from Coleridge's *The Rime of the Ancient Mariner:*

> "Hold off! unhand me, grey-beard loon!"
> *Eftsoons* his hand *dropt* he.

Archaism is also applied to the use of that which is archaic in literature and art and to the survival of a custom or attitude from the past.

archetype

The primary meaning of *archetype* is "the original model, form, or pattern from which something is made or from which something develops." Thus, one may say that the punishment of Adam, as related in the first book of the Bible ("In the sweat of thy face shalt thou eat bread, till thou return unto the ground . . . "), is an archetype of all mankind's struggle and sorrow. Coleridge's *The Rime of the Ancient Mariner* is based on the archetype of Adam's fall. Another example: Thomas Babington Macaulay referred to the British House of Commons as "the archetype of all the representative assemblies which now meet." A well-defined example of a particular type of person may be referred to as an archetype: "The archetype of a stevedore: thick-chested, bull-necked, sweaty, and profane."

In the psychology of *Jung, the word is applied to inherited ideas or modes of thought derived from the experiences of a race and present in the subconscious of an individual—the *collective unconscious of mankind. Archetype is associated with *imagery and *myth and has indeed been defined as "a *symbol, usually an *image, which recurs often enough in literature to be recognizable as an element of one's literary experience as a whole." Sophocles used the deep-seated concerns of blindness, patricide, incest, and fratricide as a grouping of archetypes in several of his plays; Milton and Dante have treated Man, an archetypal human being, in their greatest works; much of Hawthorne's and Melville's fiction derives from archetypes which represent primordial images of sin, retribution, and death.

architectonics

The science of planning and building. The term, applied to the *form or *structure of a literary work, includes consideration of the author's *purpose, the *genre selected, *style, and *tone. *Architectonics* is a critical term that expresses structural qualities of scale and emphasis.

archives

Documents or records of the claims, rights, and activities of a community, historical figure, or nation. *Archives* is also applied to a place where records and historical documents are stored. The term is now used to refer to any extensive collection of data, such as archives of the Elizabethan theater or of the presidential administration of Woodrow Wilson.

arena theater

An auditorium with seats arranged on at least three sides of a central stage. Such an arrangement is also known as *theater-in-the-round.

Areopagus

A hill in ancient Athens on which a ruling council met in judicial sessions. The term has come to mean any high tribunal or court of final authority. Milton used the word in this sense in his *Areopagitica,* a work on the subjects of *censorship and book licensing addressed to the British Parliament.

argot

Idiomatic vocabulary used by a particular class or group of people, or by members of a profession. *The Beggar's Opera* abounds in the argot of thieves, as does Dickens's *Oliver Twist.* See CANT, IDIOM, SLANG.

argument

In a specialized sense, the argument of a poem, play, or portion of a literary work is an *abstract or *summary of its content. The subject matter, central idea, or even *plot of a novel or narrative poem may also be called its argument. Milton prepared an argument for each book of *Paradise Lost,* and Coleridge used one at the beginning of *The Rime of the Ancient Mariner.* Some critics call the argument of a poem that part of its idea or *thesis which can be *paraphrased.

argumentation

All writing can be classified as argumentation, *narration, *description, or *exposition. These classifications, called *forms of discourse, are arbitrary; further, none appears in pure (unmixed) form. The purpose of argumentation is to convince a reader (or hearer) by proving the truth or establishing the falsity of an idea or *proposition. (See PERSUASION.) Formal argumentation uses these special steps: (1) establishing the proposition, (2) analyzing the proposition, (3) formulating the argument, (4) preparing the *brief (a form of outline).

Aristotelian

Based on, pertaining to, or derived from Aristotle, a Greek philosopher, pupil of Plato, and tutor of Alexander the Great.

This fourth-century-B.C. writer has had a profound effect upon all subsequent logic, literary theories, criticism, and poetry. Aristotelianism, placing emphasis upon *deduction and upon the investigation of concrete situations and objects, has obviously influenced all contemporary science. Aristotelian criticism (as contrasted with *Platonic criticism) implies a logical and objective approach that centers upon the work under consideration rather than upon its moral or social *contexts. See NEW CRITICISM.

ars gratia artis

This Latin term ("art for art's sake") was the *credo of certain writers and other artists in England during the latter half of the nineteenth century. This concept of *aesthetics was that all art is independent of *morality, a view derided by many of their contemporaries but one still held firmly by several contemporary writers, especially those who work in the fields of *existentialism and *realism.

arsis

The part of a metrical *foot that bears the stress: *AR·ti·cle, con·VEX.* See ACCENT, ICTUS.

art ballad

A *ballad of known authorship which has some claims to literary distinction, as contrasted with the *popular ballad, which is notable for its simple narrative form and primitive emotional content. A well-known poem imitating ballad technique is Coleridge's *The Rime of the Ancient Mariner;* other successful art ballads are Keats's *La Belle Dame sans Merci* and Longfellow's *The Wreck of the Hesperus.*

art epic

A term applied to such works as Virgil's *Aeneid* and Milton's *Paradise Lost,* long narrative poems somewhat more sophisticated, idealized, and consciously artistic than such popular (or folk) epics as the *Iliad,* the *Odyssey,* and *Beowulf.* The distinction between the folk epic and the art epic has broken down somewhat because many scholars now tend to believe that the former also was the work of a single poet who wrote in accordance with traditional artistic techniques. See LITERARY EPIC.

Arthurian

Connected with, or related to, a legendary king in ancient Britain, the reputed leader of the *Knights of the Round Table. King Arthur and his knights provided subject matter for a large part of medieval *romance. Scholars now believe that the legend of Arthur grew from the deeds of an actual person who was probably not a king and may not have been named Arthur. The prevailing theory is that this figure was a Welsh (or possibly Roman) leader of the Celts in Wales who led his warriors against Germanic invaders in the fifth century. The popularity of Arthurian legend and tradition reached its height in Malory's *Morte d'Arthur* (1485). Later treatment of Arthur and his followers appears in such works as Tennyson's *Idylls of the King*, Edwin Arlington Robinson's *Tristram,* and T. H. White's *trilogy *The Once and Future King.* Mark Twain wrote a *burlesque treatment of Arthurian chivalry in *A Connecticut Yankee in King Arthur's Court* (1889).

article

A written *prose *composition, usually entirely *nonfiction, dealing with a specific topic. An article customarily appears as a self-contained, independent work in a *magazine but may also be a chapter of a book or other publication.

artifact

Any object made by man. (The word is derived from Latin *arte factum,* "something made with skill.") A product of human workmanship transforming already existing materials such as clay and stone, *artifact* is a term especially applied in archaeology to relics of the past.

artificiality

A term used to characterize a literary work that is considered overly elaborate, deliberately mannered, and rigidly conventional. *Artificial* means self-conscious, studied, lacking in naturalness and spontaneity. The *Euphuism of Lyly is considered the height of artificiality. See CONCEIT, PRECIOSITY.

art lyric

A delicate, highly polished short poem usually noteworthy for triviality, conventional structure and theme, and mannered *artificiality. *Cavalier poets wrote many art lyrics; belonging to this *genre are such forms as the *rondel and the *triolet.

ascender

A *printing term referring to that part of a lowercase letter which rises above the x height of a line. Examples are *b, d, f,* and *h.* A descender is that part of a letter that descends below the x height: *p, q, j,* and *y.*

Asclepiadean

A term in classical *prosody describing a line consisting of a *spondee, several choriambi (see CHORIAMBUS), and an *iambus. Such a line is "Watch there. Over the trees, flying beyond, lost in the haze, it soars." The word is derived from the name of a third-century-B.C. Greek poet, Asclepiades, to whom such verses were attributed.

aside

A stage *convention used by a playwright to indicate words spoken by a character heard by the audience but not by other characters onstage. A novelist, short-story writer, or poet also may employ this somewhat artificial device to reveal words which are spoken aside or in a low tone so as to be inaudible to some person or persons actually present. Eugene O'Neill and a few other prominent modern playwrights resorted to asides, but the convention of the *stage whisper is somewhat rare in twentieth-century plays and fiction.

assimilation

In literature, assimilation means the merging of cultural traits from distinct groups or the process by which a writer absorbs outside influences and incorporates them into his own work. In *linguistics, assimilation is the process by which a sound becomes identical with, or similar to, a neighboring sound: *grammy* for *grandma.*

assonance

A resemblance of sound in words or syllables. *Assonance* applies especially to closely recurring vowel sounds in stressed syllables: "Twinkle, twinkle, little star, / How I wonder what you are." Assonance is a common device in poetry, particularly in the hands of a writer like Dylan Thomas or Marianne Moore. In prose and even in normal speech it is frequent but usually is accidental and not long continued.

assumption

An assumption is the act of taking for granted, or supposing, that a thing is true. The process of reading is based upon a series of assumptions. A writer assumes that his reader can see (or feel, if he is blind), that he knows something of word meanings and word order, that he has sufficient intelligence to draw messages from the page into his own mind. But the writer relies upon more assumptions than these: he assumes that ideas related to his subject need not be mentioned and depends upon his readers to understand and accept them. In *Macbeth,* Shakespeare makes the assumption that spectators (readers) will be appalled by murder and will expect such a crime to be paid for. The blackness of crime, innocence of little children, importance of good health, and nobility of Abraham Lincoln are examples of assumptions which nearly all writers might expect all readers to make. What would happen to literature if readers universally assumed that crime is excellent and praiseworthy, that all little children are sadists and beasts?

In reading, however, one must carefully check assumptions. A dishonest or vicious writer will wish his readers to overlook, and hence fail to reject, unwritten but misleading assumptions. Mussolini and Hitler and many another dictator could say, "All loyal citizens should revere their country." Most, but not all, readers would agree that this is a general truth. Relying on this assumption, dictators have then leaped to "All loyal citizens should hate anyone who opposes their government." History and literature are filled with instances of illegitimate appeals to common beliefs; everyone harbors *fallacies because of slipshod assumptions.

asterisk

A star-shaped figure (*) used in writing and *printing as a reference mark to draw attention or to indicate omission. Greek *asteriskos* means "a small star."

asymmetry

The quality or state of being uneven, not balanced. A writer may be called asymmetrical if he loads his work with false *assumptions, stresses only those so-called facts favorable to his *thesis, and fails to mention contrasting ideas or points of view. Certain modern writers and their works (for example, *existentialists) have been charged with asymmetry because only one preconceived attitude is developed.

asyndeton

A condensed expression in which words or phrases are presented in series, separated by commas only (that is, with conjunctions omitted). The best-known of all asyndetons is *Veni, vidi, vici* ("I came, I saw, I conquered"). In library science, *asyndeton* refers to the omission of cross references, as in a catalog or *index.

atavism

The reappearance in an individual, group, or nation of characteristics of a remote ancestor, or ancestors, that for some time have not been observable. "Reversion to an earlier type" is a constant theme in literature and has been for centuries.

Atellana fabula

Ancient Roman *farce played in the provinces and in Rome until the time of Augustus, the first Roman emperor (27 B.C.–A.D. 14). The term derives from Atella, a town in southern Italy, and *fabula,* a Latin word meaning a traditional tale, or *folktale. Atellana fabula was played by rude, clowning actors who spoke lines of bawdy, homely *dialogue. Related terms include *fabula palliata* (ancient Roman comedy based on Greek models), *fabula praetexta* (Roman drama with a theme based on Roman legend), and *fabula togata* (ancient Roman comedy using Greek models and native Roman subjects).

atmosphere

This term, borrowed from meteorology, is used to describe the overall effect of a creative work of literature or other example of art. It involves the dominant *mood of a selection as created by *setting, *description, and *dialogue. Thus, the setting of Thomas Hardy's novels (Egdon Heath), the description in the first paragraph of Poe's *The Fall of the House of Usher* and in the first chapter of Hawthorne's *The Scarlet Letter,* and the dialogue at the opening of Shakespeare's *Hamlet* and *Macbeth* each create the atmosphere (feeling and mood) of the entire work. Atmosphere embraces both physical and psychological details of the selection itself and the impression intended for the reader as well as his expected emotional response. See also DOMINANT IMPRESSION, TONE.

attenuation
The act of making thin, lessening, or weakening in force. Certain lengthy *novels, for example, have been called attenuated because of their excessive wordage and exhaustive listing of details.

Attic
An adjective applied to writing that is simple, clear, polished, and witty. (Attica, now a Greek province, in ancient times a Greek state, was famed for its culture, grace, and refinement.) The phrase *Attic salt* is sometimes applied to dry, delicate wit.

attitude
Manner, feeling, and position with regard to a person, situation, or tendency. The attitude of a writer to his subject matter determines the *tone of his work: pessimistic, optimistic, detached, outraged, whimsical, satirical, etc.

aubade
A poem about dawn; a piece of music sung or played outdoors at dawn. (See ALBA.) Shakespeare's "Hark! hark! the lark" and Browning's "The year's at the spring / And day's at the morn" from *Pippa Passes* are aubades. An *aube* is a song sung by a friend watching over lovers until dawn.

au courant
A French term meaning "up-to-date." Literally, the phrase means "in the current." In literature, *au courant* is applied to the latest or newest ideas, techniques, standards, and styles of writing and thinking.

audience
An audience is a group or assembly of listeners, but the word has been extended to include all spectators, as at dramatic and sports events, and also those reached by newspapers, magazines, TV and radio presentations, books, and other media of communication. Thus one may refer to Shakespeare's audience, meaning either spectators at his plays in Elizabethan times or today's readers of them; one may refer to *Life* magazine's audience or to the audience of the

London Times. In literary study, *audience* ordinarily means "readers," agents who react to a work of literature.

audio

From a Latin word, *audire,* meaning "to hear," *audio* is a term for the *sound portion of *television. *Audio* is distinguished from *video,* a term referring to the transmission and reception of *images. See VIDEO.

Aufklärung

A German word meaning "enlightenment," usually applied to the philosophical movement of the seventeenth and eighteenth centuries, called the Enlightenment, that stressed the power of human reason. Among major figures of this revival of arts and letters were Immanuel Kant and Gotthold Lessing. See AGE OF REASON.

augury

An omen, token, or indication of something that will happen. *Popular ballads, for example, are filled with auguries of impending death, treachery, shipwreck, etc. See PRESENTIMENT.

Augustan

An adjective originally applying to the age of Augustus Caesar, emperor of Rome just before and after the beginning of the Christian era. His reign marked "the golden age of Latin literature." *Augustan* is now applied to any epoch in world history during which literary culture has been great. The Augustan age of English literary history refers to the period during which Addison, Steele, and Swift flourished—largely because those writers were fully conscious of the parallels in their work to Latin literature.

authorized

Given authority or endowed with sanction. The authorized body of a writer's work is his *canon, the selections that were unmistakably written by him and published with his approval and corrections. The term appears most often in connection with the Authorized Version of the Bible, an English translation that appeared in 1611 and is known also as the King James Bible. By extension, *unauthorized* refers to literary works that do not have the sanction of their reputed authors or the guarantee and approval of literary scholars.

author's proof

A term in *printing referring to *type set in galley form and printed as a strip. (In printing, a galley is a long, narrow tray, usually of metal, for holding type which has been set.) *Author's proof* and *galley proof* are usually interchangeable terms loosely used in the printing industry. See FOUNDRY PROOF, PAGE PROOF.

autobiography

This type of writing is an account of oneself written by oneself. The author of an autobiography presents (or tries to present) a continuous narrative of what he considers the major (or most interesting) events of his life. Usually, an autobiographer reveals about himself only what he is willing to have known and remembered.

Autobiography resembles several other literary forms: *biography, *diaries, *letters, *journals, and *memoirs. A biography is the written history of a person's life composed by someone else; the other four related forms are recollections set down by the subject himself. An autobiography and a memoir are usually lengthy, organized narratives prepared for others to read, but the latter is more likely to focus on one phase of a person's life than on the whole of it. A typical memoir also emphasizes the subject's relations with notable persons or events more than most autobiographies, which are likely to be self-centered and introspective. A diary is a day-to-day or week-to-week chronicle of events and is thus closely related to a journal; the diary is usually more intimate than a journal and more deliberately chronological than autobiography. Letters are epistles, notes, and memoranda exchanged among friends and acquaintances; they afford an insight the intimacy of which varies with the personality of the writer, the identity of his correspondent, and the possibility of publication.

Of these allied types, autobiography is the most notable. Among great autobiographies are Saint Augustine's *Confessions,* Cellini's *Autobiography,* Pepys's *Diary,* Franklin's *Autobiography,* and *The Education of Henry Adams.* Also noteworthy are the strong autobiographical elements, personal and actual or imagined, in other types of fiction, notably in Defoe's *Moll Flanders* and *Robinson Crusoe,* Thackeray's *Henry Esmond,* Dickens's *David Copperfield,* Hardy's *Jude the Obscure,* James Joyce's *A Portrait of the Artist as a Young Man,* Maugham's *Of Human Bondage,* and all the work of Thomas Wolfe. Many essays, poems, and short stories are also based on autobiographical materials, a fully understandable situation since literature derives from the thought, imagination, and experience of its creators.

auto-da-fé

A term derived from Portuguese meaning "act of the faith," *auto-da-fé* refers to the public announcement of judgment passed on persons tried in the courts of the Spanish Inquisition (tribunals chiefly engaged in punishing heresy, especially widespread and severe in the sixteenth century). Such declarations to the public were followed by the execution of sentences imposed, especially the burning of heretics at the stake. By extension, *auto-da-fé* has been applied to such proceedings as the colonial witch trials in Salem, Massachusetts, and to the war guilt trials following World War II.

autonomy
Independence or freedom of the will, of action, of thought, etc. *Autonomy* also refers to self-government and to a self-governing community. When American literature ceased to rely heavily on English models for its themes, forms, and subject matter, it was said to have achieved some degree of autonomy.

autonym
One's own name. Also, *autonym* refers to a book published under the real name of the author. See PEN NAME, PSEUDONYM.

autoprompter
A term used in *television and occasionally in the making of motion pictures to refer to tape under magnifying glass that is attached to the tops of cameras. Such tape contains the actual script of the production being filmed or *cues for the use of actors and actresses when memorizing has not been possible.

auto sacramental
A medieval allegorical drama dealing with the Mass (Eucharist), usually performed on Corpus Christi Day. (See CORPUS CHRISTI.) The phrase *auto sacramental* is derived from Spanish, literally meaning "sacramental act."

autotelic
Adjective describing a work not dependent upon attainment of outside objectives. An autotelic selection speaks its own message in its own terms without reference to any external truth. Its intention and purpose have nothing to do with *didacticism or the teaching or preaching of moral, social, or political values.

avant-garde
A French term literally meaning "fore-guard," *avant-garde* is applied to writing that reveals innovations in its subject matter or style, particularly experimental treatments. As a noun, *avant-garde* refers to the advance group in any field (especially in the literary, visual, and musical arts) the productions of which are characterized by unorthodox methods.

avatar
In Hindu religion, *avatar* applied to the descent of a deity to earth in some recognizable shape. *Avatar* is applied in literature to a representation, or embodiment, that expresses concretely some attitude, view of life, or principle. Lincoln has been referred to as an "avatar of human justice" and Mark Twain as an "avatar of the *tall tale."

axiom
A self-evident truth, a universally accepted rule or principle. In logic and mathematics, an axiom is a *proposition that is assumed without proof, such as that there can be only one straight

line between two points. One of the primary purposes of
the *fable, the *parable, and the *proverb is to state axi-
omatic principles in narrative form.

B

babel

A confused mixture of sounds or voices. As recorded in the Book of Genesis, inhabitants of the ancient city of Babel began to erect a tower designed to reach heaven but were thwarted when confusion broke out in their language. *Babel,* usually spelled with a small letter, refers to any scene or situation that is noisy, turbulent, or confused.

Bacchic

An adjective referring to Bacchus, in classical mythology the god of wine and the Roman counterpart of Dionysus. (See DIO-NYSIA.) A bacchic *foot (sometimes called a bacchius) consists of one short syllable followed by two long ones or of one un-stressed syllable followed by two stressed ones. See ANTIBACCHI-US.

background music

A term referring to the musical score for a *television program or motion picture. Such music, also occasionally used in the production of stage *plays, is designed to heighten dramatic effects; it normally reflects the emotional *tones of *scenes being depicted.

background sound

A term used in the production of stage *plays, motion pictures, and *television and radio programs to refer to *sounds used to simulate a realistic setting and heighten dramatic effects. Traf-fic noises, ringing telephones, the chirping of crickets, etc., are typical background sounds.

back matter

A printing term referring to those parts of a *book that appear at the end, following conclusion of the main text. An *appendix, *bibliography, and *index constitute back matter, sometimes called "end matter." See FRONT MATTER.

Baconian

An adjective referring to the life, work, and times of the Elizabethan essayist and philosopher Francis Bacon (1561–1626). The Baconian theory attributes the plays of Shakespeare to Bacon, largely on the assumption that an unschooled countryman such as Shakespeare lacked the education, wit, and cosmopolitan knowledge necessary to create them. The theory is generally discredited; all available evidence is fragmentary and inconclusive.

bagatelle

Derived from an Italian word meaning "small possession," *bagatelle* is applied to a trifle, something of little value. The term was given by Benjamin Franklin to several of his short prose compositions, such as *The Whistle.*

balance

This term is often used in *criticism to denote the presence, or absence, of *proportion among the various elements of a literary work. A short story, for example, is said to exhibit balance if its *plot, *characterization, and *theme are handled in such a way that none is slighted, none is disproportionately accentuated. Characterization in a novel is termed balanced if favorable and unfavorable characteristics are duly noted and if some equality of treatment is provided for the *antagonist and *protagonist.

balanced sentence

A *structure in which the parts of a sentence (clauses, phrases, words) are set off in parallel position so as to emphasize contrast or similarity in meaning. Bacon's best-known remark about studies appears in a balanced sentence: "Some books are to be tasted, others to be swallowed, and some few to be chewed and digested."

ballad

A narrative poem composed in short *stanzas and designed for singing or oral recitation. A ballad usually deals with an exciting or dramatic episode. Somewhat loosely, song hits, folk music, and *folktales set to music are called ballads. The standard collection of "true" ballads is *The English and Scottish Popular Ballads,* edited by F. J. Child. See ART BALLAD, BALLAD STANZA, LITERARY BALLAD, POPULAR BALLAD.

ballade

A French verse form usually consisting of three *stanzas having the same *rhyme scheme, followed by an *envoi (postscript, conclusion). In a typical ballade, the last lines of each stanza and of the envoi are identical. Among the best-known poems in this form are Chaucer's *Ballade of Good Advice* and Rossetti's adaptation of François Villon's *Ballade of Dead Ladies,* which contains as the last line of each stanza an envoi, "But where are the snows of yester-year?"

ballad stanza

The stanzaic form of the *popular ballad consists of four lines rhyming *abcb.* Usually, the first and third lines contain four accented syllables; the second and fourth contain three. With its strong, clear beat, the ballad stanza easily and fluently adapts itself to the singing of narratives:

> There livéd a wifé at Úsher's Weĺl
> And a wéalthy wife was shé;
> She hád three stout and stalwart sóns,
> And sent them o'er the séa.

ballata

A medieval Italian verse form composed of *stanzas beginning and ending with a *refrain. A ballata was accompanied by dancing. The form is unknown in English but is closely related to the rarely appearing VIRELAY, which see.

balloon

In *cartoons and drawings, words represented as issuing from the mouth of a speaker and enclosed in balloon-shaped figures or lines are called balloons.

banality

A term applied to writing which lacks originality or freshness and is considered hackneyed, stereotyped, and commonplace. Often considered banal are stories in such *mass media as popular magazines, television, and films.

barbarism

A word or phrase used only in coarse or uneducated speech, such as *keeped* for *kept* and *hisn* for *his.* A term originally applied only to expressions felt to be alien to established customs or modes, *barbarism* is also used to refer to any uncivilized and untamed state or condition existing in life or literature. See PHILISTINE, SOLECISM, VULGARISM.

bard

Loosely a "poet," but specifically one of an ancient *Celtic order of versifiers, especially one who composed and recited heroic and adventurous poems while accompanying himself on the harp or lyre. See SKALD, TROUBADOUR.

baroque

From a Portuguese word meaning "rough pearl," *baroque* is an adjective and noun referring or applying to literature that is extravagantly ornamented, elaborately ornate, exaggerated, and high-flown. Much *metaphysical poetry is baroque, as all conceits are. The early American poet Edward Taylor wrote in a baroque style, illustrated by a poem called *Huswifery,* in which he used the *metaphor of spiritual life as a spinning wheel, God's word as man's distaff, etc.

Basic English

A simplified form of English intended as an international auxiliary language. The system consists of a total vocabulary of only 850 words (600 nouns, 150 adjectives, and 100 "operating" words, such as verbs, adverbs, conjunctions, and prepositions). See ESPERANTO.

basilisk

In classical mythology, a creature reputed to kill by its breath or glance. A basilisk was variously described as a dragon, snake, or lizard.

Baskerville

Any style of *type named for the English typographer John Baskerville (1706–1775). See PRINTING, TYPE, TYPOGRAPHY, TYPOLOGY.

bas-relief

Also called low relief, bas-relief refers to objects (such as sculpture) in which figures project slightly from the background. *Bas,* a term from French, means "low"; *relief* refers to the projection of a figure or part from the plane or ground on which it is formed. In printing, for example, relief applies to any process by which printing ink is transferred to paper or another surface from areas that are higher than the remainder of the block. See PRINTING.

bastard title

The first printed page of a book that appears after the front *endpapers and before the *title page itself. Also called a *half title, a bastard title may be the title of any subdivision of a book that is printed on a page by itself preceding that subdivision.

bathos

Applied to literature, *bathos* has two meanings: (1) *sentimentalism, mawkishness, insincere *pathos, and (2) *anticlimax, a descent from the lofty and exalted to the commonplace. The first meaning is illustrated in attempts by insipid writers to make readers sorry for public figures who have thrown away their opportunities for continuing popularity and esteem. The second meaning, "descent from the sublime to the ridiculous," a kind of anticlimax, is illustrated in Pope's witty lines from *The Rape of the Lock:*

Not louder shrieks to pitying heaven are cast,
When husbands, or when lapdogs, breathe their
last.

beast epic

A narrative in which the adventures and misadventures of animals satirize human follies and foibles. A beast epic usually
consists of a lengthy series of linked stories about contemporary
life (politics, religion, social customs, etc.) that provide satirical
comment on the depravity or stupidity of mankind. (A beast
*fable is a short *tale in which the principal characters are
animals.) The best-known beast epic is *Roman de Renart,* a
poem of 30,000 lines consisting of twenty-seven sets of stories
about Reynard the Fox. Chaucer's *The Nun's Priest's Tale* is
perhaps the greatest of all beast epics.

beat generation, beatnik

The term *beat generation* is applied to persons coming of age
after World War II who appear in rebellion against the culture
and value systems they observe (or claim to observe) about
them. American, English, French, and German writers of the
beat generation tend to express revolt in works of loose structure and colloquial diction that assert the empty qualities of
existence. For instance, the works of such American writers as
Allen Ginsberg and Jack Kerouac place them in the *coterie of
*existentialism and its offshoots. A beatnik is a member of the
beat generation, not necessarily a writer, who rejects or avoids
conventional dress, behavior, etc., as a form of social protest.
The word *beatnik* was coined from *beat* (frustrated, defeated)
and *nik,* a Russian *suffix designating an "agent" or "concerned person."

beau monde

The fashionable world of high society. A French term meaning
"fine world," *beau monde* is applied to settings and activities
such as those depicted in some of the work of Henry James and
Edith Wharton. A related term is *jet set, an ultrafashionable
social *coterie of people who apparently spend much of their
time in intercontinental travel from resort to resort.

begging the question

Taking a conclusion for granted before it is proved or assuming
in the *propositions (*premises) something that is to be proved
in the conclusion. A question such as "Should an evil man like
Smith be chosen?" assumes what is to be proved and states as
a proposition that Smith *is* evil but really *proves* nothing. See
AD HOMINEM; ad hominem argument is a form of begging the
question.

behaviorism

The doctrine and theory that consider only those facts of behavior and activity of the human and animal worlds which can be observed objectively to be fit subjects for psychological study. The response of individuals and groups to the facts of their environment is the province of all literature, but behaviorism is most apparent as a factor in the work of writers concerned with the actual and real, as distinguished from the abstract and speculative. The attempt to view, study, and represent "things as they are" is a primary aim of behaviorism and of *realism.

bel esprit
A French term used to refer to a person of unusual wit or intelligence, one with gifted intellect. Literally, *bel esprit* means "fine mind," "great intellect."

belief
Acceptance of, or assent to, that which is offered as true; a state of mind in which confidence, trust, and reliance are placed in some idea, person, or thing. Readers are usually most strongly affected by literature which seems "true" and "believable," by authors who seem to merit trust, by ideas which seem "possible" and even "sensible" and "right." Except for so-called escape literature, which entertains by removing readers temporarily into a world of *fantasy or adventure, all that one reads succeeds to the degree that an author is able to secure and nail down belief, faith, and acceptance of his *assumptions and *thesis. See VERISIMILI TUDE.

Wordsworth referred to "the willing suspension of *disbelief" to suggest what should occur when a reader is absorbed in a work of literature. Many stories and novels illustrate what Wordsworth meant: a reader, caught up in a story, forgets that it is not "true" and never really happened. Willingly, one suspends his ability to judge and evaluate and allows himself to accept ideas which, under some circumstances, he would reject. When a novel—or any type of literature—captures its reader's imagination, the author can and does use this resulting receptive frame of mind to present his philosophy, his set of ideas, his *point of view, through special techniques of literary composition. The belief inspired by all great literature is foundation for the saying that "the pen is mightier than the sword."

belles lettres
A French term literally meaning "fine letters," *belles lettres* is often used interchangeably with *literature. Usage sometimes restricts the meaning of *belles lettres* to light or even frivolous writing and to appreciative essays about literature rather than literature itself. This distinction is not entirely valid, however, because much of the work of Lewis Carroll and Mark Twain, for example, may be considered "light" and "frivolous" but definitely belongs in the category of literature.

benefit of clergy

The rites, privileges, and sanctions of a church. *Benefit of clergy* originally referred to the right claimed by church authorities to try in an ecclesiastical court any clergyman accused of a crime. More generally, the expression is applied to the formality of a marriage ceremony.

bestiary

A type of literature in which beasts, birds, reptiles, and even fish are used to impart moral lessons, foster church doctrines, and provide lessons in natural history. A typical bestiary deals with the habits and reactions of such a fabulous creature as the unicorn, the phoenix, or the siren. Presumably the phrase *crocodile tears* (a hypocritical indication of sorrow) derived from the circumstance that in an ancient bestiary a crocodile was represented as weeping while consuming his victims.

best seller

Any product that among those of its kind is selling particularly well at a given time. *Best seller* is frequently applied to a book having large sales in a particular period and also to the author of such a work.

bête noire

A French term meaning "black beast," *bête noire* refers to something that one particularly dislikes, despises, or dreads. A bête noire is a bugbear, a person, task, place, or object that causes fright, fear, or loathing. Moby Dick, a giant albino sperm whale, is a *symbol of evil in Melville's novel, but despite its color, it is also a "black beast" to the sailors who pursue it.

bias

A feeling, tendency, or inclination that prevents objective and unprejudiced consideration of a question, topic, or person. For example, Dr. Johnson's attitude toward Scotland and Scots caused him to have a bias. Fairly or unfairly, such novelists as Thomas Hardy and Ernest Hemingway have been attacked for their alleged bias against women. A bias may also be favorable. Hardy, for example, is said to have had a bias in favor of rustic life and country people; Hemingway has been acclaimed (and attacked) for his bias favoring courage and strenuous physical activity.

bibelot

A French term, *bibelot* refers to any small object of beauty, rarity, or curiosity. A bibelot may be a small household decorative object, a trinket of some kind, and, in literature, a miniature book of elegant design and workmanship.

Bible

Loosely called a book, the Bible actually is a collection, or library, of books containing *history, *poetry, *biography, *stories, *letters, and divine revelations. The word *Bible* comes from a Greek term meaning "little books" and may refer to the sacred "book" of any religion; for instance, the Bible of Muhammadans is the Koran. In Christian countries, *Bible* refers to the sacred books of the Old Testament (written at various times in the pre-Christian era in ancient Hebrew) and the New Testament (written in the Greek dialect of Mediterranean countries at the time of Christ and in the century following). Numerous translations of the Bible exist, the most famous of which is the so-called King James Bible. See AUTHORIZED.

The Bible is the best-selling book in all literature, the most quoted, the most influential and powerful. The themes and plots of works from Milton's *Paradise Lost* and Bunyan's *Pilgrim's Progress* to Faulkner's *Light in August* and Steinbeck's *The Grapes of Wrath* have been directly and subtly shaped by the unparalleled influence of the Bible upon the hearts and minds of men.

biblioclasm

The practice of mutilating or destroying books. Adolf Hitler was the most famous of all recent biblioclasts, but the fear and hatred of books, which have existed for centuries in many lands, have caused wholesale destruction of many libraries. The great library at Alexandria, Egypt, was burned in the seventh century by Muhammadan destroyers who felt that books were unnecessary, since all worthwhile knowledge was contained in the Koran.

bibliography

A list of readings on a particular subject. A bibliography of Thomas Jefferson, for instance, would consist of listings of all *secondary sources such as *biographies, books of *criticism, and magazine *articles and of *primary sources such as original *letters and contemporary *documents. In library work, *bibliography* refers to study of the history, physical description, and classification of books, graphic materials, etc.

bibliolatry

Extravagant devotion to books and excessive dependence upon them. A "bookworm" is a bibliolater or bibliolatrist. Persons who acknowledged their bibliolatry at some point in their lives include Charles Lamb and Benjamin Franklin. The term is occasionally used to refer to idolatrous reverence for the *Bible in a *literal interpretation of its meanings.

bibliomancy

The practice of opening a book, especially the *Bible or any collection of *aphorisms, to discover a verse or passage which is considered to be especially meaningful at the moment. The discovered item is then interpreted and applied to the finder's immediate situation.

bibliomania

Extreme fondness for acquiring and possessing books. A bibliomaniac collects and retains books, whereas a bibliolater reveres and reads books but may not actually acquire and keep them.

bibliophile, bibliophobe

The former term means one who loves books and possibly collects them (see BIBLIOMANIA). A bibliophobe hates, fears, and distrusts books (see BIBLIOCLASM).

Biedermeier

A term derived from the name of an imaginary nineteenth-century German poet, Gottlieb Biedermeier, author of unsophisticated minor poems. The word may be applied to any literary period notable for its acceptance of the *status quo, its restraint, and the narrow range of its artistic endeavors.

Bildungsroman

A novel concerning the youthful life and development of a major *character. *Bildungsroman* is a combination of German *Bildung* ("formation," "development") and French *roman* ("novel"). Examples of Bildungsromane are Samuel Butler's *The Way of All Flesh,* Dickens's *David Copperfield,* and Somerset Maugham's *Of Human Bondage.* See ERZIEHUNGSROMAN.

billet doux

A French term meaning "sweet little letter," *billet doux* usually refers to a love letter or a missive expressing affection and tenderness.

billingsgate

Coarse and abusive language. The term was derived from the vulgar speech often heard at Billingsgate, a fish market in London located near a gate named after a man called Billing. Shakespeare's Falstaff occasionally indulged in billingsgate when he was being especially argumentative and scornfully abusive.

binding

The covering within which the pages of a book are bound. Bookbinding consists of numerous methods of holding pages together to form a *book, *booklet, *magazine, or other multi-page piece of printed or *manuscript material. In contemporary hard-cover (so-called cloth) bookbinding, *signatures of sixteen or thirty-two pages each are bundled into folded units. These signatures are arranged in proper sequence; books are then sewed by machines that pass threads through their folds. The back of the book is treated with hot glue, and the cover is encased.

Stapling, metal-ring binding, wire-spiral binding, and plastic-comb binding are mechanical devices used for soft-covered *booklets, *brochures, *pamphlets, and similar items.

biography

A written account of a person's life or an account of the lives of any small and closely knit group, such as a family. Biography is thus a subtype of *history, "a continuous, systematic narrative of past events as relating to a particular people, country, period, or person"; a subdivision of biography itself is autobiography. Thomas Carlyle once defined history as "the essence of innumerable biographies," and Emerson wrote, "There is properly no history, only biography."

Biography has long been a popular form of reading. Sketches of kings and members of the ruling class thrilled readers some two thousand years ago with their emphasis upon martial and other adventurous deeds. Readers vicariously experienced activity, securing release and a form of escape no less popular then than they are today. Curiosity about others is as old as the human race, and its potency and prevalence apparently have increased through the centuries. Within the past century, curiosity about others, great and small, has resulted in both a major industry and a recognized literary *genre.

Eagerness to know the intimate details of others' lives, curiosity about people's attainments, about their strengths and weaknesses, their ways of speaking and thinking and acting, their human and their inhuman qualities seem as dominant as man's urge to escape or live vicariously through *fiction. This fascination with the lives of others has been cultivated as biography has become a more settled type, as it has come to be more appealingly written, as it has dealt more and more with "ordinary" people and less and less with kings and princes.

The present-day popularity of biographical writing also traces to the fact that readers have come to realize that truth is actually "stranger than fiction." It would be more correct to say that "truth is stranger than fiction *dares* to be," for some of the *complications, *ironies, and *coincidences in almost everyone's life would have to be discarded by a competent narrative writer. Put into fiction, they would seem either impossible or improbable. The biographer is restrained by no such consideration. His whole work, if properly handled, seems authentic and credible, and its reader will willingly accept more hair-raising and heart-stopping *episodes than any novelist or story writer could hope to employ. See AUTOBIOGRAPHY.

black comedy

The so-called *humor of the absurd, perverted, and morbid. Since World War II, black comedy and black humor have developed into a literary *genre. (See EXISTENTIALISM, THEATER OF THE ABSURD.) Black comedy (humor) is sometimes called "sick" because of its generally alien attitude toward contemporary *society.

blackmail

The extortion of money by the use of threats. The term (a combining of *black* and *mail*—a Middle English word for *tribute* or *rent*) is defined in law as any payment extracted by intimidation, such as threats of harmful revelations or accusations. Blackmail has been an element in English literature from early days, when plundering Scottish chiefs demanded tribute for protection from pillage.

blank verse

Unrhymed lines of ten syllables each, the even-numbered syllables bearing the accents, is called blank verse, or unrhymed iambic pentameter. (See IAMBUS, PENTAMETER, METRICS.) An example of blank verse is this line by Wordsworth:

So through / the dark/ness and / the cold /
we flew.

This form of poetry is generally considered best adapted to dramatic verse in English; it was chosen by Milton for *Paradise Lost* and ever since has been used more than any other form for serious poetry in English. Shakespeare's plays contain many lengthy passages in blank verse. (Blank verse, which is "blank" only in rhyme, is sometimes confused with *free verse.) Ordinarily, the meter of blank verse is definite and regular but does permit variations as in these lines from Shakespeare's *A Midsummer Night's Dream:*

The poet's eye, in a fine frenzy rolling,
Doth glance from heaven to earth,
    from earth to heaven;
And, as imagination bodies forth
The forms of things unknown, the poet's pen
Turns them to shapes and gives to airy nothing
A local habitation and a name.

bleed

A term in printing referring to the practice of allowing printed illustrations or ornamentation to run off (extend beyond the edges of) the page or sheet. As a noun, *bleed* is used by editors and printers to refer to a sheet or page margin trimmed so closely as to cut into textual material or illustrations.

block printing
The earliest-known form of *printing, in which impressions were taken from wood. Some typographical experts consider that printing from wood blocks (which began in China in the eighth century) rather than the invention of movable type (fifteenth century) was the true origin of printing.

blues
A melancholy song of Afro-American origin marked by the frequent occurrence of blue (flatted) notes. A blues (song) characteristically consists of three-line *stanzas (with a twelve-bar chorus and the second line repeating the first):

> Gwine lay my head right on de railroad track,
> Gwine lay my head right on de railroad track,
> Cause my baby, she won't take me back.

bluestocking
Now used to refer to affectedly intellectual females, *bluestocking* was originally applied to a woman with scholarly or literary ability, especially a member of a mid-eighteenth-century London literary circle. Apparently, the term was derived from the preference of some women of the group for blue woolen rather than black silk stockings.

blurb
A brief, laudatory advertisement or announcement. The word, coined by an American humorist, Gelett Burgess, is applied in publishing circles to the extravagant notices printed on the jackets of new books and to comments used in selling and promoting them.

Bodoni
A modern style of type based on designs created by an Italian printer, Giambattista Bodoni (1740–1813). See PRINTING, TYPOGRAPHY, TYPOLOGY.

boldface
A printing term applied to type that has thick (heavy) lines and is used for headings, emphasis, etc.

bombast
Pretentious, ranting, insincere, and extravagant language. An example of bombast from Shakespeare's *Hamlet* (act 2, scene 2):

> With blood of fathers, mothers, daughters, sons,
> Baked and impasted with the parching streets
> That lend a tyrannous and damned light
> To their vile murders. Roasted in wrath and fire,
> And thus o'er-sized with coagulate gore,

> With eyes like carbuncles, the hellish Pyrrhus
> Old grandsire Priam seeks.

bona fide

A Latin term meaning "in good faith," "without fraud or deception." In literature, the phrase is usually applied to authors or to works that appear genuine, valid, and sincere. *Bona fides* is a noun meaning "good faith," the absence of fraud and deceit, the state of being exactly as claimed.

boner

A foolish and obvious mistake or blunder. A boner in deportment, dress, or language is usually a ridiculous and embarrassing slip arising from ignorance or lack of tact. In literature, *boner* is usually applied to a grammatical, logical, or factual mistake that may have a humorous effect. See SOLECISM.

bonhomie

Open and simple good-heartedness. *Bonhomie* is a French term formed from *bon* ("good") and *homme* ("man"). In literature, the word is often applied to characters who exhibit warm geniality, good cheer, and easy friendliness. Such a character is Bob Cratchit in Dickens's *A Christmas Carol.*

bon mot

A French term with a literal meaning of "good word," *bon mot* means a "clever saying," "witticism." Speaking of possible Russian action, Winston Churchill uttered this bon mot: "It is a riddle wrapped in a mystery inside an enigma." See APHORISM.

bon vivant

A French term meaning "good liver"; a person who lives luxuriously with lively pleasure in superior food and drink. A bon vivant possesses, or claims to possess, cultivated and refined tastes.

book

A written or printed work on consecutive sheets of paper fastened together. Specifically, a book is understood to be a collection of sheets usually secured at one end or side and trimmed at the others to form a single series of uniform leaves. No agreement exists as to the number of sheets required to constitute a book or the material of the sheets themselves. Written sheets of skin, tablets of wood or ivory, and a continuous roll of parchment may be considered a book. For comment on book sizes, see FOLIO, OCTAVO, QUARTO. Also, see PAMPHLET.

bookbinding

See BINDING.

book face

A term in *printing used to refer to a style of *type suitable for the text of a *book. The basic book face (typeface) for printing the *manuscript of a *novel might differ markedly from that for a learned scientific work.

booklet

A little *book, usually one with paper covers (self-binding). (*Let* is a diminutive suffix attached to nouns.) In the printing industry, a booklet is taken to mean a small book of not more than twenty-four pages. (See PAMPHLET.) By current United States postal regulations, a book must have twenty-four pages or more to qualify for book mailing rates. Postal authorities and printing personnel consider a pamphlet smaller than a booklet, but the terms are often used interchangeably for any printed product of less than a hundred pages.

book review

A descriptive, evaluative account and discussion of a book. A book review is a form of *criticism, which is (or is generally thought should be) a process that weighs, judges, and evaluates. The primary purpose of a book review is to consider faults and excellencies and then to render careful judgment. Among types of reviews are (1) a reportorial method in which a book is presented as an item of news; (2) reportorial and critical commentary that explains, interprets, and judges a book in terms of its purpose, scope, and style; (3) the "springboard review" in which a reviewer uses a given book as a convenient starting point (or excuse) from which he launches into a critical essay that covers much more (and much less) than the specific book being considered. A springboard review of a war novel, for example, might become an analysis of the causes of international friction without comment on the particular narrative itself.

Bourbon

Specifically, *Bourbon* refers to a member of a French royal family that ruled in Spain, Naples, and France at various times from the sixteenth to the nineteenth century. Spelled with a capital or lowercase letter, *bourbon* is an adjective describing persons considered conservative or reactionary.

bourgeois

A term from French, *bourgeois* refers to a member of the so-called middle class: a businessman, shopkeeper, merchant, etc. In literature, the term is often applied to characters whose political, social, and economic attitudes are largely shaped by their concern for property values. Occasionally, *bourgeois* is applied to someone who is rigidly conventional or who lacks elegance and refinement. (See PHILISTINE.)

"Bourgeois literature" is said to appeal to "middle-class" readers, a rather meaningless statement. *Bourgeois drama* is a phrase characterizing the social sphere of the *action and *setting of a play, not a class of *audience (or readers).

bowdlerize

To amend by removing or modifying objectionable passages of a novel, play, or any piece of writing. The term is derived from the name of Thomas Bowdler, an English editor and physician who expurgated from an edition of Shakespeare's works all "indecent" and "indecorous" passages considered "unfit to be read by a gentleman in the presence of ladies." See CENSORSHIP.

boxhead

A printing term for a heading appearing at the top of a page, newspaper *column, or column of figures, enclosed in a "box" formed by lines (rules).

brachycatalectic

Term applied to a line of verse lacking one *foot or two or more *syllables. *Brachy* is a borrowing from Greek meaning "short," and *catalectic* is from Greek words meaning "to leave off," "to end." The second line of this excerpt from Thomas Hood's *The Bridge of Sighs* is brachycatalectic: "One more unfortunate / Weary of breath." See ACATALECTIC, CATALEXIS.

braggadocio

Empty boasting and bragging, or a braggart. *Braggadocio* is derived from a character of that name in Spenser's *The Faerie Queene* who has a boastful tongue but a cowardly heart. See MILES GLORIOSUS.

Brahmin

A person of culture, refinement, and intellect, especially a member of a New England family that is (or was) considered aristocratic. The term *Brahmin,* derived from Hinduism, in which it applied to members of the highest, or priestly, caste among Hindus, is sometimes used disparagingly for persons thought to be socially or intellectually aloof. Oliver Wendell Holmes said of an acquaintance: "He comes of the Brahmin caste of New England. This is the harmless, inoffensive, untitled aristocracy."

Braille

A system of writing or printing for the blind in which combinations of dots or points that can be felt represent letters and characters. The term comes from the name of a nineteenth-century French teacher of the blind, Louis Braille.

breve

A mark (˘) placed over a vowel to indicate that it has a short sound. (See MACRON.) In *prosody, a breve indicates a short or unstressed syllable.

breviary

A book of daily prayers and readings. The word, derived from a Latin term meaning "short" or "brief," applies to a collection of lessons, calendars, and outlines for services designed to help a cleric recite the Divine Office for each day and otherwise fulfill his churchly assignments.

brief

This term has several meanings, the most common of which in literature is that of an *outline (the form of which is determined by set rules) of all the *arguments and data on one side of a controversial question. *Brief* may also be defined as any concise statement in written form. (See PRÉCIS.) In legal circles, a brief is (1) a memorandum of points of law or fact for use in conducting a case, (2) a written summons calling for an answer to legal action, and (3) a written argument submitted to a court of law.

Briticism

A word, idiom, or expression characteristic of, and generally restricted to, British English as contrasted with American English. See ANGLICISM.

broadside

A sheet of paper, usually large, with printed or pictorial material on only one side, designed for distribution or posting. Beginning in the sixteenth century, broadsides were used for some three hundred years to publish news. A broadside ballad is a song (chiefly appearing in sixteenth and seventeenth-century England) written on a topical subject, printed on a broadside, and sold or sung in public. The subjects of these broadsides (or broadside ballads) were accounts of accidents, murders, and miraculous events, dying speeches of criminals, and political speeches. See BALLAD.

brochure

A term derived from a French word meaning "to stitch" (a book), a brochure is a *pamphlet or *booklet, usually paper-covered. A brochure is a treatment of a subject briefer than a *book and much less extended in scope.

bromide

A commonplace or *hackneyed expression, generalization, or notion; a trite artistic theme or device; a conventional or tiresome person. "Nobody loves a fat man" is a *bromide.* See BANALITY, CLICHÉ, PLATITUDE, TRUISM.

brouhaha

A term derived from French referring to (1) an *episode

involving confusion, excitement, or turmoil; (2) clamor attending some sensational event; (3) public concern and interest. *Brouhaha* is usually applied to excitement over relatively minor, unimportant, or ridiculous causes and happenings.

brummagem

Something cheap or inferior. The term is derived from Birmingham, England, where in the seventeenth century counterfeit coins were made and circulated and where, later, shoddy and flimsy articles were manufactured.

buckram

Coarse cloth of cotton, linen, or hemp used in bookbinding as the exterior surface (*case, *binding) of a hard-cover book. *Buckram* was probably derived from Bukhara, a city now in the Soviet Union, once noted for textiles.

bucolic

An adjective meaning rustic, rural, or unsophisticated. *Bucolic* is derived from a Latin word meaning "herdsman" and is especially applied to pastoral writing concerned with shepherds and country life. *Bucolic* is a term referring to the pastoral literature of such a writer as Virgil. See PASTORAL.

bulk

(1) The thickness of paper (cardboard, etc.) in relation to its weight; (2) the thickness of the total number of *pages in a *book or *periodical. A book printed on sheets of heavy (thick) paper may have a bulk as great as that of another book several times as long but printed on thin paper.

bull

This term, derived from a Latin word meaning "seal" or "sealed paper," is applied in literature to a formal papal document with a seal of office attached. *Bull* is sometimes loosely applied to any statement of doctrine or belief, not necessarily ecclesiastical (churchly).

buncombe

Insincere or nonsensical talk or action; also *bunkum* and *bunk*. *Buncombe* refers to a county of that name in North Carolina, the congressional representative of which justified an irrelevant and tiresome speech by saying that he was "speaking for Buncombe."

burlesque

A form of comic art, an imitation intended to ridicule by exaggeration. Burlesque is an attitude, style, or idea handled by distortion in which an important, imposing, or elevated subject is treated in a trivial way, a low or trifling subject with mock dignity. Discrepancy between style and subject matter is the essential quality of burlesque.

Chaucer's *Sir Thopas* and Cervantes' *Don Quixote* are burlesques of medieval *romance. Fielding's *Joseph Andrews* began as a burlesque of Richardson's *Pamela.* Gay's *The Beggar's Opera* and Gilbert and Sullivan's *Patience* are well-known burlesques in musical literature.

Commonly referred to as "burlesque" is theatrical entertainment, often broadly humorous and earthy, consisting of comic skits, songs, dances, and striptease acts. Such performances are usually grotesque imitations of such legitimate dramatic arts as dancing, singing, and acting. See CARICATURE, LAMPOON, PARODY, TRAVESTY.

burletta

A term derived from an Italian word meaning "jest." A burletta is a musical drama containing rhymed lyrics and resembling comic *opera. Gay's *Beggar's Opera* is a burletta as well as burlesque. Neither the term nor the form itself has been operative since the eighteenth century.

Burns stanza

A six-line *stanza usually rhyming *aaabab,* named after Robert Burns, who often used it. Here is the first stanza of Burns's *To a Mouse:*

> Wee, sleekit, cow'rin', tim'rous beastie,
> O what a panic's in thy breastie!
> Thou need na start awa sae hasty,
> Wi' bickering brattle!
> I wad be laith to rin an' chase thee,
> Wi' murd'ring pattle!

buskin

A thick-soled, laced boot or half boot. The high, heavy-soled shoe worn by ancient Greek and Roman actors, also called a *cothurnus, was associated with *tragedy rather than *comedy because buskins were thought to increase stature symbolically as well as physically. Actors in Latin comedies wore a soft shoe called a "soccus," with the result that *sock* is used to apply to comedy and *buskin* to tragedy. In *L'Allegro,* John Milton refers to "the buskin'd stage" and to Ben "Jonson's learned sock"—tragedy and comedy.

by-line

A printed line accompanying an article, news story, or dispatch that provides the name of the author.

byword

A word or phrase associated with some person, group, or organization and expressing a characteristic idea or formula. An *adage, *aphorism, *apothegm, or *maxim can be a byword, but the term is usually applied to a *motto, such as the Boy Scouts' Be Prepared.

cabal

A clique, *coterie, or small, tightly knit group of persons. (For comment on cabal in the sense of a small political group, see ACROSTIC.) In literary, theatrical, and artistic fields, persons have tended for centuries to form themselves into cabals.

cablese

Language used in cablegrams that is characterized by the omission, abbreviation, and telescoping of words. See TELE-GRAPHIC STYLE.

caccia

An ancient Italian vocal form with words that describe a hunt or the sounds of village life.

cacoëthes

A powerful impulse, or mania. This term from Greek is used most often in the phrases *cacoëthes scribendi* ("itch to write") and *cacoëthes loquendi* ("desire to speak").

cacophony

A discordant mixture of sounds or a harsh, unpleasant combination of sounds. (See EUPHONY.) In music, *cacophony* refers to the use of discords difficult to understand. Cacophony may be employed deliberately for artistic effect, as in Poe's poem *The Bells:*

> In the startled ear of night
> How they scream out their affright!
> Too much horrified to speak
> They can only shriek, shriek,
> Out of tune.

cadence

The rhythmic flow, or sequence, of sounds in writing and speaking. *Cadence* has been broadened in meaning to refer to the time, measure, sequence, or beat of any rhythmical activity (dancing, rowing, marching). Specifically, cadence suggests the particular *rhythm of *prose and *free verse and is a convenient overall term to designate the measured repetition of emphasis and accent in writing or speaking which is not altogether metrical (as in poetry). Used as a natural, inherent alternation of stressed and unstressed syllables in prose writing and in speaking, cadence is a pleasing stylistic quality; overused, it develops artificial and singsongy effects. See METRICS.

caesura

A pause, or break, in a line of verse that results from the meanings of words, the natural rhythm of language, or both. In *prosody, such a "sense pause" is marked by a double line:

A little learning // is a dangerous thing;
Drink deep, // or taste not the Pierian spring.

calligraphy

Excellent penmanship, beautiful handwriting. The significance of the term in literature derives from use of the art in medieval times, during which learned monks laboriously copied, and sometimes decorated, ancient *manuscripts.

callow

An adjective meaning "immature," "unfledged," "inexperienced." The term is sometimes applied to work produced by authors early in their careers.

calumny

Slander; false and malicious statements designed to injure the reputation and career of someone. Calumny has often played a part in the professional jealousy of authors. For example, Walt Whitman was dismissed from a government post because of the calumny directed at him by critics for his "formlessness," frank treatment of sex, and "indecency." See LIBEL, SLANDER.

Calvinism

The doctrines and teachings of John Calvin (1509–1564), a French theologian and reformer who lived in Switzerland. Calvinism is important because for some four hundred years it has deeply influenced the literature of England and the United States. In colonial days, Calvinism was influential in the development of New England culture and, through extension, American life and letters. Calvinism stresses the sovereignty of God, the supreme authority of the *Bible, and the irresistibility of God's will for man in every act of his life from cradle to grave.

calypso

A musical style of West Indian Negro origin that is influenced by jazz and exhibits a flexible accent in its frequently improvised *lyrics.

cancionero

A Spanish collection of songs and lyrical poetry. (In Spanish, *cancion* means "song.") *Cancionero* may also be applied to the collected works of a single author. See ANTHOLOGY, CHRESTOMATHY.

canon

This term from a Greek word meaning "measuring rod" or "rule" has several meanings applicable in literature: (1) a standard of judgment, a criterion; (2) the approved list of books belonging in the Christian *Bible; (3) the accepted list of works of any given author. The *Shakespeare canon,* for example, is a term applied to the thirty-seven plays established as authentic. See APOCRYPHAL.

cant

A word derived from an Old English term meaning "singer" or "song," *cant* is occasionally used to refer to the singsong, whining speech of beggars. More often, *cant* means the special language (*argot, *jargon) spoken by criminals and gypsies, and still more often it is used to refer to the speech of a particular profession or class (medical cant, legal cant). In literature, *cant* also means insincere statements, conventional but unmeant expressions of goodness and high ideals.

canticle

One of the usually nonmetrical hymns or chants, chiefly from the *Bible, sung in church services.

canto

One of the main, or larger, divisions of a long poem. Dante's *The Divine Comedy,* Spenser's *The Faerie Queene,* and Byron's *Childe Harold's Pilgrimage* are arranged in cantos.

canzone

A lyrical poem resembling a *madrigal. The term *canzone* is loosely applied to any *ballad or *song, but is properly restricted to a short poem consisting of *stanzas of equal length and of an *envoi that has fewer lines than any preceding stanza. The canzoni of Petrarch usually consisted of five stanzas and an envoi. Frequent subjects are nature, love, and melancholy.

caprice

Whimsicality; a tendency to change one's mind without apparent reason or motive. A capricious author writes erratically or deals with whimsical topics. *Peter Pan* is often referred to as a play of caprice.

caption

A heading, or title, of a chapter or article. As a printing term, *caption* refers to a legend (descriptive statement) for an illustration in a book or magazine. The purpose of a caption is to secure attention; the Latin word from which it is derived means "seizure."

caricature

This term suggests ludicrous distortion of a particular feature, or features, of the characteristics of a person or idea. The word is derived from Italian *caricare* ("to load") and may be called a "loaded" or "overloaded" representation. Caricature is more often associated with drawing, as in *cartoons, than with literature, but in each medium exaggeration is used for comic effect.

Sometimes the distortion is so gross that *irony, not *humor, is the result: "The kangaroo court is a caricature of real justice." Caricature is related to *burlesque (imitation of the dignified and grand or of the trivial by means of inverted style); to *parody (heightening of a particular feature by methods which are humorous but often less obvious, less pictorial, and less boisterous); and to *travesty (clearly and even outrageously extravagant imitation designed to mock and scorn). Notable caricaturists include Max Beerbohm, Bill Mauldin, and James Thurber.

carol

Any joyous song and hymn of religious joy, especially one dealing with the nativity of Jesus Christ (Christmas carols).

Caroline

A term applied to the literature and writers of the period of Charles I of England (1625–1649). Among poets referred to as Caroline were Herbert, Herrick, Vaughan, and the more strictly *Cavalier poets, Lovelace, Suckling, and Carew.

carpe diem

A Latin phrase meaning "seize the day." In literature, *carpe diem* refers to a *theme or *motif, chiefly in lyric *poetry, that presents youth as short-lived and urges the pursuit of pleasure. This philosophy of "eat and drink, for tomorrow we shall die" has been present in literature since the days of the first-century-B.C. Roman poet Horace. The English poet Robert Herrick stated the theory of carpe diem as well as anyone ever has:

> Gather ye rosebuds while ye may,
> Old Time is still a-flying;
> And this same flower that smiles today,
> Tomorrow will be dying.

carte blanche

This French term means unrestricted permission, unconditional authority, full discretionary power. Literally, the expression means "blank card" or "blank document."

cartoon

A sketch or drawing, usually humorous, that satirizes, symbolizes, or caricatures some person, subject, or action of popular interest. See ANIMATION, BURLESQUE, LAMPOON, PARODY, TRAVESTY.

cartouche

An ornament in the form of a scroll. *Cartouche* is usually applied to architectural forms, but sometimes the term is used in connection with bookplates and illustrations.

case

A term used in the printing industries for (1) a tray (wood, metal, plastic) for holding *type for the use of a compositor (see LOWERCASE, UPPERCASE); (2) a completed cover and spine ready to be fitted to form the *binding of a *book.

case-bound

A bookbinding term meaning "bound in hard covers." For a *case-bound* book, the cover is manufactured separately, and the sewn signatures are inserted and affixed to the cover. See BINDING.

Caslon

A term referring to old-style *type modeled after the designs of William Caslon (1692–1766), an English type founder. Because Caslon's type is legible and without distracting details, some designers and printers follow the *maxim "When in doubt, use Caslon."

cast-off

The estimate by an editor or compositor of how many *pages *copy will occupy when set in *type. *Cast-off* (with a hyphen) is used as a noun and adjective; *cast off* (two words) is the verb.

casuistry

Application of principles of ethics (rules of conduct) to particular cases of action or conscience. In literature, *casuistry* is most often used critically and disparagingly with reference to fallacious or dishonest applications of such principles. For example, Mark Twain has been accused of casuistry because of what some critics contend were the author's attitudes toward the property rights of slaveholders.

casus belli

A Latin term used to refer to an event or occurrence that results in a declaration of war.

catachresis

From a Greek word meaning "misuse," *catachresis* means a strained use of words or the employment of words under a false form derived through improper *etymology. For example, the formation of *crawfish* from *crayfish* and the use of *chronic* for *severe* are instances of catachresis. See FOLK ETYMOLOGY, IMPROPRIETY.

catalexis (catalectic)

An incompleteness in the last *foot at the end of a *verse is known as catalexis. (See ACATALECTIC, a term applied to a line that does not exhibit catalexis.) These lines by Shelley are catalectic:

> Músic, / whén sŏft / vóicĕs / díe,
> Víbrates / in thĕ / mémŏ/rý.

catalogue raisonné

A French term meaning "reasoned catalog," *catalogue raisonné* refers to a catalog (list of items) containing notes and commentaries. Such a classified, descriptive catalog would constitute, for example, a descriptive *bibliography of the works of an author.

catastasis

That part of a *play preceding the *catastrophe in which *action is at its height. *Catastasis* and *climax are usually interchangeable terms.

catastrophe

From a Greek word meaning "overturning," *catastrophe* means (1) a final event or conclusion, usually an unfortunate one; (2) a sudden and widespread calamity and disaster; (3) any misfortune, failure, or mishap. In literature, especially in *drama, *catastrophe* refers to the point at which circumstances overcome central motives and introduce a conclusion. The *resolution of a plot in which various complications are unraveled is a *denouement, a term now used more often than *catastrophe* in dramatic and narrative works.

catch

A musical *round in which the words are so arranged as to produce humorous effects. In Shakespeare's *Twelfth Night*, Sir Toby Belch and Sir Andrew Aguecheek create a ludicrous effect with their singing of a catch.

catchword

(1) A word printed at the top of a page in a reference book; (2) the first word of the following page, inserted at the bottom of each right-hand page of a book; (3) a memorable or effective word or phrase repeated so often as to become a *slogan or *motto, such as "Easy does it" or the phrase from Charles Dickens's *David Copperfield,* "Barkis is willin'."

catechism

A question-and-answer method of instruction. The term *catechism* is usually applied to an elementary book containing the principles of a given religion, presented in the form of queries and approved responses.

catharsis

This term is from a Greek word, *kathairein,* meaning "to clean," "to purify," and was used by Aristotle (384–322 B.C.) in his description of the effect of *tragedy—the purgation or purification of emotions. *Catharsis* refers to any emotional discharge which brings about a moral or spiritual renewal or welcome relief from tension and anxiety. The primary idea is that an audience—any audience—filled with confusions and unhealthy emotions, such as pity and fear, comes to see a *play developing make-believe actions that would be harmful if occurring in real life. The audience participates emotionally in the dramatic action and goes away psychologically cleansed, purged of injurious feelings and sensations. Literary critics have never agreed whether *catharsis* means that members of an audience thus learn to avoid the evil and destructive emotions of a tragic hero or that their inner conflicts are quieted by an opportunity to expend pity and fear upon such a *protagonist.

catholicity

Universality, broad-mindedness. Writers who deal with a wide range of human actions and emotions, who write of matters that concern many people of diverse social, racial, economic, and cultural backgrounds, are notable for their catholicity of understanding, taste, and purpose. It is generally agreed that Shakespeare was the world's most catholic writer of all time. Spelled with a capital letter, *Catholicity* refers to the doctrines and practices of the Roman Catholic Church.

cauda

In Latin (and in anatomy and zoology), *cauda* means "tail." In poetry, *cauda* refers to a metrically distinct group of lines at the end of a *stanza or short *poem. See CODA, ENVOI.

cause and effect

Much of what one reads is the result of cause-and-effect relations. When we read an answer to the question "Why did this happen?" we are dealing in *causes*. When we read the question "What will this do?" the answers involved deal with *effects*. A cause, therefore, is that which produces an effect, the person, idea, or force from which something results. An effect is that which is produced by some agency or cause. "The cause of their quarrel was a misunderstanding over money." "The effect of morphine is to dull pain and induce sleep."

In such literature, especially *essays and other forms of *exposition, *paragraphs are developed by a plan of cause and effect. The topic sentence of a paragraph makes a generalized statement or draws a conclusion based on data (details, ideas, suggestions) that make up the supporting material of the paragraph. Conversely, supporting material may indicate what are the results (effects) of the generalized statement in the topic sentence. For example, here is the topic of a paragraph from *The Sea Around Us,* by Rachel Carson: "The birth of a volcanic island is an event marked by prolonged and violent travail: the forces of the earth striving to create and all the forces of the sea opposing." The remainder of the paragraph is a vivid recital of specific details of the violent struggle, the causes of the travail. Again, Will Durant, in *Why Men Fight,* opened a paragraph with this topic sentence: " . . . a modern war brings complex economic results." The effects, what happens to life and property, constitute development of the remainder of the paragraph.

All life—and consequently all good literature—is concerned with why something begins to exist and why it exists the way it does. A cause is the reason. An effect is the result of the operation of a cause. Cause and effect are necessarily related: Shakespeare's Macbeth killed Duncan because of ambition and greed; the effect of the murder is the substance of a tragedy that leads to Macbeth's total ruin. Such a statement about *Macbeth* indicates that the total cause of any event is complex and involves an intricate joining of preceding forces and events; the total effects of any given cause extend beyond immediate results.

causerie

From a French word meaning "to chat," *causerie* is a name for informal talk, one usually applied to an essay or brief article on a literary topic. The causerie was named by the nineteenth-century French writer Sainte-Beuve and has been employed by Dr. Samuel Johnson, Charles Lamb, Matthew Arnold, and numerous newspaper columnists and *New Yorker* writers.

cavalier

This term has several meanings as an adjective and noun:

(1) haughty and disdainful; (2) offhand, casual, and unceremonious; (3) a horseman, especially a mounted soldier; (4) a courtly, gallant gentleman; (5) a woman's escort, or beau. In literary history, *Cavalier* refers to a follower of Charles I of England in his struggles with Parliament. The work of Cavalier poets (Carew, Lovelace, Suckling) is notable for its grace, polish, arrogance, and licentiousness. See CAROLINE.

caveat

A warning or caution. The word appears most often in the phrase *caveat emptor* ("let the buyer beware"). In legal language, a caveat is a notice to suspend a given proceeding until the notifier is provided a hearing. In literary criticism, *caveat* most often means "objection to" or "dissent."

Celtic

This term refers to a branch of language (including Irish, Gaelic, Manx, Cornish, Welsh, and Breton) that survives in Ireland, in parts of Scotland and England, in Wales, and in Brittany. *Celtic* also refers to Celts, members of an *Indo-European family now represented by the Irish, Welsh, etc., but once dominant in central and western Europe. The *Celtic renaissance* is a term applied to the late nineteenth-century movement aimed at preservation of the Celtic language, reconstruction of Celtic history, and stimulus of a new literature primarily Irish in subject matter and spirit. Among important writers of this cause were W. B. Yeats, J. M. Synge, Lady Gregory, and Padraic Colum. See FOLK DRAMA.

censorship

The repression of material on moral, ethical, religious, or political grounds. The struggle for freedom of expression by writers forms a substantial part of literary history, ranging from the arguments of Aristophanes in the fourth century B.C. to the rating of films in the late twentieth century. Possibly the most eloquent attack on *censorship* ever written was Milton's *Areopagitica:*

> As good almost kill a man as kill a good book: who kills a man kills a reasonable creature, God's image; but he who destroys a good book kills reason itself. . . . A good book is the precious lifeblood of a master spirit, embalmed and treasured up on purpose to a life beyond life.

cento

A piece of writing, especially a poem, composed of quotations from the works of other authors. One of the best-known and most humorous of all *centos* is that appearing in Mark Twain's *Huckleberry Finn:*

To be or not to be; that is the bare bodkin
That makes calamity of so long life.

certitude

Freedom from doubt; confidence and certainty in matters of opinion and faith. Authors of assurance, conviction, and firm belief—such as Dr. Johnson, Emerson, and H. G. Wells—exhibit certitude to a marked degree.

chacun à son goût

A French phrase meaning "everyone to his own taste."

chanson

A chanson is now interpreted to mean any poem written in a simple form and style and intended to be sung. The term, which is French derived from Latin, appears often in the phrase *chanson de geste* ("a song of great deeds"), an early form of French *epic dealing with legendary or historical characters such as Charlemagne.

chant

Loosely, a song, but particularly a short, simple melody characterized by single notes to which syllables are vocalized (intoned). Chants are used most often in church services for the singing of *psalms and *canticles, in which *cadence is highly important. A chant royal is a rare, complex French verse form consisting of sixty lines arranged in five stanzas of eleven verses each plus an *envoi.

chantey

Also spelled *shanty* and *chanty,* a chantey is a sailor's song, especially one sung in rhythm during the performance of work. "Blow the Man Down" is an example.

chaos

A state of utter confusion or disorder. Numerous writers, including John Milton in his *Paradise Lost,* have conceived of chaos as the infinity of space (formless matter) supposed to have existed before creation (or existence) of the universe.

chapbook

A small *book or *pamphlet of *popular ballads and *tales, sold during the eighteenth century to people on the street by peddlers, or chapmen. Chapbooks included murder cases, travel tales, accounts of witchcraft, strange occurrences, and legends. Today, *chapbook* is used in the title of numerous small books and pamphlets dealing with miscellaneous subjects.

character

This term has several meanings, the most common of which is "the aggregate of traits and features that form the nature of some person or animal." *Character* also refers to moral qualities and ethical standards and principles. In literature, *character* has several other specific meanings, notably that of a person represented in a story, novel, play, etc. In seventeenth- and eighteenth-century England, a character was a formal *sketch or descriptive *analysis of a particular virtue or vice as represented in a person, what is now more often called a *character sketch.

characterization

The creation of *images of imaginary persons in drama, narrative poetry, the novel, and the short story is called characterization. In effective narrative literature, fictional persons, through characterization, become so credible that they exist for the reader as real people. See BELIEF.

Every reader is interested in people, or should be, because people are the most important single factor in individual lives. In fiction, a reader, primarily interested in the individuals concerned, has a natural tendency to identify with the "hero" and to hate the "villain" or to feel "for" or "with" one individual or group and "against" another.

It is difficult to identify with a character whom one does not know or understand. This is why characterization is important in fiction. Before a writer can make his reader sympathize with or oppose a character, that character must come alive. The reader wants to be able to visualize him— to see him act and hear him talk. Characterization, no mere by-product, is an essential part of *plot. Character generates (causes) plot and plot results from, and is dependent upon, character. See CAUSE AND EFFECT.

Writers use any or all of several basic means of characterization: a character is revealed by (1) his actions, (2) his speech, (3) his thoughts, (4) his physical appearance, (5) what other characters say or think of him. A *flat character is a minor participant in fiction, one who is characterized briefly by only one or two of these basic methods. A *round character is one fully developed by four or five of these methods and thus takes on such added dimensions that, as readers, we come to know and to understand him as a living, breathing human being. See VERISIMILITUDE.

Without characterization, no *thesis, no *plot, and no *setting can develop genuine interest for a reader or cause him to care what happens, or does not happen, to whom, and why.

character sketch

A study of personality, *setting, or *mood which contains little *action or *plot and places emphasis on descriptive details about an individual. A perfect example of a character sketch is the third paragraph of Stephen Vincent Benét's *The Devil and Daniel Webster.*

charade

A parlor game in which players take turns at acting out in *pantomime a word or phrase. By extension, *charade* has come to mean "pretense," as, for example, Lady Macbeth's sleepwalking scene in Shakespeare's *Macbeth.*

charisma

A capacity for eliciting the enthusiastic support and approval of others through some special virtue, personal quality, or unusual ability. Charisma (from a Greek word meaning "to favor") was a special attribute of such persons as Napoleon, George Washington, and Winston Churchill. Robin Hood was a charismatic leader of his band of outlaws.

charivari

Also spelled *shivaree,* charivari is a mock serenade with pans, horns, kettles, and other noisemakers provided for a newly married couple. The term is also applied to any noisy celebration.

Chartism

A nineteenth-century political movement in England, the basic object of which was to improve the social, economic, and political conditions of the so-called lower classes. This advocacy of universal suffrage, annual meetings of Parliament, and other reforms is reflected in the work of numerous essayists and novelists, for example, the novels of Charles Kingsley and Charles Dickens. The term is derived from a document called the People's Charter.

chase

A rectangular metal frame in which *type is locked (fastened) for printing or platemaking. As a verb, *chase* means to ornament metal by embossing or engraving.

Chaucerian stanza

A seven-line *stanza in iambic *pentameter, sometimes called *rhyme royal because the form was once associated with James I of England. This is a Chaucerian stanza from book 1 of Chaucer's *Troilus and Criseyde:*

> You lovers who now bathe in happiness,
> If in your veins a pitying drop there be,
> Reflect upon the outlived heaviness
> That you have suffered, and the adversity
> Of other folk; remember feelingly
> How you, too, Love dared sometimes to displease,
> Or else you won him with too great an ease.

chauvinism

Excessive devotion to any cause or movement, especially overly zealous or belligerent patriotism. The term, derived from the name of a soldier in Napoleon's army noted for his loud patriotism, also means blind and unwavering enthusiasm for military glory. Dr. Johnson had chauvinism in mind when he remarked to James Boswell, "Patriotism is the last refuge of a scoundrel."

chef d'oeuvre

In art, literature, and music, *chef d'oeuvre* means a masterpiece. In French, the meaning is "leading work." The chef d'oeuvre of John Milton, for example, is considered to be *Paradise Lost.*

chiaroscuro

This Italian word, derived from Latin *clarus* ("light") and *obscurus* ("dark"), refers to the distribution of light and shade in a picture. In the meaning of a *sketch of varying moods, *chiaroscuro* can be applied to writings that vary in content and tone. For instance, Lamb's *Dream-Children: A Reverie* is an essay in chiaroscuro because it is playful and pathetic, gay and wistful.

chiasmus

A form of *antithesis, a reversal in the order of words so that the second half of a statement balances the first half in inverted word order. This line from Coleridge is an example of chiasmus:
Flowers are lovely, love is flowerlike.

chimera

In literature, *chimera* usually refers to an idle or vain *fancy, an unrealizable dream, an *illusion or fabrication of the mind. For example, the narrator in Poe's *The Fall of the House of Usher* has several chimerical ideas about the brother and sister who are destroyed. The concept of an unreal or horrible creature of the imagination stems from Greek mythology, in which a chimera was a she-monster emitting flames of fire.

chinoiserie

An eighteenth-century style of ornamentation characterized by delicate, intricate patterns and extensive use of *motifs thought to be Chinese. In literature, the term is applied to *themes suggestive of Oriental life and thought.

chivalry

Derived from *chevalier,* a French word meaning "horseman" or "knight," *chivalry* is a term for the customs and rules of medieval knighthood, the sum of ideal qualifications of a knight, including valor, generosity, courtesy to women and to one's foes, loyalty, and, above all, skill in the use of arms. The manners and morals incorporated in chivalry approximated a medieval religious code for the so-called upper classes. The exploits of chivalrous warriors were the subject matter of many *romances of the Middle Ages. In *The Canterbury Tales,* Chaucer portrayed a "parfit [perfect] gentle knight," and Spenser filled his *The Faerie Queene* with a colorful procession of courteous and heroic men riding over plains and through forests. Commonplaces in romantic literature are chivalrous warriors faithful to God and king, true to their ladyloves, helpful to all persons in distress, and deadly to tyrants, giants, and monsters. Scott's *Ivanhoe* and Tennyson's *Idylls of the King* carry on the ideal- istic traditions of chivalry, but more realistic concepts may be found in Malory's *Morte d'Arthur* and in the mocking passages of Cervantes' *Don Quixote* and Mark Twain's *A Connecticut Yankee in King Arthur's Court.*

choriambus

A metrical foot of four syllables, two short between two long ones. This foot is occasionally used in a verse form known as choriambics. This line from Swinburne's *Choriambics* pro- vides an illustration:

Sweet thĕ / kíssĕs ŏf deáth / sét ŏn thy̆ líps.

chorus

A group of persons singing in unison. In ancient Greece, however, a chorus meant a group of singers and dancers who participated in religious festivals and dramatic perfor- mances and who, as actors, commented on the deeds of characters and interpreted for audiences the significance of events. By Elizabethan times, this active role of the chorus was handled by a single actor who recited both *prologue and *epilogue and occasionally provided commentary be- tween acts. In Shakespeare's *King Lear,* the Fool plays a choruslike role in his comments on the action of the play. A "chorus" character appears in T. S. Eliot's *Murder in the Cathedral.* In novels, both Thomas Hardy and Sir Walter Scott often used rustic characters in the role of choruses.

chrestomathy

A collection of literary passages, often by one author. (See ANTHOLOGY.) *A Mencken Chrestomathy,* for example, con- tains selections from the book and magazine writings of H. L. Mencken.

chronicle

From a Greek word meaning "time," *chronicle* refers to a record of events and is an approximate *synonym of *histo- ry. The first outstanding book of English prose is considered to be *The Anglo-Saxon Chronicle,* begun under King Alfred in the ninth century and covering history from 60 B.C. to the twelfth century. The term *chronicle* is usually employed in reference to any systematic account or narration of events that contains little or no interpretation and analysis.

chronicle play

A *drama based on historical material usually consisting of loosely connected *episodes arranged in order of time. Chronicle plays flourished in *Elizabethan times, partly because they taught history to uneducated audiences, partly because they made much use of pageantry, battles, and other spectacular dramatic elements. Several of Shakespeare's greatest works are chronicle plays, although the term *history play* is sometimes applied to those dramas, like *Henry V,* which are considered neither *tragedy nor *comedy.

chronological order

This term means "arrangement in order of time" and is the plan and method of much narrative writing and of some *exposition and *description. When one *sentence, *paragraph, or section follows another in the time sequence of the events narrated or discussed, the resulting composition is usually clear and obviously is logical but is not always the most artistic and effective method available. See CLIMACTIC ORDER, FLASHBACK, IN MEDIAS RES.

ci-devant

A French term meaning "heretofore," *ci-devant* means "retired," "late," a person or thing of the past. (The term was originally applied to persons who had been nobles before titles were abolished during the French Revolution.) A *ci-devant* author or literary theme is one now considered old-fashioned and outdated.

cinquain

A group of five. In poetry, *cinquain* is applied to any *stanza of five lines. In form, a cinquain is analogous to the Japanese *tanka.

cipher

(1) One of the arabic numerals or figures, such as zero; (2) a person of no importance; (3) a secret method of writing depending upon such devices as the substitution and transposition of letters. The art and practice of preparing or reading messages in forms to prevent their being read by those not privy to secrets is called cryptography and appears in numerous literary works such as, for example, several of the tales of Edgar Allan Poe and Swift's *Journal to Stella.*

circa

This Latin word means "about," "around." Most often used with dates, *circa* has extended meanings of "reasonable probability" and "approximation."

circular

A letter, advertisement, statement, or notice designed for circulation among the general public. Most circulars appear as a single sheet, or *leaflet.

circumlocution

An indirect and roundabout way of speaking and writing; the use of more words than necessary to express a thought. See CONCISENESS, DEADWOOD, PERIPHRASIS, PLEONASM, TAUTOLOGY, VERBIAGE.

circumstantial evidence

Proof of facts that are offered as evidence from which other facts are to be inferred. The theory of circumstantial evidence is that certain events or circumstances are usually attended by the fact at issue and therefore provide a reasonable inference regarding the occurrence of the condition at hand. By contrast, *direct* evidence immediately establishes the fact to be proved by it.

citation

In literary and scholarly usage, *citation* means reference to an authority or precedent. The term usually refers to the act of citing *verbatim the written or spoken words of another. (See BIBLIOGRAPHY, DOCUMENTATION, FOOTNOTE, PRIMARY SOURCE, SECONDARY SOURCE.) An additional meaning of *citation* is that of an award or commendation for outstanding achievement, like those granted many authors by international, national, and local literary associations.

clairvoyance

The alleged supernatural ability to see actions or objects removed in time or space from natural (normal) viewing; sudden, intuitive knowledge and understanding of people and events. A clairvoyant character in a novel, for example, has the power to see beyond the range of natural vision and to perceive by insight matters unknown to normal persons.

classic

As a noun, *classic* means a work of literature that is universally recognized for its outstanding and enduring qualities. Thus, the *Iliad* is a classic in world literature, *Hamlet* in English literature, *The Scarlet Letter* in American literature, etc. Arnold Bennett, English novelist and essayist, has written a clear explanation of why a classic is a classic:

> A classic is a work which gives pleasure to the minority which is intensely and permanently interested in literature. It lives on because the minority, eager to renew the sensation of pleasure, is eternally curious and is therefore engaged in an eternal pro-

cess of rediscovery. A classic does not survive for any ethical reason. It does not survive because it conforms to certain canons, or because neglect would kill it. It survives because it is a source of pleasure and because the passionate few can no more neglect it than a bee can neglect a flower.

The term *classics* is usually applied to the literature of ancient Greece and Rome. The adjective *classical* means "of recognized excellence" or "in the established tradition." See CLASSICISM.

classicism

This term refers to a body of doctrine apparently derived from the qualities of early Greek and Roman culture as reflected in art and especially in literature. Classicism stands for certain ideas and attitudes such as formal elegance, correctness, simplicity, restraint, order, dignity, and proportion. Often contrasted with *realism and *romanticism, classicism places emphasis upon qualities for which the early Greeks were notable: clear, direct, simple expression of ideas in balanced and well-proportioned form; restraint of emotion and passion; an ability to think and to communicate objectively rather than subjectively. No writer can be classified as a perfect example of classicism because no writer can be so dispassionate, so calm, so objective as to forsake all of his strictly human qualities and attitudes. However, certain qualities apparent in the classical works of Homer and Virgil are traceable in much of the writing of Ben Jonson, John Milton, Alexander Pope, Matthew Arnold, and T. S. Eliot.

classification and division

These two terms denote closely related methods of analysis which underlie all thinking processes and are essential in shaping an *outline which will suggest and reveal thought. Classification determines the whole (wholes) of which a given subject is a part; to classify is to place a subject in a category or class and then to put that class into a wider class (or classes). To divide is to follow the opposite procedure of regarding the given subject as a class (whole) which can be broken down, or resolved, into subclasses (lesser units). Division is a downward movement, classification is an upward movement; both express the relation of whole and part, of class and subclass, of class and member (individual unit). See ANALYSIS, SYNTHESIS.

clausula

A word from Latin meaning "the close" and sometimes used in literary criticism in the sense of *coda or *envoi. *Clausula* is more often employed in music, however, to indicate (1) a "closing" or "conclusion" and (2) an ornamented *cadence such as those appearing in early *Renaissance *compositions.

clearness

The major aim in reading is to understand what an author is attempting to convey. The major aim in writing is to communicate to readers. Clearness, the most desirable goal in reading and writing, is not all that is involved in both processes, but it is the *sine qua non, the "without which, nothing" quality of both.

Who has not read and reread material which was obviously "correct" and seemingly well constructed without being able to understand its meaning? Lack of understanding of good literature is the fault of the reader: lack of concentration, inability or unwillingness to "think with the author," inadequate knowledge of vocabulary or of essential background information. (The "fault" may also be a matter of age or of inexperience.) A major aim of literary study is to learn to read with clarity and understanding any selection which informed judgment calls superior. One does not have to enjoy or approve every selection he reads but merely to grasp it clearly.

Effective writers of the past and present have followed the advice of Anthony Hope, author of *The Prisoner of Zenda:* "Unless one is a genius, it is best to aim at being intelligible." Even geniuses have taken pains to make their every statement believable, reasonable, and logical. Even geniuses have unfailingly seen to such matters as completeness of thought, exact *diction, proper word order, and *unity—the building blocks of clearness.

clericalism

Strict and dogmatic control of religious matters by clergymen (ordained ministers); a policy favoring the maintenance and increase of churchly power over religious and even political matters. Clericalism has played a major role in certain periods of literary history as, for example, during the struggles between Henry VIII ("Defender of the Faith") and opposing forces in sixteenth-century England and the debate over "separation of church and state" in the United States.

clerihew

A light verse form named after its inventor, E. Clerihew Bentley, an English writer. A clerihew contains pseudobiographical references to the person being *lampooned. For example, here is a clerihew composed by Bentley when he was studying chemistry:

> Sir Humphry Davy
> Abominated gravy.
> He lived in the odium
> Of having discovered sodium.

cliché

From a French word meaning "to stereotype," a *cliché* is a

word, phrase, expression, or idea that has lost its originality and impact through constant and prolonged use. For instance, "green with envy" is a cliché that expresses a common thought in *hackneyed language. Overused or *trite plots and types of *characters and methods of *characterization are also known as clichés.

cliff-hanger

A *melodramatic adventure serial (in films or magazines) in which each installment ends in *suspense. That is, the viewer or reader is left hanging in suspense (just as portrayed characters are sometimes left on the brink of a precipice) so that interest in the eventual outcome will be sustained. The term *cliff-hanger* is applied to any event, situation, or contest in which the outcome is uncertain up to the last moment.

climactic order

An arrangement in which words, phrases, or sentences are placed in ascending order of forcefulness, intensity, or importance is called climactic order. A form of *climax is attained when each succeeding idea has more force, more appeal, more interest than its predecessor. Such an arrangement prevents a sentence, a paragraph, or an entire selection from "sagging" at the end, with consequent loss of force.

climate of opinion

The prevailing attitudes, standards, temper, outlook, and environmental conditions characterizing a period or a group of people. For example, the climate of opinion in Elizabethan England was nationalistic, venturesome, and hopeful. The climate of opinion in colonial America is now considered to have been pioneering, calculating, and God-fearing.

climax

The moment in a play, novel, short story, or narrative poem at which a *crisis comes to its point of greatest intensity and is in some manner resolved is called a climax. The term is an index of emotional response from reader or spectator and is also a designation of the turning point in action. See ACT, ANTICLIMAX, CRISIS.

cloak-and-dagger

This phrase applies to a play or novel that deals with espionage or intrigue and is highly dramatic and romantic. An allied form of drama and fiction is called cloak-and-sword, a type of writing in which characters actually wear cloaks and swords, exhibit courtly manners, and engage in duels. Dumas's *The Three Musketeers* is an example of cloak-and-sword (or cloak-and-dagger) romance.

closed couplet

A *couplet (two lines), rhyming *aa,* that expresses a complete, independent statement. Such a couplet is "closed" because its meaning does not depend upon what precedes or follows:

Hope springs eternal in the human breast;
Man never is, but always to be, blessed. (Pope)

closet drama

A *play, usually in verse, more appropriate for reading than for acting. Notable examples are Milton's *Samson Agonistes* and Browning's *Pippa Passes.*

clue (clew)

A clue (or clew) is anything (act, object, facial expression, etc.) that serves to direct and guide in the solution of a problem, mystery, etc. All *detective and *mystery stories are somewhat dependent upon clues.

cock-and-bull story

An absurd, improbable narrative presented as the truth. The term probably is derived from some *fable (most fables are cock-and-bull stories) in which a cock and bull are characters. Many *tall tales are also cock-and-bull *yarns.

cockney

A native of the East End district of London, England. Persons born within the range of sound of the bells of Bow Church in this area traditionally are called cockney and have a distinct *dialect, such as the pronunciation of *lady* as *lidey.* Cockney is sometimes associated with poor taste, low birth, and rudeness of manner. Such writers as Keats and Shelley were once called members of the Cockney School because they allegedly exhibited poor taste in some of their diction and rhyming.

coda

From a Latin word meaning "tail," *coda* refers to a largely independent passage at the end of a literary or musical *composition. A coda, or tailpiece, is designed to bring a work to a successful conclusion by serving as a summation of preceding *themes or *motifs. See CAUDA.

codex

From a Latin word meaning "block of wood" or "tree trunk." A codex was originally a wooden tablet made suitable for writing with a coat of wax. When wood was replaced by parchment and paper, the term was retained for manuscript pages held together by stitching. *Codices* is a term now applied to manuscript volumes of any kind.

codicil

A supplement, an *appendix. Although usually applied to a will, *codicil* means any modification, addition, or explanation attached as a supplement to a piece of writing.

coffee-table book

A coffee table is a low bench usually placed in a prominent position in a living room. *Coffee-table book* is a disparaging term applied to a large and usually expensive art book or similar volume displayed as a *status symbol on social occasions.

cogito, ergo sum

A Latin phrase meaning "I think, therefore I am." This phrase was the underlying philosophical principle of René Descartes, seventeenth-century French philosopher and mathematician.

cognate

Formed from two Latin words meaning "born together," *cognate* means "allied or similar in nature and quality." Cognate languages, such as English and German, are both members of the so-called Teutonic branch of languages. Cognate words, occurring in different languages, are derived from the same source, as, for example, German *kalt* and English *cold.* In literature, selections that resemble each other in *theme, *mood, or subject matter are said to be cognate.

cognitive meaning

A term applied to words and statements that are capable of being perceived and consequently known; that is, to comments about reality as experienced by most people. "Water is wet" and "Two times three equals six" are statements with cognitive meaning, ideas that do not express attitude or emotion. The phrase *cognitive meaning* is important in literature because some critics hold that poetry, for example, has no cognitive meaning, that it is neither false nor true, that it expresses and arouses emotions only, that poetry does not "mean" but "is." In other words, *cognitive meaning* is the *antonym of *emotive meaning.

coherence

This word means "holding together." A literary work is coherent in that it is so closely constructed, so clearly put together, that its readers, if attentive, are never confused about the relationships of its parts. A careful writer *transfers* ideas from his own mind to those of his readers, trying always to show clear and orderly progress from beginning to end. In a fully coherent composition, one paragraph, scene, or stanza grows from the preceding one; each group dealing with one section is close-ly connected, held together, with other groups.

coinage

In a general sense, *coinage* refers to anything that is made, invented, or fabricated. In literature, *coinage* refers to words consciously and arbitrarily manufactured, as contrasted with words that have entered the language through long-standing, natural processes. For example, H. L. Mencken fabricated the word *ecdysiast* as the name of an exotic dancer who removed articles of clothing while performing. This coinage and many others now enrich the language. See NEOLOGISM.

coincidence

Two or more events or circumstances occurring at one time without any obvious causal connection create a coincidence. Despite the appearance of chance in everyone's life—an influ-ence which seems to appear and reappear—effective writers shy away from coincidence. Good literature provides a *cause for any *effect and thus prevents the reader's judging it as "improbable" or "impossible" or "preposterous." (See BELIEF.) In addition to irritating readers, repeated use of coincidence (mere chance) stretches the odds of life too much; a string of fortuitous events exceeds probability and becomes banal and unbelievable. A tightly knit chain of *cause and effect elimi-nates need for coincidence. An effective piece of narration makes less use of coincidence than life itself does simply be-cause "life is stranger than fiction dares to be." See VERISIMILI-TUDE.

cold composition

The production of written (printed) material by machines such as typewriters and photocomposing units or in any manner in which no molten metal is used to form *images. By contrast, hot composition refers to casting slugs of *type with molten metal.

collaboration

The act of "working together," the association of two or more people in a given task. Beaumont and Fletcher provide one of the best-known examples of collaboration in English literature; Gilbert and Sullivan were collaborators; dictionaries, ency-clopedias, and many other reference works result from the process of collaboration.

collage

The technique of composing a work of art by pasting together on a single surface materials not normally associated with one another, such as newspaper clippings, bottle tops or labels, theater tickets, etc. In literature, collage is illustrated in the work of such writers as John Milton, Charles Lamb, James Joyce, T. S. Eliot, and Ezra Pound, who have inserted *allusions, foreign expressions, and quotations from other writers into their essays and poems.

collate
This term means to bring together in order to compare. It refers to the critical examination of a statement or text of a manuscript so as to note points of agreement, or disagreement, between copies of that statement or text. *Collate* also means to place together in proper order the sheets of a *manuscript, *pamphlet, or *book. A collation is a careful comparison of two or more texts, editions, or printings. In older novels and plays, *collation* is sometimes used as the name for a "light meal."

collective unconscious
This is a term from psychology, largely *Jungian psychology, that applies to racially inherited ideas and concepts that allegedly persist in one's individual unconscious mind. Jung and his followers have held that typical characteristics of man's mind and spirit are conditioned by race, nation, family, and the spirit of the age in which he lives. These are combined with unique personal qualities. This psychological theory contends that the personal and the collective elements of man's *psyche are closely interrelated and that man is moved on the unconscious level to many attitudes and reactions over which he has no direct control.

colloquialism
A word or phrase used in conversation and indispensable to an easy, informal style of writing and speaking. Colloquialisms (the term is derived from Latin words meaning "to speak" and "conversation") are considered more appropriate in speech than in formal writing, but they appear often in literature, especially in *dialogue, because they provide a sense of actual talk.

colloquy
This is another name for *dialogue and conversational exchange. The word *colloquy* also means a "conference," a "speaking together," and "an exchange of opinions."

colophon
From a Greek word meaning "summit" or "finishing touch," *colophon* refers to information supplied at the end of a book about its printer, publisher, the date and place of publication, the type used, etc. More often, *colophon* is used to refer to the distinctive sign, or *emblem, of a publisher. When a publisher's emblem appears at the front of a book (usually on the *title page), it is called an *imprint.

color

This word of several meanings is used in literature to refer to a writing style that is vivid (with abundant details, fast-moving) and is filled with striking *images. *Color* is also applied to the slant of a writer, his opinions and attitudes. (See BIAS.) For instance, the work of Henry James is said to have been colored by his attitudes toward wealth, social position, and culture.

colporteur

A book peddler. A colporteur distributes pamphlets, religious tracts, and inexpensive reprints on the streets and to homes.

column

One of the several vertical blocks of print on a newspaper, magazine, or book page; the term *column* also refers to a regular department of a *periodical which usually carries the name of the author. Such a column reports or comments upon a particular field of interest (theater, politics, world affairs, etc.).

combining form

A term used in *lexicography and *linguistics for word elements (learned borrowings) that may appear independently but nearly always form parts of compound words. Examples are *hemato* (in *hematology*) and *graph* (in *lithography*). See AFFIX, PREFIX, ROOT, STEM, SUFFIX.

Linguists differ in their application of labels to word-formations, so that one expert will call a given element a prefix or suffix and another will list it as a combining form or "learned borrowing." However labeled, the roots (stems) of the following Greek and Latin expressions appear in many words, the approximate meaning of which can quickly be determined from information supplied here:

anima (life, breath)	locus (place)
aqua (water)	mater (mother)
aristos (the best)	navis (ship)
beatus (blessed)	opus (work)
bios (life)	pes, pedis (foot)
causa (cause)	petra (rock)
culpa (fault)	plus (more)
decem (ten)	polis (many)
domus (house)	populus (people)
ego (I)	sanctus (holy)
facilis (easy)	sophia (wisdom)
gramma (letter)	tacitus (silence)
hostis (enemy)	thermo (heat)
lex (law)	umbra (shade)
liber (book)	vita (life)

comedy

A ludicrous, farcical, or amusing event or series of events designed to provide enjoyment and produce smiles or laughter. More specifically, *comedy* (from Greek words meaning "merrymaking" and "singing") refers to any literary selection written in a light, familiar, bantering, or satirical style. Even more specifically, the term applies to a *play of light and amusing character that has a happy ending.

The pattern of dramatic comedy is the reverse of *tragedy. Comedy begins in difficulty (or rapidly involves its characters in amusingly difficult situations) and invariably ends happily; tragedy may, and often does, begin in happy circumstances and always ends in disaster. Not all comedies are humorous and lighthearted, although the great majority are. Occasionally, a comedy can be serious in *tone and intent as, for example, Dante's *Divine Comedy,* but even this is a comedy of a special sort because its *action begins in Hell and ends in Heaven. Comedy differs from *burlesque and *farce in that it has a more closely knit *plot, more sensible and intelligent *dialogue, and more plausible *characterization. In general, a comedy secures its effects by stressing some oddity or incongruity of character, speech, or action. When these effects are crude, the comedy is termed "low"; when they are subtle and thoughtful, the comedy is called "high." Other types of comedy are numerous; three may be mentioned: (1) comedy of *humors,* involving characters whose actions are controlled by some *whim or *humor; (2) comedy of *manners,* involving the *conventions and manners of artificial, sophisticated society; (3) comedy of *intrigue* or *situation,* depending upon plot more than characterization (such as Shakespeare's *The Comedy of Errors*).

comic relief

A humorous scene, incident, or remark occurring in the midst of a serious or tragic literary selection is referred to as comic relief. Such an intrusion is deliberately designed by a playwright or novelist to relieve emotional intensity and simultaneously to heighten, increase, and highlight the seriousness or tragedy of the action. Such an *episode, or *interlude, can enrich the tragic implications of a story, as no one knew better than Shakespeare. He provided comic relief in many of his plays, notably with the role of Mercutio in *Romeo and Juliet,* the gravedigger scene in *Hamlet,* and the episode of the drunken porter in *Macbeth.*

comic strip

A sequence of drawings usually printed in a horizontal strip (series of panels) in a newspaper or in a longer sequence of blocks in a Sunday newspaper supplement or so-called comic book. The drawings in a comic strip, appearing in color or black-and-white, relate a comic incident or an *adventure or *mystery story. The *dialogue often appears in *balloons (words enclosed in lines represented as coming from the mouth of a speaker).

commedia dell'arte

Popular Italian comedy developed during the period from the sixteenth to the eighteenth century, in which masked entertainers improvised dialogue and action from a *plot *outline based on themes associated with *stock situations and *stock characters. The term literally means "comedy of art." The characters and action in a Punch-and-Judy show constitute an example of this type of comic drama.

comme il faut

A term from French that means "as it should be," "proper," "appropriate," "suitable."

comminatory

An adjective indicating the conveying of a threat or warning, suggesting that punishment or vengeance will be forthcoming. A comminatory example of literature is one which indicates that divine vengeance and retribution are inevitable. Two works of literature largely comminatory are Milton's *Paradise Lost* and Hawthorne's *The Scarlet Letter*.

common measure

Designated by the abbreviation C.M. and frequently appearing with hymns, common measure consists of lines of fixed iambic meter that end in exact rhymes. Also called "common time" and the "hymnal stanza," common measure is most often applied to a group of four iambic lines rhyming *abab* or *abcb*.

commonplace book

A book in which quotations in prose and verse are entered as remarks and ideas for further consideration. The writer of a commonplace book, as distinguished from the keeper of a *diary or author of a *journal, may make irregular entries concerning various topics. A commonplace book may consist entirely of an author's own sayings or wholly of excerpts from the writings and comments of others. Jefferson and Emerson compiled commonplace books of genuine interest to themselves and to later readers.

commonwealth

This term refers to a group of sovereign states and their associated dependencies, as, for example, the British Commonwealth of Nations. Certain states of the United States refer to themselves as commonwealths rather than as states: the Commonwealth of Virginia. In English literary history, the term (with a capital letter) refers to the period between the execution of Charles I in 1649 and the restoration of the monarchy under Charles II in 1660. During most of this time, England was governed by Parliament under the direction of Oliver Cromwell, the Puritan leader, with John Milton as Latin Secretary of the Commonwealth government.

comp

A contraction of several different longer words, loosely used to mean (1) a compositor (of type); (2) the act of composing (type, literature, music); (3) a complimentary ticket to a theatrical or film performance; (4) a compilation (*anthology) of any sort; (5) accompanying a *jazz soloist with spaced chords to punctuate *rhythm.

comparison and contrast

A method used to place together and thus bring into relief two or more persons, ideas, or circumstances so as to establish their similarities and dissimilarities. Skilled writers frequently use comparison and contrast to describe characters and places, to explain *plot situations, and to make clear their *themes and purposes. For example, in describing the leading female character in *The Return of the Native,* Hardy wrote, "In her movements, in her gaze, she reminded the beholder of the feathered creatures who lived around her home." In its broadest sense, *comparison* embraces the meaning of *contrast* since it involves or implies not only likenesses but differences. See ANALOGY, CONTRAST AND COMPARISON, CONTRAPUNTAL, COUNTERPOINT.

compassion

A feeling of sympathy or sorrow for someone who is beset by misfortune or suffering, accompanied by a desire to lessen that misfortune or suffering. Many writers have exhibited compassion in their work, for example, Charles Dickens in *Oliver Twist* and *Hard Times* and Abraham Lincoln in most of his speeches and letters.

compendium

A brief treatment or account of a subject. (See ABRIDGED, UNABRIDGED.) A compendium is also an inventory or list.

compensation

A form of substitution, a means of supplying omissions in verse. Compensation usually involves unstressed syllables, the absence of which is compensated for by a rest, or pause, as in Tennyson's lines:

Break, break, break
On thy cold grey stones, O Sea!

Despite the fact that the second of these lines has seven syllables and the first only three, the lines are metrically equivalent because of pauses following each of the words in the first line.

complaint

A *lyric poem that comments on the misery of the speaker (the poet), usually involving either the fickleness of his beloved, the dreadful state of the world, or his general unhappiness. Well-known complaints are Chaucer's *To His Empty Purse* and Surrey's *Complaint of a Lover Rebuked.*

complication

A difficult issue or situation, appearing sometimes suddenly, which changes existing plans, methods, or attitudes. In literature, a complication consists of a detail of *character or *situation entering into and twisting or changing the main thread of a *plot. Specifically, in plays and stories it is that part of the narrative in which entanglement of affairs caused by the *conflict of opposing forces is developed and explained. Complication, usually the middle part of a story or play, develops the conflict already set forth: it "ties the knot tighter" by placing further obstacles in the path of the *protagonist, by mentioning further misunderstandings, by raising additional problems. The second act of a five-act tragedy is often called "the act of complication." See ACT.

composition

The act of composition is the formation of a whole by creating, ordering, and arranging its parts. A composition is any literary, musical, or artistic product which reveals some plan and form. Every literary selection is a composition in one form or another: poem, essay, novel, play, short story, letter, biography, etc. In schools, the term is applied to any written exercise but especially to a piece of writing which exhibits a plan, care in preparation, and a definite *purpose or *thesis. See COMP.

compos mentis

A Latin phrase meaning "being in possession of one's mind," *compos mentis* means "sane," "mentally sound." The phrase *non compos mentis* ("mentally incapable") appears more frequently in literature than *compos mentis.*

comprehensive

This is an adjective most often applied to *biography or *history that is of large scope, that involves or covers much, that details everything concerned. Edward Gibbon's *The Decline and Fall of the Roman Empire,* a history in six volumes, has been termed comprehensive. No single work of literature really deserves such a judgment, but perhaps the thirty-seven plays of Shakespeare do approximate a comprehensive treatment of man's will, intellect, and passions.

comstockery

Moral censorship of the fine arts and literature. Comstockery (named after Anthony Comstock, an American writer and reformer) is often intense, overly zealous condemnation and attempted suppression of outspoken works that are not necessarily salacious. See CENSORSHIP.

con amore
An Italian phrase most often used as a musical direction, *con amore* means "with love," "with tender zeal and enthusiasm."

con brio
An Italian phrase frequently used in music, *con brio* means "vigorously," "with energy," "vivaciously."

conceit
A fanciful *image, an elaborate *metaphor in which a writer describes a person or idea by use of an *analogy which often seems farfetched and even startling. A beautiful woman, for example, is discussed as a rose or as a marble statue. Some conceits are merely fanciful, some remarkably ingenious, some artificial, some highly intellectual; some seem appropriate, striking, effective; others appear false and misleading. Effective or not, conceits have been common in literature, especially poetry, from the time of Petrarch (1304–1374) to the present.

John Donne, noting that his love was about to destroy a flea which had extracted blood from both himself and her, wrote:

> Oh, stay, three lives in one flea spare,
> Where we almost, yea, more than married are.
> This flea is you and I, and this
> Our marriage bed, and marriage temple is.

Shakespeare uses several conceits and simultaneously satirizes them in the opening of one of his sonnets:

> My mistress' eyes are nothing like the sun;
> Coral is far more red than her lips' red;
> If snow be white, why then her breasts are dun;
> If hairs be wires, black wires grow on her head.

conciseness
The expression of thought in economical, terse language. A concise statement is brief in form, however *comprehensive it may be in scope. *Conciseness* is derived from a Latin term meaning "to cut short" and suggests that brevity adds to the force and appeal of expression. See PLEONASM, TAUTOLOGY.

In Shakespeare's *Hamlet,* old Polonius announces:

> Therefore, since brevity is the soul of wit,
> And tediousness the limbs and outward flourishes,
> I will be brief.

Polonius was really a garrulous, tiresome man, and yet he was making an important comment. He was *not* saying that brevity (conciseness) is the center and heart of "humor." In this *context, *wit* means "understanding" or "wisdom." That is, Polonius (Shakespeare) was saying that being concise, to the point, is the only way to express genuine thought effectively. Lincoln's Gettysburg Address contains 267 words. The Ten Commandments require 75 words. The Golden Rule contains 11 words.

concordance

With the general meaning of "agreement" and "harmony," *concordance* is most often applied to an alphabetical *index of topics or subjects and to lists of passages or words in an important book (such as the *Bible) or the complete works of Chaucer, Shakespeare, Milton, etc.

concreteness

Effective writers achieve concreteness in their work by giving it a quality of reality, specific elements that the reader can see, hear, feel, smell, or taste. Even emotions and sensations are made to seem tangible. A literary artist ordinarily does not merely "tell" about the characters he portrays; he "shows" them in their actions and thoughts.

For example, Shakespeare, in describing the intensity and brooding countenance of Cassius in *Julius Caesar,* not only notes these characteristics but writes "Yond Cassius has a lean and hungry look." Thus are made vivid and unmistakable the unhappiness and frustration of a man who "thinks too much." For another example, "jealousy" is referred to in *Othello* as "the green-eyed monster"; in *Romeo and Juliet,* the hero remarks that no one can understand the depth of his love for Juliet because no one has ever loved as he does: "He jests at scars that never felt a wound."

Writers possess the ability to abstract and to generalize and frequently use these powers. But their aim is to move, not merely inform; to portray, not merely philosophize. They make *abstractions on occasion, but more often they leave abstraction and conclusions for the reader to draw for himself. In most writing, the primary aim of the author is to make the reader *feel* and then to *think;* as the French writer Guy de Maupassant put it, "The public is composed of numerous groups who cry to us [authors]: 'Console me, amuse me, make me sad, make me sympathetic, make me dream, make me laugh, make me shudder, make me weep, make me think.' " Normally, only writing which possesses concreteness can achieve these effects. See ABSTRACT DICTION, ABSTRACTION, BELIEF.

condensation

From Latin words meaning "to thicken together," *condensation* applies to a shortened version of a longer work, especially a novel or play. See *ABRIDGED, ABSTRACT, APERÇU,

BRIEF, CONSPECTUS, EPITOME, PRÉCIS, REDACTION, RÉSUMÉ, SUMMARY, SYNOPSIS.

confession

This term means an acknowledgment, an avowal, a disclosure of some sort. In a literary application, *confession* does not necessarily imply an admission of sin or wrongdoing. De Quincey's *Confessions of an English Opium Eater* and the *Confessions of Saint Augustine* resemble *autobiography far more than they do the vulgar forms of "confession stories" found in *pulp magazines. Rousseau's *Confessions* and George Moore's *Confessions of a Young Man* disclose autobiographical details not usually revealed, but they primarily express their authors' most profound convictions and deepest thoughts.

A *confessional* usually refers to a place set apart for the hearing of confessions by a priest.

confidant

A confidant (feminine, *confidante*) is a person to whom secrets and intimate thoughts are entrusted, an intimate friend or acquaintance with whom one feels free to discuss secret or private matters. Dramatists and novelists have often used a confidant rather than employing an *aside or *soliloquy to reveal the thoughts of major characters and to summarize events not shown onstage or not revealed in a *flashback. Usually a minor character, a confidant thus enables a writer to show the *protagonist in more intimate detail than otherwise would be possible: as confidant, Dr. Watson reveals much about Sherlock Holmes, Horatio about Hamlet, and Lady Macbeth about her husband.

conflict

The opposition of persons or forces upon which the *action depends in drama and fiction is called conflict. Dramatic conflict is the struggle which grows out of the interplay of opposing forces (ideas, interests, wills) in a *plot; conflict may be termed the material from which a plot is constructed.

One type of conflict is *elemental,* or *physical:* a struggle between man and the physical world. It represents man versus forces of nature: the difficulties and dangers, for example, faced by explorers, navigators, astronauts. Rain, cold, heat, wild beasts in the jungle, treacherous tides—these are constant obstacles to mankind. Such elemental conflicts are frequently found in films, in melodramatic television plays, and in *pulp magazines; occasionally, combined with other ingredients, they appear in narrative or dramatic masterpieces.

Another type of conflict is *social:* a struggle between man and man. Much popular fiction is based on social conflict: two men trying to win the love of a girl; the competition of businessmen; a girl having difficulties with her parents over her conduct; racial and religious prejudices, etc.

A third kind of conflict is *internal,* or *psychological:* a struggle between desires within a person. External forces may be important and other characters may appear in the narrative, but the focus is always upon the central figure's inner turmoil.

A variant form of social conflict is a *protagonist's struggle against society, as in some of the novels of Dickens, George Eliot, and Theodore Dreiser. A fifth kind of conflict is man's struggle against fate and destiny as, for example, in a play by Sophocles or a novel by Thomas Hardy. But most conflicts are basically physical, social, or internal—or combinations of these three. Conrad's *Youth* contains elements of all three kinds of conflict, but the primary one is physical; so, too, Stevenson's *Treasure Island* is primarily, although not wholly, a plotted narrative based on physical conflict. All of Hardy's novels contain elements of each kind of conflict, but the dominant struggle is usually social (between man and man or between man and society). The great tragedies of *Macbeth* and *Hamlet* contain elements of each kind of conflict, but the basic one in each instance is internal.

conjugation

The changes in the form and uses of a verb to show number, person, etc.: I *am,* you *are,* he *is;* I *am* seeing, you *are* seeing, they *are* seeing.

connoisseur

A French term, originally from Latin and meaning "knower," a connoisseur is a person competent to pass judgment in some art or field of knowledge, especially in matters of taste. A connoisseur is a perceptive, discerning judge, particularly in the fine arts and literature.

connotation

The suggestions and associations which have surrounded a word as contrasted with its bare, literal meaning, its *denotation. For example, the denotative meaning of *gold* is "a malleable, ductile, yellow trivalent and univalent metallic element," but its connotative meaning is associated with color, riches, power, happiness, greed, luxury, evil, and misery. These suggestions and implications beyond the core meaning of *gold* constitute its connotation, its "plus" or "added" associations. A mother is "a female parent," but everyone adds his private and personal meanings to the word as well as group meanings of national or racial origin and even universal concepts of the term.

To a good writer, both denotations and connotations are important. He uses words with exact and specific meanings, but he knows that insensitiveness to the connotative values of words will rob his work of charm and effectiveness. If he never uses connotation, his writing will be flatter, more insipid, than it should be.

Scientists and philosophers tend to use words in their denotative meanings; literary artists rely upon connotation for beautiful effects and deepest meanings. An essayist (Robert Thouless) has illustrated this distinction by quoting these lines from Keats's *The Eve of St. Agnes:*

Full on this casement shone the wintry moon
And threw warm gules on Madeline's fair breast.

He then shows how all beauty and richness are destroyed by substituting neutral, denotative words:

Full on this window shone the wintry moon,
Making red marks on Jane's uncolored chest.

consonance

Having a general meaning of "accord" and "agreement," *consonance* is used in *prosody to refer to the correspondence of consonants, especially those at the end of a word. A kind of *rhyme, consonance is illustrated in a phrase such as "dis*cuss* and then dis*miss.*" See ALLITERATION, ASSONANCE.

conspectus

A survey; a general or comprehensive view; a *digest or *summary that retains the overall pattern of a larger work but condenses its contents sharply. See ABRIDGED, ABSTRACT, APERÇU, BRIEF, EPITOME, PRÉCIS, REDACTION, RÉSUMÉ, SUMMARY, SYNOPSIS.

construct

As a verb, *construct* (accented on the second syllable) means "to form by putting together," "to frame," "to devise." As a noun, *construct* (accented on the first syllable) refers to a complex idea or *image formed from several less complex images and ideas. For example, the construct of the "waste land" depicted in some of T. S. Eliot's poems is based upon his concepts of observed frailties, imperfections, and foibles in mankind.

conte

A French term, *conte* originally applied to any *short story or *tale, especially one dealing with legendary, extraordinary, and highly imaginative events. In general use, *conte* is but a name for a compact, brief story, such as those written by Guy de Maupassant.

contents

The thing, things, or substance in a receptacle or enclosed space is called *content,* usually in plural form, *contents.* Thus, one refers to the topics, ideas, statements, or facts in a book, document, letter, or other literary selection as its content (contents). The term is generally synonymous with *subject matter* or *substance.* A *table of contents is a condensed enumeration, a systematic arrangement of a book or other document.

context

The part, or parts, of a passage of writing or speaking preceding or following a particular word or group of words is referred to as *context.* The context of a group of words is nearly always so intimately connected as to throw light upon not only the meaning of individual words but the sense and purpose of an entire passage or selection.

The surroundings of any statement often change, extend, or amend the meaning which seems apparent in the statement itself. For example, Cardinal Newman's famous essay *Definition of a Gentleman* begins with this statement: "Hence it is that it is almost a definition of a gentleman to say he is one who never inflicts pain." But it is unfair and unwise to quote Newman's definition without recalling the *almost* in the statement; the author explains in the context, in every statement which follows, that even one who inflicts no pain is not an ideal gentleman unless he holds religious convictions.

Certain passages in the Bible and in many other great works of literature in themselves seem cruel or obscene but, taken in context, have different meanings. One basic test for *pornography is determining the intent, purpose, and character of an entire work—the complete selection in context—rather than focusing upon a particular passage notable for its profanity or obscenity. "Quoting out of context" and "reading out of context" are considered serious faults in literary criticism.

continuity

The state or quality of being continuous, uninterrupted, of unbroken persistence or occurrence is called continuity. Thus one speaks of the continuity of ancient Greece, meaning Greek life for a period of centuries and the connection of that life with modern-day living. More specifically, one refers to the continuity of a novel, or short story, meaning its unbroken thread of events, the links in the chain of narrative constituting a fictional *plot.

Continuity is also a name for a detailed *scenario or "shooting script" showing *dialogue, scenes (shots), and transitions in a TV presentation or motion picture.

contraction

A drawing together or into smaller size, *contraction* most often refers to a shortened form of a word or phrase: *I'll* for *I will* or *I shall, exam* for *examination.* The term is sometimes applied to a literary selection which covers a major theme in comparatively brief space.

contrapuntal

Primarily a term used in music, *contrapuntal* means "composed of two or more independent melodies sounded together." A term derived from Latin words meaning "point against point," *contrapuntal* is an adjectival form of *counterpoint. The method by which one theme in a novel, for example, is developed and balanced against another is contrapuntal and constitutes a kind of counterpoint. Another example is Shakespeare's use of contrapuntal character development in contrasting Hamlet's indecisiveness with his desire for revenge.

contrast and comparison

A standard rhetorical device by which authors note similarities and differences in the actions and reactions of characters, in descriptions of settings, and in results of *cause and effect relations. For example, Dylan Thomas's line "I see the boys of summer in their ruin" uses comparison and contrast to suggest youth and age, hope and despair, life and death. See COMPARISON AND CONTRAST.

contretemps

A term from French literally meaning "counter" (against) and "time," *contretemps* is used to refer to an embarrassing mishap, an inopportune occurrence. One of the most fateful contretemps in literature is the sudden knocking at the gate in act 2 of *Macbeth,* which startles the murderers and leads to premature discovery of the killing of Duncan. Literature is filled with such contretemps as overheard conversations, detected falsehoods, unexpected invasions of privacy, and social blunders.

control

As both noun and verb, *control* refers to command, direction, authority, and regulation. In science and *literature, *control* may mean a standard of comparison (see ARCHETYPE, PROTOTYPE), but in writing, *control* most often refers to the authority and mastery which an author exercises in the handling of subject matter (*characters, *plot, etc.).

controlling image

A *metaphor or *image which persists throughout a literary work and determines its form and nature. The controlling image of Thurber's *The Secret Life of Walter Mitty,* for example, is that of a timid, depressed, and badgered man who seeks to escape humdrum routine. The controlling image of much of Faulkner's writing is decadence; of Hemingway's, courage under pressure.

conundrum

A *riddle or anything that puzzles, *conundrum* is a term used to refer to an unsolvable problem, but most often it poses a question the answer to which involves a play on words. A typical conundrum is "Where is tennis mentioned in the Bible?" Answer: "When Joseph served in Pharaoh's court."

convention

A literary practice which has become an established means of expression, an accepted technique. Literature makes use of scores of conventions, such as the fainting heroine of sentimental fiction, the despair of a rejected lover, a bragging coward as a *stock character, the set pattern of rhyme in much poetry, love at first sight, the *fading of an image on a motion-picture screen to indicate a lapse of time, etc. When a set of conventions is characteristic of a group of writers, the word *tradition* is used: the *classical* tradition, the *pastoral* tradition, the *Puritan* tradition, etc. See BELIEF, DRAMATIC CONVENTION.

conversation piece

Any object that arouses comment because of some unusual or outstanding quality; a group portrait of fashionable people in a landscape or indoor setting. In literature, *conversation piece* is usually applied to *drama in which talk seems more important than *plot or *theme. Many of Oscar Wilde's plays are conversation pieces because characters in them do little but speak wittily and pungently. George Bernard Shaw wrote several plays notable for their *dialogue rather than their plot or entertainment value.

copy

In its most general sense, *copy* means an imitation, transcript, or reproduction of an original, but in literature it refers to any *composition, whether handwritten or typed, that is intended for printing. In journalism, *copy* applies to the appeal or newsworthiness of a person or event ("A human interest story is always good copy").

copy editing

The act of preparing a *composition, *manuscript, or *document for publication. Copy editing involves attention to spelling, punctuation, sentence structure, clarity and accuracy of expression, etc.

copyright

The exclusive right, granted by law for a fixed period, to produce, dispose of, and otherwise control copies of a literary and artistic work. In the United States, a copyright extends for twenty-eight years, is renewable once, and thus controls for fifty-six years. In England, regardless of the date of initial publication and copyright, protection continues for fifty years after the author's death.

copywriting
The preparation of material for appearance in advertisements or publicity releases.

coronach
A funeral *dirge, a poem or song of lamentation. A Gaelic word, *coronach* means "a crying out together." Canto 3 of Sir Walter Scott's *The Lady of the Lake* is called "Coronach," one stanza of which begins:
> The hand of the reaper
> Takes the ears that are hoary,
> But the voice of the weeper
> Wails manhood in glory.

Corpus Christi
Literally, the body of Christ. A Corpus Christi play was a medieval religious drama performed as part of a procession on the fiftieth day after Easter.

corrigendum
An error to be corrected. *Corrigendum* especially refers to an error in print. *Corrigenda* applies to a list of corrections of errors in a book or other publication.

cosmic
Immeasurably extended in time or space. *Cosmic* is used to refer to events and concepts such as those in Dante's *Divine Comedy* and Milton's *Paradise Lost* that are vast, universal, and even outside the earth.

costume piece
Another name for a *historical play and *historical novel, *costume piece* is applied to works of literature that rely heavily on *pageantry, romantic action, and methods of dressing. See CHRONICLE PLAY, CLOAK-AND-DAGGER.

coterie
A group of persons associated because of similar interests and purposes. One of the most famous coteries in literature was called the Sons of Ben, a group of seventeenth-century poets who attempted to continue the literary ideals of Ben Jonson (1572–1637), the Elizabethan playwright. The *beat generation is a somewhat loose but populous kind of coterie. See CABAL.

cothurnus
A high-soled boot worn by actors in ancient Greek tragedies. See BUSKIN.

counterplot

A secondary *theme in a play or novel used as a variation of the principal theme or in contrast to it. A counterplot (also called a subplot) constitutes a related but separate action. Counterplots appear in several of Shakespeare's plays, such as *Hamlet, King Lear,* and *Henry IV.* In the last-named, the activities of Falstaff and his companions are the counterplot, whereas the principal theme is the putting down of a political rebellion. In *Hamlet,* the struggle between Laertes and Hamlet is the counterplot to the primary conflict between Hamlet and Claudius. In *King Lear,* the dominant figure of the counterplot (Edmund) actually determines the outcome of the principal action.

counterpoint

In music, counterpoint is the art of combining melodies; in literature, counterpoint is the art and technique of playing off complementary and opposing *characters, *themes, or *plots against each other. In a novel entitled *Point Counter Point,* Aldous Huxley moves from one set of individuals to another, balancing each life against its "counterpoint." The lives of these people repeat the same patterns in different forms. See CONTRAPUNTAL.

counterword

A term or expression that is used with a meaning much less specific than its original one. Such words as *awful* and *terrific* are counterwords, that is, imitation tokens or coins.

coup de grace

A French term literally meaning "blow of mercy," *coup de grace* refers to any finishing or decisive action or stroke, such as one delivered mercifully to end suffering.

coup de théâtre

A "stroke concerning the theater," coup de théâtre is an unexpected, surprising turn in a play which produces an amazing or sensational effect. In an Elizabethan play, *The White Devil,* a character is shot by his sister and mistress. The audience, expecting his death, is shocked when the "wounded" man, discovering that neither woman intends to follow him in death, leaps to his feet shouting, "I am not wounded."

couplet

A pair of successive lines of verse, especially a pair that rhyme and are of the same metrical length.

> Words are like leaves; and where they most
>   abound,
> Much fruit of sense beneath is rarely found. (Pope)

See CLOSED COUPLET, DISTICH.

courtesy book

A book defining and explaining the ideals, training, duties, and conduct of persons planning or intending to serve at court in medieval times. A courtesy book, usually written in *dialogue, explains, for instance, the etiquette of *courtly love and the duties and responsibilities of a courtier. See ETIQUETTE BOOK.

courtly love

The chivalric, romantic code and philosophy of love and lovemaking. Courtly love was illicit, secret, discreet, never promiscuous, and always dedicated. A system of courtly love is revealed in Chaucer's *Troilus and Criseyde* and in several romances about King Arthur, Queen Guinevere, and Lancelot. See ARTHURIAN.

Coventry

A city in central England with many historic associations. One of the most important series of *mystery plays was called the Coventry Mysteries because they were first and most often produced in Coventry. To "send someone to Coventry" is to refuse to associate with him, to ignore him, although the phrase may have originated during periods when political prisoners were sent to Coventry for safekeeping.

Cowleyan ode

A poem in which the rhyme scheme and stanzaic pattern are irregular. This form of *lyric was named after Abraham Cowley (1618–1667), an English poet who first used it. The best-known Cowleyan ode in English is Wordsworth's *Ode on Intimations of Immortality from Recollections of Early Childhood;* the first lines of the first stanza read:

> There was a time when meadow, grove,
> and stream,
> The earth, and every common sight,
> To me did seem
> Appareled in celestial light,
> The glory and the freshness of a dream.

cradle book

A printed book produced during the first years of printing. See INCUNABULA.

craftsmanship

The skill, dexterity, and technique of one who practices a trade or art. An author who writes with professional ability and who is artful and careful is said to possess craftsmanship.

credibility

That which is capable of being believed; the condition or state of being trustworthy. See BELIEF.

credit line

A notice (line of *copy) acknowledging the *source or origin of published or exhibited material. Although a *footnote is sometimes referred to as a credit line, the term most often appears in newspaper usage to indicate the authorship of a news story.

credo

A Latin word ("I believe"), *credo* means any formula of belief or any statement or system of accepted opinion. Because *credo* is the first word of both the Apostles' Creed and the Nicene Creed, it is used as a name for these creeds. One of the best-known credos in American literature appears at the end of Thomas Wolfe's *You Can't Go Home Again.* It begins: "I believe that we are lost here in America, but I believe we shall be found. And this belief, which amounts now to the catharsis of knowledge and conviction, is for me—and I think for all of us—not only our own hope, but America's everlasting, living dream. . . ."

cri de coeur

A French phrase meaning a call or cry from the heart. Each of the *monologues of Hamlet is a cri de coeur, a heartfelt plea or protestation.

crisis

A turning point, for better or worse, in an acute disease, a love affair, a military campaign, or any activity. The term can refer to the point of time when it is decided whether a course of action or an affair shall be stopped, be modified, or proceed and also applies to an emotionally significant event or radical change of status in an individual's life.

In *drama and *fiction, a crisis occurs when opposing forces creating *conflict interlock in a decisive *action on which the *plot will turn. Such a brief period of time may occur more than once in a given novel or play, each crisis resulting in a climax; a crisis is essentially a structural element of plot, whereas a climax (always produced by a crisis) is primarily an index of emotional response from reader or spectator. One of several major crises in *Hamlet* occurs in act 3, scene 2, when Claudius sees the play-within-a-play. The resulting climax consists of Claudius's emotion, fright, and guilty departure. See ACT, CLIMAX.

criterion

A standard of judgment or criticism; an established principle or rule for testing. From a Greek word meaning a "judge," *criterion* is used in literary circles to indicate the standards by which a work should be judged, such as beauty, insight, depth, force, and clarity. The plural form is *criteria.*

criticism

Thoughtful, many-sided evaluation and *analysis. *Criticism* comes from Greek *kritikos,* meaning a "judge." Thus criticism is a process which weighs, evaluates, judges. Contrary to some opinion, it does not deal only with faults. Sound criticism mentions good qualities as well as bad, virtues as well as faults. It does not set out to praise or condemn; rather it weighs faults and excellencies and then passes a considered judgment.

In his *Principles of Literary Criticism,* I. A. Richards says:

> The qualifications of a good critic are three. He must be an adept at experiencing, without eccentricities, the state of mind relevant to the work of art he is judging. Second, he must be able to distinguish experiences from one another as regards their less superficial features. Third, he must be a sound judge of values.

Subjective criticism judges a literary work solely in terms of the critic's personal reaction to it. *Impressionistic* criticism, like subjective criticism, is primarily concerned with a critic's reactions and impressions. *Ethical* criticism applies principles of *morality; *historical* criticism reconstructs the standards and settings of the period in which a work was produced; *biographical* criticism centers on the author rather than the work; *comparative* criticism sets up parallels between different works; *objective* criticism is nonexistent since, as Anatole France once wrote:

> The good critic is he who recounts the adventures of his soul in the presence of masterpieces. Objective criticism no more exists than objective art, and those [critics] who suppose that they are putting anything but themselves into their work are the dupes of the most fallacious illusion.

critique

An *article or *essay evaluating a literary or other work of art. *Critique* is but another name for a *review. However, the best-known title using the word is Kant's *Critique of Pure Reason,* which, although a review, is also a demonstrated system concerning man's *a priori knowledge in scientific matters and a vigorous argument which removes religion and immortality from the sphere of reasoning and places them in the realm of faith.

cross reference

A note or statement directing a reader from one part of a book, section, index, or the like to a word or other item in another part.

cubism

A style of painting and sculpture that emphasizes the formal *structure of a work of art and the reduction of natural forms to geometric equivalents. Cubist poetry attempts to fragment the elements of an experience and then to rearrange them in a new *synthesis. Some of the poetry of E. E. Cummings and Archibald MacLeish exhibits traces of cubism.

cue

In general usage, *cue* means a hint or guiding suggestion. In theatrical language, a cue is anything said or done, on or behind the stage, that is followed by a specific line or particular action.

culture

The quality in a society or individual that springs from an interest in, and acquaintance with, what is generally considered excellent in the arts, letters, scholarly pursuits, and social manners. The English essayist, poet, and critic Matthew Arnold once wrote, "Culture [is] acquainting ourselves with the best that has been known and said in the world." In sociological language, *culture* refers to the sum total of ways of living built up by a group of people and handed down from one generation to the next.

cuneiform writing

Wedge-shaped characters, impressed in clay and baked. Cuneiform characters were used by ancient Persians, Assyrians, and Babylonians, perhaps as long as 6,000 years ago.

curiosa

*Books or *pamphlets dealing with unusual subjects. (See ESOTERIC.) *Curiosa* is most often used in connection with *pornography and erotica. See EROTICISM.

curse

This word, derived from an *Old English term meaning to "call down wrath," is a *malediction, the expression of a wish that evil, misfortune, or doom shall befall someone. *Curse* also applies to retribution for evil as in the most famous instance in all literature, "the curse of Cain." God's curse upon Cain, who murdered his brother Abel, is stated in Genesis 4: "And now art thou cursed from the earth, which hath opened her mouth to receive thy brother's blood from thy hand. When thou tillest the ground, it shall not henceforth yield unto thee her strength; a fugitive and a vagabond shalt thou be in the earth." See IMPRECATION.

cursive

A term in printing meaning "in flowing strokes resembling handwriting." In literature, *cursive* refers to writing apparently performed in a casual, offhand manner without attention to detail, such as a hasty *sketch or *informal essay. The adjective *cursory* is a *synonym of *cursive.*

curtain

In the theater, a curtain is a set of hanging drapery for concealing part or all of a *stage from audience view. *Curtain* is applied also to the end of a *scene or *act, which is indicated by the falling or closing of a curtain. A curtain *call* is the appearance of performers at the end of a theatrical performance in response to applause. A curtain *lecture* is a scolding administered in private by one person to another. A curtain *line* is the last line of *dialogue in a scene or act. Curtain *music* is music played before the raising of a theater curtain or before the beginning of a performance or act. A curtain *raiser* is a short play presented before the main performance. A curtain *speech* is the final statement of an act or scene or a brief speech by an actor, author, or producer following a performance.

cut

In radio and television, *cut* means to stop recording or transmitting a scene, broadcast, or orchestral number. *Cut* also means to abridge or shorten, to edit by omitting something. A cut version of a literary work is an *abridged selection. In printing, a cut is an engraved plate or block, or a picture or illustration printed from it.

cutback

A return in the course of a story, novel, or film to earlier events. See FLASHBACK.

cycle

Originally meaning "circle," *cycle* is applied to any group of poems, plays, or narratives about a central figure, theme, or major event. Accounts of the Trojan War, the Charlemagne *epics, and the *romances associated with King Arthur and the *Knights of the Round Table are cycles

cynicism

Distrust, doubt, or contempt for accepted standards of conduct, especially honesty and morality. A cynical writer (such as Oscar Wilde or George Bernard Shaw) holds a low opinion of mankind in general or at least disbelieves in the sincerity of human motives. Any individualistic writer who scorns ordinarily accepted standards and ideals is considered a cynic. Well-known novels that exhibit cynicism are Samuel Butler's *The Way of All Flesh,* Somerset Maugham's *Of Human Bondage,* and Sinclair Lewis's *Main Street.* See MENIPPEAN.

D

dactyl

A metrical foot of three syllables, one stressed syllable followed by two unstressed ones, as in the words *Washington, yesterday,* and *humanly.* Each of the first three feet in both lines of this excerpt from Browning's *The Lost Leader* is a dactyl:

dadaism

The style and artistic techniques of an early twentieth-century group in Paris which emphasized and exploited incongruous, bizarre, and accidental effects in their writings (and paintings). The followers of dadaism (sometimes spelled with a capital letter) challenged and even denied established *traditions and *canons of art, morality, social customs, and thought. Dadaism, derived from French meaning "hobby horse" and a childish reduplication of *da* ("giddap"), was a form of conscious madness that later developed into *surrealism.

dagger

A printing term for a reference mark shaped like a dagger (†), a *symbol employed to key text matter to a *footnote or other material. See ASTERISK.

daimon

A little-used term for *daemon* or *demon.* In classical mythology, a daimon or daemon was a god, a minor deity, such as the genius, or controlling force, of a place or of a man's spirit.

dance of death

A procession in which the living are led to their graves by the dead or by Death itself. This allegorical representation stressing the inevitability of death and the equality of all men at their end originated in Germany in the fourteenth century as a kind of *morality play. A series of *woodcuts by Hans Holbein (1497–1543) represents Death dancing before and after many sorts of persons, beginning with Adam and Eve. Saint-Saëns (1835–1921), the French composer, and Moussorgsky (1839–1881), the Russian, have used this theme in their work. W. H. Auden (1907–   ), the Anglo-American poet, called a satiric poetic *drama on "the decline" of the English middle classes *The Dance of Death*.

Dark Ages

This phrase is sometimes loosely applied to the whole of the Middle Ages from about A.D. 476 to the *Renaissance. Scholars avoid the term because it is vague and because the period thus covered was actually one of considerable activity in intellectual, cultural, scientific, and artistic pursuits. The phrase is primarily a reference to the earlier part of the Middle Ages (from the fifth to the eleventh century).

dead metaphor

A term used to refer to a word that began as a *metaphor (an implied comparison) but is now accepted in a literal meaning, such as *telecast* (a television broadcast). The term is applied also to metaphors that are archaic or obsolete, such as *baker's dozen* for *thirteen.*

deadwood

This word refers generally to anything considered useless or burdensome. *Deadwood* is a convenient label for words and phrases that add little or nothing to the selections in which they appear. To some modern readers, many slow-paced, highly detailed English novels of the eighteenth and nineteenth centuries seem filled with deadwood. See CONCISENESS, VERBIAGE.

debacle

A sudden downfall, or collapse; a general dispersion or breakup. Macbeth met with a debacle when Lady Macbeth died and he had to confront an advancing army. See CATASTROPHE, CLIMAX, CRISIS.

débat

A French term literally meaning "strife" and "argument," the débat is a kind of literary *composition, especially popular in medieval times, in which two or more characters discuss and debate some subject. The debaters are (were) usually *allegorical figures who argue some topic in theology, politics, *courtly love, or *morality. The term is now occasionally used to refer to an extended philosophical argument engaged in by two opposing characters in a literary work.

decadence

In a general sense, *decadence* refers to any period in literary or art history considered inferior to a preceding period. The period following Shakespeare, for example, was notable for such decadent qualities as sensationalism, loss of poetic power, and a lowered standard of *morality.

Decalogue

This is a name for the Ten Commandments, the precepts spoken by God to Moses as recounted in the Biblical books Exodus and Deuteronomy. *Decalogue,* composed of two Greek *combining forms meaning "ten words," is sometimes applied to any formal statement of procedure, doctrine, or opinion such as the constitution and bylaws of an organization.

decasyllable

A word or a line of verse containing ten syllables. This line from Pope's *An Essay on Criticism* is decasyllabic:
    True ease in writing comes from art, not chance.

decima

A Spanish *stanza form originated during the *Renaissance and consisting of eight ten-syllable lines.

deckle edge

A term applying to the irregular, untrimmed edge of hand-made paper, often used for ornamental effects in stationery and books.

declension

In a general sense, *declension* means a sloping, bending, or moving downward. In linguistics, *declension* refers to the *inflection (change) in nouns and pronouns to indicate their case and number.

décor

A term referring to a mode or style of decoration. In the theater, *décor* is used as an approximate *synonym for scenery and scenic decoration. In literature, the term is sometimes applied to the *settings of novels and short stories and to the dress and behavior of characters in fiction.

decorum

An observance or requirement of polite society or anything that is proper and fitting. In literature, *decorum* is a critical term describing that which is suitable to a subject, character, or setting. In *Paradise Lost,* for instance, fallen angels speak in a dignified, highly rhetorical style that fits the occasion. In *Huckleberry Finn,* characters speak and act in informal, colloquial ways that are appropriate to their stations in life and therefore are "decorous."

dedication

Commitment to a cause or ideal as, for example, Shakespeare's dedication to the theater as a playwright and actor. The dedication of a book is a prefixed inscription (note) that states the affection or respect of the author for a named person (or persons).

deduction

Two common methods of thinking are deduction and *induction. The former seeks to establish a specific conclusion by showing that it conforms to, is allied with, or "leads down from" a general truth or principle, a *premise. In deduction, movement of thought, expressed or implied, is always from the general to the particular. For example, if one accepts the general principle that most Danes have blue eyes, it may be deduced that Hans, a Dane, probably has blue eyes.

Induction seeks to establish a general truth, a principle, a premise. The inductive process begins by using observations of a number of facts; it classifies these facts, looks for similarities among them, and from a supposedly sufficient number of those particulars draws a conclusion or leads "into" or "up to" a principle. Once stated, the principle is supported by other facts and particulars: movement of thought is always from the particular to the general. For instance, if one knows hundreds of Danes, most of whom have blue eyes, he may conclude (induce) from these specific cases that most Danes have blue eyes.

Through induction (inductive reasoning) the laws (principles, generalized statements) of science have been arrived at. Through deduction (deductive reasoning) they are applied in particular situations—the development of a vaccine or the manufacture and launching of space rockets. As in science, so in writing: all literature is based upon deductive or inductive processes of thought. See ARGUMENTATION, SYLLOGISM.

de facto

A Latin phrase meaning "in fact," "in reality." *De facto* implies "actually existing," and when a condition exists without legal authority, the situation is distinguished from that implied by *de jure ("by right").

definition

From the standpoint of logic, a definition is made only by placing the term to be explained in the class or kind to which it belongs (genus) and then providing a statement of individual characteristics which distinguish the term from other members of the genus. Thus, *Braille* (the term) is a system of writing for the blind (genus) in which characters are represented by raised dots (differentia).

A definition need not be formal in order to make clear the meaning of a term, act, idea, or situation. Many definitions appearing in literature overlook both genus and differentia and merely present examples or instances. Some definitions explain what something is not rather than what it is. Some compare and contrast the term being defined with something known and familiar through the use of a *simile or *metaphor.

For comment on a famous definition, see CONTEXT. For an example of a definition, see CLASSIC.

definitive

In literature, *definitive* has two meanings: (1) complete and reliable—in reference to a study, text, examination, biography, or the like; (2) providing a final answer or solution.

A definitive edition is the author's own, final, and chosen text or the apparently most accurate text of an anonymous work. See COMPREHENSIVE.

degeneracy

A decline or deterioration of moral, mental, or physical qualities. Literature is filled with descriptions of individuals whose deeds and thoughts steadily become lower than, and inferior to, standards considered normal. At one time or another, the novel, drama, poetry, etc., have been described as in a state of degeneracy. A degenerate is a person who exhibits morbid traits and tendencies, especially a sexual pervert.

de gustibus non est disputandum

A Latin term meaning "there is no disputing about tastes." The phrase is usually shortened to *de gustibus* ("about tastes") and is used to explain (or minimize) variations in personality and reaction that cause people to differ widely.

deism

The religion of those who believe in the existence of God on the evidence of nature and reason only. Followers of deism reject the divinity of Jesus Christ, supernatural revelations, and the inspiration of the *Bible. Deists believe that God created the world but has since remained indifferent to creation. Deism arose from the scientific movement which developed after the discoveries and theories of Copernicus, Columbus, Galileo, and others.

The effects of this "natural religion," or rationalistic *point of view, on literature have been great. Strong evidences of deism are apparent in Pope's *An Essay on Man,* in much of the poetry of Wordsworth and Shelley, in Gibbon's *The Decline and Fall of the Roman Empire,* and in Thomas Paine's *The Age of Reason.* Much of the literature of the Revolutionary period in America is deistic, notably some of the writings of Benjamin Franklin and Thomas Jefferson.

déjà vu
A French phrase meaning "already seen." *Déjà vu* is used to refer to a trite, unoriginal story situation or to dated film making. In psychology, *déjà vu* applies to the illusion of having previously experienced something being encountered for the first time.

de jure
A Latin phrase meaning "according to law," "by right." See DE FACTO.

delineation
Describing or outlining with care and precision; sketching or tracing in detail. The delineation of a character involves portrayal of his appearance, characteristics, personality traits, motives, and acts. The delineation of an event refers to a *description that is detailed and precise.

delusion
A false belief or opinion. Literature is filled with descriptions of persons whose minds and judgments are mistaken in some way. For example, Don Quixote, deluded by his reading of romances of *chivalry, decks himself in rusty armor and cardboard helmet to roam the world as a knight-errant. Shakespeare's Othello, for another instance, suffers a delusion about his wife's faithfulness and innocence with a resulting unwarranted jealousy that leads to tragedy. In psychiatry, *delusion* refers to a persistent, dominating mental conception that is false and unreasonable. See ILLUSION.

denotation
The specific, exact, and concrete meaning of a word independent of any associated or secondary meanings. See CONNOTATION.

denouement
This term, derived from a French word meaning "to untie," refers to the outcome or result of any complex situation or sequence of events. More specifically, it is applied to the final outcome or unraveling of the main dramatic *complications in a play, novel, or other work of literature. Denouement is an ingenious untying of the knot of an *intrigue that involves some explanation of the secrets and misunderstandings connected with the *plot. In drama, *denouement* is the term most often applied to comedies, *catastrophe to tragedies.

de rigueur
A French term, *de rigueur* applies to anything that is strictly

required by etiquette, fashion, or usage. For example, it was de rigueur for a medieval knight to be loyal to his lord, kindly to the poor, courteous to women, etc. See NOBLESSE OBLIGE.

derivative

An adjective meaning "not original," "secondary," "taken from something else." *My Fair Lady* is a derivative form of George Bernard Shaw's *Pygmalion,* the idea for which was derived (received, obtained) from the classical myth about a sculptor and king who carved an ivory statue, fell in love with it, and prayed that it be brought to life.

dernier cri, le

A French term literally meaning "the last cry." *Le dernier cri* is used in English to mean "the latest word" and, in literature, applies to the newest mode and current fashion in style, technique, or subject matter.

descender

See ASCENDER.

description

A *form of discourse which tells how something looks, tastes, smells, sounds, feels, or acts. It deals with things, people, animals, places, scenes, moods, and impressions. The primary purposes of description are to portray a sense impression and to indicate a *mood. It tries to make the impression or mood as vivid, as real, as lifelike for the reader as it was for the writer when he received the impression or observed the mood.

Description is not often an independent form of writing. Except in travel "literature," it rarely stands alone. Often, however, a paragraph of description appears in a longer work, such as this one from O. Henry's short story *A Municipal Report:*

> Eight-sixty-one Jessamine Street was a decayed mansion. Thirty yards back from the street it stood, outmerged in a splendid grove of trees and untrimmed shrubbery. A row of box bushes overflowed and almost hid the paling fence from sight; the gate was kept closed by a rope noose that encircled the gate-post and the first paling of the gate. But when you got inside you saw that 861 was a shell, a shadow, a ghost of former grandeur and excellence.

Description is most effective when used in short passages as an aid in explaining or narrating something. But although its part is minor, its function is important. The great value of description is that it brings something to life; it creates a vivid impression for the reader or hearer. Everyone lives in a world of *images, not *abstractions, and responds to the graphic and

the concrete. Good description, always graphic and concrete, is made so by the use of abundant details.

Depth and richness of description depend upon the ability
of the writer to receive, select, and express details. Some details
are based upon visual reproduction—color, movement, and
form—and others convey impressions of tastes, touches, smells,
and sounds. Nevertheless, to catalog all pertinent information
about an object is not to describe it. The result of this process
is only a mass of raw material from which the reader must
formulate his own impression. The writer of good description
uses plentiful detail, but he tries to produce a single effect, a
*dominant impression. His primary purpose is to convey the
impressions which he received when he saw or felt or tasted or
smelled whatever it is that he is describing. These impressions
form a pattern which must be supported by details but not
obscured by them. See BELIEF, CHARACTERIZATION, EXTRANE-
OUS, SETTING, VERISIMILITUDE.

details

Items or particulars concerning persons and their actions,
events and their consequences, settings and their appearances.
All types of literature are based upon details of various sorts.
Effective writers avoid *generalizations and supply plentiful
details from their unusually keen powers of observation and
their retentive memories. See CONCRETENESS.

detective story

A narrative (*short story or *novel) in which a *mystery is unraveled by a detective through the assembly and interpretation
of *clues. The detective story had its origin in Edgar Allan Poe's
The Murders in the Rue Morgue in 1841; Poe firmly established the type in several other tales of similar sort. *Conventions of this form of light entertainment include such details as
the perfection of the crime, the stupidity of police, the bril-
liance or diligence of the detective, and a striking *denouc-
ment. A basic rule of the detective story is that clues from which
a solution can be obtained must be given to the reader precisely
as and when the detective receives them. In a sharply limited
sense, Sophocles and Shakespeare might be called detective
story writers, since *Oedipus Rex* and *Hamlet* involve a *hero
trying to clarify a situation involving a murder.

Among notable writers of this form may be mentioned
Poe, Sir Arthur Conan Doyle (the Sherlock Holmes stories),
S. S. Van Dine (Philo Vance), Ellery Queen, Dashiell Ham-
mett, and Dorothy Sayers.

determiner

A person or event that settles and decides an issue or
problem. (See ACT, ACTION, DEUS EX MACHINA.) A character
who says or does something that causes, affects, or controls
the *plot of a narrative is called a determiner. In *linguis-

tics, a determiner is a word (such as *a, an, the,* and *your*) that limits or describes the noun with which it appears.

determinism

The philosophical doctrine that all facts and events are determined by outside causes, that results and effects are controlled by natural laws. Determinists believe that human choices and decisions are regulated by external sources and that man's will is free and therefore able to function only in the sense that it is uncompelled. Determinism is related to *naturalism in that both theories embrace the idea that what a person thinks, does, and says is directed by heredity and environment over which he has little or no control.

detritus

From a Latin term meaning "a rubbing away," *detritus* refers to the remains of anything broken down or destroyed. Considering the moral, mental, and physical collapse of Macbeth, one can refer to the fragments and ruins of his career, of his hopes and plans, as detritus. Literary critics who consider *dadaism to be rubbish have called it the detritus of World War I.

de trop

A French term meaning "too much," "too many," "not wanted," "in the way." For example, some modern writers consider as de trop such qualities or ideals as frugality, hard work, honesty, and religious belief of any sort.

deus ex machina

A Latin phrase meaning "god from a machine." The term is a name for the literary device of resolving the arrangements of a *plot by the intervention of outside or supernatural forces or by an unexpected and unprepared-for trick or *coincidence. *Deus ex machina* is often used to refer to any artificial, forced, or improbable method used to untangle the difficulties of a play or novel. An example occurs in *The Threepenny Opera,* a comic work in which Mac the Knife is saved from hanging by a proclamation from Queen Victoria.

deuteragonist

In classical Greek drama, the character second in importance to the protagonist, especially one serving as the antagonist. (See AGON, ANTAGONIST, PROTAGONIST, TRITAGONIST.) In *The Adventures of Huckleberry Finn,* the slave Jim is the deuteragonist and Tom Sawyer is the tritagonist.

devil's advocate (disciple)

One who, for the sake of argument, presents or defends an opposing point of view or an evil cause. Both *devil's advocate* (supporter) and *devil's disciple* (follower) refer to an adverse critic, to a detractor, to one who argues against a plan or idea considered sound and good. In Roman Catholicism, the phrase is applied to an official appointed to present arguments against the beatification or canonization of a person as a saint. In this sense, a devil's advocate is not a whitewasher of the wicked but a blackener of the good. One of George Bernard Shaw's plays that illustrates this role is entitled *The Devil's Disciple.*

diacritical

A word meaning "distinctive," "serving to distinguish or set apart." A diacritical mark is a point or sign added or attached to a letter to distinguish it from another of similar form, to give it a particular sound value or emphasis, such as a *diaeresis.

diaeresis

A word from Greek meaning "division," *diaeresis,* also spelled "dieresis," refers to (1) the separation of two adjacent vowels, dividing one syllable into two; (2) a sign (¨) placed over the second of two adjacent vowels to indicate separate pronunciation, as in *naïve;* (3) the division made in a line (or verse) by *coincidence of the end of a *foot and the end of a word. See CAESURA.

dialect

The language of a particular district, class, or group of persons; the sounds, grammar, and diction employed by people distinguished from other persons either geographically or socially. A major technique of *characterization is the use by persons in a narrative of distinct varieties of language that indicate their educational, social, and geographical status. When a novelist or playwright reproduces the sounds, word choices, and speech rhythms of characters, he gives an illusion of reality to fictional characters. Without exception, all writers of *dialogue generally acknowledged to be proficient have differentiated between characters through the skillful use of dialect.

dialectics

This word of Greek origin means "argument" and is usually applied to debates over the nature of truth. Dialectics is also a form of *materialism which places matter over mind and is used as a *synonym for "dialectical materialism," a philosophy of history that stresses the constantly changing nature of reality.

dialogue

This word means "a conversation," "a speaking together." Dialogue involves an exchange of opinions or ideas and is used in narrative poetry, short stories, novels, and plays to reveal characters and to advance action. Some works of literature are composed wholly of conversation: a dialogue of Plato, for example.

diary

A daily record, especially of the writer's (keeper's) own attitudes, observations, and experiences. *Diary* also refers to a book for keeping such a record. As an intimate record of thoughts and events, a diary is not usually intended for publication, but many famous ones have been published: those of Samuel Pepys, Jonathan Swift, and William Byrd, for example. See AUTOBIOGRAPHY, BIOGRAPHY.

diatribe

A bitter, sharp, and abusive attack upon and criticism of some person, act, or condition. Originally a diatribe was a *dialogue about some matter of philosophy, but as such conversations became more violent and faultfinding, the term assumed its present meaning.

dibrach

A poetic foot of two unaccented (short) syllables. A dibrach is also called a *pyrrhic foot.

diction

The style of speaking and writing as reflected in the choice and use of words. Diction refers to the selection and arrangement of words in statements and to the accuracy, emphasis, and distinction with which they are spoken and written.

dictionary

A book containing a selection of the words of a language, arranged alphabetically, providing information about spelling, pronunciation, meanings, origins, etc. Sometimes a dictionary is restricted to word lists of special interest, such as dictionaries of art, of science, of medicine, etc.

A modern dictionary is not an "authority" in any exact meaning of the word. It does not prescribe or dictate, except in the sense that it records and frequently explains the comparative standing of words and phrases as regards national, reputable, and current usage.

didacticism

From a Greek word meaning "to teach," *didacticism* means the practice, art, or science of providing instruction. In literature, *didacticism* refers to the use of writing for teaching, for offering guidance in moral, religious, and ethical matters. Since all literature exists in order to communicate, the didacticism of a given selection depends upon the *purpose of the author. If a writer's primary intention is to provide instruction, his work is didactic; if he is concerned more with artistic qualities and techniques than with a message, his work, no matter how instructive, is considered nondidactic. For instance, Upton Sinclair's *The Jungle* is a novel of didacticism because the author was intent upon pointing out the social and economic injustices then prevailing in the meat-packing industry. Hawthorne's *The Scarlet*

Letter teaches much about the universal subject of sin, but it is primarily a psychological *romance notable for its narrative appeal. See PROPAGANDA, PURPOSE.

dies irae

A Latin phrase meaning "day of wrath," *dies irae* was used often in eighteenth- and nineteenth-century English literature to refer to the Last Judgment (the final trial of all mankind, the end of the world). Spelled with capital letters, the phrase is the title of a medieval hymn in Latin commonly sung at a requiem mass and on All Souls' Day.

diffuse

An adjective applying to writing that is lengthy, wordy, aimless, and rambling. To modern readers, many *double-decker novels of the eighteenth and nineteenth centuries seem diffuse.

digest

A collection of classified, condensed matter, usually dealing with historical, literary, scientific, or legal concerns. In legal language, a digest is an *abstract (summary statement) of some body of law. As a verb, *digest* means "to condense, abridge, summarize." See ABRIDGED, ABRIDGMENT.

digraph

A pair of letters representing a single speech sound, such as *ea* in *beat* and *th* in *wrath.*

digression

When applied to writing, *digression* refers to a passage or section that departs from the central *theme or basic *plot of a selection. To some readers, lengthy or seemingly unimportant passages of *description in a novel appear to be digressions. An *epic simile is a form of digression. Laurence Sterne's *Tristram Shandy* contains a section entitled "Digression on Digressions."

dilemma

A situation requiring a choice between two equally undesirable alternatives. Every character in literature who faces a *conflict of some sort also faces a dilemma, although his choices may not be restricted to only two. One of the most notable dilemmas in all literature confronted Hamlet: how could he avenge his father's death and shame his mother without himself committing a mortal sin?

dilettante

A person who takes up an activity, art, pursuit, or subject merely for amusement and in a superficial, desultory way. A dilettante is a dabbler, an amateur who pursues an art as a pastime but not with serious intent. The term is also applied to a lover of the fine arts, especially music and painting.

dime novel

A cheap, *melodramatic, or sensational work of fiction, usually paperbound. (Dime novels were sold for ten cents during the period of their greatest popularity, 1850–1920.)

dimeter

A verse (line) of two metrical feet. Thomas Hardy's poem *The Robin* is in dimeter:

When Ĭ / descénd
Tŏwardś / thĕir brínk
Ĭ stánd / aňd loók
Aňd stoóp / aňd drínk.

diminuendo

A term signifying a gradual reduction in loudness or in force. In music, *diminuendo* is an *antonym of *crescendo,* which suggests an increase in volume. After the final *climax in some plays and novels, what follows is sometimes said to be written in diminuendo style. When a writer has passed his period of greatest power and creativity, his career (such as that of John Milton) may be said to be in diminuendo, or eclipse.

Dionysia

Dramatic festivals held periodically in honor of Dionysus, in classical mythology the god of wine, drama, and fertility. Dionysus was the Greek name for Bacchus; Bacchanalia was the Latin (Roman) name for Dionysia. In Dionysian orgies Greek drama was born, both *tragedy and *comedy. In the latter days of Greek power and through the Roman era, Dionysia were characterized by debauchery and drunkenness; hence the word *bacchanalian* (drunken) and the current use of *Dionysian* to describe any ribald, intoxicated, and convivial orgy.

diphthong

The combination of two vowel sounds pronounced in one syllable: *ou, oi, au,* etc. *Diphthong* is derived from a Greek word meaning "having two sounds." See DIGRAPH.

dipody

A term in *prosody, *dipody* refers to a group of two metrical feet in which one of the two accented syllables bears primary *stress and the other secondary stress. *Dipody* usually refers to any pair of feet treated as a unit.

dirge

A lyrical poem or song expressing mourning for the dead.

Dirge is a term now applied to any kind of solemn, mournful music. (See ELEGY, THRENODY.) In Shakespeare's *The Tempest,* Ariel sings a dirge for Ferdinand's lost father:

> Full fathom five thy father lies;
> Of his bones are coral made;
> Those are pearls that were his eyes:
> Nothing of him that doth fade,
> But doth suffer a sea-change
> Into something rich and strange.
> Sea nymphs hourly ring his knell:
> Ding-dong.
> Hark! now I hear them—Ding-dong, bell.

disbelief

Refusal to believe or to accept something as true. The incredulity of readers is a constant concern of all writers, because unless they can secure acceptance for the characters they portray and the actions they narrate, their work fails to communicate. See BELIEF, SUSPENSION OF DISBELIEF, VERISIMILITUDE.

discord

As applied to literature, *discord* has three distinct but related meanings: (1) any confused or harsh sound, such as that caused by uneuphonious words; (2) lack of harmony or concord between characters in a selection or between the separate parts of a literary work; (3) strife or dispute between contending characters who have different aims or hold conflicting opinions. Some elements of the second and third meanings of *discord* appear in every work of literature involving *conflict.

discursive

An adjective applied to writing that seems rambling as it passes aimlessly from one subject to another. Some *informal essays appear discursive, such as a few by Charles Lamb, who occasionally wandered wherever his ideas and fancy led him.

disparate

A term applied to writers or to literary selections that are dissimilar, essentially different, basically unlike each other. Disparate authors, for instance, are Henry James and Theodore Dreiser, who differed widely in their choice of subject matter, style, diction, and literary techniques.

display type

Printing characters (*type) larger than body type and used in headings, advertisements, etc. The term is generally used to refer to any type larger and heavier than that customarily used for straight text matter.

dissertation

A formal *treatise, a learned *essay or *thesis. *Dissertation* (derived from a Latin term meaning "discussion ") can be applied to any formal discourse in speech or writing, but it has also been loosely used in the title of a *discursive *personal essay, Charles Lamb's *A Dissertation upon Roast Pig.*

dissolve

In motion pictures and *television, the momentary overlapping of an *image (scene, shot) with that of another and the gradual elimination of the first image. Also called a "lap dissolve," the term characterizes the overlapping process during which one shot fades out and another fades in. See FADING.

dissonance

A harsh or inharmonious sound. In this sense, *dissonance* is a synonym for *cacophony. (Also, see CONSONANCE, an *antonym for *dissonance.)* On occasion, a writer may deliberately employ a combination of harsh-sounding words in order to create a desired effect, as in these lines from a poem by Gerard Manley Hopkins:

> For how to the heart's cheering
> The down-dugged ground-hugged grey
> Hovers off, the jay-blue heavens appearing
> Of pied and peeled May!

distich

A synonym for *couplet, a distich is a pair of verse lines making complete sense. Usually, the lines of a distich rhyme, as in this couplet from Milton's *Il Penseroso:*

> These pleasures, Melancholy, give,
> And I with thee will choose to live.

disyllabic

An adjective meaning "consisting of two syllables." *Repent* is a disyllabic word.

dithyramb

Originally, a dithyramb was a choral song or chant sung during festivals and sacrifices dedicated to Dionysus. (See DIONYSIA.) The term is now applied to literary expression, both verse and prose, that employs unrestrained, passionate, wild, or excited language. Dithyrambic verse appears in Dryden's *Alexander's Feast,* a chorus of which reads:

> With ravished ears
> The monarch hears,
> Assumes the god,
> Affects to nod,
> And seems to shake the spheres.

ditty
A loosely applied term that refers to a poem designed for singing and to any short, simple song. The name is most often used for popular melodies and for songs sung by sailors. See CHANTEY.

divertissement
A French word meaning "entertainment," "recreation," or "amusement." The term is applied to brief acts or short ballets performed in the course of dramatic productions. In literature, *divertissement* refers to any brief work that is light in tone and primarily designed to please or to cause laughter.

divine afflatus
Poetic inspiration; an elevation of mind and spirit preceding creative composition during which the poet (or other writer) is felt to be receiving aid from a divine source. *Divine afflatus* is now largely used in a contemptuous sense to imply that the receiver of such an alleged gift overvalues the worth of his efforts. See AFFLATUS.

divine right
This phrase is usually expressed as "the divine right of kings"—a saying implying that the right of monarchs to rule comes directly from God and not the consent of subjects. Some writers have contended that they (and all authors) have a divine right to compose whatever they please in any style and manner that they choose. The divine right of kings is an *anachronism; the divine right of authors is debatable.

division
The marking off (or separation) of a whole into its parts. Every worthwhile selection in literature is an artistic whole, but each reveals division of some sort. For example, most poems are divided into *stanzas; most plays have separate *acts; most novels are presented in chapters; the thought units of essays are arranged in separate paragraphs. Only a creative artist can know how and why he divided the parts of his work while he was evolving it, but readers are dependent upon division in order to grasp separate parts, the sum of which dictates their responses to a selection.

doctrinaire
As a noun, *doctrinaire* applies to a person who attempts to apply some theory or doctrine without due regard for practical considerations or the beliefs of others. As an adjective, *doctrinaire* refers to those whose actions and attitudes are controlled by preconceived theories. A doctrinaire person is

dogmatic, fanatical in his insistence that others accept a given point of view. One of the more doctrinaire (dogmatic, opinionated) writers in literature was Dr. Samuel Johnson, who had a fixed code of critical and social beliefs which he was vigorous in advancing.

document

A written or printed paper that provides information or evidence of some sort. Historians, biographers, and some novelists rely on documents as the *source of their own writing. See PRIMARY SOURCE, SECONDARY SOURCE.

documentary

A term used in the making of motion pictures and production of television shows to refer to a dramatically structured film of an actual event or of a play providing the impression of an actual event. A documentary is based on actual *sources, on documentary proof or evidence that is factual and informative. See DOCUMENT.

documentation

The use of *documentary evidence; the citing of *documents as proof or backing for statements made. A formally written paper is said to be documented when it is accompanied by *footnotes and a *bibliography. All histories, biographies, and formal essays rely to some extent upon documentation, the *citation of authority for statements expressed and conclusions reached.

doggerel

A term applied to verse that is crudely written, loose or irregular in measure, and that usually exhibits comic or burlesque qualities. Doggerel is any poorly executed attempt at poetry that deals with trite subject matter, is overly sentimental, and is monotonous in form. The *epitaph on Shakespeare's tomb is doggerel, sometimes cited as unworthy of his genius and possibly not composed by him:

> Good friend, for Jesus' sake forbear
> To dig the dust enclosed here!
> Blest be the man that spares these stones,
> And cursed be he that moves my bones.

dogma

A settled and established opinion, belief, or principle. Dogma is also a specific doctrine or tenet laid down by some authority such as a church, a society, a monarch, or a government. Dogma is not necessarily faulty or harmful, but dogmatism (the arrogant assertion of opinions as truths) is rare in worthwhile literature. In *The Way of All Flesh,* Samuel Butler wrote, "It is in the uncompromisingness with which dogma is held and not in the dogma or want of dogma that the danger lies."

dolce far niente

An Italian phrase literally meaning "[it is] sweet to do nothing." In English, the phrase refers to "pleasing inactivity," "indolence," "a lazy, pleasurable way of living."

domestic tragedy

A dramatic composition dealing with a serious and somber theme that involves middle-class or lower-class characters, settings, and conflicts. A domestic tragedy is not concerned with the problems of persons of high rank but with events in the lives of everyday, contemporary people. Since the eighteenth century, dramatists have slowly but increasingly become aware that tragic events do occur in the lives of others than heroes of lofty estate. Plays dealing with the fate of lowly people are more common in the twentieth century than ever before, among them such domestic tragedies as O'Neill's *Desire under the Elms,* Arthur Miller's *The Death of a Salesman,* and Tennessee Williams's *The Glass Menagerie.*

dominant impression

The most important and influential effect upon a reader of a literary selection. (See CONTROLLING IMAGE, EXTRANEOUS.) The dominant impression of one reader may differ from that of another, but many readers will agree that the dominant impression received from *Othello* is that of the power of jealousy to destroy one's character; from *Macbeth,* the ruinous effects of ambition and ruthlessness; from *King Lear,* the destructive force of fury and the redemptive qualities of unselfishness and forgiveness.

doppelgänger

A word from German meaning, literally, "double-walker." The term refers to a ghostly double or to the counterpart of a living person. An amusing short story by Edward Everett Hale (1822–1909), an American clergyman and author, is entitled *My Double and How He Undid Me.* See ALTER EGO.

Doric

The best synonyms for *Doric* are *simple* and *unpretentious.* The term is derived from Doris, a small country in Greece, the inhabitants of which spoke in a rustic "Doric" *dialect. The first *pastoral poets wrote in this dialect; centuries later, John Milton used "Doric lay" in *Lycidas* as a synonym for "pastoral poem": "With eager thought warbling his Doric lay." Because the Doric dialect was rustic and because Doric architecture is notable for strength and simplicity, such unpretentious selections of literature as several of Wordsworth's "nature" poems are referred to as Doric.

dos-à-dos

An archaic term from French meaning "back to back." The term is used in square dancing and, occasionally, to refer to two *books bound back to back. In dos-à-dos *binding, the back cover of one volume serves as the back cover of the other, with the fore edges of one next to the spine of the other.

dossier

A French term meaning "bundle of papers," *dossier* refers to a group of *documents on the same subject. The term is usually applied to a complete set of items of detailed information about an individual. Some novelists have prepared in advance dossiers on leading characters scheduled to appear in their novels.

double-decker novel

A double-decker is something with two decks or tiers, such as a ship, bed, bus, sandwich, or cake. *Double-decker novel* is a term that refers to any narrative work of great or excessive length. In the nineteenth century the term applied to the *serial (in installments) publication of a work, the final issue of which appeared in two parts.

double entendre

A French phrase referring to a word or phrase with a "double meaning." Usually, one of the two possible meanings of a double entendre is indelicate, risqué, or suggestive. In *Macbeth,* Lady Macbeth, making plans for the visit of Duncan, remarks, "He that's coming must be provided for." She was speaking as hostess and as assassin-to-be. See EQUIVOQUE.

double negative

An expression in which two negative words are used to express a single negation: *can't hardly, haven't scarcely, can't help but.* The double negative is now out of style and is considered illiterate, but the construction appears often in English literature, dating to Elizabethan times. In Latin, two negatives in the same construction made an affirmative; such expressions were not out of style when they were used: Jane Austen was not being "ungrammatical" when she wrote, "There was *none* too poor or too remote *not* to feel an interest."

double rhyme

A rhyme of two syllables of which the second is unstressed, such as *motion* and *notion.* An example of double rhyme appears in these lines:

> Others aver, to him, that Handel
> Is scarcely fit to hold a candle.

(See FEMININE RHYME.) The work of Ogden Nash, for example, is filled with double and even triple rhymes (*fortunate* and *importunate*).

double talk

Speech using nonsense syllables in rapid *patter along with standard words. A variant form of double talk is the use of a nonexistent word in an otherwise sense-making statement.

down center

A stage direction which indicates the part of the stage in which action takes place. This guidance is relative to the position of an actor facing the audience. *Down center* means in the center of the front half of the stage nearer the audience.

downstage

See DOWN CENTER. *Downstage* is a stage direction for action in that part of the stage nearest the audience but does not specify whether action is to the left, right, or center. The half of the stage farthest from the audience is upstage.

drama

A composition in prose or verse presenting in *pantomime and *dialogue a narrative involving *conflict and usually designed for presentation on a stage. Drama, derived from a Greek word (*dran*) meaning "to do," "to act," was referred to by Aristotle as "imitated human action," a definition that remains serviceable. Drama presupposes a theater, actors, and an audience; in order to be fully experienced, a play should be seen and heard, not merely read.

Drama arose from religious ceremonies (see DIONYSIA); both *comedy and *tragedy evolved from such varied themes in those ceremonials as fertility, life, and death. Medieval drama largely evolved from rites commemorating the birth and resurrection of Jesus Christ. (See MIRACLE PLAY, MORALITY PLAY, MYSTERY PLAY.) Beginning with the Renaissance, dramatic elements were widened, developed, and emphasized in so many and diverse ways that drama today bears only a faint resemblance to its beginnings. Nevertheless, a play is fundamentally what it was more than 2,000 years ago: a picture of human life revealed in successive changes of events and told in dialogue and *action for the entertainment and instruction of an audience.

dramatic convention

A device employed in a play as a substitute for reality which the audience is supposed to accept as genuine and real. (See BELIEF, SUSPENSION OF DISBELIEF.) The *chorus in Greek plays is a dramatic convention. The *curtain which opens and closes the stage is a convention, as is the *stage itself, which must be regarded as the actual scene or geographical setting of action. Actors must be accepted as real persons involved in a dramatic story. In real life, persons rarely talk to themselves in lengthy, rhetorical *monologues, another dramatic convention. A *soliloquy (the act of talking as if alone) is a dramatic convention. So is the *aside (a remark that the audience, but not other actors on the stage, is supposed to hear). Even the *theater itself is a convention by reason of its invisible fourth wall through which the audience views interior action.

Every type of literature makes use of generally accepted devices, but those of drama are more numerous. more imaginative, and more demanding of the viewer (or reader) than those of any other literary form.

dramatic illusion

An illusion is something that deceives by producing a false impression. In psychological terms, an illusion is a perception (understanding, recognition) that represents what is perceived in a way different from the way it is in reality. A dramatic illusion refers to the conventions of plays (see DRAMATIC CONVENTION) that intentionally and necessarily present as real several persons, scenes, speeches, and acts that are actually illusory. When one witnesses a production of *Macbeth*, he sees it in a modern theater, but through a dramatic illusion he understands that the real setting is Scotland in the eleventh century. The audience at a production of a Shakespearean tragedy by dramatic illusion accepts a stage filled with dead and dying persons, but it knows that these dead persons will live and again die in other performances.

All literary illusions, including those of drama, involve something imagined; without them, literature would be impossible to create, understand, and enjoy. See ILLUSION.

dramatic irony

A condition in which the audience is made aware of information unknown to some of the actual characters in a play. This information may involve the real identity of a character, his true intentions, or the probable outcome of action; because the audience possesses knowledge which characters do not, it is able to measure words and deeds against a clear standard and understanding. A striking example of putting into a speaker's mouth words that have a different meaning for the audience occurs in *Macbeth* when the drunken porter jests about being the porter at the gate of Hell. In *Othello*, an *allusion to the villain as "honest Iago" is an instance of dramatic irony. In Sophocles's *Oedipus Rex*, Oedipus seeks throughout the play for the murderer of Laius, only to find that he himself is guilty. See IRONY.

dramatic monologue

A poetic form in which a single character, speaking to a silent auditor at a critical moment, reveals both a dramatic situation *and* himself. This kind of poem was brought to a high level of excellence by Robert Browning in such selections as *My Last*

Duchess and *Soliloquy of the Spanish Cloister.* T. S. Eliot's *The Love Song of J. Alfred Prufrock* is a recent example of the dramatic monologue.

dramatic poetry

A term applied to poetry that employs dramatic form, such as the *dramatic monologue. By extension, the term refers to plays written partly in verse and partly in prose (as were many of Shakespeare's productions) and to such poetic dramas as Shelley's *The Cenci* and Maxwell Anderson's *Winterset.* See CLOSET DRAMA.

dramatis personae

A Latin term ("masks of the drama") meaning "characters of the play." Frequently printed at the beginning of a published play or in the program for a live production is a list of characters with indications of their relationships.

dramaturgy

The craft and techniques of dramatic composition. *Dramaturgy* is usually employed to refer to dramatic art in its entirety, including the writing, producing, and acting of plays. In Greece, a dramaturge was "a maker of plays."

Drang nach Osten

A German term meaning "drive to the east." The phrase refers primarily to German imperialistic policy that from the twelfth to the fourteenth century extended its influence to eastern and southeastern Europe. *Drang nach Osten* again became a rallying cry for the German government before and during World War II.

dream vision

Also referred to as a "dream allegory," a dream vision is a device used in narrative verse that presents a story as though it were told by someone who falls asleep and dreams the events of the poem. This type of "vision literature" was especially popular during the Middle Ages. The term *dream allegory* is more exact when, as occurred frequently, physical struggles in the narrative involved moral and spiritual conflicts and when characters bore such names as Hypocrisy and Fear. *The Romance of the Rose* (thirteenth century), Dante's *Divine Comedy,* Chaucer's *The Book of the Duchess* (and other poems by Chaucer), and *Piers Plowman* are dream visions.

A dream allegory provides the framework (see FRAME STORY) for Bunyan's *Pilgrim's Progress* and Edward Bellamy's *Looking Backward.* In *Alice's Adventures in Wonderland,* Alice dreams about a world inside a rabbit hole. Joyce's *Finnegans Wake* is one long dream.

dry humor

A form of wit that depends primarily upon reserve and

*understatement for its effects. A man with a broken leg, asked if it hurt, might reply with dry humor, "Only when I laugh." See HUMOR, WIT.

dulce et decorum

A Latin phrase meaning "sweet and fitting." The complete phrase *dulce et decorum est pro patria mori* means "sweet and fitting it is to die for one's country." In abbreviated or full form, the expression is sometimes used in literature in its literal meaning but more often in anger or irony. A vivid and shocking description of soldiers undergoing a gas attack ("flound'ring like a man in fire or lime") and dying hideous deaths appears in a poem by Wilfred Owen entitled *Dulce et Decorum Est*. The last four lines:

> My friend, you would not tell with such high zest
> To children ardent for some desperate glory
> The old lie: *Dulce et decorum est*
> *Pro patria mori.*

dumb show

(1) A scene enacted without words. Such performances were common in Elizabethan drama, where they were usually symbolic or allegorical interpretations of the main action of the play. (2) A *play-within-a-play presented partly in *pantomime, such as that appearing in *Hamlet,* act 3, scene 2.

dummy

A representation or copy; a rough draft. In *printing, the term usually refers to sheets folded and made up to show the size, shape, form, sequence, and general style of a contemplated *book, *pamphlet, etc.

duodecimo

A book size resulting when a sheet of paper is folded and cut so as to form twelve leaves (twenty-four pages). The term is derived from Latin *duodecim* ("twelve").

duologue

(1) A synonym for *dialogue, a conversation between two persons. (2) A dramatic performance in the form of a dialogue limited to two speakers; a short scene with two actors only.

duplicity

Deceitfulness in speech or conduct; speaking or acting in different ways concerning the same matter. Literature is filled with characters who exhibit duplicity, usually with an intent to trick or deceive other characters.

dust jacket

See JACKET.

Dwiggins, William A.
American type and book designer (1880–1956) who designed such clean typefaces as Caledonia and Electra for *Linotype composition.

dysphemism
Substitution of an offensive or disagreeable word or expression for an inoffensive or agreeable one. A dysphemism is the opposite (*antonym) of a *euphemism. Examples: *old bag* for *woman, went to hell* for *died.*

ecce homo

A Latin phrase meaning "behold the man." These were the words with which Pontius Pilate presented Jesus Christ to his accusers; the phrase has become a *cliché to signify a person or condition presented as an object lesson or *fait accompli. In art, *ecce homo* means any representation of Christ crowned with thorns.

echo allusion

A form of *allusion (reference, mention) that varies a well-known saying. For example, Oscar Wilde wrote an echo allusion of Abraham Lincoln's famous utterance: " . . . but democracy means simply the bludgeoning of the people by the people for the people."

echo verse

Poetry (or, more likely, *doggerel) in which a line has its closing syllables echoed with a different meaning in the following line. These lines from Jonathan Swift's *A Gentle Echo on Woman* are illustrative:

Shepherd: Echo, I ween, will in the words reply,
And quaintly answer questions: shall I try?
Echo: Try.
What must we do our passion to express?
Press.

eclectic

An adjective meaning "choosing from various sources." An eclectic author does not follow any one system in his attitudes, philosophy, and view of life but selects and uses what he considers the best (or most suitable) of several systems or elements. An eclectic novelist, for example, might characterize the same individual with *irony at one time and gentle *humor at another. Parts of his novel may be realistic and earthy, other parts sentimental or symbolic, etc.

eclogue

From a Greek word meaning "selection," *eclogue* refers to a *pastoral or *idyllic poem that praises country life. The best-known eclogue in English literature is Spenser's *The Shepheardes Calender.* W. H. Auden's *Age of Anxiety* and Robert Frost's *Build Soil* are examples of twentieth-century eclogues.

economy

In literature, *economy* refers to the efficient and sparing use of words to express ideas and emotions. *Economy* is a *synonym for *conciseness and an *antonym of *verbosity. Such writers as Francis Bacon, Ralph Waldo Emerson, and Ernest Hemingway are noted for economy, whereas Henry Fielding, Charles Dickens, and Thomas Wolfe are not. In general, poetry is more likely to exhibit economy than prose is. In poetry, which consists of words in their best possible use, "each word must carry twenty other words upon its back."

edition

(1) The *format (shape and size) in which a literary work is published; (2) the whole number of impressions (copies) of a book, magazine, or newspaper printed from a set of type in one continuous run; (3) a version of any work (printed or not) that is publicly presented, as, for instance, the latest edition of a play or opera. *Edition,* from a Latin word meaning "to give out," is loosely and inexactly used in both publishing and general circles. If a new "printing" involves no changes in the text or illustrations, or only minor corrections, the result is not a new edition but an *impression.* A thorough revision resulting in a noticeably different version is a *new edition.* A *first edition is the book as it is (was) originally published.

editorializing

Setting forth a position or opinion on some subject; injecting personal interpretations or explanations into an otherwise objective, detached, or factual account. Literary artists obviously have attitudes, ideas, and points of view, but rarely are these now stated directly as pronouncements by the author. *Editorializing* does appear in numerous novels, essays, and poems of the eighteenth and nineteenth centuries, but the bulk of all literature of whatever period is designed to cause readers to form opinions and make inferences rather than tell them *what* to think or what authors believed. A standard rule implicit in the work of most writers is "Show, don't tell." *Editorializing* is prevalent in *essays and *articles of *persuasion and, of course, in newspaper editorials and *columns.

editorial we

The plural pronoun *we* is often used by editors and other writers as a substitute for a repetitive *I.* The editorial *we,* a device well established in newspaper writing, occasionally appears in fiction and other forms of literature largely published prior to the twentieth century. More recent writers (and readers) consider this *convention both artificial and pretentious. See ENALLAGE.

Edwardian

An adjective applying to the reign of Edward VII of England, who ruled from 1901 to 1910. As a literary term, *Edwardian* is sometimes used to characterize the self-satisfaction of this period, or its extravagance and opulence. The Edwardian era was notable for the powerful reaction of its writers to the alleged propriety and conservatism of the *Victorian age. Distrust of authority and basic doubt concerning established principles of conduct and authority were hallmarks of the Edwardian period. It has been noted that, in this "English" era, the best poet writing in English may have been William Butler Yeats, an Irishman; the best dramatist, G. B. Shaw, another Irishman; and the best novelist, Joseph Conrad, an expatriated Pole.

effect

The mental, emotional, and spiritual impression an author attempts to create in and upon his readers' minds and hearts. See CAUSE AND EFFECT, CONTROLLING IMAGE, DOMINANT IMPRESSION.

effectiveness

A quality (or group of qualities) in writing which enables an author to produce effects and results intended or expected. (See CONTROLLING IMAGE, DOMINANT IMPRESSION.) The positive and even dynamic qualities which have the power to produce lasting effects include such diverse matters as insight, understanding, interest in and knowledge of human nature, technical skill, and, above all, powerful desire and ability to communicate directly, clearly, and imaginatively with and to the hearts and minds of readers.

effete

An adjective meaning worn-out, tired, weak, exhausted of energy or vigor. *Effete* also means sterile, unable to produce, and decadent. The term is most often applied to society in general at some particular time, but it is also used to characterize literary works and authors judged to be below acceptable standards of vigor, taste, and imaginative force. In the sense of *decadence, much of the work of Swinburne and Wilde, for example, has been called effete.

e.g.

An abbreviation of the Latin phrase *exempli gratia, meaning "for example," "for the sake of example."

egalitarian

A term implying belief in the equality of all men. An egalitarian writer develops characters who may be unlike in heredity, social status, education, and traits of personality, but his work nowhere asserts that men are basically unequal, that they do not exhibit correspondence in degree, value, ability, etc. Possibly no completely egalitarian (also *equalitarian*) writer ever lived, but Abraham Lincoln came close to exhibiting this belief in some of his letters and speeches, and Walt Whitman frequently endorsed the concept in his writing.

ego, egoism

One's conscious self is one's ego; the word *ego* may also be defined as that trait or component of personality that most immediately and directly controls thoughts and behavior. That is, *ego* is the "I" or "self" of any person; *ego* is "a person" feeling, thinking, and distinguishing itself from the selves of others.

Ego can also mean "conceit" and "self-love," in which senses it is a *synonym for *egotism.* The ego and egotism of a writer like George Bernard Shaw were evidenced in his tendencies to make himself, his deeds and thoughts, the object of others' attention, interest, and conversation. Egoism also emphasizes concentration on oneself, implies self-interest, and is the opposite of *altruism.

For many understandable reasons, most writers are egotists. All characters in literature who seek attention for themselves, who usually are scornful of others' interests and opinions, and who are generally self-assertive, self-important, and filled with self-esteem may be termed egotists, egoists, or persons with inflated egos.

Einfühlung

A German term which is an approximate *synonym for empathy (the projection of one's own feelings into an object, scene, or situation). (See EMPATHY, SYMPATHY.) In German, the word means "a feeling into." If, for instance, a reader actually "feels" like washing his hands along with Pontius Pilate or Lady Macbeth, he is experiencing Einfühlung.

eisteddfod

A gathering of Welsh *bards and *minstrels, a conclave (or congress) of persons attempting to promote use of the Welsh language and the singing of Welsh songs. *Eisteddfod* is sometimes applied to any session of similarly minded persons attempting to promote a cause or idea.

elaboration

The development and expansion of a literary work. *Elaboration,* derived from a Latin word meaning "labor," suggests hard work and an abundance of details. An elaborated plot or character is one that is carefully and fully developed.

elegant variation

A form of *jargon; specifically, the practice of using different words and *metaphors as elaborate and artificial substitutes for a term being discussed. The coiner of the phrase, Sir Arthur Quiller-Couch, explains elegant variation in his *On the Art of Writing:*

> In an essay on Byron, Byron is (or ought to be) mentioned many times. But [the writer] has a blushing sense that to call Byron Byron twice on one page is indelicate. So Byron, after starting bravely as Byron, turns into "that great but unequal poet." [Later] he becomes "the gloomy master of Newstead"; overleaf he is reincarnated into "the meteoric darling of society"; and so proceeds through successive waters [forms, embodiments]—"this archrebel," "the author of *Childe Harold,*" "the apostle of scorn," " . . . the martyr of Missolonghi," "the pageant-monger of a bleeding heart."

elegy (elegiac)

A mournful, melancholy poem, especially a funeral song or *lament for the dead. (See DIRGE, THRENODY.) Among well-known elegies are Gray's *Elegy Written in a Country Churchyard,* Shelley's *Adonais,* Tennyson's *In Memoriam,* Milton's *Lycidas,* and Walt Whitman's *When Lilacs Last in the Dooryard Bloom'd.*

Elegiac, an adjective suggesting the expression of sorrow and regret, refers also to *meter. Elegiac meter consists of a line of dactylic *hexameter followed by one of *pentameter, as explained and illustrated in Coleridge's lines:

> In the hexameter rises the fountain's silvery column;
> In the pentameter aye falling in melody back.

The elegiac *quatrain in verse is iambic pentameter rhyming alternately, as in these lines from Gray's *Elegy:*

> Can storied urn or animated bust
> Back to its mansion call the fleeting breath?
> Can Honor's voice provoke the silent dust,
> Or Flattery soothe the dull cold ear of Death?

elision

From a Latin term meaning "a striking out," *elision* refers to the omission of a vowel at the end of one word when the next word begins with a vowel and also to the dropping of a vowel, consonant, or entire syllable in pronunciation. Elision may also involve the striking out of an entire passage. (See ABRIDGED, UNABRIDGED.) Elided words common in literature include *I'll, doesn't, th', ne'er, o'er, e'er.*

elixir of life

A substance or concoction believed during the *Middle Ages to be capable of prolonging life indefinitely or of changing any metal into gold. Both *elixir* and *elixir of life* are sometimes used to refer to a cure-all, a panacea, an all-powerful remedy, and the height or greatest excellence of anything.

Elizabethan

In English history and literature, the name given to that part of the *Renaissance which occurred during the reign of Elizabeth I (1558–1603). It was an era of religious controversy, commercial growth, and nationalistic expansion during which *drama and *lyric poetry reached their highest levels.

ellipsis

(1) The omission of a word or words that a reader must supply for full understanding; (2) a mark (or marks) to indicate the omission or suppression of words, phrases, etc. The bracketed (nonappearing) word in these lines from Pope's *An Essay on Criticism* illustrates ellipsis:

> Authors are partial to their wit, 'tis true,
> But are not critics [partial] to their
> judgment too?

The ellipsis periods shown in the quotation from Quiller-Couch under ELEGANT VARIATION are elliptical marks indicating the omission of words.

elocution

(1) A stilted, artificial manner of speaking, (2) a person's manner of speaking or reading aloud; (3) the study and practice of oral delivery, including voice and body control. Elocution, once a subject of concern and interest, is now an *archaism except in speech study.

eloquence

The art of using language with fluency, appropriateness, and power. All great writers are eloquent, but the term is usually applied to those authors who seem to have made a studied practice of writing and speaking with deliberately *rhetorical *purposes. See ORATION.

Elysium

In classical mythology, Elysium (or the Elysian fields) was the home of the blessed after death. In literature, *Elysium* refers to any place or state of perfect happiness, as suggested in these lines from Keats's *Lines on the Mermaid Tavern:*

> Souls of Poets dead and gone,
> What Elysium have ye known,
> Happy field or mossy cavern,
> Choicer than the Mermaid Tavern?

emblem

A sign, design, figure, or *symbol that identifies or represents something, such as the emblem of a society or organization. Spenser's *The Shepheardes Calender* shows the influence of emblems. The casket scene in Shakespeare's *The Merchant of Venice* is a form of emblem literature.

An emblem book is a collection of emblems in book form usually dealing with particular *themes. Such books contained pictures, the symbolic meaning of which was expressed in accompanying verse or prose.

em dash

A dash one em long. In *printing, *em* originally referred to the portion of a line of type occupied by the capital letter M in type of the same size. An em is now considered the square of any size of type used as the unit of measurement for matter printed in that type size (either the length of an em dash or the area of an em squared—an em quad). An *en* is half the width of an em.

emendation

A correction; the removal of an error or flaw. See COR-RIGENDUM.

emotive meaning

The emotion that a reader or listener associates with a word or phrase. An emotive meaning is one with an emotional *connotation of approval or disapproval. Literature is filled with emotive meanings because it is made up of language designed to excite emotion. See COGNITIVE MEANING, CON-NOTATION, DENOTATION.

empathy

Identification with an object and sharing in its physical and emotional sensations. Empathy involves ascribing the feelings and attitudes present in oneself to the plight of characters in a literary work and the conditions of their lives. When a reader physically and emotionally feels hunger, cold, and misery as he reads of the overworked and half-starved central character in Dickens's *David Copperfield,* he is experiencing empathy. Keats revealed his empathic nature when he wrote that "if a Sparrow comes before my Window, I take part in its existence and pick about the gravel." Burns's poem *To a Mouse* ("Wee, sleekit, cow'rin', tim'rous beastie") is a poem built upon empathy. See EIN-FÜHLUNG, SYMPATHY.

emphasis

The stress laid upon, or the significance and importance attached to, a *character, *setting, or *theme. *Emphasis* refers to the intensity and force of expression with which a writer develops an idea, reveals a character, unfolds a plot, or stresses a concept. See CONTROLLING IMAGE, DOMINANT IMPRESSION, EFFECTIVENESS.

empiricism

The practice of drawing rules of behavior and practice not from theory but from experience; the doctrine that all knowledge is derived from the act of living. An empirical method of writing is "experimental," especially important in *naturalism and in certain *avant-garde approaches, such as *Theater of the Absurd. An empirical judgment of literature is considered "untrained," "without proper foundation."

enallage

The substitution of one grammatical form for another, such as the plural for the singular in *editorial we. The best-known example of enallage in literature occurs in Shakespeare's *Richard III:* "But me no buts."

enchiridion

A handbook, a manual, a small volume to be carried in the hand. The term is straight from Greek.

enclitic

An adjective applying to a word that has no independent accent and thus leans heavily on another term. Such enclitic words are *prithee* from *pray thee* and *'twas* from *it was.*

encomium

An expression of praise; a poem or speech that pays tribute to someone. Encomium is a synonym for *eulogy. Encomiastic verse praises or glorifies people, ideas, or objects, as in these lines from Wordsworth's *Ode to Duty:*

> Stern Lawgiver! yet thou dost wear
> The Godhead's most benignant grace;
> Nor know we anything so fair
> As is the smile upon thy face.

encyclopedia

A book (or set of books) containing articles on various topics. An encyclopedia is arranged alphabetically; it may cover all branches of knowledge or all aspects of one subject. The term is derived from a Greek word meaning "circular" or "well-rounded."

endpapers

Sheets of paper, often ornamented or colored, folded to form two leaves, one of which is pasted flat inside either cover of a book, the other forming a *flyleaf (a blank leaf in the front or back of a book).

end rhyme

*Rhyme that occurs at the end of verses (lines) of poetry. This duplication of similar sounds at the ends of lines is normally expected in English verse. See FEMININE RHYME, INTERNAL RHYME, RHYME.

end-stopped line

A line of poetry in which a grammatical pause (such as the end of a phrase or clause) coincides with the end of the line. Each of the twelve lines is end-stopped in Bradstreet's *To My Dear and Loving Husband,* which begins:

If ever two were one, then surely we.
If ever man were loved by wife, then thee;
If ever wife was happy in a man,
Compare with me ye women if you can.

See RUN-ON LINE.

en famille

A French term meaning "in the family."

English sonnet

Better known as the Shakespearean sonnet, an English sonnet is a fourteen-line poem with a *rhyme scheme of *abab, cdcd, efef, gg.* See SONNET, SHAKESPEAREAN SONNET.

enigma

An enigma is (1) a saying, question, or picture that contains a hidden meaning or (2) a puzzling hard-to-explain event, situation, person, or nation. For example, Hamlet has been called the most enigmatic character in literature because his motives, thoughts, and actions are so puzzling. See CIPHER, RIDDLE.

enjambement

The running on of thought from one line, couplet (pair of lines), or *stanza to the next. Enjambement, a French term equivalent to "striding over," occurs with the use of *run-on lines. These lines from Milton's *Paradise Lost* illustrate enjambement:

But see! the angry victor hath recalled
His ministers of vengeance and pursuit
Back to the gates of Heaven . . .

Enlightenment

Another term for the *Age of Reason, a philosophical movement of the seventeenth and eighteenth centuries which stressed the powers of human reason and was marked by political, religious, and educational unrest.

en passant
A French term meaning "by the way," "in passing."

enthymeme
A *syllogism (argument) in which one *premise (proposition) is unexpressed. An enthymeme is illustrated in the statement "All men are mortal; therefore, Shakespeare was mortal." The omitted premise is "Shakespeare was a man."

entr'acte
(1) The interval between two acts of a theatrical or operatic performance or (2) the entertainment provided during this peiod. *Entr'acte,* a French term, also refers to a piece of music or a short *sketch prepared for use on such an occasion.

entre nous
A French term meaning "confidentially," "between ourselves."

envoi
Also spelled *envoy,* an envoi is a postscript to a prose composition (see CODA) or a short *stanza concluding a poem. For an example of an envoi in verse, see BALLADE.

epanaphora
A *synonym for *anaphora.* An epanaphora is a rhetorical device involving the repetition of a word (or words) at the beginning of successive lines, stanzas, paragraphs, etc. See ANAPHORA.

ephemeral
An adjective meaning short-lived, transitory. An ephemeral literary work or author lasts but a short time in popular or critical favor. Many literary movements and causes also have proved ephemeral—for instance, *dadaism.

epic
A lengthy narrative poem in which action, characters, and language are on a heroic level and style is exalted and even majestic. Major characteristics of an epic are (1) a setting remote in time and place, (2) an objective, lofty, dignified style, (3) a simple plot, (4) a central incident (or series of incidents) dealing with legendary or traditional material, (5) a theme involving universal human problems, (6) a towering hero of great stature, (7) superhuman strength of body, character, or mind, (8) supernatural forces entering the *action. Among noted epics are the *Iliad* and the *Odyssey* by Homer; the Spanish *Cid; Beowulf;* Virgil's *Aeneid;* Dante's

Divine Comedy; Milton's *Paradise Lost;* Longfellow's *Hiawatha;* Benét's *John Brown's Body.*

epic simile
A *simile (likeness, comparison) developed in a lengthy passage. As an elaborated comparison, an epic simile is longer, more detailed, and more ornate than a simple *metaphor. The object, image, or picture developed in an epic simile creates an impression that temporarily at least obscures the principal thread of the story. The epic simile, patterned after the elaborate *digressions appearing in Homer's work, is sometimes referred to as the *Homeric simile.

Epicurean
A term referring to the philosophy of Epicurus, a third-century-B.C. Greek thinker, who held that the highest good in life is pleasure, pleasure being broadly interpreted as freedom from pain or disturbance. Literature is called *Epicurean* when it emphasizes a search for pleasure as, for instance, in some of the works of Oscar Wilde and A. C. Swinburne. Epicureans actually avoided *hedonism through their belief that pleasure derives from such qualities and traits as honesty, integrity, and prudence.

epidiplosis
A rarely used rhetorical device by which an author begins and ends a sentence with the same word.

epigone
An undistinguished imitator or follower of an important literary artist. *Epigone* is from a Greek phrase meaning "born afterward." In a sense, every dramatist since Shakespeare has been something of an epigone, as every epic poet since John Milton has been.

epigram
A witty, ingenious, and pointed saying that is expressed tersely. (Originally, an epigram meant an inscription, or *epitaph.) Coleridge once defined an epigram as "A dwarfish whole, / Its body brevity, and wit its soul." Francis Bacon's remark "I would live to study and not study to live" is an epigram. See ADAGE, APHORISM, APOTHEGM.

epigraphy
The study and interpretation of ancient inscriptions. *Epigraphy* is derived from *epigraph,* a quotation or note of *dedication. The science of epigraphy made possible the decipherment of ancient Egyptian inscriptions on the famous Rosetta Stone now in the British Museum.

epilogue
(1) A concluding part added to such a literary work as a novel,

play, or long poem; (2) a speech to be delivered at the conclusion of a dramatic performance. An epilogue is related to the *peroration (eloquent conclusion) of a speech and is contrasted with *prologue (introductory speech). See AP-PENDIX, CODA.

epiphany

Spelled with a capital letter, Epiphany is the name of a Christian festival, observed on January 6, commemorating the revelation of Jesus Christ to gentiles through the Wise Men (Magi). In literature, *epiphany* means an intuitive and sudden insight into the reality and basic meaning of an event; the term also refers to a literary work, or part of a work, that symbolically presents such a moment of perception and revelation. In this latter meaning, *epiphany* was used by James Joyce as a term for "a sudden spiritual manifestation," first revealed in his *Stephen Hero,* which was expanded into *Portrait of the Artist as a Young Man.*

epiphora

The repetition of a word (or words) at the end of two or more successive phrases, clauses, verses, etc., such as "I should do Brutus wrong, and Cassius wrong." *Epiphora* is another term for the less-used word *epistrophe.* See ANAPHORA.

episode

An incidental event or happening within a longer prose or verse narrative. An episode occasionally is a *digression but usually is a unified narrative passage integrated within the main plot.

episodic

An adjective which refers to a literary work made up of a number of thematically related but loosely connected scenes, incidents, or stories. Tennyson's *Idylls of the King* is episodic in structure, and so are many *double-decker novels, especially those of the eighteenth and nineteenth centuries.

epistemology

A study of the theory of the method of knowledge; a branch of philosophy that delves into the origin, methods, and limits of animal and human knowledge. Epistemology was a basic concern of such an author as John Locke, whose *An Essay Concerning Human Understanding* was the first major presentation of *empiricism.

epistle

A letter, especially a formal one characterized by *didacticism. An epistle differs from an ordinary or conventional letter in that it is consciously literary and is deliberately planned for publication. The term *epistle* is applied to several books of the *Bible, to formal letters of *dedication, and to published comments on political and religious matters.

epistolary

A term usually applied to a novel written in the form of a series of letters; also, epistolary friendships are prominent in literary history. The epistolary form of a novel allows the author to present several points of view without injecting himself into the narrative, but the structure seems awkward and unreal to many modern readers. The first epistolary novel in English was Richardson's *Pamela* (1740).

epitaph

A brief poem or other form of writing praising a deceased person; a commemorative inscription on a tomb or monument. Many writers, notably Dr. Johnson and John Milton, wrote dignified and moving tributes to the dead in the form of epitaphs, and Shakespeare possibly wrote an epitaph for his own tomb (see DOGGEREL). John Gay's grim self-epitaph on his tomb in Westminster Abbey is as follows:

Life is a jest and all things show it.
I thought so once, and now I know it.

epitasis

A term once used to designate the rising *action of a play, that part of a drama, following the *protasis, in which the main action is developed. (For the position of epitasis in drama, see ACT, COMPLICATION.) The term applies to dramatic action in a play, novel, or short story that is in preparation for the *catastrophe.

epithalamion

A bridal song; a poem in honor of a bride and bridegroom. The best-known marriage hymn (song, poem) in English is Spenser's *Epithalamion.* The most famous epithalamion in world literature is the Biblical Song of Solomon (Song of Songs).

epithet

A word or phrase applied to a person or thing to show a quality or characteristic, such as the "Age of Reason," "William the Conqueror," and "Richard the Lionhearted." An epithet may involve abuse or contempt but is not necessarily a form of *invective. Homer used many epithets, including "rosy-fingered dawn," "swift-footed Achilles," and "all-seeing Jove."

epitome

(1) A *summary or condensed statement, especially of a literary work. See ABRIDGMENT, ABSTRACT. (2) A representative of some greater subject, body, or quality that is typical of the whole, as in these lines from Dryden's *Absalom and Achitophel:*

A man so various, that he seemed to be
Not one, but all mankind's Epitome.

e pluribus unum

A Latin term meaning "one out of many." It is the *motto of the United States.

epoch

A particular period of time marked by distinctive character- istics, events, and features. In literature, epoch is properly employed to mean the starting point of a new period, one that is distinguished by startling or striking events. See ERA.

epode

From a Greek term meaning "additional song" or "after- song," *epode* means (1) a kind of lyric verse in which a long line (or stanza) is followed by a short one; (2) the *stanza sung by a Greek *chorus while standing still. See ANTISTROPHE, STROPHE.

eponym

The name of someone so commonly associated with a spe- cific characteristic or quality that the name itself stands for the attribute. Eponyms include the following: Caesar for *dictator,* Marquis de Sade for *sadism,* Helen for *beauty,* Blue- beard for *woman killer,* Hercules for *great strength.* See PAT- RONYM.

equivocation

The use of a word or expression in two or more meanings, usually with the intention of deceiving or misleading the reader (or hearer). Equivocation is a deliberate use of *am- biguity involving different senses of the same expression at different points in writing or speaking. Shifting the meaning of words is illustrated in this question: "Should every citizen of the United States vote the Republican ticket because this is a great republic, or should he vote the Democratic ticket because this is a great democracy?"

equivoque

(1) A play on words; (2) an evasive answer that can be interpreted in more than one way. Equivoque is illustrated in a statement such as "Nothing is too good for this man." If an equivoque is deliberately misleading, it becomes *equivocation. See DOUBLE ENTENDRE.

era

A period characterized by a new order of things, a point of time marked by characteristic or distinguishing features of some sort. *Era* is frequently used interchangeably with *ep- och but actually is a period extending from a point in time marked by a particular beginning.

Eros

The ancient Greek god of love, identified by the Romans and later peoples as Cupid. Spelled with a small letter, *eros* is a synomym for desire and sensuous love; in psychiatry, *eros* refers to the *libido.

eroticism

The sexual or amatory (lovemaking) quality or character of literature. *Eroticism* refers to the use of sexually arousing or suggestive *allusions, *settings, and *situations and to the condition of being sexually aroused or excited. Erotic literature ranges from the sentimental to the pornographic, but erotica (literature dealing with sexual love) deals with fleshly desire, attraction, and fulfillment. Shakespeare's *Hamlet, Romeo and Juliet,* and *Antony and Cleopatra* have a "love interest," but emphasis on sexual drive and desire varies in intensity in ascending order of their listing here.

erratum

A term from Latin meaning an error in printing or writing. (See BONER, CORRIGENDUM.) The plural of *erratum* is *errata.*

Erziehungsroman

A synonym for *Bildungsroman, a novel about the formative years of the central character. *Roman,* a French word for "novel," is combined with German *Erziehung,* which means "upbringing." See KÜNSTLERROMAN.

escapism

The desire or tendency to avoid reality and to seek entertainment and release in fantasy or imaginative situations. The appeal of escapism is suggested in this comment from Sir Philip Sidney's *Defence of Poesy:* "He cometh unto you with a tale which holdeth children from play and old men from the chimney-corner." Escape literature enables the reader to forget or put aside his troubles and to live vicariously in another world. Although sometimes of inferior quality, television shows, detective and mystery stories, films, and radio programs provide diversion from the tediousness and the anxieties of daily living.

esoteric

An adjective applying to literary works that are understood by, or are intended for, a select circle of readers who have special interests or knowledge. An esoteric work is secret and mysterious. Occasionally the term is applied to literary selections that seem unusually abstruse and recondite, such as Joyce's *Ulysses* and some of the poetry and criticism of T. S. Eliot. See OBSCURANTISM.

Esperanto

An artificial language concocted in 1887 by a Russian

philologist and intended for universal use. The word *Esperanto* is derived from French and Spanish words meaning "the hoping one" and "hope"; the language is based on the commonest words in the most important European languages. In Esperanto, grammar is simple, pronunciation is easy, and spelling is phonetic, but it provides scant promise of becoming a universal language. See BASIC ENGLISH.

esprit

Sprightliness of spirit, wit, lively intelligence. Esprit, a French word derived from a Latin term for "spirit," appears most often in the phrase *esprit de corps* (a sense of common interests, responsibilities, and aims developed among a group of associated persons). See COTERIE.

essay

A short literary *composition on a particular *theme or topic, usually in prose and generally thoughtful and interpretive. Because the term *essay* is applied loosely and widely, no fully acceptable definition is possible. Some essays are descriptive, narrative, or argumentative; some are whimsical, humorous, or satiric; some are biographical, critical, or historical; some are objective, some subjective.

One basic division is helpful: "formal" and "informal" compositions. See FAMILIAR ESSAY, FORMAL ESSAY, INFORMAL ESSAY, PERSONAL ESSAY.

Montaigne first used the word *essay* in 1580 for informal reflections on himself and mankind in general. Francis Bacon's *Essays* (1597) were written as "counsels for the successful conduct of life and the management of men." Since the seventeenth century, English essayists, such as Addison, Goldsmith, Lamb, Hazlitt, Steele, and Chesterton, have poured out prose compositions on various topics. Essayists of other countries, including the United States, have been no less prolific.

*Articles in magazines, editorials (see EDITORIALIZING), *columns, *book reviews, and some forms of *criticism are also essays of a sort.

essence

The basic, real, and unvarying qualities and characteristics of a literary work and its significant individual features. Thus, the essence of Shakespeare's work is its inward nature, its fundamental substance, its essentials at their very bottom. In *Biographia Literaria,* Coleridge wrote:

> *Essence,* in its primary signification [meaning], means the principle of *individuation* [individual existence], the inmost principle of the possibility of anything, as that particular thing. It is equivalent to the *idea* of a thing, whenever we use the word "idea" with philosophic precision.

eternity

Infinite time; duration without beginning or end. Finite minds cannot really embrace eternity, but writers have been absorbed with it, as contrasted with mortal life, since the start of recorded history. A seventeenth-century English poet, Henry Vaughan, expressed a conception of eternity in *The World* that is more understandable than those of most authors:

> I saw Eternity the other night,
> Like a great ring of pure and endless light,
> All calm, as it was bright;
> And round beneath it, Time, in hours, days, years,
> Driven by the spheres
> Like a vast shadow moved; in which the world
> And all her train were hurled.

ethnic

An adjective applying to the cultural, religious, racial, or linguistic traditions of a people or country. *Ethnic group* is a sociological term applied to a group of people of the same race or nationality who share a common and distinctive culture.

ethos

(1) The *moral* element in dramatic literature that determines a character's actions rather than his thought or emotion; (2) the character (principles, beliefs, traditions) of a person, group, community, or nation; (3) the major customs and practices of a society; (4) the fundamental spirit of a culture. Thus, for example, one speaks of the democratic ethos of the American people.

etiquette book

Another name for *courtesy book. *Etiquette* is a more apt word than *courtesy* to describe a book that deals with the conventional requirements of social behavior and the accepted codes of usage prevailing in polite society. By extension, Lord Chesterfield's *Letters to His Son* is a kind of etiquette (or courtesy) book, and so is much of Benjamin Franklin's *Autobiography,* a work undertaken to instruct the author's son about business, society, and ways of living.

et tu, Brute

Latin for "and thou, Brutus," allegedly the dying words of Julius Caesar spoken as his longtime friend Brutus stabbed him. *Et tu, Brute* has extended meanings of "and you, too," "you of all people," and "even you," phrases spoken in surprise, bewilderment, or resignation.

etymology

(1) The study of the origins of words; (2) an account of the

history of a particular word. *Etymology,* derived from Greek terms meaning "true sense" and "word," is simply defined as a study of historical linguistic changes in words. See FOLK ETYMOLOGY.

eulogy

A formal *composition or speech in praise of someone, especially an *oration in honor of a deceased person. *Eulogy* also means "high praise" and is a *synonym for *encomium. Related terms are *dirge, elegy, monody, panegyric,* and *threnody.* One of the best-known eulogies in literature is Mark Antony's "funeral oration" for Brutus as it appears in Shakespeare's *Julius Caesar:*

> This was the noblest Roman of them all.
> All the conspirators, save only he,
> Did that they did in envy of great Caesar;
> He only, in a general honest thought
> And common good to all, made one of them.
> His life was gentle, and the elements
> So mix'd in him that Nature might stand up
> And say to all the world, "This was a man!"

euphemism

The use of an indirect, mild, or vague word or expression for one thought to be coarse, offensive, or blunt. *Euphemism* is from a Greek phrase meaning "the use of words of good repute or omen." In recent years, effective writers who mean "prison" are likely to say so and not "correctional institution." If they mean "dead," they will not likely write "deceased" or "the late." Euphemisms are usually vague and wordy, as is evident in this comment by Elizabeth Barrett Browning on the insanity of a fellow poet: "Discord fell on the music of his soul; the sweet sounds and wandering lights departed from him." See PARRHESIA.

euphony

A pleasant-sounding, harmonious combination of sounds. *Euphony,* from a Greek word meaning "sweet-voiced," is an *antonym of *cacophony. All good poetry is euphonious except when an author deliberately strives to achieve a harsh, strident effect. The following lines from Tennyson's *Lotus-Eaters* have a pleasing sound:

> There is sweet music here that softer falls
> Than petals from blown roses on the grass,
> Or night-dews on still waters between walls
> Of shadowy granite, in a gleaming pass . . .
> And in the stream the long-leaved flowers weep,
> And from the craggy ledge the poppy hangs in
>   sleep.

euphoria

A feeling of well-being. *Euphoria* usually implies a state of contentment, happiness, or ecstasy that has little or no basis in truth or reality. A euphoric writer, such as James M. Barrie or William Saroyan, is prone to overlook harsh or uncomfortable realities and to concentrate on *fantasy or *escapism. Much of the exuberant poetry of Walt Whitman stemmed from his euphoric love for life and for people.

Euphuism

An affected and artificial style of writing or speaking which flourished during the sixteenth century. Euphuism takes its name from John Lyly's *Euphues,* which was designed to reveal how elegant and polished English prose could be. The principal characteristics of euphuism are excessive use of *alliteration, *antithesis, *allusions to mythological and real persons, and *conceits. See BAROQUE, FINE WRITING, PRECIOSITY, PURPLE PROSE.

eureka

An exclamation of discovery or triumph, *eureka* means "I have found (it)." *Eureka* was the alleged exclamation of Archimedes, the Greek mathematician, physicist, and inventor, when he finally found a method of ascertaining the amount of alloy in the golden crown of a king; fittingly, Eureka is the *motto of California.

evidence

A ground or reason for belief; proof; that which tends to prove or disprove something. For instance, in order for a character to be accepted as kindly or cruel, evil or good, generous or grasping, winsome or repulsive, a writer provides evidence of his characteristics and personality traits. To persuade readers to a belief or cause of action, an essayist will give evidence (factual statements, *documentation) to support his point of view. *Detective and *mystery stories and plays rely heavily upon evidence in their development of *plot. All literature is based upon the evidence of an author's senses, intuition, and insight.

evocation

A calling forth, or calling up, of memories and sensations; the suggestion or production through artistry and imagination of a sense of reality. Evocation, a primary tool and technique of all writers, relies heavily upon evocative writing that elicits associations, images, and reactions from readers.

exactness

Strict accuracy, precision, and correctness. *Exactness* in literature applies to a writer's *diction and sentence structure and even more forcefully to the use of logical thought processes, scrupulous development of character, and accurate recounting of events. See CLEARNESS, EFFECTIVENESS, REALISM.

exaggeration

Overstatement; magnifying beyond the limits of truth; disproportionate representation. In literature, exaggeration usually takes the form of *hyperbole, a rhetorical device involving an extravagant statement or *figure of speech not intended to be taken literally, such as "The discussion lasted for an eternity." The work of such authors as A. A. Milne, Sir James M. Barrie, Mark Twain, Ogden Nash, and James Thurber contains numerous examples of both exaggeration and hyperbole. The device of overstatement is illustrated in Byron's *The Destruction of Sennacherib:*

> Like the leaves of the forest when summer is green,
> That host with their banners at sunsct were seen.

Byron's *simile is intended to convince the reader that the number of soldiers involved was great, but actually the leaves in a forcst would be counted in the hundreds of millions.

example

One of a number of things; a part of something taken to reveal the characteristics of the whole; a pattern or model. In literature, example most often applies to an instance serving for illustration and to a specimen illustrating a principle or rule. Macbeth is an example of an overly ambitious man; Hamlet is an example of an introspective, indecisive person; *Macbeth* and *Hamlet* are examples of *Elizabethan *tragedy.

ex cathedra

A Latin phrase that means "from the chair." The term is used to mean "with authority" and "from the seat, or source, of authority." A papal *bull, for instance, is an ex cathedra statement.

excelsior

A Latin term, *excelsior* means "ever upward." It is the *motto of New York State. *Excelsior* is sometimes used as a rallying cry to urge man forward to higher and nobler attainments, as exemplified in the theme of a poem entitled *Excelsior,* by Henry W. Longfellow.

excursus

A detailed discussion of some point in a book, especially such a statement appearing as an *appendix. An excursus is usually considered a formal, lengthy *digression from a principal theme or narrative account. A lengthy explanatory *footnote, which frequently appears in a work of *history or *biography, is an excursus.

exegesis

Critical interpretation and explanation of a literary work. *Ex-*

egesis is usually applied to an *analysis of an unusually difficult passage in poetry or prose; the term refers especially to interpretations and explanations of selections from the *Bible. See EXPLICATION.

exempli gratia

A term meaning "for example," "for the sake of example," "for instance." In older literature, especially *formal essays of the eighteenth and nineteenth centuries, the phrase was often spelled out; in later writing, it is usually abbreviated to e.g.

exemplum

A Latin word meaning "example," *exemplum* is used in English to apply to an anecdote that illustrates or supports a moral issue or that teaches a lesson of some sort. An *example of such a moralized tale is Chaucer's *The Pardoner's Tale,* a kind of narrative *sermon intended to prove that the love of money is the root of all evil. See ANECDOTE, DIDACTICISM, FABLE, INCIDENT.

exhibitionism

Displaying of one's abilities, appearance, or mannerisms in such a way as to attract attention. Authors who seek the limelight, who speak or act in order to gain publicity, indulge in exhibitionism. Among such writers have been mentioned Dr. Samuel Johnson, Charles Dickens, Walt Whitman, Oscar Wilde, William Saroyan, and Ernest Hemingway. Certain characters in literature make a display of themselves: Falstaff, Cyrano de Bergerac, Dumas's three musketeers, Professor Henry Higgins in Shaw's *Pygmalion,* etc. Some literary historians regard as forms of exhibitionism such movements as dadaism, existentialism, imagism, and surrealism.

exhortation

The act of advising, urging, or cautioning others. *Exhortation* applies in literature to any statement, speech, or address conveying urgent advice or recommendations. For example, in act 3 of *Hamlet,* Hamlet exhorts visiting actors about the most effective way to present a play by means of which he wishes to establish the guilt of King Claudius. Nearly all of Benjamin Franklin's *Autobiography* is an exhortation about how life should be lived.

existentialism

The belief that man forms his *essence, his essential being, in the course and pattern of the life he elects to lead. *Existentialism* is a loose term with several meanings, but it is normally applied to writing that emphasizes man's responsibility for forming his own nature and that stresses the prime importance of personal decisions, personal freedom, and personal goals. The doctrine of existentialism holds that man is completely responsible for himself because he has a free will to do exactly as he pleases. If man follows social, political, or moral conventions and refuses to make his own decisions and choices, existentialists claim that he is contemptible.

Existentialism had its beginnings in the work of a Danish theologian, Søren Kierkegaard, in the nineteenth century, but it owes its greatest popularity and influence to the French novelist-philosopher Jean-Paul Sartre, who declared that "man is alone in a godless universe." Sartre and his post–World War II followers insist that the universe is meaningless, a concept that produces anxiety, loneliness, acute discomfort, and despair.

Sartre's existentialism, like that of Albert Camus, Simone de Beauvoir, Samuel Beckett, and Franz Kafka, among others, is largely atheistic, but a form of Christian existentialism which holds that possibilities for altering human nature and society are great has been set forth by such writers as Jacques Maritain, Paul Tillich, and Gabriel Marcel. Both groups of existentialists are (1) concerned with man's essential being and nature, (2) convinced that thought and reason are insufficient to understand and cope with the mysteries of living, (3) conscious that anguish and despair are the common lot of everyone, and (4) fixed in the belief that a sense of *morality depends upon posititve and active participation in life.

ex libris

A Latin phrase meaning "from the library (books) of" and used as a bookplate to indicate ownership.

exodus

A departure, emigration, or going out of a large number of people, such as is described in the Biblical book of Exodus (the trek of Israelites from Egypt under the leadership of Moses). In Greek drama, *exodus* referred to the final scene in both tragedy and comedy.

exordium

The beginning of anything. In literature, *exordium* refers to the introductory part of an essay, formal article, or speech. See INVOCATION, PRELUDE.

exoticism

The state or condition of strangeness, unusualness, or foreignness. Literary works exhibit exoticism if they are striking in effect and deal with exciting, glamorous, or far-off settings, characters, and customs. Some of the stories and novels of Herman Melville, Robert Louis Stevenson, Joseph

Conrad, James Branch Cabell, Joseph Hergesheimer, and Somerset Maugham are exotic.

expletive

(1) A syllable, word, or phrase used to fill out a statement or to provide some sort of emphasis; (2) an interjectory word, usually profane. Expletives fitting both definitions are common in literature, especially in *dialogue, which is often loaded with such fillers as *you know, sort of, like,* and swear words of varied sorts.

explication

Explanation, interpretation; the act of making meaning clear and plain. *Explication* appears in the phrase *explication de texte* ("explanation of text"), an approach to literary *criticism involving close and detailed study, *analysis, and *exposition of the text of a selection. In such explication, a critic concentrates on language, style, and the interrelations of parts to the whole so as to make plain the meaning and *symbolism of the text.

explicit

An adjective meaning "clearly stated," "distinct," "fully and clearly expressed." An explicit literary work leaves nothing merely implied (that is, implicit) but is unequivocal, definite, and unreserved in its language and meaning. For example, many modern works of literature are so explicit in their description of the actions and language of characters that their taste and total effect have been severely questioned. See NATURALISM, REALISM.

exposition

In writing, exposition is that *form of discourse that explains, defines, and interprets. It embraces all *composition, both oral and written, that does not primarily describe an object (*description), tell a story (*narration), or maintain a position (*argumentation). *Exposition* is also applied to the beginning portion of a *plot in which background information is set forth. For example, Shakespeare provides details about characters and situation at the beginning of each of his plays, notably *Henry V, Richard III, Romeo and Juliet,* and *Othello.*

Magazine articles, editorials, and essays usually consist almost wholly of exposition; plays, novels, short stories, and a considerable quantity of poetry contain some exposition along with other more dominant elements of discourse.

ex post facto

A Latin term meaning "from what is done afterward." In English, the phrase is used to mean "subsequently," "retrospectively," "from or by following action." An ex post facto law is one passed after an occurrence which, if applied to the facts of this event, would change the legal situation.

expressionism

A term with several meanings variously applied to different forms of artistic work, *expressionism* is impossible to define exactly and succinctly. In the so-called fine arts (painting, sculpture, etc.) it involves techniques in which forms derived from nature are exaggerated or distorted and in which colors are intensified to express emotion. In drama, *expressionism* applies to a style of playwriting and production emphasizing emotional content, the subjective reactions of characters, and symbolic or abstract representations of reality. In novels and short stories, *expressionism* involves the presentation of an objective outer world through the intensified impressions and moods of characters. In poetry, the movement is evidenced by distortions of objects and by dislocations of generally accepted ideas of time and space.

In brief (but not with total accuracy), expressionism in modern literature can be referred to as any deliberate distortion of reality. The following selections are notable for expressionistic tendencies and techniques: Strindberg's *Dream Play;* Eugene O'Neill's *The Emperor Jones;* Tennessee Williams's *The Glass Menagerie;* James Joyce's *Ulysses* and *Finnegans Wake;* T. S. Eliot's *The Waste Land.* See ANGST, IMPRESSIONISM, REALISM, THEATER OF THE ABSURD.

expurgate

To alter or amend by removing passages from a work; to purge or cleanse of moral offensiveness by deleting material considered objectionable. An expurgated edition of some of Shakespeare's works, *Tales from Shakespeare* (Charles and Mary Lamb), was designed to introduce Shakespeare to children without offending their moral sensibilities; see BOWDLERIZE.

extempore

An adjective and adverb from Latin literally meaning "out of the time" and now used to suggest "on the spur of the moment," "offhand," "without preparation or planning." To speak extempore is to speak without notes of any kind. The term has largely been supplanted by *extemporaneous,* an adjective also meaning "impromptu," "made for the occasion," "improvised."

extraneous

An adjective meaning "irrelevant," "not pertinent or applicable," "unneeded and unnecessary." *Extraneous* applies to material in literary selections that appears to be "introduced from without" and that does not fit properly into the principal *theme, *conflict, or *setting of the selection itself. A *digression is often extraneous, but in well-constructed literary works, nothing that does not contribute to the author's *purpose and the hoped-for *dominant impression of the reader is allowed to intrude. Edgar Allan Poe once wrote:

A skillful literary artist has constructed a tale. If wise, he has not fashioned his thoughts to accommodate his incidents; but having conceived, with deliberate care, a certain unique or single *effect* to be wrought out, he then invents such incidents—he then combines such events as may best aid him in establishing this preconceived effect. If his very initial sentence tend not to the outbringing of this effect, then he has failed in his first step. In the whole composition there should be no word written, of which the tendency, direct or indirect, is not to the one pre-established design.

extrapolation

The extension or projection of known information by estimate or inference. Extrapolation, a term in statistics, is constantly involved in literary selections because inferences about character and forthcoming events are based on facts already revealed. Extrapolation is at work whenever a reader says, "I knew that would happen" or "I felt sure that he would react just this way," etc. See CAUSE AND EFFECT.

extrasensory

An adjective meaning "not perceptible by the normal senses," "supernatural." An extrasensory perception is something "felt" or "sensed" by intuition rather than through sight, sound, hearing, etc. Effective writers try to "show" what they mean, but they and the characters whom they develop rely constantly on inner feelings and emotions directly traceable to what they receive through extraordinary insights. See AFFLATUS.

extravaganza

In the nineteenth century, *extravaganza* was applied to the elaborate production of any fanciful subject, especially a fairy tale, employing song and dance. Currently, an extravaganza is a dramatic or musical composition (such as comic opera or a musical comedy) notable for its light theme, loose structure, and elaborate costuming and staging. See BURLESQUE, CARICATURE, MUSICAL COMEDY.

extrinsic

A term meaning (1) outward or external; (2) not essential or inherent. The *subplot of a play, for example, may be considered extrinsic. See EXTRANEOUS.

eye rhyme

Also called sight rhyme, eye rhyme is a form of agreement apparent in spelling but not in sound. Examples of eye rhyme (half rhyme, *slant rhyme*) are *love* and *move; have* and *grave; watch* and *patch; bead* and *bread.*

F

fable

A short, simple story, usually with animals as characters, designed to teach a moral truth. (See ALLEGORY, APOLOGUE, BESTIARY, PARABLE.) Fables with animals as principal characters are sometimes called beast fables, such as Kipling's *Jungle Books* and *Just So Stories,* Joel Chandler Harris's stories from Uncle Remus, and George Orwell's *Animal Farm. Fable* is also occasionally applied to stories about supernatural persons, to accounts of extraordinary events, to legends and myths generally, and to outright falsehoods.

fabliau

A sort of smoking-room story, popular with medieval French and English poets. A fabliau, always humorous and frequently ribald, conventionally was told in eight-syllable verse that satirized the faults of clergymen and women. Fabliaux are less serious than fables but do present moral lessons through bawdy situations. Chaucer's *Canterbury Tales* includes several fabliaux: stories by the Friar, the Miller, the Reeve, the Cook, the Manciple, etc.

fabula

See ATELLANA FABULA.

facetiae

A term from Latin meaning amusing or witty remarks or writing. Facetiae are usually coarse, objectionable, or indecent.

facile

A word meaning "moving, acting, or working with ease," "easily done," smooth-flowing," and "fluent." *Facile,* an adjective applied to writers whose performance seems glib and superficial, is a sharply critical term for prolific authors whose output is notable for its quantity rather than its quality, depth, and insight.

facsimile

An exact copy of a book, manuscript, or painting. *Facsimile,* a synonym for *replica* and *reproduction,* is related to *verbatim. Facsimile* also applies to the transmission of printed and visual materials by radio and telegraph.

factitious

An adjective meaning "manufactured," "made by art." *Factitious* is applied to writing judged to be artificial and contrived. Much *light verse, for example, seems forced, feigned, and engineered and is therefore labeled "factitious."

fading

In motion pictures and *television, *fading* means "appearing gradually." *Fading in* applies to bringing up (making an *image brighter or clearer in a gradual process). *Fading out* reverses the process of a fade-in in that it gradually makes an image more and more indistinct until complete disappearance.

fairy tale

A story about elves, dragons, sprites, hobgoblins, and other magical creatures. These supernatural "spirits" are usually represented as having mischievous temperaments, unusual wisdom, and power to regulate the affairs of man in whatever fashion they choose. The most famous writers or compilers of fairy tales were the Grimm brothers (Germany) and Hans Christian Andersen (Denmark). The term *fairy tale* is also applied to a misleading or incredible account, belief, or statement.

fait accompli

A French term meaning "a thing already done," "an accomplished fact." For instance, before Shakespeare attained popularity and eminence as a playwright, his success as an actor on the London stage was a fait accompli.

fallacy

From a Latin word meaning "to deceive," *fallacy* names a false or misleading notion, belief, or argument. In logic, a fallacy is any of various kinds of erroneous reasoning that make arguments unsound. Literature is peopled with characters who entertain fallacious ideas that lead to comic or tragic situations. For example, both Don Quixote and Othello were ruled by fallacies, with vastly different outcomes. See DEDUCTION, INDUCTION, LOGIC, PATHETIC FALLACY, SYLLOGISM.

falling action

The part of a play that follows the *climax (the moment of highest and most intense interest). Falling action is equivalent to the *resolution or *denouement of a drama, which leads to the *catastrophe. See ACT, ACTION.

familiar essay

A term applied to the more intimate and subjective kind of *personal essay. (See ESSAY.) A familiar essay is light in manner and tone, often humorous, occasionally whimsical, and always deft and polished in its approach to personal experiences, problems, and prejudices. Among noted familiar essayists may be mentioned Oliver Goldsmith, Charles Lamb, Robert Louis Stevenson, and E. B. White.

fancy

This word is often considered a synonym for *imagination,* the forming of mental images of what is not actually present in the senses. In modern literary criticism, however, imagination is considered "creative" and "organic," whereas fancy is considered "logical," "mechanic," or "*factitious." This distinction was first noted by Coleridge in his *Biographia Literaria:*

The *fancy* brings together images which have no connection natural or moral, but are yoked together by the poet by means of some accidental coincidence.

Fancy also has a meaning of superficial love or liking for something attractive, as is suggested by a song from Shakespeare's *The Merchant of Venice:* "Tell me where is fancy bred. / Or in the heart or in the head?"

fantasy

Extravagant and unrestrained imagination; the forming of weird or grotesque mental *images. *Fantasy* is applied to a literary work the action of which occurs in a nonexistent and unreal world (such as fairyland) and to a selection that involves incredible characters (as Maeterlinck's *The Blue Bird* does). *Science fiction and *utopian stories are forms of fantasy.

farce

A farce is (1) a foolish show, a ridiculous sham; (2) a light, humorous *play in which the *plot depends upon a carefully exploited situation rather than upon character development. A farce is usually considered to be a boisterous *comedy involving ludicrous *action and *dialogue. Farce is a mainstay of many television and motion-picture comedians, but farcical scenes occur in such well-wrought plays as *The Taming of the Shrew, Twelfth Night,* and *A Midsummer Night's Dream.*

farrago

A confused mixture, a hodgepodge, a medley. In literature, a farrago is a collection of *light verse or humorous *prose. The term is also applicable to *vaudeville and to certain kinds of *musical comedy.

fascism

The philosophy, principles, and methods of a governmental system involving a dictator with total power. In fascism opposition to, and criticism of, the government are forcibly suppressed, industry is regimented, and aggressive *nationalism and racism are encouraged. Fascism has played an important role in world literature since the establishment of a fascist government in Italy (1922–1943) by Benito Mussolini. Two works dealing with totalitarianism of the general sort represented by fascism are George Orwell's *Animal Farm* and *1984.* See MARXIST, PROLETARIAN.

fatalism

(1) Acceptance of all things and events as inevitable; submission to *fate; (2) the philosophical doctrine that all happenings are the result of *predestination. The lives of major characters in nearly all of Thomas Hardy's works (*The Return of the Native, Jude the Obscure,* etc.) are ruled and regulated by both meanings of *fatalism* cited here.

fate

A word meaning "destiny," "fortune," "lot." Although often used lightly, *fate* emphasizes the irrationality and impersonal (cold) character of events. Approximate synonyms for *fate* occasionally appearing in literature include *karma, kismet, chance,* and *luck.*

"The three Fates" and "the cruel Fates" are phrases also appearing in literary works. Ancient Greeks and Romans believed that these Fates controlled the birth, life, and death of everyone: Clotho (who held the distaff), Lachesis (who spun the thread of life), and Atropos (who cut the thread when life was ended).

fatuous

A term applied in modern criticism to writing judged to be silly, foolish, and inane. *Fatuous* is also used to characterize literary selections that seem unreal and illusory. (See ILLUSION.) Serious critics have termed as *fatuous* many current *best sellers, films, and *television productions.

feminine ending

An unaccented syllable at the end of a line of poetry. In the following line from Shakespeare's *The Merchant of Venice,* the *-ats* of *ducats* constitutes an unstressed eleventh syllable in a line of iambic pentameter:

And Í / bĕ pléased / tŏ gíve /
tĕn thóus/ănd dúcăts.

feminine rhyme

A rhyme extending over two or more syllables. Feminine
rhyme is "double" if it includes two syllables, "triple" if it includes three. In a humorous poem by John Millington Synge,
feminine two-syllable rhymes include *sister* and *blister, liver*
and *give her.* A three-syllable rhyme is illustrated by *hamper-
ing* and *pampering.* See DOUBLE RHYME, MASCULINE ENDING.

feral

(1) Wild, not domesticated or cultivated; existing in a natural
state; (2) ferocious, brutal, characteristic of wild animals. *Feral*
is used in each of these senses in various literary applications.
For instance, the characters in William Golding's *Lord of the
Flies* revert to a feral state; Macbeth's course of action is feral
in that it is brutal and results in many deaths.

festina lente

A Latin phrase which means "make haste slowly."

Festschrift

A term composed of two German words meaning "feast" or
"festival" and "a writing." A Festschrift is a volume of *essays,
*articles, and *sketches contributed by several authors in honor
of someone, usually a colleague or friend, and published on the
occasion of an important occurrence, such as the retirement of
the person being honored.

fetishism

Belief in, or use of, some object regarded with awe as being the
embodiment or residing place of a powerful spirit or force. The
magical and ecstatic rites associated with voodooism, for instance, are a form of fetishism. In psychiatry, the term refers to
a compulsive use of some object or part of the body as a stimulus
in the act of attaining sexual pleasure (a lock of hair, a shoe,
underclothing, one's feet, etc.). In literature, a fetish is any idea
or object that calls forth unqualified respect, reverence, or devotion; for example, feudal knights made a fetish of duty and
loyalty to their leader.

feudalism

The social and economic system prevailing in Western Europe
during a large part of the *medieval period. The entire system
was based upon force, with every landholder the tenant and
servant of some greater landlord. As rent, various groups (bar-
ons, knights, etc.) paid to their superiors "service" which consisted of military aid, or actual property, or both. Socially, two
principal groups existed: (1) knights, higher clergy, lords and (2)
free renters, serfs, peasants.

Feudalism, which broke down in the fifteenth century, was primarily responsible for the ideals of *chivalry and was powerfully influential in medieval *romances and romantic *epics. An exceptionally clear picture of the social, ecclesiastical, and political order of feudalism is revealed in Chaucer's *Tho Canterbury Tales.*

feuilleton
A French term, feuilleton is a form of light literature (fiction, criticism, verse) that resembles vers de société in tone and purpose. It is so named after the page of a French newspaper given over to such material. See LIGHT VERSE, VERS DE SOCIÉTÉ.

fiction
From a Latin word meaning "to make," "to mold," fiction is imagined and invented literary *composition. Fiction may or may not be based on history and fact, but its distinguishing characteristic is that it is fashioned to entertain and, somewhat secondarily, to instruct. Effective fiction makes readers *think,* but the primary purpose of all fiction, effective or ineffective, is to make readers *feel.* The term is usually applied to *novels and *short stories, but *drama, the *epic, *fables, *fairy tales, *folklore, and *parables contain fictional elements. *Nonfiction includes *autobiography, *biography, the *essay, and *history, but, as currently written, these types frequently contain strong fictional components. See IMAGINATION, NARRATION.

fictitious
A term meaning (1) imaginatively produced, created by the imagination and (2) false, not genuine. All fiction is fictitious, or fictional, but is not necessarily "false" in the sense that it is untrue to life.

figurative, literal
These words, often confused, have directly opposite meanings. *Figurative* means "not literal," that is, metaphorical, ornate, rhetorical, and based on or making use of *figures of speech. *Literal* means "true to fact," "actual," "not exaggerated," "in accordance with strict meaning." See CONNOTATION, DENOTATION.

figurative language
Deliberate and intentional departure from normal word meanings or word order so as to gain freshness and strength of expression. Figurative language is writing (or speech) that makes use of one or more figures of speech, such as *metaphors and *similes. The basic purposes of figurative language are to employ ornamental devices for comparing

dissimilar things and for creating sounds and *images. See CONNOTATION, DENOTATION, FIGURES OF SPEECH.

figures of speech

Expressive uses of language in which words are used in other than their literal senses so as to suggest and produce pictures or *images in a reader's (hearer's) mind. Figures of speech may be divided into three classes: (1) *imagined similarities,* such as those in an *allegory, *allusion, *conceit, *simile; (2) *suggestive associations* in which one word is linked with another as, for example, *golden* with *youth, happiness,* and *wealth:* *hypallage, *hyperbole, *metonymy, and *synecdoche; (3) *appeals to the ear and eye,* as in *alliteration, *anacoluthon, and *onomatopoeia.

Figures of speech may also be grouped into (1) "figures of thought" in which words retain their meanings but not their rhetorical patterns, as in an *apostrophe, and (2) *tropes, in which words undergo a definite change in meaning, as in a *metaphor.

Another useful classification of figures of speech is (1) those that actually involve a comparison (*analogy, *personification, *trope) and (2) those that do not normally compare anything (*hyperbole, *litotes, *irony).

filmstrip

A length of film containing a series of transparencies for projection on a screen. A filmstrip can also consist of still photographs to be projected as slides.

fin de siècle

A French expression meaning "end of the century." The term is generally used to mean a period free from social and political conventions and traditions, a meaning derived from the transitional era of the 1890s, when writers were trying to escape the "bonds" of Victorianism. (See VICTORIAN.) Because the artistic temper of this period was confused, fin de siècle now has such opposed meanings as "decadent" and "up-to-date." See DECADENCE, EDWARDIAN.

fine arts

Visual arts such as architecture, painting, sculpture, watercolor, and ceramics. The fine arts are those created with concern for aesthetic values rather than utility (the practical arts, useful arts). Every fine art is subject to judgments concerning its beauty and meaningfulness.

finesse

Adroit and artful management; delicacy or subtlety in action, performance, skill, and discrimination. The finesse of a great dramatist, for example, is revealed in his handling of *character development, his *dialogue, his building up of *conflict, his *verisimilitude, etc.

fine writing

Composition which is mistakenly thought to be free from all impurities because it has been polished to perfection. Actually, fine writing is affected and overcareful as a result of the use of pompous and polysyllabic words, *euphemisms, etc. See AFFECTATION, EUPHUISM, RHETORIC.

first edition

(1) The whole number of copies of a literary work printed first, from the same *type, and issued (published) together; (2) an individual copy of a work from this number; (3) the first printing of a newspaper for a given date. See EDITION.

five-act formula

A term applied to the custom of writing plays in five acts of approximately equal length and playing time. In the nineteenth century, a German novelist and journalist, Gustav Freytag, described the structure of a five-act play as a pyramid, with action rising and falling as suggested under the entry ACT.

flagrante delicto

A Latin term meaning "while the crime is blazing." In literature and in law, the phrase means "while the crime is, or was, being committed." When a character is apprehended while performing an unlawful or immoral act, he is said to be "in flagrante delicto."

flaps

See JACKET.

flashback

A scene inserted into a *play, *novel, or *short story representing an earlier event. A flashback is a narrative device that flashes back to the presentation of an incident that occurred prior to the opening scene of a literary work. Such a flashback may be developed through a reverie, a recollection by a character, a dream sequence, or dialogue. Nearly all of Edna Ferber's *Ice Palace* consists of a flashback; Arthur Miller's *Death of a Salesman,* Thornton Wilder's *The Bridge of San Luis Rey,* the film *Citizen Kane,* and Somerset Maugham's *Cakes and Ale* make extensive use of flashbacks. See IN MEDIAS RES, SWITCHBACK.

flat character

A term coined by E. M. Forster (in *Aspects of the Novel,* 1927) to designate a person who appears in a literary work as little more than a name or as someone who is presented with a single trait. A flat character is not fully developed, lacks complexity, never surprises the reader by what he does or says, and may be referred to as a *type or *caricature. Conversely, a *round character has depth, complexity, full development, and is capable of convincingly surprising the reader time and again. All great works of literature that present characters at all contain both flat and round characters, just as life itself does. Macbeth is a round character; King Duncan is a flat character. See FOIL.

fly (flies)

A *fly* (or *flies*) refers to space above the stage, used mainly for storing equipment and scenery. Such material is "flown" (raised and lowered) through the use of ropes.

flyleaf

A blank leaf in the front or back of a *book. See ENDPAPERS.

focus

A central point of attention, activity, or attraction. In every literary work, the author selects an individual, a group, a situation, or an idea and directs his and the reader's attention to it. In a short story, focus is usually not shifted from one person or situation, but in a novel, play, or long narrative poem, the center of attention may be altered many times. See CONTROLLING IMAGE, DOMINANT IMPRESSION, PURPOSE, THEME.

foil

A person or thing that, by contrast, makes another seem better or more prominent. Using one character as a foil to another brings out the qualities of both. For example, the Fool is a foil in *King Lear;* Hotspur and even Falstaff are foils to Prince Hal in *Henry IV.* Several dozen princes, princesses, and counts are foils in Tolstoi's *War and Peace.* See FLAT CHARACTER.

folio

A term with several meanings, the most common of which is that of a book with a large *format, one having pages more than 30 centimeters (about 12 inches) in height. *Folio* also means (1) a sheet of paper folded once to make two leaves (four pages) of a book; (2) a page number of a book.

Shakespeare's plays were first collected and published in 1623 in a folio edition, so called because of the size of the pages of the volume.

folk ballad

An anonymous storytelling poem handed down orally from generation to generation. See BALLAD, POPULAR BALLAD.

folk drama

In a general sense, folk drama consists of dramatic activities of the folk (the so-called common people), in popular festivals and religious rites. In medieval England, the meaning of the term was widened to include plays about such popular folk heroes as Saint George and Robin Hood. The term *folk drama* now refers to plays written by dramatists on folk themes that reveal the attitudes, problems, language, and customs of "everyday" people rather than those of high estate. Much of the drama of the Irish literary movement—plays by Lady Gregory, J. M. Synge, and others—belongs in this classification, and so do the "peasant plays" of Pirandello as well as plays by such American writers as Paul Green that reflect the lives of mountain people and Negroes.

folk epic

A composition by an unknown author, or authors; a selection assumed to be the work of a group of unknown persons. A folk epic, synonymous with popular epic, grew out of early national history, was founded on primitive beliefs, and focused attention on a noble hero. See ART EPIC, EPIC, LITERARY EPIC.

folk etymology

A fanciful explanation for the origin and derivation of words. Folk etymology consists of false or unlearned modification of words (*Welsh rarebit* from *Welsh rabbit*) and of irrelevant *analogy (*bridegroom* from *bridegome*). See ETYMOLOGY.

folklore

The long-standing and traditional beliefs, legends, and customs of a people. *Folklore,* derived from *Anglo-Saxon *folc* ("people") and *lar* ("learning"), once embraced only orally transmitted materials but now includes written accounts of traditions, literature, craftsmanship, and folk habits. Much folklore is contained in *ballads, *beast epics, *fairy tales, *maxims, *myths, *old wives' tales, and *riddles. In the United States, folklore covers such diverse items as *Amerind materials, work songs, *chanteys, Negro spirituals, and *tall tales.

folktale

A legend or narrative originating in, and traditional among, a people, especially one forming part of an oral *tradition. The term covers a wide range of materials from outright *myths to *fairy tales. *The Thousand and One Nights* is a famous collection of folktales. Some of the stories about Paul Bunyan, Davy Crockett, Pocahontas, Johnny Appleseed, and Daniel Boone are folktales.

font

A complete assortment of *type of one face and size.

fool

A silly or stupid person. In *drama, a fool is a court jester, a professional clown who sometimes hides wit and understanding beneath a cloak of foolishness. In some literary works, like *Twelfth Night* and *King Lear,* the simplicity of such a *stock character causes his remarks to clarify and deepen the underlying meanings of events. Wherever a fool appears in literature, his basic role is that of a *foil.

foot

A group of syllables constituting a metrical unit of verse, a set pattern of stressed and unstressed sounds. In English, a foot most often consists of accented and unaccented syllables in one of five principal groupings:

1. The *iambic* foot (or *iamb*) consists of an unstressed syllable followed by a stressed (long) syllable: *today, about, repeat.* Most English verse falls into an iambic pattern.

2. The *trochaic* foot (*trochee*) consists of a stressed syllable followed by an unstressed (short) syllable: *meter, pleasant, daily.*

3. The *anapestic* foot (*anapest*) consists of two unstressed syllables followed by a stressed syllable: *intercede, for the nonce.*

4. The *dactylic* foot (*dactyl*) consists of a stressed syllable followed by two unstressed syllables: *silvery, national, penitent.*

5. The *spondaic* foot (*spondee*) consists of two stressed syllables: *thirteen, deadbeat.*

These lines from Coleridge are illustrative:

> Trōchĕe / trīps frŏm / lōng tŏ / shōrt;
>
> From long to long in solemn sort
>
> Slōw Spōn/deē stālks; / strōng foōt! /
>   yēt ĭll / ablĕ
>
> Ēvĕr tŏ / cōme ŭp wĭth / Dāctyl trĭ/syllăblĕ.
>
> Ĭam/bĭcs mārch / frŏm shōrt / tŏ lōng;
>
> With ă leāp / ănd ă boūnd /
>   thĕ swĭft Ăn/ăpaĕsts thrōng.

For comment on less common kinds of feet, see AMPHIBRACH, AMPHIMACER, ANTIBACCHIUS, BACCHIC, PYRRHIC.

footnote

An explanatory or proof-citing note or comment referring to a specific part of the main text of a work. A footnote, so-called because it is normally placed at the bottom (foot) of a page, is usually indicated in the text by a superior number. By extension, *footnote* refers to any minor but related comment upon, or afterthought to, a main statement. See DOCUMENTATION, SOURCE.

forensics

The art and study of *argumentation. *Forensics* applies to formal debates and public discussion carried on in oral or written form. Forensic medicine, a phrase appearing in *detective and *mystery stories, is the application of medicine to questions of law, especially in court proceedings. Forensic psychiatry is the use of techniques and knowledge in determining legal insanity.

foreshadowing

Showing, indicating, or suggesting beforehand. In a literary work, foreshadowing provides a hint of what is to occur later. For instance, the early appearance, conversation, and actions of the three witches in *Macbeth* foreshadow the *atmosphere of danger and gloom that runs throughout the play. See NARRATIVE HOOK, PROLEPSIS.

foreword

Introductory remarks in a book, article, or other type of *composition. *Foreword* is synonymous with *preface* in that both provide comments upon, or explanations of, what is to follow and both are usually less formal in tone than the following text. *Foreword* is a less learned word than *preface, *prologue, and *prolegomenon, but each of these terms names introductory remarks designed to put a reader into a proper frame of mind for understanding and appreciating the work he is about to read. Also see EXORDIUM, PREAMBLE, PROTASIS.

form

The manner and style of arranging and coordinating the parts of a *composition, the structural pattern of a work of art. *Verse form* applies to the organization of rhythmic units in a line; *stanza form* applies to the organization of verses in a poem; *novel form* applies to the arrangement of *incidents and *episodes in chapters or other divisions, etc.

In literature, such expressions as *ballad form, elegy form, short-story form,* and the like apply to categories called *genres.

Form is more than an external scheme imposed upon subject matter; it should be considered the entire structural integration of expression and thought. The form of a successful literary work is shaped from within more than it is imposed from without. As a result, in genuine works of literature shape (form) and substance are one. See GENRE, STRUCTURE, STYLE.

formal essay

A serious, carefully organized, logically developed *composition designed to inform or persuade. See ESSAY.

format

The general physical appearance and makeup of a book, magazine, or newspaper: shape, size, typeface, binding, quality of paper, margins, bulk, etc. *Format* has been extended in meaning to refer to the organization, type, style, or plan of such diverse items as buildings, meetings, business operations, and social activities. See BOOK, FOLIO, MAGAZINE, TYPOGRAPHY.

forms of discourse

An old-fashioned term for the types into which thought and expression are classified according to their primary purpose. The traditional forms of discourse—*argumentation, *description, *exposition, and *narration—are artificial divisions made for the purpose of analyzing literary *composition. For further discussion, see each of these four forms of discourse.

formula

In literature, *formula* means a fixed and conventional method of developing a *plot. A stereotyped plot pattern appears in many motion pictures, *television plays, *Western stories, and *slick magazines. Well-known formulas (formulae) include the "redemption" theme (a dissolute or wayward person recovers his manhood); the Cinderella story (a poor, virtuous girl wins her man from a rich, predatory rival); the "country bumpkin" plot (an unsophisticated person defeats a "city slicker" rival), etc.

In a sense, all literary selections follow a formula of some sort, but genuine literature does not do so slavishly and always exhibits qualities and ingredients that transcend hackneyed situations and stereotyped action and characterization.

foundry proof

*Proof pulled for final checking before printing plates are made; proof taken from a form that has been locked up and made ready for plating. (A proof is a trial impression of composed type; *foundry* here means an establishment that produces type in molten metal.)

fourteener

A verse form, especially an *iambic line, consisting of fourteen syllables. George Chapman's translation of the *Iliad* (which inspired Keats's *On First Looking into Chapman's Homer*) was written in this meter. See HEPTAMETER, SEPTENARY.

frame

In motion pictures and *television, *frame* refers to one of the successive small pictures on a *filmstrip. In motion pictures, frames may appear at a rate of thirty per second. In television, *frame* also refers to a single traversal by the electron beam of all the scanning lines on a TV screen. In *bookbinding, a frame is an ornamental border stamped on the cover (*case) of a book.

frame story

A story within a narrative setting, or frame. (See STORY-WITHIN-A-STORY.) The *convention of using a framework for separate narratives has been employed for many centuries. Certain stories in *The Thousand and One Nights* interrupt other stories being related. Boccaccio's *The Decameron* is a collection of 100 tales developed on a central framework. The general setting of Chaucer's *The Canterbury Tales* is a frame; stories the pilgrims tell along the way are frame stories.

free association

Writing in which one thought leads to another. Such "triggering of ideas" may be used in *interior monologue and in *stream of consciousness writing. Many *informal essays, such as some by Charles Lamb, G. K. Chesterton, and Hilaire Belloc, are partly composed of ideas apparently brought into consciousness by a random connection with something already written. In *psychoanalysis, an uncensored expression of ideas and impressions passing through the mind of a person being treated is used as a means of gaining access to unconscious thought processes.

free lance

A writer, performer, or designer who is not compensated on a regular salary basis. A free-lance writer independently prepares material for eventual sale to a publisher, often without any advance guarantee of financial reward. One who advocates a cause without personal attachment or allegiance also is known as a free-lancer.

free verse

Verse that lacks regular meter and line length but relies upon natural rhythms. Free verse is "free" from fixed metrical patterns but does reveal the *cadences that result from alternation of stressed and unstressed syllables. Some writers and critics contend that free verse by its very irregularity provides added force to thought and expression. Conversely, Robert Frost once remarked, "Writing free verse is like playing tennis with the net down." For further discussion, see VERS LIBRE.

Freudianism

The doctrines and psychoanalytic theories of Sigmund Freud (1856–1939), an Austrian physician (neurologist), with regard to the diagnosis and treatment of neurotic and psychopathic states, the interpretation of dreams, etc. The influences upon literature of Freud's exploration of the subconscious and his emphasis on the sex drive of human beings have been profound and long-lasting. A Freudian writer searches for *symbols in his characters' dreams, speech, and actions. Such a follower of Freudianism is concerned with developing the *libido, repressed anxieties, and inmost thoughts of characters. Strong elements of Freudianism appear in James Joyce's *Ulysses* and *Finnegans Wake,* in several of the plays of Eugene O'Neill, Tennessee Williams, and Edward Albee, and in much of the work of William Faulkner. See JUNGIAN, SURREALISM.

frontispiece

An illustrated leaf preceding the *title page of a *book. *Frontispiece,* derived from Latin words meaning "front" and "to look at," is also an architectural term for the façade of a building.

front matter

All matter that precedes page 1 of a book. It may include a *frontispiece, *half title, *title page, *copyright, *preface, *foreword, list of illustrations, list of tables, and *table of contents. See BACK MATTER.

function words

Words such as conjunctions and prepositions used as markers (indications) of word relationships. Function words have relatively little meaning of their own but do serve (function) to point out the relationships of other words. Such elements are known also as "empty words," "form words," and "structure words."

fundamental image

A central figure or object around which a literary work is organized. When a writer singles out an aspect or feature of an object or idea being described or discussed, he develops a fundamental image intended to reduce a possibly complex whole to a unifying base. In describing the Battle of Waterloo, Victor Hugo used the shape of the letter A to explain the positions of opposing armies. Another fundamental image is illustrated in this paragraph from Thomas Hardy's *The Dynasts:*

> The nether sky opens, and Europe is disclosed as a prone and emaciated figure, the Alps shaping like a backbone, and the branching mountain chains like ribs, the peninsular plateau of Spain forming a head. Broad and lengthy lowlands stretch from the north of France across Russia like a grey-green garment hemmed by the Ural Mountains and the glistening Arctic Ocean.

See CONTROLLING IMAGE, DOMINANT IMPRESSION.

fustian

(1) A stout fabric of cotton and flax; (2) inflated, exaggerat-

ed, turgid language. Although fustian is mentioned often as wearing apparel in Thomas Hardy's Wessex novels, the term is most often applied in literature in its second sense of *bombast and ranting language. These lines appear in Pope's *Epistle to Dr. Arbuthnot:*

> Means not, but blunders round about a meaning;
> And he whose fustian's so sublimely bad,
> It is not poetry, but prose run mad.

futurism

A style developed by a group of Italian artists early in the twentieth century in which forms derived from *cubism were employed to represent dynamic motion and rapid movement. In literature, futurism is an approach to writing and a theory of art in which speed, power, and violence are portrayed and in which hostility to the past and to all traditional forms of expression is advocated. See CUBISM, DADAISM, EXPRESSIONISM, SURREALISM.

G

Gaelic

A *Celtic language, especially the speech of ancient Ireland. See ANGLO-SAXON, CELTIC.

Gallicism

A French expression or *idiom used in another language. A statement such as *je ne sais quoi* ("I don't know what") employed in English to mean "an indefinable, elusive, or pleasing quality" is a Gallicism. The term, which also applies to any French linguistic characteristic or pecularity, is derived from Gaul, an ancient name for France.

gargantuan

An adjective meaning "enormous," "gigantic." *Gargantuan* is derived from the name of a kingly giant who consumed prodigious amounts of food and drink in Rabelais's satirical novel *Gargantua and Pantagruel* (1534).

gasconade

Boastful talk, extravagant bluster. *Gasconade* is derived from Gascony, a former province in France, the natives of which were considered boasters and braggarts. Vainglorious *fiction and *cloak-and-dagger literature often contain gasconade. See MILES GLORIOSUS.

gatefold

An inserted page, larger than the trim size of a *book or *periodical, folded one or more times so as not to extend beyond the edges.

gazette

A newspaper; a news sheet, published periodically, which offers accounts of current events, dispatches, legal notices, appointments, etc. In Great Britain, *gazette* is sometimes used as a verb meaning "to announce," "to publish," or "to list" in an official government journal. The term comes from the name of an Italian (Venetian) coin (the price of the paper or newssheet).

gazetteer

A geographical *dictionary. A gazetteer is an alphabetically arranged collection of information about continents, countries, rivers, cities, mountains, etc.

gemination

The immediate repetition of a word or phrase for rhetorical effect ("May he hang by the neck until he is *dead, dead, dead*"). Gemination, which has a basic meaning of "doubling," is used in *linguistics to refer to the repetition of a consonant in spelling and pronouncing a word: *cattail, drunkenness.*

generalization

A statement (or belief) based on only a few facts, statistics, or examples; the characterization of an attitude, trend, or principle in general terms without reference to specific details. Most effective authors avoid generalizations because they are vague and indefinite: "All Frenchmen are crafty"; "English people are reserved"; "Nothing succeeds like success." (See LOGIC.) However, writers do express what they consider "general truths" during and after the development of numerous specific details and events.

general semantics

A systematic study of the relations between words and people's actions, of the connections between words (as symbols) and human behavior. (See SEMANTICS, WORD.) General semantics is concerned with word meanings in more than their "dictionary sense"; it involves several kinds of verbal and nonverbal meanings and the importance of those meanings in private lives and public affairs.

General semanticists claim that the meanings of words reside in the person who uses them or responds to them. For example, a student of general semantics has suggested that one cannot find in a dictionary the meaning of a particular sunset; that the true meaning of *sunset* lies in oneself, in one's thoughts and feelings, in what one says, thinks, and does about a sunset. That is, general semantics asserts that the true meanings of words are no more in the words themselves than the meaning of an elm tree is in an elm. The thoughts and images of many poets and novelists reflect this concept of word meanings. For example, a literary artist, instead of a general semanticist (the late Wendell Johnson), might have written that the meanings of *a green meadow* are "the children who chase butterflies across it, the artist who paints it, the cows which graze upon it, or the old soldier who remembers the battle that once was fought across its green slopes."

generic

An adjective meaning "general," "common to or characteristic of an entire group or class." In literature, *generic* applies to that which is common or universal in a category (such as "lyric poems") or a group (such as "novelists"). Thus, one might refer to a generic tendency among poets to use rhythmic language or among novelists to place characters in situations involving *conflict.

genre

A category or class of artistic endeavor having a particular form, technique, or content. *Genre,* a word from French, is a synonym for *type* and *kind.* Among genres in literature are included the *novel, the *short story, the *essay, the *epic, etc. The term *genre* is somewhat loose and general; for instance, *poetry* suggests a genre, but so do *lyric, *pastoral, *ode, *elegy, and *sonnet.

In painting, *genre* is applied to works that deal with everyday life in realistic techniques. See FORM, TYPE.

genteelism

From a Latin word meaning "well-bred" and a French word meaning "elegant," *genteelism* is applied to literary works notable for their polished style and graceful form. In current literary criticism, *genteelism* is often used with mocking or scornful reference to what are considered false standards of refinement. (See AFFECTATION.) The term can be a synonym for *euphemism, as illustrated in the use of *limb* for *leg* and *serviette* for *napkin.* The phrase *genteel tradition* is applied to attitudes of correctness and conventionality in writing more common in the eighteenth and nineteenth centuries than they are today.

Georgian

An adjective applying to the reigns of the four Georges (1714–1830), with particular reference to the styles of architecture, crafts, and arts current in England during that period. In literature, *Georgian* is a vague term of doubtful usefulness since it has been loosely applied to all British writers living in that era as well as to authors during the later reign of George V (1910–1936) and even that of George VI (1936–1952).

georgic

An adjective meaning "agricultural," *georgic* is used as a noun to designate a poem about farming and allied aspects of rural life. The *Georgics* of Virgil (first century B.C.) deals with such topics as rural life, weather forecasting, animal husbandry, and beekeeping.

germane

A term often used in literary criticism, *germane* means "pertinent," "belonging," "relevant." In an effective literary work, all topics, ideas, and events are closely and significantly related and appropriate and are therefore germane. See EXTRANEOUS, EXTRINSIC, INTRINSIC, IRRELEVANCE.

gest (geste)

An old-fashioned name for a *metrical romance involving warfare and adventure. *Gest,* derived from a Latin word meaning "deeds" or "exploits," now occurs more often in the form of *geste* (see CHANSON). A thirteenth-century collection of stories, the *Gesta Romanorum* (deeds of the Romans), has been widely used as a source book by later writers, including Shakespeare.

gestalt

A unified whole; a pattern or form that has a *structure not accounted for by the sum of its parts. Gestalt psychology teaches that physiological and mental acts do not occur through reflexes, stimuli, and sensations but through gestalts (wholes) operating separately and independently. In literature, *gestalt* applies to a manner of *composition, such as that illustrated by Coleridge's insistence that poetry and prose exhibit a characteristic "construction" (or gestalt). (See FORM.) By this theory, a poem is a composition in patterned language not explained by the rhythm, rhyme, stanzaic structure, etc., that function distinctly, although interrelatedly. See INTENTIONAL FALLACY.

ghost writer

One who prepares speeches, papers, articles, or books for another person who is named as, or presumed to be, the author. Such a writer is an "unseen spirit" or "invisible hand," often referred to by phrases like "edited by" and "as told to."

gibberish

A term for (1) meaningless or unintelligible speech or writing and (2) language that is learned, affected, and pretentious. *Gibberish,* an example of *onomatopoeia, is a blend of *gibber* ("foolish chatter") and *English.* See DOUBLE TALK, GLOSSOLALIA, GOBBLEDYGOOK, JABBERWOCKY.

gleeman

A wandering entertainer, a strolling singer or minstrel. See JONGLEUR, SCOP, SKALD, TROUBADOUR.

gloria in excelsis

A Latin phrase meaning "glory in the highest." The term appears most often in the title of a *hymn, *Gloria in Excelsis Deo* ("Glory be to God on high").

gloss

An explanation or definition of a difficult, unusual, or technical word or passage. A gloss may appear as a *footnote, as a note in the margin of a *manuscript, or in a special kind of *appendix called a *glossary. The word *gloss* is sometimes used in the sense of providing a false appearance or explanation; to "gloss over" something is to excuse or explain it away. See ANNOTATION, VARIORUM.

glossary

A list of terms in a special field, subject, or area of interest and usage, accompanied by definitions. A glossary consists of a series of *glosses (verbal interpretations, explanations, and definitions). Many scientific and technical works contain an appended glossary.

glossolalia

A "gift of tongues," ecstatic speech uttered in excitement or hysteria. Glossolalia consists of unintelligible utterances expressed during worship services of various religious groups noted for their emotional fervor. The term is from Latin words meaning "tongue" and "chatter." See GIBBERISH.

gnomic

An adjective applied to terse statements of general truth; a characteristic of writing that is didactic, moralistic, aphoristic, and sententious. *Gnomic,* derived from a Greek term meaning "judgment," "opinion," or "wisdom," is applied to all *maxims, to some *fables and *proverbs, and to many of the "wise" statements of Francis Bacon, Benjamin Franklin, Emerson, Thoreau, and Robert Frost.

In ancient Greece, a group of "gnomic poets" dealt with ethical and philosophical matters in pithy sayings and excessive moralizing. Gnomic elements appear in modern poetry, such as that by Carl Sandburg, W. H. Auden, and Archibald MacLeish.

gnostic

Knowing; possessing knowledge, especially that of spiritual matters. Among early Christians, a Gnostic was a member of a sect that claimed superior knowledge about religious affairs. The term is related to *agnostic,* one who holds that all claims to knowledge are uncertain, especially those concerning ultimate causes and the essential nature of everything, including God.

goat

From early times, the goat has been associated with the idea of sin and with devil lore. In older literature, the devil himself was often shown as a goat, and the animal has frequently been used as a symbol of lust and lechery. A scapegoat is a person made to bear the blame for others or to suffer in their place.

gobbledygook

Wordy, inflated, obscure, and often unintelligible language. *Gobbledygook,* a special kind of *fine writing or *jargon, is a term coined by a former United States congressman who had grown weary of involved government reports and bulletins. Apparently he had in mind the throaty sounds uttered by a male turkey; the term is a fanciful formation from *gobble.*

golden age

This term is variously applied, but it often refers to a period in Latin literature (70 B.C.–A.D. 14) during which Cicero, Horace, Virgil, and Ovid wrote. (See AUGUSTAN.) The golden age of Greek literature came in the fifth and fourth centuries B.C. In general, *golden age* refers to that period in the life of a nation or an individual to which is attributed special excellence or happiness, real or imagined.

Gongorism

An affected, artificial, and heavily ornamented style of writing. Gongorism, derived from the name of an early seventeenth-century Spanish poet, Góngora, makes use of *bombast, *conceits, *paradoxes, and *puns and has some of the characteristics of *Euphuism.

gospel

A term of several meanings, *gospel* is a name for (1) glad tidings, good news; (2) something regarded as true and wholly believed; (3) a doctrine of prime importance; (4) the story of Jesus Christ's life and teachings as recorded in the first four books of the New Testament.

Gothic

An adjective of varied meanings derived from *Goth,* the name of a Germanic tribe of ancient and medieval times. *Gothic* refers to (1) a style of architecture originating in France and persisting from the twelfth to the sixteenth century, characterized by ribbed vaults, pointed arches, flying buttresses, ornamental gables, and fine woodwork and masonry; (2) anything pertaining to the *Middle Ages and therefore erroneously considered crude and barbaric; (3) a style in literature characterized by gloomy *settings, violent or grotesque *action, and a *mood of decay, degeneration, and *decadence.

The Gothic novel was a late eighteenth- and early nine-teenth-century kind of *fiction noted for the qualities indicated in the third definition above. Popular romantic and thrill-evoking works in this *genre include Walpole's *The Castle of Otranto,* Radcliffe's *The Mysteries of Udolpho,* Lewis's *The Monk,* and Mary Shelley's *Frankenstein.*

Götterdämmerung

A German term formed from words meaning "gods" and "twilight," usually translated "twilight of the gods." In English, the expression is used to refer to collapse and destruction accompanied by disorder and violence. The resounding defeat of Austrian and Russian armies in the Battle of Austerlitz, as described in Tolstoi's *War and Peace,* has often been referred to as a Götterdämmerung.

Goudy

Frederic William Goudy (1865–1947) was a famous and prolific designer of printing types in the United States.

graffiti

Words or phrases written on the walls of buildings, on sidewalks, and in public rest rooms. *Graffiti,* the plural of *graffito,* was originally a term in archaeology referring to ancient drawings. The word is derived from an Italian term meaning "scratch" that is based on a Greek word meaning "to write."

Grail, Holy

A cup (chalice), or dish, which, in medieval *legend, was used by Jesus Christ at the Last Supper and in which were received the last drops of His blood at the Cross. The Holy Grail, which appears often in literature as a *symbol for Christian purity, formed a cycle of tales. Search for the Holy Grail was the source of many adventures of the *Knights of the Round Table. The framework of Tennyson's *Idylls of the King* firmly fixes the legendary history of the cup to the *Arthurian cycle of romance and adventure.

grammar

A statement, or series of statements, of the way a language works. Grammar discusses the forms of words, their use in phrases, clauses, and sentences, their tenses, cases, and other changes in form. The word *grammar,* which comes from Greek *gramma* ("letter," "written symbol"), means the basic *structure of an entire language. English grammar, for instance, is "the English way of saying things." See LINGUISTICS, WORD.

Graveyard School

A phrase used to refer to a group of eighteenth-century English poets who wrote gloomy poems about death and life after death. These writers, reacting against others who avoided all thoughts of death, the grave, and "the mystery of the future," tried to create an *atmosphere of "pleasing gloom." Gray's *Elegy Written in a Country Churchyard* is a restrained example of graveyard poetry which, as one critic has said, reflected "the joy of gloom, the fondness for bathing one's temples in the dank night air, and the musical delight of the screech owl's shriek." The expression *graveyard writing* is sometimes applied to work that is pessimistic, foreboding, and despairing of man's fate.

gravure

A printing process involving engraving by means of photography. Many current *periodicals are produced by *rotogravure and *photogravure. *Gravure* also refers to a print or plate produced by such a process and to a metal or wooden plate used in photogravure. See PRINTING.

Grub Street

The former name of a London street in Cripplegate (changed in the nineteenth century to Milton Street). In his *Dictionary,* Samuel Johnson notes that this street was "much inhabited by writers of small histories, dictionaries, and temporary poems, whence any mean production is called *grubstreet.*" The term is applied to any form of literary hackwork (routine writing done for money only).

Grundy, Mrs.

A conventional, narrow-minded person critical of any breach of propriety. The name is taken from that of a nonappearing character in an eighteenth-century play by Thomas Morton, concerning whom questions such as "What will Mrs. Grundy say?" and "What will Mrs. Grundy think?" are constantly asked. Mrs. Grundy is a *symbol of social *convention.

hack

A person who, solely for money, exploits his creative ability in the production of unimaginative work. See GRUB STREET.

hackneyed

Adjective applied to words or ideas made commonplace. *Hackneyed* is derived from the idea of a horse or carriage let out for hire and therefore worn out in service. See BANALITY, CLICHÉ, STEREOTYPE, TRITENESS.

hagiography

Writing about, and critical study of, the lives and legends of saints. Hagiography is a subtype of *biography. *Hagiology* is a related term with the same meaning as *hagiography*.

haiku

A form of Japanese verse usually employing *allusions and *comparisons. A haiku is composed of three lines containing a fixed number of syllables, usually seventeen or nineteen:

O cricket, from your cheery cry
No one could ever guess
How quickly you must die.

See IMAGISM, TANKA.

half rhyme

Imperfect rhyme, the result of *assonance or *consonance: *years, yours; somewhere, summer.* See NEAR RHYME, RHYME, SLANT RHYME.

half title

The first printed page of a book. It contains the title of the book, together sometimes with a *blurb or quotation, and precedes the full *title page. The title of a subdivision of a book, when printed on a page by itself, is also called a half title. See BASTARD TITLE, FRONT MATTER.

halftone

A photoengraving term designating a process in which gradation (shading) of tone is secured by a system of minute dots that are produced by a screen placed in the camera in front of a plate.

hallucination

A false notion, belief, or impression. A hallucination is a *delusion or *illusion, an apparent experience of one's senses that is nonexistent outside the mind. For example, Lady Macbeth was hallucinating (having a hallucination) during the sleepwalking scene in act 5, scene 1, of *Macbeth.* Many characters in literature have experienced a "wandering of the mind," the primary meaning of the Latin term from which *hallucination* is derived.

hamartia

An error in judgment. Hamartia, derived from a Greek word meaning "fault," is sometimes known as "the tragic flaw" because it represents a fatal weakness that causes the downfall of a *protagonist in *tragedy. This hamartia may be caused by inherited weakness, by faulty character traits, or by poor judgment; whatever the cause, the result is action, or inaction, that leads to destruction and death. (See CAUSE AND EFFECT, TRAGEDY.) Rashness is the character flaw that caused Oedipus to kill his father; ignorance led to his marrying his own mother. The hamartia (or tragic flaw) of Macbeth is ambition; of Othello, jealousy. See HUBRIS.

harangue

A passionate and vehement speech, especially one delivered to a crowd and designed to rouse emotions. In Shakespeare's *Julius Caesar,* Antony's speech over the body of Caesar is an example of the harangue. The term has been extended in meaning to include any long and pompous speech or heated oral attack. Adolf Hitler achieved and temporarily maintained political eminence by haranguing public gatherings. See DIATRIBE, TIRADE.

harlequin

A comic character, a buffoon. A harlequin was originally a masked actor in Italian comedy, a mixture of wit and childishness, dressed in multicolored tights. A harlequinade is a *farce or *pantomime in which a harlequin (sometimes spelled with a capital letter) plays the principal role. See COMMEDIA DELL'ARTE.

harmony

In literature, harmony is the *proportion of separate parts

of a selection to each other and to the whole. The term refers to the combination of elements (such as *theme, *setting, *characterization, *action) that are brought together in such ways as to reveal their basic *unity. Such an agreement of parts is applied to both subject matter and treatment. See ATMOSPHERE, CONSONANCE, MOOD, TONE.

haruspex

An ancient Roman priest who practiced the foretelling of future events, reading signs from the entrails of animals killed in sacrifice. That such fortune-tellers were not held in universal esteem even in their own time is suggested by Cato's remark, "I wonder how one haruspex can keep from laughing when he sees another." A haruspex was a kind of soothsayer, such as the witches in Shakespeare's *Macbeth.*

headband

A band of silk or other material glued to the head or tail of the back (spine) of a *book, or to both, to protect and strengthen the *binding.

head rhyme

A *synonym of *alliteration. Head rhyme is based on *assonance or *consonance. The line "Apt alliteration's artful aid" is an example of head rhyme, or "beginning rhyme," which may occur in successive words or successive lines of verse.

heavy

(1) A dramatic role (or an actor) representing a dignified, solemn, and imposing person; (2) an actor who plays villainous parts or characters. Iago, for instance, is the heavy in *Othello.*

hedonism

The belief and doctrine that pleasure and happiness are the highest and greatest good which man can hope to attain. *Hedonism* also implies devotion to pleasure as a way of life. The word, derived from a Greek term meaning "pleasure," is closely related to *Epicurean. See CARPE DIEM, DOLCE FAR NIENTE.

hegira

A flight or journey. Spelled with a capital letter, *Hegira* refers to the flight of Muhammad from Mecca to Medina in 622. *Hegira* is now applied to a trip of any sort, especially one to a place considered congenial and desirable. See EXODUS.

Hellenism

(1) Imitation or adoption of ancient Greek customs, art, thought, etc.; (2) the characteristics of Greek culture from the fourth to the first century B.C.: (3) ancient Greek culture and ideals. *Hellenism,* from a Greek word meaning "similarity to

the Greeks," is a loose and broad term, for it refers to admiration (and to admirers) of Greek art, architecture, sculpture, philosophy, tribal customs, and language—indeed to everything concerning ancient Greek civilization. Related words are *Hellene* (a Greek), *Hellenic, Hellenize* (to make Greek in character), *Hellenist* (a person who adopts Greek speech, customs, etc.), and *Hellenistic.*

hemistich

A half line of verse or a line of less than the usual length. *Hemistich* refers to that part of a line of poetry preceding or following a *caesura (pause, break). These lines from Pope's *An Essay on Criticism* are illustrative:

> Trust not yourself; // but your defects to know,
> Make use of ev'ry friend—// and ev'ry foe.

hendecasyllabic

Adjective applied to a line of verse of eleven syllables. *Hendecasyllabic* is derived from a Greek term meaning "eleven" and another Greek word from which *syllable* is formed. A line from Tennyson illustrates hendecasyllabic verse: "Like the skater on ice that hardly bears him."

hendiadys

A figure of speech in which a complex idea is expressed by two words joined by *and. Hendiadys* is Greek for "one by means of two" or "one through two." The device occurs in this passage from the Psalms: "Such as sit in darkness and in the shadow of death, being fast bound in misery and iron." The idea of the last three words is one: the iron (shackles) *is* the misery.

heptameter

A line of verse consisting of seven *feet. This is a line in heptameter from Walt Whitman's *When Lilacs Last in the Dooryard Bloom'd:*

> Ever / return/ing spring, / trini/ty sure /
> to me / you bring.

heptastich

A *stanza or *poem consisting of seven lines. For an example of a heptastich, see CHAUCERIAN STANZA.

heresy

Opinion or belief differing from orthodox or accepted doctrine. *Heresy,* derived from a Greek word meaning "to choose," was originally applied to churchly and religious systems but is now used to refer to any attitude and point of view that differ from generally accepted ideas and *conventions. A heretic is anyone who does not conform to and with an established doctrine or principle.

hero, heroine

In classical mythology, a hero was a man of godlike prowess and goodness who came to be honored as a divinity. Later, a hero was a warrior-chieftain of special strength, ability, and courage. Still later, a hero was an immortal being, a demigod. For several centuries, a hero has been considered a man of physical or moral courage, admired for bravery and noble deeds. A heroine is a female hero.

Somewhat incorrectly, *hero* and *heroine* are sometimes considered the principal characters in a story, film, play, or novel. See AGON, ANTAGONIST, PROTAGONIST.

heroic couplet

Two rhyming lines of verse in iambic *pentameter. This simplest form of English *stanza is so called because it was frequently used for *epic poetry and poetic *drama. This is a heroic couplet from Pope's *Essay on Man:*

> Laugh where we must, be candid where we can;
> But vindicate the ways of God to man.

heroic drama

A form of *tragedy and *tragicomedy that developed in England late in the seventeenth century. Heroic drama, often in verse, was characterized by *bombast in dialogue, violent *conflict, and *spectacles involving passionate love and savage warfare. Dryden's *The Conquest of Granada* is an example of this type.

heroic line

An iambic *pentameter line, called heroic because used so often in *epic poetry and other narratives involving heroes engaged in adventure, warfare, and death.

heroic stanza

A *quatrain (four lines) in iambic pentameter. Gray's *Elegy Written in a Country Churchyard* is composed in heroic stanzas:

> Far from the madding crowd's ignoble strife,
> Their sober wishes never learned to stray;
> Along the cool sequestered vale of life
> They kept the noiseless tenor of their way.

heterodoxy

Belief in doctrines and principles not generally accepted and established. *Heterodoxy,* an *antonym of *orthodoxy, is often applied to theological and churchly principles and ideas but also refers to the support of literary movements that are unconventional or generally discredited. (See HERESY.) For example, *dadaism and *existentialism may be considered examples of heterodoxy.

heuristic

An adjective applying to any course of action that stimulates interest, furthers investigation, and causes one to discover something for himself. *Heuristics,* the science or technique of finding things, comes from a Greek term meaning "to discover." The major purpose of most great literature is heuristic in that it is designed to enable readers to find out for themselves the real meaning of life and living.

hexameter

A line of verse consisting of six *feet. Longfellow's *Evangeline* is written in hexameter:

This is the / forest pri/meval. The / murmuring /
   pines and the / hemlocks
Bearded with / moss, and in / garments green, /
   indis/tinct in the / twilight

hexastich

A *stanza or *poem of six lines. Each of the four stanzas in Wordsworth's *I Wandered Lonely as a Cloud* is a hexastich. This is the last stanza of the poem:

For oft, when on my couch I lie
In vacant or in pensive mood,
They flash upon that inward eye
Which is the bliss of solitude;
And then my heart with pleasure fills,
And dances with the daffodils.

hiatus

An interruption or break in the continuity of an action, series, or work; a missing part; a gap. In language, hiatus is a pause due to the coming together, without pause or break, of two vowel sounds: *ride over, coordinate. Hiatus* is an *antonym of *elision.

hierarchy

(1) Any system of persons or objects ranked one above another; (2) a government by ecclesiastical (church) rulers; (3) the power or dominion of a person who rules or has authority. *Hierarchy* usually refers to an individual or group of persons with high position and substantial influence. The existing power structure in society, currently referred to as the Establishment, is a form of hierarchy.

hieroglyph

A character standing for a word or sound. A hieroglyph is a *symbol, a conventionalized picture of a tree, bird, reptile, animal, etc., that formed part of a way of writing on ancient Egyptian monuments. Hieroglyphics is a form of picture writing. The term has been loosely extended to refer to any writing that is difficult to understand. See CIPHER.

historical novel

A narrative in *novel form characterized by an imaginative reconstruction of historical personages and events. Writers have combined *fiction and *history for many centuries, but Sir Walter Scott firmly established the *type in *Ivanhoe, Kenilworth,* etc. Prominent historical novels include Thackeray's *Henry Esmond,* Dickens's *A Tale of Two Cities,* Tolstoi's *War and Peace,* Dumas's *The Count of Monte Cristo,* Hervey Allen's *Anthony Adverse,* and Margaret Mitchell's *Gone with the Wind.*

historical play

A *drama dealing with events from *history, especially critical and crucial episodes in the career of a ruler or outstanding military personage. A historical (or history) play is synonymous with chronicle play, although the latter is more likely to deal with incidents involving only one major character and to make greater use of pageantry (coronations, battle scenes, state funerals) than the former. See CHRONICLE PLAY.

historical present

The present tense used in narrating a past occurrence as though the event were happening at the time of narration. Such a device provides a sense of immediacy, of being present, and for that reason appears frequently in literature. The historical present is used in the player's speech in *Hamlet* (act 2, scene 2) and in much of Carlyle's *The French Revolution,* as is illustrated in this passage:

> ... The drums drown the voice. "Executioners, do your duty!" The Executioners, desperate lest themselves be murdered ... seize the hapless Louis; six of them desperate, him singly desperate, struggling there; and bind him to their plank. Abbé Edgeworth, stopping, bespeaks him: "Son of St. Louis, ascend to Heaven." The Axe clanks down; a King's life is shorn away. It is Monday the 21st of January, 1793. ...

history

A branch of knowledge dealing with past events; a connected and continuous account of previous happenings ordinarily presented in *chronological order. Primarily concerned with direct *exposition, history is considered "literature" only in the hands of such skilled craftsmen as Gibbon, Macaulay, Carlyle, and Parkman. These sentences from Macaulay's *The Perfect Historian* are illuminating:

> The perfect historian is he in whose work the character and spirit of an age is exhibited in miniature. He

relates no fact, he attributes no expression to his characters, which is not authenticated by sufficient testimony. But, by judicious selection, rejection, and arrangement, he gives to truth those attractions which have been usurped by fiction. . . . He shows us the court, the camp, and the senate. But he shows us also the nation. He considers no anecdote, no peculiarity of manner, no familiar saying, as too insignificant for his notice which is not too insignificant to illustrate the operation of laws, of religion, and of education, and to mark the progress of the human mind. . . .

See AUTOBIOGRAPHY, BIOGRAPHY, HISTORICAL NOVEL, HISTORICAL PLAY.

holism

A philosophical concept (theory) that whole entities (fundamental components or elements of reality) have an existence other than that of the sum of their parts. *Holism* is based upon a learned borrowing from Greek *holo-,* meaning "entire" or "whole."

holograph

(1) Something wholly written by the person in whose name it appears; (2) a document such as a deed, will, or letter in the author's handwriting. The holograph of James Joyce's *Finnegans Wake* has proved important to literary scholars and critics because it reveals the creative process at work. See ALLONYM.

Homeric

A term referring to the eighth-century-B.C. Greek epic poet, the reputed author of the *Iliad* and *Odyssey*. Because of the stature of this writer and the majesty and grandeur of his works, *Homeric* is used to mean "imposing," "grand," "of heroic dimensions." For instance, Homeric laughter is loud, hearty, and room-shaking.

A Homeric epithet is a descriptive phrase that accents a dominant trait of a character, such as "swift-footed Achilles," "Odysseus, sacker of cities," and "laughter-loving Aphrodite." See EPITHET.

A Homeric simile is an extended figure of speech, a figurative comparison which develops parallel likenesses over several lines of verse. See EPIC SIMILE.

homiletics

The art and practice of preaching. Homiletics, from a Greek word meaning "to converse with," is that branch of practical theology dealing with the preparation and delivery of *sermons. (See DIDACTICISM.) Among noted preachers in literature may be mentioned Saint Augustine, Saint Thomas Aquinas,

Jonathan Swift, John Donne, Jonathan Edwards, John Wesley, and Phillips Brooks.

homily

A moralizing discourse; a sermon explaining some part of the *Bible with accompanying instruction for the congregation. In *As You Like It,* Shakespeare refers to a preacher: "O most gentle pulpiter! What tedious homily of love have you wearied your parishioners withal, and never cried 'Have patience, good people'!" See SERMON.

homograph

A word of the same written form as another but of different origin and meaning. The term, composed of two Greek elements meaning "the same" and "to write," is illustrated by *homer* (a unit of measure, a home run in baseball); *wound* (injury, the past tense of *wind*); *sole* (only, part of a shoe). See HOMONYM.

homologous

Corresponding in position, attitude, or structure; having the same or a similar relation. An *adage and a *proverb are homologous sayings.

homonym

A word like another in sound but different in meaning, origin, and often in spelling: *bare, bear; meet, meat; male, mail; led, lead.* See HOMOGRAPH.

homophone

A word pronounced the same as, but differing in meaning from, another, whether spelled the same way or not: *air, heir; key, quay; tier, tear.*

homostrophic

Following an identical stanzaic pattern throughout a selection. *Homostrophic,* literally meaning "one *strophe," is a synonym of *Horatian when applied to odes and other long poems. Keats's *Ode to Autumn* is a homostrophic poem consisting of three stanzas of eleven lines each, each line five feet in length. See HORATIAN, PINDARIC.

honi soit qui mal y pense

A French term meaning "shamed be the one who thinks evil of it" or, somewhat more commonly and inexactly, "evil to him who evil thinks."

Horatian

A reference to Horace (65–8 B.C.), Roman poet and satirist. In literature, *Horatian* applies to the poetic style and diction of Horace. An ode is Horatian when each of its stanzas follows the same metrical pattern, as, for instance, Keats's *Ode to a Nightingale* does. See HOMOSTROPHIC, PINDARIC.

hornbook

A single sheet of paper containing the alphabet or simple religious or moralistic comments, covered with a thin sheet of transparent horn and fixed in a frame with a handle. Hornbooks were widely used in England and America up to the eighteenth century for teaching children to read. See ABECEDARIAN, ABECEDARIUM, PRIMER.

hors de combat

A French term translated as "out of the fight," "disabled," "no longer able to contest or resist."

howler

A mistake, especially an embarrassing one, in speech or writing. See ANACHRONISM, BONER, IRISH BULL, MALAPROPISM, SOLECISM.

hubris

Arrogance; excessive self-pride and self-confidence. *Hubris,* a Greek term for "insolence," referred to the emotions in Greek tragic heroes that led them to ignore warnings from the gods and thus invite *catastrophe. Hubris is that form of *hamartia or *tragic flaw that stems from overbearing pride and self-assumed superiority. In Sophocles's *Antigone,* Creon rejects warnings from the blind prophet Tiresias, and consequently suffers the death of Antigone and the self-destruction of his wife and son. The play ends with these words about hubris from the leader of the *chorus:

Wisdom is the supreme part of happiness; and reverence toward the gods must be inviolate. Great words of prideful men are ever punished with great blows and, in old age, teach the chastened to be wise.

Hudibrastic

Referring to *Hudibras,* by Samuel Butler, a seventeenth-century *mock heroic poem. *Hudibrastic* implies a playful, *burlesque style, such as that of much *doggerel. Hudibrastic verse is humorous or satiric and is filled with "wise" sayings and farfetched rhymes. Here are a few lines from *Hudibras* itself:

Beside, he was a shrewd philosopher,
And had read every text and gloss over;
Whate'er the crabbed'st author hath
He understood by implicit faith;
Whatever skeptic could inquire for,
For every *why* he had a *wherefore;*
Knew more than forty of them do,
As far as words and terms could go.

humanism

Any system of thought or action in which human interests,

values, and dignity are held to be dominant. Humanism implies devotion to the concerns of mankind; it is an attitude of mind that concentrates upon the activities of man rather than upon the supernatural world, the world of nature, or the so-called animal kingdom. Historically, humanism was a *Renaissance doctrine, born in fourteenth-century Italy, which stressed the essential worth, dignity, and potential of man as contrasted with an older view that man was wicked, worthless, and doomed to destruction both in this life and in that to come. Renaissance humanists, deriving their beliefs from study of ancient poets, historians, and philosophers, came to believe that man was indeed the center of the universe and that he was capable of living a life of reason, dignity, morality, and even happiness. In a more specific sense, humanism involves devotion at any time, including the present, to those studies that deal with the life, thought, and literature of ancient Greece and Rome. Advocates of humanism in literary history range from Petrarch, Thomas More, Erasmus, and Sir Philip Sidney to Shakespeare, Milton, and Goethe.

humanities

A term applied specifically to the classical languages and literatures of Greece and Rome and more broadly to subjects distinct from the physical and social sciences: art, literature, music, and philosophy. See QUADRIVIUM, SEVEN LIBERAL ARTS, TRIVIUM.

humor

A comic quality causing amusement. *Humor* is also applied to the faculties of seeing, understanding, or expressing what is amusing and laughter-producing and to a mood or frame of mind ("in a good humor today"). Humor consists primarily of the recognition and expression of peculiarities, oddities, and absurdities in a situation or action.

Humor is not always light and mirth-provoking, despite its ever-present capacity for perceiving and stating what is amusing or ridiculous. George Eliot, a nineteenth-century English novelist not noted for humor, wrote, "Humor is thinking in jest while feeling in earnest." Joseph Addison once said that Good Sense was the father of Wit and that Humor was the offspring of Wit and Mirth. For a discussion of differences between wit and humor, see WIT.

humors

In ancient and medieval physiology, four liquids of the body—blood, phlegm, yellow bile, black bile—were called humors. These liquids were allied with four elements: the blood, like air, was warm and moist; phlegm, like water, was cold and moist; yellow bile, like fire, was hot and dry; black bile, like earth, was cold and dry. In these ancient beliefs, one's emotional and physical condition was affected by the condition of one's humors. Good health and a perfect temperament resulted when no one humor was dominant. This conception of humors in Elizabethan times came to mean "mood," "disposition," or "peculiarity" and is helpful in understanding such characters as, for example, Hamlet, King Lear, Lady Macbeth, Jaques, and scores of other Shakespearean personages. In *Every Man out of His Humour,* a satirical comedy (1599) by Ben Jonson, appear these lines:

> The choler, melancholy, phlegm and blood . . .
> Receive the name of humours. Now thus far
> It may by metaphor apply itself
> Unto the general disposition:
> As when some one peculiar quality
> Doth so possess a man that it doth draw
> All his effects, his spirits, and his powers,
> In their confluxions, all to run one way,
> This may be truly said to be a humour.

hymn

A *song or *ode in praise or honor of God or any deity, of a nation, or of an ideal. A typical hymn is a lyric poem in verse form designed to be sung, and hence a direct means of emotional expression. In literature, hymns are often songs of praise in honor of any outstanding or exalted person, such as Ben Jonson's *Hymn to Diana.* Shelley's *Hymn to Intellectual Beauty* is an example of a tribute to an ideal. Oliver Wendell Holmes and John Greenleaf Whittier were notable American writers of hymns on religious and moral themes.

hypallage

A *figure of speech in which an *epithet (descriptive term) is applied not to an apparently appropriate noun but to another. Hypallage occurs in Virgil's phrase "the trumpet's Tuscan blare" (rather than the more usual "Tuscan trumpet's blare") and in Keats's line in *Ode to a Nightingale:* "The murmurous haunt of flies on summer eves" (rather than "the haunt of murmurous flies"). See METONYMY, OXYMORON.

hyperbaton

A *figure of speech in which words are transposed from their natural order. *Hyperbaton* is employed to increase *emphasis, as in Shelley's "Hail to thee, blithe Spirit! / Bird thou never wert" (*To a Skylark*) and in Shakespeare's *Othello:* "Yet I'll not shed her blood, / Nor scar that whiter skin of hers than snow."

hyperbole

Obvious and deliberate exaggeration; an extravagant statement. Hyperbole is a figure of speech not intended to be taken literally. *Exaggeration for the sake of *emphasis is a common poetic and dramatic device: in *Hamlet,* Shakespeare wrote, "If thou prate of mountains let them throw millions of acres on us . . . " and in *Macbeth:*

No; this my hand will rather
The multitudinous seas incarnadine,
Making the green one red.

See EXAGGERATION, IRONY, LITOTES.

hypocorisma

A Greek term usually appearing in English as *hypocorism* and meaning "baby talk," "the use of pet names." In literature, hypocorism usually consists of using nicknames, such as Will for William, Dick for Richard, etc.

hypothesis

A *proposition assumed as a *premise; an assumption, guess, or conjecture. John Stuart Mill, a nineteenth-century English philosopher, explained *hypothesis* in these words: "It appears, then, to be a condition of the most genuinely scientific hypothesis that it be of such a nature as to be either proved or disproved by comparison with observed facts." Something is said to be hypothetical when it is "supposed" or "assumed."

hysteron proteron

A *figure of speech in which what logically should come last comes first. *Hysteron proteron* is from Greek words meaning "later earlier." Examples: *bred and born* for *born and bred, thunder and lightning* for *lightning and thunder.* See HYPER-BATON.

I

iambus

A poetic foot of two syllables, the first unaccented, the second accented. The iambus is the most common metrical foot in English. *Iamb* is a shortened form of *iambus,* the adjectival form of which is *iambic.* These lines by Richard Lovelace consist of iambic feet:

> Ĭ cóuld / nŏt lóve / thĕe, Déar / sŏ múch
> Lŏved Í / nŏt hón/oȓ móre.

ibidem

A Latin word meaning "there the same" and used in English to mean "in the same place," "in that very place." *Ibidem,* usually shortened to *ibid.,* appears often in *footnotes and other *citations where it is used to mean "on the same page in the same chapter of the same book" as a previously mentioned *source. *Ibid.* is also employed to refer to printed sources other than books. See LOC. CIT.

icon

An *image, picture, or other representation. In some religious sects, an *icon* refers to a painting or related likeness of some sacred personage such as Christ, the Virgin Mary, an angel, or a saint.

iconoclasm

The act of destroying or attempting to weaken traditional institutions and established ideas and ideals. *Dadaism and *existentialism, for instance, are forms of iconoclasm. An iconoclast is a destroyer or breaker of images, one who attacks cherished traditions, beliefs, and institutions. See ICON, IMAGE.

iconography

See ICON. *Iconography* (1) has the conventional meanings pertaining to an image (see IMAGE, SYMBOLISM); (2) means subject matter in such arts as painting and sculpture with reference to the *conventions about revealing subjects in artistic representation; (3) means the study of subject matter and its significance in all visual arts.

ictus

The accent, or stress, that falls on a syllable. *Ictus* does not refer to the accented syllable but to the accent (stress) itself. See ACCENT.

id

A psychoanalytical term referring to that part of the *psyche (spirit) that is the source of instinctive energy (action). According to analysts, one's id provides impulses that seek satisfaction in pleasure and is controlled, if it is controlled, by one's *ego and *superego (social ideals, conscience). The term *id* (and its implications) appears often in twentieth-century literature. See FREUDIANISM, JUNGIAN, LIBIDO.

idée fixe

A French term meaning "fixed idea." An idée fixe is a persistent, powerful, and obsessive idea from which one cannot escape. Such a fixation can be a delusion, a falsity, such as the idée fixe which Othello had about the unfaithfulness of Desdemona. In Melville's *Moby Dick,* Captain Ahab has an idée fixe about the white whale that had deprived him of a leg in an earlier encounter.

identical rhyme

Rhyme created by the repetition of a word. The device is illustrated in lines 2 and 4 of this *stanza from Coleridge's *The Rime of the Ancient Mariner:*

> He holds him with his skinny hand;
> "There was a ship," quoth he.
> "Hold off! unhand me, grey-beard loon!"
> Eftsoons his hand dropt he.

The recurrence of two words which sound exactly alike but have different spellings and meanings is called rime riche; it is shown in these lines from Chaucer's *The Canterbury Tales:*

> The hooly blisful martir for to seke [seek],
> That hem hath holpen whan that they were
>   seeke [sick].

identification

(1) A process by which a person ascribes to himself the characteristics and qualities of someone else; (2) an intense feeling of "oneness" with another person. In literature, a reader must

identify to some degree with a character (or characters) in a work in order to care about what happens, why, and to whom. See BELIEF, EMPATHY, READER IDENTIFICATION.

ideograph

A written symbol that represents an idea or object directly rather than a particular word or speech sound. The Chinese language, for instance, is written in ideographs. A stick figure, a diagrammatic drawing representing a human or animal, often used in statistical work, is an ideograph.

ideology

The body of doctrine, *myth, *tradition, and *symbol that represents the beliefs and attitudes of an individual, group, class, etc. *Ideology* is usually applied to a political or cultural plan, such as that of democracy, or *fascism, or *expressionism, along with methods for putting it into operation. The basic beliefs, *points of view, and life experiences of an author form a part of his ideology and thus shape his literary products.

id est

A Latin term meaning "that is" and often abbreviated to i.e. See EXEMPLI GRATIA.

idiolect

The language or speech pattern of an individual at a particular period of his life. Because no such thing as total conformity in pronunciation, for instance, is possible, every speaker of every language has an idiolect, his individual way of pronouncing that differs, however slightly, from the pronunciation of everyone else.

idiom

(1) A language, dialect, or style of speaking peculiar to a people; (2) the constructions or expressions of one language whose structure is not matched in another language. The word *idiom* meant, in original Greek, "a private citizen, something belonging to a private citizen, personal." By extension, *idiom* has come to mean "individual" and "peculiar." Idiomatic usage in English, for example, refers to expressions that conform to no grammatical precedents or principles but are laws unto themselves. *Idiom* has been widened in meaning to apply to a distinct style or character, such as the modern idiom or the idiom of *naturalism or *existentialism or *polyphonic prose, etc.

idola

False *images of the mind. *Idola* is the plural of *idolum,* or *idol,* something to which strong attachment is given and which is an object of passionate devotion. In his *Novum Organum* (1620), Francis Bacon classified the principal fallacies of people into *idola tribus, specus, fori, theatri* ("idols of the tribe, cave, market, theater").

idyll

A composition in prose or verse describing *pastoral scenes and events or any simple, appealing, and charming *incident; also spelled *idyl.* An *idyll* is an idealized story of happy innocence. The *Idylls* of Theocritus, a third-century-B.C. poet, described the primitive, rustic life of Sicilians. Tennyson's *Idylls of the King* lacks descriptions of rustic life, but in *tone and *mood is idyllic (simple, poetic, pleasing). John G. Whittier's *Maud Muller* is a well-nigh perfect example of an idyll. See ARCADIA, GEORGIC, PASTORAL.

i.e.

An abbreviation of Latin *id est, meaning "that is."

ignis fatuus

Also referred to as "will-o'-the-wisp" and "friar's lantern," *ignis fatuus* is a Latin term meaning "foolish fire." The phrase applies to a flitting phosphorescent light seen at night over marshy ground, caused by the combustion of gas from decomposed organic matter. In literature, *ignis fatuus* is used to refer to something that is misleading and deluding, as in the Earl of Rochester's lines:

Reason, which fifty times to one does err,
Reason, an ignis fatuus of the mind.

illiteracy

A word or expression not accepted in either informal or formal speech and writing, such as *disremembered* and *youse.* Characteristic of uneducated speech, illiteracies appear in literature in the dialogue of persons being characterized as unlettered or ignorant. In a more general sense, *illiteracy* means the lack of ability to read and write.

illuminated manuscript

Sheets that contain writing and are decorated with color. Before the invention of printing (fifteenth century), devotional, religious, and other texts were copied on paper, parchment, or other writing surfaces by scribes in monasteries. Capital letters were drawn in combinations of colors (gold, red, blue, etc.), and pages were embellished by floral designs and representations of religious figures. See CALLIGRAPHY, INCUNABULA, MANUSCRIPT.

illusion

(1) An impression of what is perceived that is other than true; (2) a false mental *image or conception which may be something imagined or a misinterpretation of a real appearance. An illusion may be harmful but quite often is harmless, pleasing, and even useful. For instance, an audience at

a play has to experience illusions of reality in order to grasp what is happening. See BELIEF, CONVENTION, DELUSION, DIS-BELIEF, DRAMATIC ILLUSION, SUSPENSION OF DISBELIEF.

image

(1) A physical representation of a person, animal, or object that is painted, sculptured, photographed, or otherwise made visible; (2) the mental impression or visualized like-ness summoned up by a word, phrase, or sentence. An author can use *figurative language (such as *metaphors and *similes) to create images as vivid as the physical pre-sence of objects and ideas themselves. When Andrew Mar-vell wrote in *To His Coy Mistress:*

> But at my back I always hear
> Time's wingèd chariot hurrying near;
> And yonder all before us lie
> Deserts of vast eternity . . .

he was describing the transience of life and mystery of the future in the images of a hurrying vehicle and limitless deserts.

The image is a distinctive and essential element, a basic ingredient, of nearly all imaginative prose and poetry. See CON-CRETENESS, CONNOTATION, FIGURATIVE LANGUAGE, IMAGERY, METAPHOR, SIMILE, SYMBOL, TROPE.

imagery

The forming of mental *images, figures, or likenesses of things; the use of language to represent actions, persons, objects, and ideas descriptively. Any effective writer, especially a poet, is a maker of pictures in words, but he can, and does, appeal to senses other than sight. For instance, Edgar Allan Poe com-bined both a visual and a nonvisual image in

> Along the ramparts plumed and pallid
> A wingèd odour went away.

Coleridge resorted to auditory imagery in these lines:

> And now 'twas like all instruments,
> Now like a lonely flute;
> And now it is an angel's song,
> That makes the heavens be mute.

Also, imagery can be both figurative and literal, as in these lines from a sonnet by Wordsworth:

> It is a beauteous evening, calm and free,
> The holy time is quiet as a Nun
> Breathless with adoration; the broad sun
> Is sinking down in its tranquillity.

See CONNOTATION, FIGURATIVE LANGUAGE, IMAGE, METAPHOR, SIMILE, SYMBOL, TROPE.

imaginative writing

Composition which is dependent upon the formation and expression of mental *images and concepts stored in the memory and upon the ability to recombine former experiences and observations in the creation of new impressions aimed at a specific goal. In general, *poems, *plays, *short stories, and *novels are judged to be imaginative writing, although many such selections are based upon observed realities and recorded facts. *Biography, *history, *essays, and *articles are usually judged to be less imaginative than so-called creative or fictional writing, but many selections in these *genres are heavily dependent upon their author's ability to see inner relationships through powers of the mind that constitute imagination. See FANCY.

imagism

The theory and practice of a group of early twentieth-century poets in Great Britain and the United States who believed that poetry should employ the language of common speech, have complete freedom in subject matter, create new rhythms, and present clear, precise, and concentrated *images. Ezra Pound, Richard Aldington, and Amy Lowell were adherents of imagism and were known as imagists. Carl Sandburg's *Fog* ("The fog comes / on little cat feet") is an imagist poem.

imbroglio

A complicated and difficult situation; an intricate and perplexing state of affairs. *Imbroglio* also applies to a bitter misunderstanding or disagreement between persons or groups. Involved in an imbroglio were the houses of Montague and Capulet in Shakespeare's *Romeo and Juliet.* See BROUHAHA.

imitative words

Expressions that imitate the sound made or associated with the referent (the object or action named). An imitative word, such as *buzz* or *clattered,* is also referred to as *onomatopoeia, which occurs in these lines from Alfred Noyes's *The Highwayman:*

> Tlot-tlot; tlot-tlot! Had they heard it?
> The horse-hoofs ringing clear;
> Tlot-tlot; tlot-tlot, in the distance?
> Were they deaf that they did not hear?

A notable example of imitative words appears in Tennyson's *The Princess:*

> The moan of doves in immemorial elms,
> And murmuring of innumerable bees.

immanence

A word naming a feeling, sensation, or belief that is inherent, that lodges within a person's mind and heart. *Immanence* refers to a thought or conviction that is indwelling, that seems a part of the innermost life of one's spirit. In literature and philosophy, an immanent mental act is one that takes place within the mind of the subject without producing any external effects. An inner realization of the presence and power of God, for instance, was a matter of immanence for Dante, Milton, John Donne, and Hawthorne, among scores of great writers. The ideas about guilt, repentance, and retribution that revolved in Hamlet's mind were immanent. See INDIGENOUS.

imperfect rhyme

Resemblance in the sound of words that is not true or exact. Imperfect rhyme, also known as *approximate rhyme, *half rhyme, *near rhyme, and *slant rhyme, is illustrated in lines 1 and 3, 2 and 4 of this passage from William Butler Yeats:

Heart-smitten with emotion I sink *down*
My heart recovering with covered *eyes;*
Wherever I had looked I had looked *upon*
My permanent or impermanent *images.*

implication

Something suggested or implied as naturally to be understood. In literature, an implication is a meaning or understanding that is to be arrived at by the reader but that is not fully and explicitly stated by the author. When Hawthorne, in *The Scarlet Letter,* makes clear the religious fervor and strong conscience of the young minister Arthur Dimmesdale, there is an implication that a sense of self-guilt will lead this "sinner" to destruction. When wine is poisoned in the final scene of *Hamlet,* there is an implication that death will follow. See EXPLICIT, IMPLICIT, INFERENCE, INNUENDO.

implicit

(1) Not specifically stated; (2) absolute, unreserved. In the first of these meanings, *implicit* is the adjectival form of *implication. When, for example, in the first act of *King Lear* both Goneril and Regan merely pretend filial love and Cordelia responds honestly, it is implicit (not expressly said) that only Cordelia is dutiful and trustworthy. The second meaning of *implicit* is illustrated in Dante's *The Divine Comedy* by the author's total acceptance of the desirability of Christian salvation.

import

Another word for *meaning* or *implication. The import of a literary work is related to its *theme, its *purpose. The phrase *true import* means "essential message," "true significance."

imprecation

A curse; the calling down of evil upon someone. (See CURSE.) An imprecation occurs in *King Lear* (act 1, scene 4) when Lear, thinking that Cordelia does not truly love him, says:

> Hear, Nature! hear, dear goddess, hear!
> Suspend thy purpose, if thou didst intend
> To make this creature fruitful!
> Into her womb convey sterility!
> Dry up in her the organs of increase,
> And from her derogate body never spring
> A babe to honour her! If she must teem,
> Create her child of spleen, that it may live
> And be a thwart disnatur'd torment to her! . . .
> Turn all her mother's pains and benefits
> To laughter and contempt, that she may feel
> How sharper than a serpent's tooth it is
> To have a thankless child!

impression

(1) the process, or result, of *printing from *type; (2) a printed copy from type or plates; (3) one of a number of printings made at different times from the same set of type. See EDITION.

impressionism

A literary practice which does not stress reality but rather the impressions of the author (or one of his characters). *Impressionism* may also be defined as an artistic theory which claims that the dominant purpose of literature is to explain effects upon intellect, feelings, and conscience rather than to provide detailed descriptions of objective *settings and events. Impressionism is a personal style of writing in which the author develops characters and paints scenes as they appear to him at a given moment rather than as they are (or may be) in actuality. For instance, the so-called camera-eye passages in John Dos Passos' *U.S.A.* are impressionistic. In Joyce's *Portrait of the Artist as a Young Man,* much is revealed about Stephen Dedalus's feelings but little about his physical surroundings and activities. See EXPRESSIONISM, IMAGISM, STREAM OF CONSCIOUSNESS, SYMBOLISM.

imprimatur

An official license to print or publish a *book, *pamphlet, etc. *Imprimatur* is a Latin term meaning "let it be printed" or "let it be made by pressing upon something." Specifically, an imprimatur is a license issued by a censor of the Roman Catholic Church. See NIHIL OBSTAT.

imprint

Information (publisher's name, place and date of publication) appearing on the *title page (or elsewhere) in a book. *Imprint* also has the meaning of fixing firmly in the mind or memory; for example, a great work of literature makes an imprint on readers. See COLOPHON.

impromptu

An adjective meaning "made or done without previous preparation," "improvised," "suddenly or hastily concocted." A speech or written composition is impromptu when it is quickly made ready or delivered. See AD LIBITUM, EXTEMPORE.

impropriety

Something that is incorrect, inappropriate, not suitable. In language, an impropriety is an erroneous expression, the improper use of a word, such as saying or writing *literal* when *figurative* is meant or saying *eats* for *food*.

improvisation

The act or result of hasty and offhand preparation; written material composed on the spur of the moment. See EXTEMPORE, IMPROMPTU.

incantation

(1) The chanting of words thought to have magical power or (2) words that possess a charm or cast a spell. Incantation is illustrated by the mumblings and chants of the witches in *Macbeth*. Ariel's song ("Full fathom five thy father lies") from Shakespeare's *The Tempest* is an incantation as well as a *dirge.

incarnate

(1) Represented in the flesh, as when reference is made to "the Devil incarnate"; (2) personified or typified; for example, chivalry incarnate is the theme of Tennyson's *Idylls of the King*. In literature, *incarnate* is used in both of these senses and also with the meaning of "putting into or representing in concrete form." Iago is evil incarnate in *Othello;* Jim, a concrete example of slavery in Twain's *Huckleberry Finn,* is an incarnate *symbol. *Incarnation* also refers to the assumption of human form by a deity, as, for example, the incarnation of God in Jesus Christ.

inchoate

An adjective with several meanings: just begun, incomplete; imperfect; rudimentary; not properly organized. Will Durant built his ten-volume history of civilization from an inchoate mass of material. The work of the American novelist Thomas Wolfe has often been referred to as inchoate. Applied to writing in any of the meanings listed, the term is not always complimentary although it is not necessarily faultfinding.

incident

An event or occurrence; a distinct piece of *action. An incident is a short narrative dealing with a single situation. When incidents are strung together in connected fashion, they become *episodes in a *plot.

incoherence

A quality of writing or speech that is disconnected, rambling, and without logical *structure. Under the stress of powerful emotions, characters in literature sometimes become incoherent and are unable to speak and act in understandable, logical ways. Some *informal essays approach incoherence in structure and thought—Lamb's *Dissertation upon Roast Pig* and *Dream-Children* have been cited as examples—but effective writing, despite outward appearances, is always coherent, ordered, and unified in some fashion. See COHERENCE.

incremental repetition

A form of iteration (uttering repeatedly) occurring in writing, especially in the *ballad. *Incremental* refers to "addition," "gain," and "the process of increasing"; coupled with "repetition" it suggests "cumulative growth." An important structural device of the ballad, incremental repetition applies to the use of *refrains but even more to the repetition of *stanzas with increments—either additions or changes in key words to indicate advancement of the story. The opening stanzas of a *popular ballad, *The Demon Lover,* illustrate incremental repetition:

> "Oh where have you been, my long, long love,
> This long seven years and more?"
> "O I'm come to seek my former vows
> Ye granted me before."
>
> O hold your tongue of your former vows,
> For they will breed sad strife;
> O hold your tongue of your former vows,
> For I am become a wife."

incubus

An imaginary demon or evil spirit (especially one in male form) supposed to descend upon sleeping persons. *Incubus* is generally used to refer to a nightmare or to any thought or situation that weighs upon and oppresses a person. The demon lover who spirited away a young wife and destroyed her (see INCREMENTAL REPETITION) is a form of incubus. In another sense, the hasty remarriage of Hamlet's mother is an incubus for him. See SUCCUBUS.

incunabula

Books produced in the earliest stages (before 1500) of printing from movable type. Incunabula comes from a Latin word meaning "swaddling clothes" and is a synonym for *cradle books. A famous incunabulum (singular) is Caxton's edition of *The Canterbury Tales,* printed in 1478.

index

An alphabetical listing (with page numbers) of all topics treated in a book, appearing in, or constituting, the *back matter of a work. An index should be distinguished from a *table of contents because of its position in a book, its primary purpose, and its detail. The plural of *index* is *indexes* or *indices.* Sometimes referred to as "the Index" is *Index Librorum Prohibitorum* (list of prohibited or forbidden books), published for adherents of the Roman Catholic faith.

indigenous

Native, inherent, natural. An indigenous literary work, for example, is one that originated in and that characterizes a particular region or country. The dialect poems of Robert Burns are indigenous to Scotland; *The Scarlet Letter* is indigenous to colonial, Puritan New England.

Indo-European

A family of languages including, among others, the Germanic, Hellenic, Slavic, and Italic branches. Some specific languages in this family, which has been "formed" by many correspondences in sound and meaning, are German, Yiddish, English, Welsh, Latin, Italian, Spanish, French, Greek, Russian, and Polish—all of them culturally or politically important. The Indo-European family of languages forms the largest and most important category into which tongues related by common origin can be placed. See LANGUAGE, LINGUISTICS.

induction

A form of reasoning (thinking) from the specific to the general. Induction tries to establish a general truth from the observation of specific facts. From a sufficient number of these facts, or particulars, the inductive process of reasoning reaches a principle or conclusion. For instance, a novelist may provide a dozen or several hundred "facts" about the actions, thoughts, and comments of a given character. From these particulars, general ideas and understandings about the personality and characteristics of that individual are induced by both author and reader. Most narratives in prose and poetry involve the process of induction, although a *problem novel or play may begin with a general thesis (belief) and then provide supporting details. See DEDUCTION.

Induction is also an *archaism (an outmoded term) for an *introduction, *preamble, or *prologue. (See FRAME STORY.) In *A Mirror for Magistrates,* Thomas Sackville's Induction (1563) describes how the poet was led into Hell, where exist the souls of those whose lives form the subject matter of the *Mirror* itself. In *The Taming of the Shrew,* Shakespeare, in a prefatory section called Induction, presents a drunken tinker, Christopher Sly, who becomes convinced that he is a nobleman; for him, a play, the *Shrew* itself, is presented.

in extremis

A Latin term meaning "on the outer edges," "at the uttermost limit." The phrase is used to mean "in extremity," "near death."

infantilism

The persistence of childish traits in an adult. *Infantilism* may apply to physical, mental, or emotional characteristics. Characters in literature who present babyish or childish attitudes or who seem unable to cope with life on a so-called grown-up level are infantile. A classic example of infantilism is provided in James M. Barrie's play *Peter Pan,* about a boy who never grew up.

inference

A judgment or conclusion based on evidence presented; the forming of an opinion which possesses some degree of probability according to facts already available. An *implication gives grounds for an inference. For instance, the taut, worried actions and remarks of the central character in Stevenson's *Markheim imply* that he intends to do harm to the dealer whose shop he has entered; from these actions and remarks, the reader *infers* that a robbery, a murder, or some other criminal act will result. See EXPLICIT, FORESHADOWING, IMPLICIT, INNUENDO.

infinity

That which is immeasurably great, unlimited and unbounded, endless and inexhaustible. (See ETERNITY.) The meanings of *infinity* and *eternity* are hinted at in these lines from William Blake because they are related to *world* and *heaven:*

> To see a world in a grain of sand
> And a heaven in a wild flower,
> Hold infinity in the palm of your hand
> An eternity in an hour.

Both Dante in his *Divine Comedy* and Milton in *Paradise Lost* made valiant attempts to deal with infinity, but man's finite (measurable, limited) mind cannot conceive of time and space without bounds and without endings.

inflection

A change in the form of a word to express different grammatical uses. (See CONJUGATION, DECLENSION.) *Inflection* also refers to a change in the *pitch or *tone of a person's voice. See INTONATION.

informal essay

A *composition without set *form or obvious *pattern which also goes by the names of *familiar essay, light essay, and *personal essay. Subject matter for an informal essay is infinite; it may reflect any of a thousand *moods or feelings.

In his *preface to *Essais,* Montaigne clearly explained the purpose and aim of this form of writing:

> Reader, lo is here a well-meaning book. . . . I have proposed unto myself no other than a familiar and private end. I have no respect or consideration at all, either to thy service, or to my glory. . . . I desire . . . to be delineated in mine own genuine, simple, and ordinary fashion, without contention, art, or study. . . .

Although informal essays make no pretensions to learning or instruction, nevertheless the best of them are stylistically polished and imply far more than they state. For example, Swift's *A Modest Proposal* and Defoe's *Shortest Way with the Dissenters* are ironic and thought-provoking informal essays.

informality

That which is not according to customary, prescribed, or official forms; something irregular or casual. In literature, characters often speak or act with informality. Certain authors attempt an informal style by the use of *colloquialisms, *humor, and a generally relaxed approach. Many *personal essays and newspaper *columns are characterized by informality.

infra dig

An abbreviation of the Latin term *infra dignitatem* ("beneath one's dignity"). *Infra dig* means "undignified," "demeaning," "degrading."

inherent

An adjective meaning "existing in something as a permanent element, quality, or attribute." For instance, inherent in all the work of Chaucer and Shakespeare are these authors' deep love, understanding, and tolerance of humanity.

in loco parentis

A Latin phrase meaning "in the place of a parent." In English, the phrase means "replacing a parent," as one might speak of the function of a college, school, church, orphanage, etc.

in medias res

A Latin phrase meaning "in the middle of things." The term applies to the literary device of beginning a narrative well along in the sequence of events. The device, a *convention in *epic poetry and often used in novels, short stories, drama, and narrative poetry, is designed to attract immediate attention and secure prompt interest. For example, Homer's *Iliad* begins in the final year of the Trojan War, the beginning of which is recounted later in the epic. When a story is begun at some point other than its chronological opening, a *flashback (or series of flashbacks) is also employed.

innate

Inborn, native, existing in one from birth. Shakespeare's poetic and dramatic genius was innate. Innate characteristics of Abraham Lincoln were humility and nobility of spirit. See IN-HERENT.

innuendo

A word derived from a Latin term suggesting a "hint" and used in English to refer to an indirect suggestion or intimation of some kind. An innuendo is a way of implying something without actually stating it. In Robert Frost's *Mending Wall,* there is an innuendo that "good fences" perpetuate prejudice, prevent understanding, and avoid companionship more than they make "good neighbors":

> He will not go behind his father's saying,
> And he likes having thought of it so well
> He says again, "Good fences make good
>   neighbors."

insensate

An adjective meaning "without feeling or sensitivity." In literature, an insensate character may be not only insensitive but also without sense, judgment, or understanding. Except for the hero and heroine, the Capulets and Montagues in *Romeo and Juliet* are insensate.

intaglio

(1) A printing process in which a design or text is engraved in the surface of a plate so that when excess ink is removed, the remaining ink stays in grooves and is transferred to paper. Intaglio printing is used with etchings and engravings. (2) A gem, seal, or piece of jewelry cut with a sunken design. See BAS-RELIEF, PRINTING.

intellectual

A term meaning "appealing to or engaging" the powers and faculties of one's mind, but also used to refer to a person engaged in mental labor as distinguished from a manual worker, businessman, etc. Not all authors are intellectuals, but those who rely on their mental powers more than on emotions and feelings may be so designated. Shakespeare was *intellectual* but not so much *an intellectual* as, for example, Francis Bacon, Sir Isaac Newton, Charles Darwin, or Albert Einstein.

intentional fallacy

A term used to describe the so-called error of judging the meaning and success of a literary work in terms of the author's expressed purpose in writing it. (See AFFECTIVE

FALLACY.) In this phrase, *intentional* does not mean "deliberate" but instead refers to the intention of the writer. Two modern critics (Wimsatt and Beardsley) have claimed that "the poem is not the critic's own and not the author's. It is detached from the author at [its] birth and goes about the world beyond his power to 'intend' about it or control it." See FALLACY.

Inter alia
A Latin phrase meaning "among other things." A related term, *inter alios,* means "among other persons."

interior monologue
A form of writing which represents the inner thoughts of a character. It records the internal, emotional experience of an individual, reaching downward to unspoken levels where *images represent emotions and sensations. The Molly Bloom section at the end of James Joyce's *Ulysses* is an example of interior monologue in which the author seems not to exist and the reader directly "overhears" the thought flowing through the character's mind. In plays by Eugene O'Neill and novels by William Faulkner, the authors present, guide, and even comment on impressions passing through the minds of characters. See STREAM OF CONSCIOUSNESS, a related term which applies more to subject matter than to the technique (interior monologue) of presenting inner thoughts (see MONOLOGUE).

interlinear
Situated or inserted between lines. *Interlinear* also applies to books with the same text set in different languages, as, for instance, an interlinear Bible set in alternate lines of Latin and English.

interlude
(1) An intervening episode, incident, space, or period of time; (2) a short dramatic sketch introduced between the acts of plays or given as part of another entertainment. *Interlude,* which comes from Latin words meaning "between play," is applied to any interruption of the main plot of a novel or play and to a break in a lecture or essay.

internal rhyme
Correspondence in sound created by two or more words in the same line of verse; rhyme falling in the middle as well as at the end of the same metrical line. (See LEONINE VERSE.) Internal rhyme appears in the first and third of these lines from Shelley's *The Cloud:*

> I silently *laugh* at my own *cenotaph,*
> And out of the caverns of rain,
> Like a child from the *womb,* like a ghost

from the *tomb,*
I arise and unbuild it again.

interpolation

The altering of a text by inserting new material or editorial comment. For instance, references to the Bible and to Christian life that appear in the *Old English poem *Beowulf,* a pagan *epic, are interpolations by persons who made later copies of the work.

intonation

The melody or pattern of pitch changes in speech; the manner of producing musical tones. *Intonation* also applies to the opening of a *chant. The term is used to refer to anything said or recited in a singing voice. See JUNCTURE, PITCH, STRESS.

in toto

A Latin phrase meaning "in all." Related meanings are "wholly," "entirely," "with no exceptions or omissions."

intrigue

Deceitful plans, underhanded plotting. *Intrigue* involves crafty or secret dealings and is applied, for example, to plays that have intricate plots. *The Way of the World,* by William Congreve, is a comedy of intrigue.

intrinsic

Belonging by its very nature. The *play-within-a-play by which Hamlet made certain of the guilt of King Claudius is an intrinsic part of *Hamlet.* See EXTRINSIC.

introduction

A preliminary part of an *essay, *article, *book, etc., leading up to the main part. An introduction to a book is a formal preliminary statement or guide to the book. See FOREWORD, PREFACE, PROLEGOMENON.

invective

Abuse; accusation or denunciation. See CALUMNY, CURSE, IMPRECATION, MALEDICTION.

inversion

Reversal of the usual or natural order of words. (See ANASTROPHE.) Inversion occurs often in poetry for *emphasis and also to accommodate *meter, as in Coleridge's *Kubla Khan:*
A damsel with a dulcimer
In a vision once I saw.

in vino veritas

A Latin phrase meaning "in wine there is truth." The phrase is used to suggest that an intoxicated person is freed from restraint and inhibitions and hence is more likely to tell the truth than if he were sober.

invocation

The act of calling upon a deity, spirit, or person for protection, aid, inspiration, or assistance of some kind. Invocation (derived from a Latin term meaning "to call") has become a literary *convention in which a writer, usually a poet, calls on a *muse for help and divine guidance. At the beginning of *Paradise Lost,* John Milton directs an invocation to Urania, the muse of astronomy and epic poetry:

> Sing, Heavenly Muse . . . I thence
> Invoke thy aid to my adventrous song,
> That with no middle flight intends to soar
> Above the Aonian mount . . .

Ionic

(1) A metrical foot with two long and two short syllables. Ionic meter is rare in verse written in English but is frequent in the Latin odes of Horace; (2) a term applying to one of the classical orders in ancient Greek architecture: fluted columns, molded bases, richly ornamented figures, etc. See DORIC.

ipse dixit

A Latin phrase meaning "he himself said it." In English, the expression applies to any assertion made without proof. An ipsedixitism is an emphatic, dogmatic statement.

ipso facto

A Latin term meaning "by the fact itself." The expression is used to mean "by the nature of the deed," "by the act itself." When Faust sold his soul to the devil, he became an ipso facto debtor with an obligation that eventually had to be met. The term is generally used to mean "absolutely," "irrespective of external considerations."

Irish bull

A paradoxical statement that seems to make sense but is really absurd. When an Irish bull is unintentional, it is a *boner: "Deep down, Falstaff was a very shallow person." In *nonsense verse, however, Irish bulls are used deliberately for humorous purposes, as in Edward Lear's *The Jumblies:* "They went to sea in a sieve, they did" and in Lewis Carroll's *The Walrus and the Carpenter:*

> The sun was shining on the sea,
> Shining with all his might;
> He did his very best to make
> The billows smooth and bright—
> And this was odd, because it was
> The middle of the night.

irony

A *figure of speech in which the literal (*denotative) meaning of a word or statement is the opposite of that intended. In literature, irony is a technique of indicating an intention or attitude opposed to what is actually stated. Aristotle defined *irony* as "a dissembling toward the inner core of truth"; Cicero supplied a simpler and more helpful explanation: "Irony is the saying of one thing and meaning another." Sometimes called the most ironic writing in all literature is Jonathan Swift's *A Modest Proposal,* in which the author "recommends" that the Irish sell their babies to English landlords for food. Among devices by which irony is achieved are *hyperbole, *litotes, *sarcasm, *satire, and *understatement.

Socratic irony is so called because Socrates adopted another's point of view in order to reveal that person's weaknesses and eventually to ridicule him. Another form of irony with a special meaning is *dramatic irony.

irrelevance

Something that is unconnected, not applicable, inappropriate, unsuitable. An irrelevant remark, *episode, or *incident is one that does not belong in the selection in which it appears because it is not *germane to the subject being discussed or to the *plot being developed. See EXTRINSIC, INTRINSIC.

Italian sonnet

A poetic form, also called Petrarchan, consisting of fourteen lines divided into an *octave (eight lines) and a *sestet (six lines), usually rhyming *abbaabba, cdecde* (or *cdcdcd*). One of the best-known of all Italian sonnets is Keats's "On First Looking into Chapman's Homer." See PETRARCHAN, SONNET.

italics

A style of printing types in which letters usually slope to the right. Italics are used in many literary selections to differentiate between varying kinds of material, to secure greater *emphasis, to denote words as words, etc. In handwritten *manuscripts, underlining is a method of italicizing words.

ivory tower

A place, situation, or attitude toward life that is remote from practical, worldly affairs. The phrase, first used by Sainte-Beuve, a nineteenth-century French literary critic, suggests aloofness, disdain for practical considerations, and indifference to everyday existence and to all matters that are outside one's restricted circle of interests. Poets, for example, have often been called ivory-tower dwellers, but in *A Defence of Poetry* Shelley referred to them as "the unacknowledged legislators of the world."

jabberwocky

A *parody of language consisting of meaningless syllables or words. *Jabberwocky,* applied to unintelligible speech and writing, appears delightfully in Lewis Carroll's poem by that name in *Through the Looking-Glass.* The first stanza is

> 'Twas brillig, and the slithy toves
> Did gyre and gimble in the wabe;
> All mimsy were the borogoves,
> And the mome raths outgrabe.

See DOUBLE TALK, GIBBERISH, GOBBLEDYGOOK, IRISH BULL, JARGON, NONSENSE VERSE.

jacket

A detachable paper cover, often colored and illustrated, for protecting the *binding of a *book. Sometimes referred to as a dust jacket, such a cover usually bears the title of the book, the author's and the publisher's names, and perhaps other information and decoration designed to provide sales appeal. The parts of the jacket that fold inward are called front and back jacket flaps.

Jacobean

Referring or applying to the reign of King James I of England (1603–1625). *Jacobean,* a term applied to the literature (especially drama), furniture, art, and architecture of that period, is derived from Jacobus, the Latin form of James. The literature of this era was really a late flowering of Elizabethan writing, although toward the end of James's reign, *cynicism and *realism began to flourish. During this *epoch, many of Shakespeare's greatest plays were written; John Donne, Ben Jonson, and Francis Bacon were at the peak of their creative powers; the King James Bible appeared in 1611. See BIBLE; ELIZABETHAN.

jargon

A term of several meanings, *jargon* usually applies to (1) unintelligible or meaningless writing and talk (see GIBBERISH); (2) the diction (vocabulary) of a particular trade, profession, or group: legal jargon, educational jargon, plumber's jargon, etc. (see ARGOT); (3) mixed speech for communication between persons who do not know each other's language, such as *pidgin English and *lingua franca. In a famous lecture, "Interlude: on Jargon," Sir Arthur Quiller-Couch, an English critic and novelist, extended the meaning of *jargon* to include the use of *polysyllabication (big words) and *circumlocutions (indirect, roundabout expressions).

jazz

A term usually applied to a kind of music that originated in the South (New Orleans) early in the twentieth century and has developed in numerous increasingly complex styles. Jazz has a strong but changeable rhythmic pattern; it stresses solo and group *improvisations on basic chords and tunes; it is marked by a sophisticated melodic progression of chords. The term *jazz* has several meanings in literature, but principally it refers to the atmosphere of freedom from restraint and revolt against moral traditions that prevailed in the United States during the second and third decades of the twentieth century. A representative example of this literary approach is F. Scott Fitzgerald's *Tales of the Jazz Age* (1922).

je ne sais quoi

French for "I don't know what." For additional comment on this phrase, see GALLICISM.

jeremiad

A mournful *complaint, an expression of sorrow, a lamentation denouncing evil. *Jeremiad,* named after the Old Testament prophet Jeremiah, refers to any literary work which contains prophecies of destruction or complaints about the state of society and the world. Jonathan Edwards's *sermon *Sinners in the Hands of an Angry God* is a jeremiad.

jestbook

An *anthology (collection) of jokes and witticisms, satirical *anecdotes, *epigrams, and ribald stories. Jestbooks (or jokebooks) have been popular since the first one, *A Hundred Merry Tales,* appeared in England in the sixteenth century.

jet set

A social set of people who travel on jet airlines from one fashionable amusement place to another. In recent years, numerous novels and films dealing with the jet set have appeared. See CARPE DIEM.

jeu d'esprit

A French term meaning (1) a witticism or *wisecrack and (2) a literary work showing intelligence or *wit rather than depth. *Jeu d'esprit* literally means "play of spirit," a quality found in plays by such dramatists as Oscar Wilde and Noel Coward and in novels and stories by Peter De Vries, S. J. Perelman, and scores of other twentieth-century authors in England and the United States.

jig

A rapid, lively dance. The term appears in numerous eighteenth- and nineteenth-century novels dealing with rustic life, such as those by Thomas Hardy. In *Elizabethan times, a jig was an amusing dramatic *interlude with words sung to the accompaniment of dancing. In *Hamlet,* the title character says of Polonius: "He's for a jig or a tale of bawdry [obscenity]."

jingle

A piece of verse that repeats sounds, contains numerous rhymes, and frequently is humorous, lighthearted, and nonsensical. *Nursery rhymes ("Hickory, dickory, dock" and "To market, to market") are jingles.

jongleur

A wandering entertainer in medieval France and Norman England who sang songs, often of his own composition, and told stories. A jongleur resembled a *gleeman and *minstrel. See TROUBADOUR.

journal

(1) A newspaper or any *periodical published for a learned society, profession, organization, or legislative body; (2) a daily personal record of occurrences, observations, and experiences. (See AUTOBIOGRAPHY.) Notable journals have been kept by such writers as Daniel Defoe, Charles Darwin, and André Gide. The term has also been loosely applied to fictitious history (Defoe's *Journal of the Plague Year*) and to such writings as Boswell's *Journal of a Tour to the Hebrides* (travel) and Jonathan Swift's *Journal to Stella* (letters).

journalese

A style considered characteristic of newspaper writing. Journalese, not applicable to all newspaper writing, is notable for its use of *hackneyed language, *neologisms, careless sentence structure, *jargon, raciness, and occasional *affectation.

juncture

(1) A point of time, especially one that is critical or important because of circumstances; (2) a term in *linguistics referring to

a distinctive sound feature marking the boundary of a word or expression. For example, the word *well* requires a pause, before or after, in a statement such as "The person who can do this *well* deserves our thanks." If a pause (juncture) occurs before *well,* the adverb modifies *deserves;* if a pause occurs after *well,* the adverb modifies *can do.*

Jungian

A term referring to Carl Gustav Jung (1875–1961), a Swiss psychiatrist. Jung supported many of the ideas, theories, and methods of Freud (see FREUDIANISM), but he differed from his mentor in many important ways. Jungian psychology largely rejects the ideas of infantile sexuality and wish fulfillment that are a part of Freudianism and holds that Freud's psychoanalytic principles were overly concrete and one-sided. Jung introduced the concept of the *collective unconscious and was largely responsible for a theory of human types divided into introverted and extroverted kinds of behavior. Jungian psychology has been influential in the lives and works of many twentieth-century authors because it tries to explain irrational forces of the present day and to throw light on the *primeval and often impersonal terrors that confront mankind.

Juvenalian

Resembling the Roman satirist Juvenal (A.D. 60–140). A Juvenalian writer (such as Jonathan Swift) is noted for his pungent *realism, or biting *satire, or both.

juvenilia

Literary compositions produced in an author's youth, typically marked by immaturity of style, thought, and subject matter. For instance, Lord Byron's *Hours of Idleness,* published when the writer was eighteen, was first entitled *Juvenilia.* The term is also applied to literary productions intended for the young.

juxtaposition

A term often used in literary criticism, meaning placing together, or side by side, for *comparison and contrast.

kabuki

Popular drama of Japan, developed in the seventeenth century, that is characterized by elaborate costuming, stylized acting, and rhythmic dialogue. In Japanese, *kabuki* means "music and dancing with spirit and style." Kabuki is distinguished from *noh (or nō), the classical and lyrical drama of Japan.

kaleidoscope

An optical instrument by means of which continually changing forms can be viewed. In literature, the term *kaleidoscopic* is applied to *compositions that are complex and varied, constantly shifting from one set of relations to another. The action of most novels of *suspense and of *detective stories is so rapidly changing as to be called kaleidoscopic.

karma

Destiny. See FATE.

keening

A wail or lamentation, especially a lament for the dead. A one-act play, *Riders to the Sea,* by John M. Synge, an Irish dramatist, is based upon the keening (mourning) of an old mother for her missing son. When her only other son is also drowned, the central character ceases to keen because she has nothing else to lose and nothing more to fear. See DIRGE.

kenning

A conventional, poetic phrase used for, or in addition to, the usual name of a person or object. Originally an Icelandic term, a kenning is a stock phrase, a picturesque metaphorical compound, such as *wave traveler* for *boat, the helmet of night* for *darkness,* and *whale's path* for *ocean.* See EPITHET, HOMERIC, METAPHOR.

King's English

Educated or "correct" English grammar and usage. Despite the fact that several English sovereigns have not been able to speak English at all, it has long been fitting to think of the ruler's language as above reproach; Chaucer wrote "God save the king, that is lord of this language." The King's (or Queen's) English is always "proper," and the phrase is sometimes used to mean "the linguistic currency of the realm."

kismet

One's appointed lot. See FATE.

Knights of the Round Table

A legendary order of knights created by King Arthur. (See ARTHURIAN; CHIVALRY; GRAIL, HOLY.) According to Sir Thomas Malory (1400–1471) and his *Morte d'Arthur,* 150 knights had seats at a table where none was at the "head." These knights ventured into all then-known countries in search of adventure. Among them, Sir Modred was a model of treachery, Sir Lancelot of bravery and of frailty in love, Sir Gawain of courtesy, Sir Galahad of chastity, etc.

Künstlerroman

From German *Künstler* ("artist") and French *roman* ("novel"), *Künstlerroman* refers to a narrative which traces the development of the author (or that of an imagined character like the author) from childhood to maturity. (See BILDUNGSROMAN, a *synonym for this term.) Most such novels depict the struggles of a sensitive, artistic child to escape from the misunderstandings and *bourgeois attitudes of his family and youthful acquaintances.

L

labor omnia vincit
Latin for "work conquers all." This is the motto of Oklahoma.

lacuna
A missing part in a manuscript, a break of some sort. *Lacuna* also means "a gap" or "a blank space"; the plural, *lacunae,* refers to obliterations resulting from tears or fadings.

laissez faire
French for "allow to act." In English use, *laissez faire* means noninterference in the affairs of others and applies especially to freedom of action. In economic, political, and social affairs, this phrase refers to the doctrine that government should intervene as little as possible.

lament
An expression of grief or sorrow; a poem, such as a *dirge or an *elegy, that indicates mourning. The laments of King David for Saul and Jonathan (in the Old Testament) are deeply emotional and painful. A modern example of a lament is Shelley's *A Lament,* the first stanza of which is

> O World! O Life! O Time!
> On whose last steps I climb,
> Trembling at that where I had stood before;
> When will return the glory of your prime?
> No more—Oh, never more!

laminated
Formed or set in thin layers. A laminated *book is one covered with lightweight plastic sheeting which adheres to the *jacket or binding material of the book.

lampoon

A sharp *satire, in prose or verse, directed against an individual or an institution. A lampoon severely ridicules the character, intentions, or behavior of a person or a society. Lampoons appeared often in the seventeenth and eighteenth centuries but are less common today because of *libel laws. Pope's *Epistle to Dr. Arbuthnot* is a series of lampoons in which the author defends himself against "the vicious or the ungenerous" persons who had attacked "my person, morals, and family."

language

The body of words and the systems applying to their use that are common to a people of the same community, area, nation, or culture. Language, derived from a Latin word meaning "tongue," involves communication by voice and written systems through the use of those signs and symbols that are called *words.

The term *language* applies to the general patterns of vocabulary, *syntax, and *usage characteristic of a people or race and should be distinguished from such levels and varieties of language as *argot, *cant, *dialect, *jargon, *vernacular, *gobbledygook, *King's English, *localisms, *slang, and *vulgarisms. The phrase *language arts* involves reading, composition, speech, spelling, and dramatics.

lap dissolve

See DISSOLVE.

lares et penates

A Latin phrase usually spoken and written as "lares *and* penates" and meaning one's most valued household or personal belongings. In ancient Roman beliefs, lares and penates were spirits who watched over a house or community. One's cherished possessions of any sort are his lares and penates.

Latinism

An idiom or use of words imitative of Latin. Using *et* rather than *and* in the immediately preceding entry is a Latinism. *Polysyllabication frequently results from the use of Latinisms; for instance, one might say, "Secure the portal and extinguish the illumination" rather than "Lock the door and put out the light."

laureate

Crowned with laurel as a mark of honor and esteem. (The foliage of laurel—a small evergreen tree or shrub—for centuries has been considered an *emblem of victory or distinction.) *Laureate* is applied to anyone who has been honored for achieving distinction in a particular field. See POET LAUREATE.

laus Deo

A Latin phrase meaning "praise (be) to God"; familiar in the Latin Vulgate *Bible. *Laus Deo* is the title of a poem by John G. Whittier written to celebrate the passage of the constitutional amendment abolishing slavery:

> Ring and swing,
> Bells of joy! On morning's wing
> Sound the song of praise abroad!
> With a sound of broken chains
> Tell the nations that He reigns,
> Who alone is Lord and God.

lay

A short lyric or narrative poem intended to be sung. *Lay* (also spelled *lai* and *ley*) comes from a German word meaning "song," but its meaning has been expanded to include historical narrative poems (ballads) such as Sir Walter Scott's *The Lay of the Last Minstrel* and Macaulay's *The Lays of Ancient Rome*. See BALLAD.

lead

A journalistic term applying to a short *summary which serves as an *introduction to a news story, *article, or other *copy.

leaflet

A small flat or folded sheet of printed matter. A leaflet has fewer leaves (or pages) than a *brochure, *pamphlet, or *book.

legend

A tradition or story handed down from earlier times and popularly accepted as true. *Legend* originally denoted a story about a saint but is now applied to any fictitious tale concerning a real person, event, or place. A legend is likely to be less concerned with the supernatural than a *myth, but *legend* and *myth* are related terms. (Also, see FABLE.) A well-known legend forms the basis of Washington Irving's short story *The Legend of Sleepy Hollow*.

Legend is also a name for brief explanatory comments accompanying photographs, maps, paintings, etc. See CAPTION.

legitimate theater

Professionally produced stage plays as distinguished from *television, motion pictures, burlesque, ballet, puppetry, and vaudeville. The term derives from the fact that when the British Parliament in the eighteenth century authorized only three "legal theaters," other producers evaded the law by calling their offerings *pantomimes or concerts. See BURLESQUE, BURLETTA, PUPPETRY, VAUDEVILLE.

leitmotiv

A term from German, literally meaning "leading motive." It

refers to the *theme or *motif associated throughout a musical drama with a particular situation, person, or idea. *Leitmotiv* (also spelled *leitmotif*) is often applied to the dominant *impression, *controlling image, or recurring *theme of a literary selection, as, for instance, the "practicality" of Franklin's *Autobiography* or the "revolutionary spirit" of Thomas Paine.

leonine verse
A kind of verse in which the last word rhymes with the last word before the *caesura (pause, break). W. S. Gilbert's "Oh, a private *buffoon* is a light-hearted *loon"* is an example of leonine rhyme, or verse. The name is derived from that of a French poet, Leoninus, who wrote numerous lines containing this kind of rhyme. See INTERNAL RHYME.

Lesbian
A term referring to Lesbos, a Greek island in the Aegean Sea (now called Mytilene). The word in the sense of "highly sensual" or "erotic" was derived from the reputed character and literature of the inhabitants of Lesbos. More specifically, *lesbian* refers to a female homosexual. See SAPPHIC.

letterpress
In the United States, *letterpress* is a printing term referring to matter that is reproduced (printed) from letters or type in relief, rather than plates, *woodcuts, etc. In Great Britain, *letterpress* is used for reading matter as distinguished from illustrations. The term is loosely employed to refer to *typography and to *printing in general. See OFFSET PROCESS.

letters
(1) A general term given to literature (see BELLES LETTRES); (2) the profession of literature ("a man of letters"); (3) communications in writing, such as notes and *epistles exchanged between friends, business firms, etc. (See AUTOBIOGRAPHY, EPISTLE, EPISTOLARY.) The correspondence of Charles Dickens, Charles Lamb, Robert Louis Stevenson, Oliver Wendell Holmes, Abraham Lincoln, and Winston Churchill is genuine literature, a *genre which is revealing, entertaining, and often creative and moving.

lexicography
The writing and compiling of *dictionaries. The term, derived from Greek, involves intricate processes of preparing word lists and presenting them as "entries" consisting of pronunciations, spellings, derivations, meanings, illustrative quotations, etc. (See DICTIONARY.) Samuel Johnson, himself a noted lexicographer, defined his role as that of "a writer of dictionaries, a harmless drudge," but he also wrote, "I am

not so lost in lexicography as to forget that words are the daughters of earth and that things are the sons of heaven" —Johnson's way of echoing an earlier writer (George Herbert), who said, "Words are women, deeds are men." See LEXICON.

lexicon
(1) A wordbook or dictionary; (2) the vocabulary of a particular language, activity, social class, etc. The first of these meanings is explained in the entry for *dictionary;* the second is illustrated in these lines from Edward Bulwer Lytton's play *Richelieu:*

In the lexicon of youth, which fate reserves
For a bright manhood, there is no such word
As "fail."

libel
Written or printed words or pictures that defame or that maliciously or damagingly misrepresent. See CALUMNY, SLANDER.

libido
Usually applied to the sexual instinct, *libido* refers to all the instinctual energies and desires that are derived from the *id (spirit, self). A libidinous person is lustful, lewd.

library
A depository, a treasury of the written word and the graphic portrayal of thought preserved in *manuscripts, pictures, and print. The word *library* is also applied to a place where books and other materials are stored, to a set of books of similar character, and to a commercial enterprise, such as a rental library, that lends books for a fixed charge.

libretto
The text (words) of an *opera or similar musical *composition, such as a cantata or oratorio. Libretto, derived from an Italian word meaning "little book," often takes the form of a *pamphlet or booklet containing the *story, *tale, or *plot of the musical work.

ligature
A term from printing that refers to a character of two or more letters joined together and cast in one piece, such as *ff* and *ffl.*

light verse
Verse designed to entertain, amuse, or please. Light verse is ordinarily distinguished by its *wit and the subtlety and perfection of its *form rather than by depth or genuine significance. Light verse includes *doggerel, *epigrams, *limericks, *nonsense verse, *parodies, and *vers de société. Among noted contemporary American writers of light verse are Ogden Nash and Richard Armour.

limbo

A place or state of oblivion to which persons or objects are supposedly relegated when they are cast aside, forgotten, or out of date. In literature, limbo is occasionally referred to as a region presumably on the border of heaven or hell that is the abode of unbaptized infants and of righteous people who died before the coming of Jesus Christ.

limerick

A form of *light verse, a *stanza of five lines rhyming *aabba*. Limerick takes its name from a county in Ireland and social gatherings there at which *nonsense verse was set out in facetious *jingles. The tendency of limericks to become naughty is commented upon in this limerick by Morris Bishop:

> The limerick's furtive and mean;
> You must keep him in close quarantine,
> Or he sneaks to the slums
> And promptly becomes
> Disorderly, drunk, and obscene.

limited edition

An edition of a book limited to a specific number of copies. Copies of a limited edition are usually numbered. See EDITION.

line drawing

A drawing done in line (pen, pencil, brush, crayon) providing gradations in tone through changes in width and compactness.

line of verse

A phrase referring to a single line of metrical language. Strictly speaking, a verse is a line; *verse* means "a turning" and is properly applied to the method by which one line "turns" into another. (See VERSE.) In English, lines of poetry (verses) are measured in feet. See FOOT, METER, METRICS, PROSODY.

lingo

(1) Language and speech that are strange or foreign; (2) specialized speech or language peculiar to a particular activity, profession, class. (See ARGOT, CANT, JARGON.) *Lingo* is usually applied derogatorily to a foreign language, as in this *doggerel by Thomas Hood:

> Never go to France
> Unless you know the lingo,
> If you do, like me,
> You will repent, by jingo.

lingua franca

An Italian term literally meaning "Frankish tongue" (West Germanic language of the ancient Franks, whence the name of France). *Lingua franca* applies to any language that is used for communication among speakers of other languages. Actually a species of Italian mixed with French, Arabic, and Greek, *lingua franca* refers to any jumble of assorted languages. Molière, a French dramatist, used examples of lingua franca in *The Bourgeois Gentleman.*

linguistics

A term derived from a Latin word meaning "tongue" or "language," linguistics is the science of *language. More specifically, linguistics is a systematic study of *etymology, *phonetics, *morphemes, *syntax, and *semantics. More generally, linguistics is a deliberate, purposeful, conscious activity of the whole mind and its means of communication by speech.

Linotype

A typesetting machine that casts solid lines of type from matrices that are selected and controlled by an operator at the keyboard.

lipogram

A written work composed of words that avoid using one or more letters or of words employing only one vowel. A lipogram is a contrivance, a literary stunt obviously without literary value.

litany

(1) A form of prayer consisting of a series of *invocations with identical responses in succession; (2) the supplications (appeals) in the Book of Common Prayer of the Church of England; (3) a recitation that is ceremonial and repetitive. *Litany* is also applied to any prolonged, monotonous statement or account.

literal, figurative

The former means "word for word" and "exact." *Figurative* means "not literal," "metaphorical," "in a manner of speaking." See FIGURATIVE, LITERAL.

literary agent

A person who acts for an author in finding a publisher, arranging contract terms, and handling *subsidiary rights.

literary ballad

Another name for ART BALLAD, which see. A literary ballad is of known authorship and has some claim to literary distinction. See BALLAD, POPULAR BALLAD.

literary epic

An extended narrative poem, exalted in style and heroic in theme, that is modeled to some extent upon early epics of unknown authorship. (See EPIC.) The literary epic is more artistically perfect than a popular, or *folk, epic but is not necessarily more vigorous or appealing. See ART EPIC.

literature

Writings in which expression and *form, in connection with ideas and concerns of universal and apparently permanent interest, are essential features. (See BELLES LETTRES, CLASSIC, LETTERS.) *Literature* is frequently, but unwisely, applied to any kind of printed material, such as circulars, leaflets, and handbills. The term is correctly reserved for prose and verse of acknowledged excellence, the value of which lies in its intense, personal, and superb expression of life in its varied meanings.

> In the civilization of today it is undeniable that, over all the arts, literature dominates, serves beyond all.
>
> Walt Whitman

> Literature is an investment of genius which pays dividends to all subsequent times.
>
> John Burroughs

> Life comes before literature, as the material comes before the work. The hills are full of marble before the world blooms with statues.
>
> Phillips Brooks

lithography

The process of producing designs on prepared stone and taking impressions from this. In lithography today, substances other than stone, such as zinc and aluminum, are used.

litotes

A form of *understatement in which something is affirmed by stating the negative of its opposite. *Litotes,* from a Greek word meaning "small" or "plain," is an *antonym of *hyperbole and a near synonym for *meiosis. To say that a person is "no amateur" affirms the speaker's belief that he is a professional. In *Paradise Lost,* when Milton writes that his poem "with no middle flight intends to soar," he is saying that he expects his work to reach the highest levels imaginable.

littérateur

A literary man, one who devotes himself to the study or writing of literature. *Littérateur* is often applied to an amateur or *dilettante rather than to a dedicated, professional student, creator, or critic of *literature.

little magazine

A term applied to literary *journals of small circulation. The typical little magazine is underfinanced, short-lived, of small *format, and experimental in its approach to prose and poetry. Little magazines flourished in the United States, England, and France in the 1920s, but most of them ceased publication before the outbreak of World War II. Despite spotty records, these periodicals at one time or another provided first publication for Sherwood Anderson, Hart Crane, E. E. Cummings, T. S. Eliot, William Faulkner, Ernest Hemingway, Ezra Pound, Gertrude Stein, and Thornton Wilder.

little theater

Noncommercial drama, usually experimental and directed to the tastes and interests of limited audiences. Such semiprofessional or frankly amateurish productions, normally supported by community resources (talent and money), seek artistic rather than financial success. Writers who to some degree were products of the little theater movement in various countries include George Bernard Shaw and John Galsworthy (England), J. M. Synge and William Butler Yeats (Ireland), Ivan Turgenev (Russia), Eugene O'Neill, Paul Green, Thornton Wilder, and Clifford Odets (United States).

liturgical drama

Plays performed as part of church services. (*Liturgical* refers to public worship.) *Liturgical drama* applies particularly to the Mass (Holy Eucharist) and its forms of worship. The term is also applied to *mystery plays and *morality plays performed in *medieval times. See QUEM QUAERITIS.

liturgy

Ritualistic worship in the Christian Church. *Liturgy* applies to the *form, *order, and manner of religious services, especially those dealing with the sacrament of Holy Communion.

local color

A term applied to writing which develops and promotes the mannerisms, dress, speech, and customs of a particular region. (See COLOR.) Writers who are local colorists try to be informative about the peculiarities of a given region and emphasize *verisimilitude of details about *dialect, local geographical features, and the like. See REGIONALISM.

Details of Yorkshire life are emphasized in novels by the Brontës; Thomas Hardy's novels contain much of the local color of Wessex; Bret Harte, Mark Twain, Joel Chandler Harris, Sarah Orne Jewett, and Robert Frost concentrated on special American regions in their efforts to deal with life in its larger aspects and wider applications.

locale

The *setting (scene) of a novel, play, or motion picture. See REGIONALISM.

localism

A manner of speaking, pronunciation, usage, or inflection that is peculiar to one locality. A localism may be a word or phrase that is used and understood in a particular section or region but that may not be in national use. (See PROVINCIALISM, REGIONALISM.) Localisms, which can also include *dialect, appear in every language; in American English they can be illustrated by such terms as *down-Easter* (native of New England, especially of Maine); *corn pone* (corn bread); *maverick* (an unbranded animal); *rustler* (cattle thief).

loc. cit.

An abbreviation of the Latin phrase *loco citato,* meaning "in the place cited." *Loc. cit.* appears often in references such as *footnotes to indicate the exact passage covered by a previous *citation not immediately preceding. See IBIDEM, OP. CIT.

locution

Any saying, phrase, or expression. *Locution* more particularly refers to a special or peculiar way of making a statement, such as the use of an *idiom.

logic

The art, science, or technique of reasoning; a systematic investigation of the truth or falsity of an idea or argument. *Logic* is usually considered to mean "sound judgment" and "the making of correct *inferences." (See DEDUCTION, INDUCTION, PREMISE, SYLLOGISM.) Logic may be called the "rule" or "standard" by which one evaluates the statements of others and by which one judges the soundness of one's own thinking.

Offenses against "straight and clear thinking" that violate "correct reasoning" have occurred often in literature and presumably will continue to do so. Among these faults may be mentioned (1) hasty *generalizations, (2) *begging the question, (3) *non sequitur, (4) *post hoc, (5) *bias, and (6) faulty *analogy.

Logic is an important study in itself, ranging from consideration of careless phrasing to the *canons and *criteria of philosophical, scientific, and literary methods first set forth by Aristotle in the fourth century B.C. and constantly revised and refined ever since. Two quotations from *literature will throw light upon the problem of *logic:*

> He was in logic a great critic,
> Profoundly skilled in analytic.
> He could distinguish and divide
> A hair 'twixt south and southwest side;
> On either which he would dispute,
> Confute, change hands, and still confute.
>
> Samuel Butler, *Hudibras*

> "Contrariwise," continued Tweedledee, "if it was so,
> it might be; and if it were so, it would be; but as it isn't,
> it ain't. That's logic."
>
> Lewis Carroll, *Through the Looking-Glass*

logical order

A method of developing an idea in which a general statement is followed by details and particulars or in which an
*effect is first stated and then followed by details. See
CAUSE AND EFFECT, DEDUCTION, INDUCTION, LOGIC, ORDER.

logorrhea

Incoherent, repetitious speech. Logorrhea, derived from
Greek words meaning "flow " and "discharge" of words, is
an acute kind of *prolixity and *verbosity. In the first two
scenes of act 2 of *Hamlet,* Polonius is afflicted with logorrhea: he speaks at length, forgets what he has been saying,
starts a definition, cannot finish it, and generally talks ver-
bosely with many wanderings of thought.

long measure

Four lines of iambic *tetrameter which form a *stanza of a
*hymn. In hymnbooks, this phrase is abbreviated to L.M.
See BALLAD STANZA, COMMON MEASURE.

loose sentence

A sentence that is grammatically complete at one or more
points before its end. Most sentences, whether written or
spoken, are loose because they do not end with completion
of main statements but continue with additional words,
phrases, or clauses. See PERIODIC SENTENCE.

lost generation

The generation of men and women who came of age during or just after World War I (1914–1918). The term derives
from Gertrude Stein's comment to Ernest Hemingway,
"You are all a lost generation." Hemingway, himself a member of the lost generation, used the phrase as a *motto and
*theme for his novel *The Sun Also Rises* (1926). Members of
this lost generation, who found themselves without emotional or cultural stability in a time of social unheaval, included
F. Scott Fitzgerald, Louis Bromfield, Hart Crane, and John
Dos Passos. See BEAT GENERATION.

lowercase

A term referring to letters that are written or printed in
small (i.e., not capital) letters. The term, largely used in
*printing, comes from reference to a pair of trays, or cases,
holding types in compartments: the upper one for capital
letters and the lower one for small letters. *Lowercase* has
been extended to refer to a person, event, or object of
comparatively less importance or significance than some-

thing else. For example, a critic might refer to a *flat character as a "lowercase person."

lucidity

The quality of being clear, intelligible, easily understandable. *Lucidity* in literature refers to writing that is characterized by clear perception and understanding and is comprehensible to readers. See CLEARNESS, ESOTERIC, RECONDITE.

lullaby

A song used to lull a child to sleep. A lullaby is a cradlesong. Tennyson's song from *The Princess* is a lullaby:

> Sweet and low, sweet and low,
> Wind of the western sea,
> Low, low, breathe and blow,
> Wind of the western sea!
> Over the rolling waters go,
> Come from the dying moon, and blow,
> Blow him again to me;
> While my little one, while my pretty one, sleeps.

lyric

(1) A poem having the form and musical quality of a song; (2) a short, subjective poem with a songlike outburst of the author's innermost thoughts and feelings; (3) an adjective meaning "spontaneous," "rapturous," "undisciplined." *Lyric* is derived from Greek, Latin, and Middle English names for a musical instrument (the lyre) dating back to ancient Greece. As a noun or adjective, *lyric* is applied to any poem expressing personal emotion, to any short poem that does not primarily tell a story, and to *prose or *verse that is characterized by a direct, spontaneous outpouring of intense feeling.

lyrics

The words of a *song. See LIBRETTO.

M

macabre

An adjective meaning "ghastly," "grim," "horrible." *Macabre* is also used to pertain to or to represent death, especially in its more gruesome aspects. Most *Gothic novels are macabre; so are such stories as Edgar Allan Poe's *The Cask of Amontillado* and *The Masque of the Red Death.*

macaronic

Composed of a mixture of languages. Macaronic verse mingles two or more languages in humorous, *burlesque style. For instance, an unknown writer altered the Mother Goose rhyme "Sing a song of sixpence, pocketful of rye" into this macaronic (mixture like a dish of macaroni) *doggerel:

Cane carmen sixpence, pera plena rye,
De multis atris avibus coctis in a pie.

macrocosm

The great world; the universe considered as a whole. (See MICROCOSM.) *Macrocosm* is sometimes used to refer to the total, complete, and complex structure of something; for example, Homer's *Iliad* has been said to be a macrocosm of warfare and Milton's *Paradise Lost* a macrocosm of man's sin and loss of Paradise.

macrology

Excessive wordiness. (See CIRCUMLOCUTION, DEADWOOD, PERIPHRASIS, PLEONASM, TAUTOLOGY, VERBIAGE.) Macrology is a stylistic fault and does not appear in literature except when used to characterize someone who talks a great deal. See LOGORRHEA.

macron

A line placed over a vowel to indicate a long sound. See BREVE.

madrigal

(1) A part song without instrumental accompaniment, usually for five or more voices and making much use of *contrapuntal effects; (2) a lyric poem, usually short and frequently concerning love, suitable for being set to music. Italian in origin, the madrigal was both fashionable and popular from the sixteenth century on in Italy, France, and England.

This song from Shakespeare's *Measure for Measure* is a madrigal:

Take, oh, take those lips away,
That so sweetly were forsworn;
And those eyes, the break of day,
Lights that do mislead the morn:
But my kisses bring again, bring again;
Seals of love, but sealed in vain, sealed
    in vain.

magazine

A publication issued periodically, usually with a paper cover and containing *articles, *essays, *stories, or *poems by different writers. *Magazine* comes from a French word (*magasin*) meaning "store" or "storehouse" and has the general meaning of *miscellany or collection. See JOURNAL, LITTLE MAGAZINE, PERIODICAL, PULP MAGAZINE, SLICK MAGAZINE.

magnum opus

A Latin term that in English means "great work," "masterpiece," or "major production." In the sense of an author's most important work, *Remembrance of Things Past* might be called the magnum opus of Marcel Proust, and *War and Peace* that of Leo Tolstoi. See CHEF D'OEUVRE.

makeready

A term from *printing identifying the process of preparing a form for printing. Makeready specifically applies to adjustments necessary to equalize the *impression (compensate for low and high spots in the printing form).

malapropism

The act or habit of using words ridiculously. A malapropism results from ignorance or from confusion of words similar in sound. Mrs. Malaprop, a character in Richard B. Sheridan's play *The Rivals,* made such remarks as "I would have her instructed in geometry that she might know something of the contagious countries" and "If I reprehend anything in this world, it is the use of my oracular tongue."

mal de mer
A French term meaning "seasickness."

malediction
A *curse; an imprecation; a damning; *slander. *Malediction,* derived from Latin words meaning "speaking evilly," is illustrated under the entries for CURSE, DOGGEREL (Shakespeare's epitaph), and IMPRECATION.

malevolence
Ill will, malice, hatred. *Malevolence* comes from Latin terms meaning "spiteful" and "ill-disposed." Iago, in *Othello,* has been called the *personification of malevolence, but thousands of other villains rival Iago's claim to this dubious distinction. See VILLAIN.

mammon
(1) Material wealth, riches; (2) a *personification of riches in the shape of a deity or spirit. In the Syriac (Aramaic) language, *mammon* means "riches"; in this sense it appears in the New Testament (Matthew 6:24): "Ye cannot serve God and Mammon." In *Paradise Lost,* Milton makes Mammon an evil spirit:
... Mammon led them on,
Mammon, the least erected Spirit that fell
From Heaven; for even in Heaven his looks
    and thoughts
Were always downward bent, admiring more
The riches of Heaven's pavement, trodden gold,
Than aught divine or holy.

manifesto
A public declaration of motives, opinions, and intentions. The Preface to Victor Hugo's *Cromwell* has been called the manifesto of French *romanticism; a world-famous statement of theory is the *Communist Manifesto* (an 1848 pamphlet by Karl Marx and Friedrich Engels); the Declaration of Independence (July 4, 1776) is an American manifesto.

mannerism
A characteristic or habitual way of doing something, a distinctive style or quality. In literature, *mannerism* applies to qualities which distinguish an author's style, such as Macaulay's use of *balanced sentences and William Faulkner's intricate, lengthy, convoluted passages. Mannered styles of writing include *Euphuism, *Gongorism, and *Marinism.

manqué
A French word meaning "fallen short," "having failed." *Manqué* is applied to authors who appear unsuccessful or unfulfilled because of lack of talent, circumstances, or a

character defect. A poet manqué is a versifier who has "missed."

manuscript

A *letter, *document, or *book written by hand; writing as distinguished from print. *Manuscript* comes from Latin words meaning "written by hand," but the term is now applied to an author's *copy of a work, whether in longhand or typewritten, that is used as the basis for typesetting.

märchen

A German word for *folktale and *fairy tale. *Märchen,* both singular and plural, applies to the collection of stories by Jacob and Wilhelm Grimm. See FOLKLORE.

marginalia

Notes and comments written on the border (margin) of a page by the author or by an editor or reader. See RUBRIC.

Marinism

A style of writing named for a seventeenth-century Italian poet, Giovanni Marino. Marinism is a florid, bombastic style marked by extravagant *metaphors, *antithesis, and *conceits. An example of Marinism, which is related to *Euphuism and *Gongorism, is contained in these lines by Richard Crashaw, a seventeenth-century English poet, in which he compares a woman's tear-filled eyes to

Two walking baths, two weeping motions,
Portable and compendious oceans.

Mariolatry

Idolatrous worship of the Virgin Mary. Mariolatry is apparent in Chaucer's *Prioress's Tale* (in *The Canterbury Tales*). The term has been extended to refer to the idealization and exaltation of woman as woman.

Marxist

A follower of, and believer in, the theories of Karl Marx (1818–1883), a German philosopher, economist, and socialist. A Marxist subscribes to Marxism, a system of thought which expounds the doctrine that throughout history the state has exploited the masses, that class struggle has always been the principal means for effecting historical changes, that the capitalist system contains the seeds of its own decay, and that, after a period of dictatorship by the proletariat, a socialist order and classless society will emerge. Marxists and Marxism have played important roles in world literature since the Russian Revolution of 1917.

masculine ending

A line of verse in which the final syllable is stressed (accent-

ed), as in these lines from Ben Jonson's *Fancy:*
> And Fancy, I tell you, has dreams that have wings,
> And dreams that have honey,
> and dreams that have stings.

A closely related term is *masculine rhyme,* correspondence of sound limited to a single stressed syllable, as in the preceding quotation and in the words *disdain* and *complain, marsh* and *harsh.* See FEMININE ENDING, FEMININE RHYME.

masochism

(1) The act of turning one's destructive tendencies upon oneself; (2) the tendency to find pleasure in submissiveness, meekness, and self-denial; (3) gratification gained from pain and deprivation that are self-inflicted or sought out. Masochism, named after a nineteenth-century German novelist, Leopold von Sacher-Masoch, has been noticeable in twentieth-century fiction and drama, such as some of the work of William Faulkner and Tennessee Williams. In psychiatry, *masochism* refers to the condition in which sexual gratification depends on physical pain, suffering, and humiliation.

masque

A form of entertainment in sixteenth- and seventeenth-century England consisting of dancing and *pantomime and, later, of added *song and *dialogue. As a kind of semidramatic, elaborate, and aristocratic *spectacle, the masque flourished in the hands of such writers as Ben Jonson and such stage designers as Inigo Jones. Shakespeare's *Tempest* contains a masque (act 4) in which *pastoral and mythological figures entertain Ferdinand and Miranda. The best-known of all masques is John Milton's *Comus* (1634). See ANTIMASQUE.

mass media

Forms of communication that reach large numbers of people. (*Media* is the plural of *medium,* meaning "agency," "means," "instrument.") Mass media include *television, films, newspapers, radio, and *slick magazines.

materialism

A philosophical theory that regards matter and its movements as constituting the universe and insists all phenomena of whatever kind are traceable to material (physical) agencies. Materialism gives attention to, and places emphasis upon, material needs, considerations, and objects and minimizes, neglects, or rejects spiritual values. Many writers of *naturalism, such as Émile Zola, James Joyce, and Theodore Dreiser, advocated materialism.

matériel

As distinguished from *personnel, matériel* refers to the sum or total of items and objects used or needed in any business or operation. Often employed in novels and films about war, *matériel* refers to arms, ammunition, and equipment in general.

matin
(1) A morning song; (2) one of the seven canonical (established by *canon) hours of the Roman Catholic Church, a midnight order of service sometimes recited at daybreak; (3) public morning prayer in the Church of England. See ALBA, AUBADE.

matrix
A term of several meanings, *matrix* is used in literary circles to refer to that which gives origin or form to something or which encloses it; for example, Rome was the matrix of Western European civilization, and British common law was the matrix of American jurisprudence. In this sense, Puritanism may be said to have been the matrix, the shaping force, of Hawthorne's *The Scarlet Letter.*

In printing, matrix (plural *matrices*) has the meanings of a mold in which the face of a type is cast and the impression from which a plate for printing may be made. The term is frequently abbreviated to "mat."

maxim
An expression of a general and practical truth. A maxim is an *adage, an *aphorism, an *apothegm. Maxims prefixed to Benjamin Franklin's *Poor Richard's Almanac* include such comments as "He that goes a borrowing goes a sorrowing," "It is hard for an empty sack to stand upright," and "He that riseth late must trot all day."

measure
A term for "metrical unit" and specifically for the short rhythmical movement and arrangement in poetry known as the *foot. *Measure* also refers to the width to which a *column or page of printed matter is set.

medieval
An adjective applying to the *Middle Ages, which is precisely the meaning of *medieval* in Latin (*medius,* "middle," and *aevum,* "age"). Scholars have never agreed about the exact period referred to as medieval or as the Middle Ages, but loosely both terms apply to the time in European history between classical antiquity (the late fifth century) and the *Renaissance (about 1350). More exactly, *medieval* refers to the later part of this period (after 1100) and may extend to 1500. See CHIVALRY, DARK AGES, FEUDALISM.

Medieval has come to mean "antiquated," "outmoded," or "old-fashioned" and is often used in these meanings in modern literature.

megalomania

An obsession with doing extravagant, reckless, or grand things. In *psychiatry, megalomania is a form of mental illness marked by false ideas of greatness, power, wealth, etc. Literature is filled with megalomaniacs, persons with *delusions about themselves and their roles in life: Don Quixote, Satan, Faust, Lady Macbeth, Julius Caesar, Alexander the Great, Benedict Arnold, Adolf Hitler, etc.

meiosis

The use of *understatement, a synonym for *litotes. *Meiosis,* from a Greek word meaning "leveling" or "lessening," is used to give the idea that something is less in importance or size than it really is. This rhetorical device is ordinarily used for humorous or satiric effects. When John Dryden referred to honor as "an empty bubble," he was making an ironic *understatement about one of mankind's most cherished ideals.

melodrama

A form of play that intensifies sentiment, exaggerates emotion, and relates sensational and thrilling action. Melodramas, from Greek words for *song* and *drama,* were originally romantic plays with music, singing, and dancing, but they evolved in the eighteenth century into productions with elaborate but oversimplified and coincidental *plots, touches of *bathos, and happy endings. Until recent years, touring companies of actors presented melodramas all over the United States, plays such as *Ten Nights in a Barroom.* The sensational elements of melodrama are present in *Gothic novels and in current films, *Western stories, and *television crime plays.

memoir

A biographical or autobiographical *sketch; a record of facts and events connected with a subject, period, or individual; a commentary on one's life, times, and experiences. *Memoir,* usually spelled *memoirs,* is derived from the Latin word for "memory" or "remembering." An author's memoirs usually focus attention on personalities and events known to, or experienced by, the writer. For example, several of the books published by such recent world figures as Winston Churchill and Dwight D. Eisenhower are memoirs. See AUTOBIOGRAPHY, BIOGRAPHY.

memorabilia

Ideas or points worthy of note. *Memorabilia* is derived from a Latin word meaning "memorable" or "things to be remembered." The official library of any former president of the United States, for example, is a collection of memorabilia. So too are the notebooks often kept by authors that contain thoughts, ob-

servations, and suggested items for possible later use. See
AUTOBIOGRAPHY, BIOGRAPHY, COMMONPLACE BOOK, MEMOIR.

ménage à trois

A French phrase referring to an arrangement involving a
married couple and the lover of one of them, all three
occupying the same household. The phrase means
"household of three."

Menippean

Cynical, distrustful, contemptuous. *Menippean* is derived
from the name of a Syrian writer, Menippus, who lived in
the third century B.C. and whom Lucian, a later Greek
satirist, called the "the greatest snarler and snapper of all
the old dogs." (The word *cynic* is derived from a Greek
term meaning "doglike," that is, snarling, "like a cur.") See
CYNICISM.

mens sana

Latin for "sound mind." *Mens sana* is sometimes followed by
in corpore sano ("in a sound body").

mesostich

From Greek words meaning "middle" and "line of poetry,"
mesostich is a composition in which certain middle letters
in successive lines form a word when put together. See
ACROSTIC.

metamorphosis

A complete change in character, appearance, or circumstances. *Metamorphosis* also applies to a change in form,
structure, or substance caused by witchcraft or magic. Stevenson's story *The Strange Case of Dr. Jekyll and Mr. Hyde* is
based on metamorphosis. So, too, are *fairy tales in which a
prince is changed into a toad, a pumpkin into a coach, etc.
In a somewhat less drastic sense, nearly every important
character in literature undergoes a degree of metamorphosis during the course of the action in which he plays a role.

metaphor

A figure of speech in which a word or phrase is applied to
a person, idea, or object to which it is not literally applicable. A metaphor is an implied *analogy which imaginatively
identifies one thing with another. A metaphor is one of the
*tropes, a device by which an author turns, or twists, the
meaning of a word. For example, Martin Luther wrote "A
mighty fortress is our God, / A bulwark never failing";
mighty fortress and *bulwark* are metaphors. Wordsworth
wrote metaphorically when he said of England that "she is
a fen of stagnant waters." In *Song of Myself,* Walt Whitman
wrote that *grass* seemed to be "the beautiful uncut hair of

graves." See ANALOGY, CONNOTATION, DEAD METAPHOR, FIGURATIVE LANGUAGE, MIXED METAPHOR, SIMILE, TROPE.

metaphysics

Investigation of, and speculation about, objects, ideas, and realms beyond what can be known from direct observation and experience. Metaphysics is a branch of philosophy that deals with first principles, such as *cosmic affairs, *eternity, and *ontology.

Metaphysical poetry is a term applied to writing that is highly intellectual and philosophical, that makes extensive use of ingenious *conceits (imaginative *images), and that usually combines intense emotion with mental ingenuity. The outstanding metaphysical poet in English literature was John Donne; among leading American poets of this school may be mentioned Edward Taylor and T. S. Eliot. For examples of metaphysical poetry, see CONCEIT.

metathesis

The transposition of letters, *syllables, or *sounds. Metathesis is one of the processes that change *language; for instance, Modern English *bird* was *brid* in *Old English, *drugath* in Old English is now *drought,* etc.

metempsychosis

The passage of the soul from one body to another. *Metempsychosis* also refers to the rebirth of the soul at death in another body with human or animal form. Many ghost stories and *fairy tales involve characters who reappear in different forms at different times and in different places. In Dickens's *A Christmas Carol,* Scrooge receives a visit from the ghost of his late partner, an act of metempsychosis. See NECROPHILIA.

meter

The term *meter* is a poetic *measure that refers to the *pattern of stressed and unstressed *syllables in a *line, or *verse, of a *poem. The number of syllables in a line may be fixed and the number of stressed syllables may vary, or the stresses may be fixed and the number of unstressed syllables may vary. The number of stresses and syllables is fixed in the most frequent forms of meter in English verse, although actually this basic pattern occasionally varies so as to avoid sounding like a metronome. In some modern poetry, regular meter is largely forsaken, and *cadence is employed to approximate the flow of speech.

These meters are most commonly used in English poetry: iambic (˘ -), trochaic (- ˘), anapestic (˘ ˘ -), dactylic (- ˘ ˘). Every such metrical unit, or group of syllables, is called a *foot; the number of feet in a line of poetry determines its name; for example, a verse of three feet is called *trimeter and one of five feet is called *pentameter.

These lines are from Longfellow's *The Jewish Cemetery at Newport:*

> Gone are the living, but the dead remain,
> And not neglected; for a hand unseen,
> Scattering its bounty, like a summer rain,
> Still keeps their graves and their
> remembrance green.

It is impossible to read this stanza without hearing its rhythm. The meter is iambic pentameter, the most common meter in English and American verse.

> Gŏne āre / thĕ lĭv/ĭng, bŭt / thĕ dēad / rĕmaīn,
> Ănd nŏt / nĕglĕct/ĕd; fŏr / ă hānd / ŭnseēn ...

Here are the meters (metrical patterns) of several other poems:

Iambic pentameter

> Thĕ cūr/fĕw tōlls / thĕ knēll / ŏf pārt/ĭng dāy,
> Thĕ lōw/ĭng hērd / wĭnd slōw/lў o'ēr / thĕ lēa,
>
>> Gray, *Elegy Written in a Country
>> Churchyard*

(Note that in the second line, the prevailing meter is iambic, but not every foot is.)

Iambic tetrameter and iambic trimeter

> Yĕt thĭs / ĭncōn/stăncў / ĭs sūch
> Ăs yōu / tŏo shāll / ădōre;
> Ĭ coūld / nŏt lŏve / thĕe, Dēar, / sŏ mŭch
> Lŏved Ī / nŏt Hōn/ŏr mōre.
>
>> Lovelace, *To Lucasta, on Going to
>> the Wars*

Trochaic tetrameter

> Whў sŏ / pāle ănd / wān, fŏnd / lŏvĕr?
> Prĭthĕe, / whў sŏ/ pāle?
> Wĭll, whĕn / lōokĭng / wĕll can't / mŏve hĕr,
> Lŏokĭng/ ĭll / prĕvāil?
>
>> Suckling, *Why So Pale and Wan?*

(The second and fourth lines indicate a variation in prevailing kind of foot and line length that is characteristic of much poetry.)

Dactylic tetrameter

> Jūst fŏr ă/ hăndfŭl ŏf / sīlvĕr hĕ/ lĕft ŭs,
> Jūst fŏr ă/ rībănd tŏ / stĭck ĭn hĭs / cŏat ...
>
>> Browning, *The Lost Leader*

(The prevailing foot is dactylic, but in each line the last foot is altered without destroying rhythmic effect.)

Anapestic tetrameter

Nŏt ă wōrd / tŏ eăch ōth/er̆; wē kēpt /
thĕ grēat păce
Nĕck by̆ nĕck, / str̆ide by̆ str̄ide, /
nĕver̄ chāng/ĭng ŏur plāce . . .

Browning, *How They Brought the Good
News from Ghent to Aix*

method acting

A theory and technique of performing in which the actor identifies as closely as possible with the character to be presented and renders that role in an individualized, relatively quiet, and natural manner. See STANISLAVSKI METHOD.

metonymy

A figure of speech in which the name of one object or idea is used for another to which it is related or of which it is a part. Thus, "the crown" or "scepter" may refer to a ruling monarch, "the bottle" may mean milk or strong drink, "the fleet" may stand for sailors, etc. "The tailor sews a fine seam" means that he does good tailoring. The Biblical verse "In the sweat of thy face shalt thou eat bread" illustrates metonymy: "sweat of thy face" means hard work and "bread" means food. In John Milton's line "When I consider how my light is spent," *light* stands for sight, vision, ability to see. See SYNECDOCHE.

metrical romance

An *adventure story in verse. The term is applied to such works as *Sir Gawain and the Green Knight,* Chaucer's *The Knight's Tale* (in *The Canterbury Tales*), and Sir Walter Scott's *The Lady of the Lake.*

metrics

The science of *meter. *Metrics,* the systematic study and investigation of the patterns of *rhythm in poetry, is a synonym for *prosody. See METER, SCANSION.

microcosm

A little world, a world in miniature. *Microcosm* is often used to refer to mankind or society as an *epitome (summary or miniature version) of the world or the universe. For example, Thornton Wilder's *Our Town* presents through the lives of a few inhabitants of a tiny New England village a microcosm of the beauty and terror of life throughout the world. See MACROCOSM.

Middle Ages

The period in European history from about the end of the Roman Empire (476) to the beginnings of the Renaissance (about 1350). For further comment, see MEDIEVAL.

Middle English

The English language as spoken and written after the Norman Conquest (1066) and preceding the *Renaissance in England. The dates commonly given are 1100 and 1500, but these are only approximate.

For an illustration of Middle English, here is the Lord's Prayer approximately as it appeared in John Wycliffe's translation in the fourteenth century:

> Oure fadir that art in heuenes, halwid be thi name; thi kyngdom cumme to; be thi wille don as in heuen and in erthe; ȝif to vs this day ouer breed oure other substaunce; and forȝeue to vs oure dettis as we forȝeue to oure dettours; and leede vs nat in to temptacioun, but delyuere vs fro yuel. Amen.

miles gloriosus

A Latin term meaning "a boastful soldier." The braggart warrior was a *stock character in Greek and Roman comedy (Plautus wrote a play entitled *Miles Gloriosus* in the second century B.C.) and has remained a dramatic figure ever since. The best-known miles gloriosus in literature is Shakespeare's Sir John Falstaff (*Henry IV,* Parts 1 and 2). Sergeant Bilko of television fame carries on the *tradition of the bragging coward, and so does an officer in George Bernard Shaw's *Arms and the Man.*

milieu

Environment, condition, medium. *Milieu,* a term from French, also means surroundings, sphere, element, and background. The milieu of an author is the physical setting of his life and the intellectual climate of his times. The milieu of Shakespeare was the theatrical world of Elizabethan London. The milieu of William Faulkner was rural and small-town Mississippi. See AMBIENCE, SETTING.

millennium

A period of 1,000 years. More specifically, *millennium* refers to the thousand years during which Christ will reign on earth as recounted in the *Bible (Revelation 20). The term has been extended to mean any period of general happiness and well-being.

Miltonic

A reference to John Milton, English poet (1608–1674), considered to rank with Shakespeare and Chaucer among the greatest poets of all time in English literature. The adjective is sometimes applied to authors who serve their government (as Milton did); to writers with strong ethical and moral beliefs; to defenders of free speech and haters of *censorship; to authors whose style is dignified and lofty (Milton has been called "the God-gifted organ-voice of England").

A Miltonic sonnet is a fourteen-line poetic form (see SON-NET) which has the same *rhyme scheme for the *octave (first eight lines) as the *Petrarchan sonnet (*abbaabba*) but does not pause after the octave and does not follow a fixed rhyme scheme in the *sestet (final six lines). *On His Blindness* ("When I consider how my light is spent . . . / They also serve who only stand and wait") is a Miltonic sonnet.

mime

(1) A form of popular *comedy developed in Italy in the fifth century B.C. which presented events of everyday life through dances, gestures, and *dialogue; (2) *pantomine, the art of portraying a character or mood by the use of gestures, facial expressions, and bodily movements. The term *mime* is now most often used as a verb meaning to imitate or copy in action or speech and as a noun meaning an actor, a professional entertainer, who is clever in mimicking or imitating others. Charlie Chaplin was a mime in silent movies for many years. See DUMB SHOW, MIMESIS, PAN-TOMIME.

mimesis

A Greek word for "imitation." In the *Poetics,* Aristotle first stated the principles of mimesis by commenting that *trage-dy is an imitation of *action, not mere mimicry but the selection, arrangement, and presentation of acts that reveal the relation of art and life. Hamlet's speech to the players (*Hamlet,* act 3, scene 2) reveals the principles of mimesis:

> . . . the purpose of playing, whose end, both of the first and now, was and is, to hold, as 'twere, the mirror up to nature; to show virtue her own feature, scorn her own image, and the very age and body of the time his form and pressure.

mimetic

An adjective that refers to mimicry. A mimetic literary selection is one that places primary emphasis upon the creation of imagined actions and *dialogue in such ways as to make unmistakable their reality, their actuality. See BELIEF, MIMESIS, NATU-RALISM, REALISM, VERISIMILITUDE.

miniature

A representation or *image of something on a small or reduced scale. In art and literature, *miniature* usually refers to a small painting, especially a portrait on ivory or *vellum, to the illumination (decoration) in *manuscripts or *books, and to books of less than usual size.

minnesinger

A "singer of love." *Minnesinger,* derived from German words for *love (Minne)* and *sing,* refers specifically to a group of *medieval German lyric poets. See MINSTREL, TROUBADOUR.

minstrel

(1) A musician, singer, or poet; (2) a professional entertainer of the *Middle Ages who was attached to one great household or who wandered about the countryside; (3) an itinerant comedian with blackened face. See GLEEMAN, JON-GLEUR, TROUBADOUR, VAUDEVILLE.

mirabile dictu

A Latin phrase meaning "wonderful to say." *Mirabile dictu* means "marvelous to relate," "incredibly," "unbelievably."

miracle play

A *medieval dramatic form dealing with Biblical stories or the lives of saints. Miracle plays were usually presented in a series, or *cycle, such as dramas dealing with the Virgin Mary, the fall of man, the creation of the world, etc. In France, a religious drama that dealt with a religious or moral but non-Biblical theme was known as a mystery play, but elsewhere *miracle* and *mystery* have been synonymous terms. *Sister Beatrice,* by the Belgian writer Maurice Mae-terlinck (1862–1947), is a modern example of the miracle play. See MORALITY PLAY, MYSTERY PLAY.

miscellany

A group of various unselected items; a medley. In literature, *miscellany* refers to a collection of literary compositions by several authors, dealing with various topics and assembled in a book. The first such volume was a medley of *Elizabe-than *songs and *sonnets published in England in 1557 and known as *Tottel's Miscellany.* An *anthology and a *chres-tomathy are forms of miscellany.

mise-en-scène

The stage setting of a play. A French term, *mise-en-scène* refers to the scenery and stage properties of an acted play, to the arrangement of actors and the handling of technical equipment. With a literal meaning of "putting in the scene," *mise-en-scène* is used to refer to the surroundings or environment of any event. See AMBIENCE, MILIEU, SETTING.

missal

A book of prayers or devotions. *Missal* refers specifically to a book containing the rites and prayers used by a Roman Catholic priest in celebrating Mass.

Mitteleuropa

Central Europe. A German term, *Mitteleuropa* has been used by historical and political writers to refer to the continent of Europe under German domination. The term also implies a concept of European politics before World War I (1914–1918).

mixed metaphor

A use in the same expression of two or more *metaphors (implied analogies, comparisons) that are incongruous or illogical, as referring to someone as "a well-oiled cog in the beehive of industry" or to an administration that "will put the ship of state on its feet." Effective writers rarely mix metaphors; when they do, the mixing is usually deliberate and effective. For example, in *Lycidas,* Milton referred to corrupt clergymen as "Blind mouths! that scarce themselves know how to hold / A sheep-hook."

mnemonics

The art of developing or improving the memory; a device that serves as an aid to remembering. *Mnemonics* (used as a singular noun) comes from a Greek word meaning "relating to memory" or "mindful." The *jingle "Thirty days hath September" is a mnemonic device.

mock epic

A long, humorous poem in which a slight or trivial subject is treated in a lofty, exalted, and heroic manner. A mock epic is a mockery, an imitation, a *burlesque of *epic presentation and subject matter. Chaucer's *The Nun's Priest's Tale* (from *The Canterbury Tales*) is a mock epic. Jonathan Swift's *The Battle of the Books,* a prose satire, and Pope's *The Rape of the Lock* are mock epics. From the last-named, these lines narrating the emotions of a girl from whose head a lock of hair is snipped illustrate a mock epic approach:

> Then flashed the living lightning from her eyes,
> And screams of horror rend the affrighted skies.

mock heroic

A term closely related to mock epic, *mock heroic* refers to the *style* of a kind of *satire that treats "ordinary" characters and events in the ceremonious manner and lofty language usually reserved for major happenings and elevated personages. *Mock heroic* refers more to *style than to *form (see MOCK EPIC); for instance, Joseph Fielding's *Tom Thumb* is a play written in a mock heroic manner. Mock heroic passages occur in Byron's poem *Don Juan.* Oscar Wilde's drama *The Importance of Being Earnest* contains *dialogue in which characters discuss with great solemnity numerous trivial occurrences.

modulation

A word with the general meaning of "adjustment" or "regulation," *modulation* has two special applications in literature and speech. (1) It can apply to rhythmical *measure, such as a variation from the basic metrical pattern of accents and stresses; see, for example, the quotations from Gray, Suckling, and Browning under the entry METER. (2) The inflection (varying, changing) of the *stress or *pitch of the voice: depending upon which word is stressed, the statement "Babs is here" can have three entirely different meanings as the result of voice modulation. In music, *modulation* refers to a change of key in a passage.

modus operandi

Latin for "mode of operating or working." *Modus operandi* is used to refer to a method, a plan, a scheme for doing, acting, or performing. A similar term, *modus vivendi,* means "manner of living" and is sometimes applied to a temporary arrangement between persons pending a final settlement.

monger

A person who acts in a contemptible or petty way, such as a "gossipmonger" or "tastemonger."

monody

(1) A poem in which one person laments the death of another (see DIRGE, ELEGY, THRENODY); (2) an *ode sung by an actor in Greek tragedy. *Monody* comes from a Greek term meaning "singing alone." In an *introduction to *Lycidas,* Milton wrote, "In this monody, the author bewails a learned friend, unfortunately drowned...." Matthew Arnold referred to his *lament entitled *Thyrsis* as "a monody, to commemorate the author's friend, Arthur Hugh Clough, who died at Florence, 1861."

monograph

*A composition on a single subject, such as a *biography, the *history of a city, or a study of the works of one author. *Monograph,* from Greek terms meaning "one writing," is usually applied to a detailed and documented written investigation of a limited field of inquiry. See DISSERTATION, TREATISE.

monologue

From Greek terms meaning "one word" or "one speech," *monologue* refers to a speech by one person. (See DIALOGUE.) In *drama, *monologue* refers to a form of entertainment by a single speaker or to an extended part of the text of a play uttered by an actor. (See SOLILOQUY.) A device used to reveal the flow of thoughts through a character's

mind in plays or novels is called *interior monologue. (See
STREAM OF CONSCIOUSNESS.) In everyday life, *monologue* is
sometimes used disparagingly to refer to the remarks of
someone who talks glibly and incessantly. See LOGORRHEA.

monometer

A one-foot line of verse. Monometer, rare in verse in English,
is illustrated in this sad fifteen-line poem by Robert Herrick,
written in *iambic *feet (see METER):
Thus I / Passe by / And die: / As One / Unknown /
And gone: / I'm made / A shade, / and laid / I'the grave: /
There have / My Cave. / Where tell / I dwell, / Farewell.
Also, see AMPHIMACER.

monopody

A line (verse) consisting of one *foot. See MONOMETER, under
which entry monopody is illustrated.

monosyllable

A word of one syllable, such as *yes* and *no.* To speak in monosyllables is to use simple language. A line in Pope's *An Essay
on Criticism* illustrates the use of monosyllables: "And ten low
words oft creep in one dull line." Ben Jonson's praise of Shakespeare is also monosyllabic: "He was not of an age but for all
time."

montage

A combination of elements that forms a unified whole, a single
*image. (See COLLAGE.) *Montage* is used in literature as a device to establish a *theme or create an *atmosphere through a
series of rapidly presented impressions or observations. In
U.S.A., John Dos Passos used what he referred to as "newsreels,"
but they are actually montages. The device of montage, frequently used by writers of *impressionism, appears in the *interior monologue of novels and plays and in motion-picture and
*television productions.

mood

A word coming from *Old English *mod* that meant "heart,"
"spirit," and "courage," *mood* refers to a disposition of mind,
a feeling, an emotional state. The *mood* of a literary work refers to its predominating *atmosphere or *tone. (Comment on
mood appears also under the entries for CONTROLLING IMAGE
and DOMINANT IMPRESSION.) Every major work of literature has
a prevailing mood, but many also shift in mood to achieve
*counterpoint, to provide *comic relief, or to reflect changing
circumstances in *plot.

mora

A unit of metrical time equal to the sound of a short *syllable.
Mora, from Latin meaning "delay," "space of time," is represented by a *breve (˘).

moralist

A person who teaches or preaches the rules and principles of right conduct. A moralist is concerned with distinctions between right and wrong, with ethical behavior, with honest and honorable dealing. Most writers of *exempla, *fables, *parables, and *sermons are moralists. So, too, are such writers as John Bunyan, Francis Bacon, Lord Chesterfield, Benjamin Franklin, and many others from whose works one can infer the moral principles that are stated or implied.

morality

Acceptance of, and conformity to, rules of right conduct; moral or virtuous behavior. Morality is what a *moralist advocates, a doctrine or system of morals. Except for works of *decadence and *pornography, all literature is involved with morality, although this quality may be only implied. For instance, despite the treachery, deceit, cunning, and murders involved in worthwhile *tragedies, they are plays of morality because their essential message is that "the wages of sin is death."

morality play

An *allegory in dramatic form current from the fourteenth to the sixteenth century. Most morality plays employed personified *abstractions of vices and virtues (Shame, Lust, Mercy, Conscience). A morality play, unlike *miracle and *mystery plays, did not necessarily use Biblical or strictly religious material and was more concerned with *morality than spirituality. The best-known of all morality plays is *Everyman* (fifteenth century). The *theme of this drama is the summoning of Everyman (everyone) by Death. On his passage to Death, Everyman discovers that, of all his supposed friends, only Good Deeds will go with him. Other characters in the play are Fellowship, Kindred, Knowledge, Strength, and Beauty.

morocco

A fine, pebble-grained leather, originally made in Morocco from tanned goatskin. Books bound in genuine morocco leather are rare and expensive.

morpheme

A term in *linguistics for the smallest meaningful unit in a language. A morpheme may be a word (*it*), a *prefix or *suffix (*ad-, -ism*), or an *accent (*PER·mit, per·MIT*).

motif

A recurring *theme, idea, or subject in a literary work (or musical *composition). A motif is closely related to *dominant impression, the unifying thread in a work. The abduction of a princess or queen by a fairy lover is a motif in some medieval *romances and *fairy tales. The dullness and drabness of life are a motif in James Joyce's *Dubliners.* In Thomas Wolfe's novels, the motif is that of a lost boy, a searcher for something (for a father, a belief, a way of life) to which he can cling.

motivation

Reasons and explanations for action through the presentation of convincing and impelling causes for that action. Motivation consists of the psychological impulses and drives which impel a character in literature to act as he does. The motives supplied to characters by novelists and dramatists are combinations of temperament and circumstance that realistically account for what they do, do not do, say, and do not say. When suitable motivation of characters is supplied by the imaginative ability and understanding of an author, a reader *knows* and fully accepts the emotional and circumstantial forces that made their deeds inevitable. Readers can accept the fact that Othello smothers Desdemona when he thinks her unfaithful; motivation for this act has been supplied by revealing the intensity of his pride and jealousy. See BELIEF, CHARACTERIZATION.

mot juste

An expression from French meaning "the exact word." *Mot juste* applies to the precise expression required to convey an intended meaning. Guy de Maupassant, in telling of the assistance given him by Gustave Flaubert, once wrote:

... having laid down the truth that in the entire world there are no two grains of sand, two flies, two hands, or two noses exactly alike, he compelled me to describe an object so particularized as to distinguish it from all others of its species and class. He used to say ... "make me see by *a single word* wherein a cab horse differs from the fifty others that go before and come after him."

Another French term for the same idea is *mot propre* ("appropriate word").

motto

An especially appropriate word or saying attached to or inscribed on an activity, institution, or undertaking; a *maxim adopted as an expression of a guiding principle or basic aim.

Then conquer we must, for our cause it is just,
And this be our motto: "In God is our trust!"

The Star-Spangled Banner, stanza 4

movement

In literature, *movement* applies to a progressive development of ideas toward a particular result, conclusion, or end; it suggests a literary trend which has definite characteristics.

For example, *cubism, *dadaism, and *imagism were literary movements.

Movement is also a term referring to *action in a play, novel, short story, or narrative poem. Thus a novel is spoken of as having slow or weak movement (as a novel by Henry James) or rapid, forceful movement (as a typical *detective story).

muckraking

Searching for and exposing alleged or actual corruption, scandal, etc., in politics, public life, and industry. (The term was formed from the idea of using a rake on muck, dung, or filth.) The term *muckrakers* has been applied to a group of American writers who, during the first decade of the twentieth century, exposed corruption in business and governmental operations. Lincoln Steffens was a leading muckraker; so, too, was Upton Sinclair in novels such as *The Jungle* and *The Octopus.*

multum in parvo

A Latin term for "much in little." The expression is used to refer to a great deal contained in a small space. For example, a poem of only a few words which expresses a profound idea or truth may be described as multum in parvo. See GNOMIC, MICROCOSM.

mumbo jumbo

(1) An object of superstitious reverence or awe; (2) meaningless *incantation or *ritual; (3) senseless or pretentious *language designed to obscure or confuse, such as *gobbledygook. *Mumbo jumbo* is derived from the name of a West African tribal god who was considered by natives to be the guardian of their villages, a masked man who fought evil and enforced tribal laws.

mummery

(1) A dramatic performance or ceremony performed by persons wearing masks or fantastic disguises; (2) any activity regarded as false, absurd, or pretentious. Mummery, an integral part of festivities engaged in in certain localities at New Year's, the beginning of Lent, Christmas, etc., is a farcical presentation, a kind of *pantomime. See MASQUE.

muse

(1) The genius or powers characteristic of a literary artist; (2) the goddess regarded as inspiring a poet or other writer. *Muse,* especially when capitalized, refers to one of a number of goddesses in classical mythology, specifically the nine daughters of Zeus who presided over various arts: epic poetry, lyric poetry, history, music, dance, tragedy, religious music, comedy, and astronomy. Homer began the *Iliad* by appealing to a muse; in book 7 of *Paradise Lost* Milton requests a muse to "descend

from heaven"; the *prologue to Shakespeare's *Henry V* begins "O for a Muse of fire that would ascend / The bright-
est heaven of invention." See AFFLATUS.

musical comedy

A play with music. A typical musical comedy is based on a slight
*plot, presents songs and dances in solo and group perfor-
mance, and is lighthearted, whimsical, or satiric. Such a production is a combination of light *opera, *vaudeville, and
*burlesque. Notable musical comedies include *The Merry
Widow, Show Boat, Oklahoma!, South Pacific,* and *My Fair
Lady*.

music of the spheres

A music that cannot be heard by human ears, formerly
supposed to be produced by the movements of heavenly
bodies. A sixth-century-B.C. Greek philosopher and mathematician, Pythagoras, observed that the *pitch of notes
depends on the rapidity of vibrations and that the planets
move at different rates; therefore, he concluded, they must
make sounds. In act 5, scene 1, of *The Merchant of Venice,*
Lorenzo says:

There's not the smallest orb which thou behold'st
But in his motion like an angel sings.

mutatis mutandis

A Latin phrase meaning "with the necessary changes having been made." The expression appears occasionally in
eighteenth- and nineteenth-century prose and is still used in
legal *jargon to mean "with respective differences having
been noted."

mystery play

A dramatic form, especially popular during the *Middle
Ages, which dealt with Biblical stories, such as the "mystery" of the life, death, and resurrection of Jesus Christ.
Mystery plays were so called for another reason: the French
word *mystère* means "craft," and many "mysteries" were
performed by members of craft guilds, such as the ship-
wrights' guild, the stationers' guild, etc. Although some
scholars make a distinction, the terms *mystery play* and
miracle play are now used interchangeably. See MIRACLE
PLAY, MORALITY PLAY.

mystery story

A mystery is anything that is kept secret or that remains
unknown or unexplained. A mystery story is a form of
*narration in which the methods, details, and motives of a
crime are entertaining and baffling. More exactly, the term
mystery story can be applied to a DETECTIVE STORY (which
see), to a *Gothic tale or novel (terror, frightening events),

and to a novel of *suspense (excited uncertainty). Most speakers mean detective story when they refer to a mystery, since any tale of *adventure involving a criminal act that is not immediately explained is a mystery story. In this sense, Stevenson's *Treasure Island* is a mystery story, although of a kind different from Dashiell Hammett's *The Thin Man* or Raymond Chandler's *The Long Goodbye.*

mysticism

(1) Obscure thought or speculation; (2) the beliefs and ideas of persons who claim to have immediate intuition and insight into mysteries beyond normal understanding. Mysticism takes many forms in the mental, spiritual, and emotional lives of authors, but varied aspects of it are traceable in the works of William Blake, Samuel Taylor Coleridge, Herman Melville, and Walt Whitman. In the opinion of many students of literature, *transcendentalism is a form of mysticism.

myth

(1) A legendary or traditional story, usually one concerning a superhuman being and dealing with events that have no natural explanation; (2) an unproved belief that is accepted uncritically; (3) an invented idea or story.

A myth usually attempts to explain a phenomenon or strange occurrence without regard to scientific fact or so-called common sense. The myth, appealing to emotion rather than to reason, dates from ancient times when rational explanations were neither available nor apparently wanted. A myth is less "historical" than a *legend and less concerned with *didacticism than a *fable, but all three forms are *fictitious stories, many of which have persisted through *oral transmission.

mythopoesis

The making of *myths. A mythopoeic writer consciously makes a mythic *frame or background for his work. For instance, in *The Plumed Serpent,* D. H. Lawrence used ancient myths of Mexico to explain the primal behavior and blood consciousness that ruined the lives of sophisticated Europeans. In a sense, Melville's *Moby Dick* is a created myth, because its action is a symbol of primeval conflict. William Butler Yeats, T. S. Eliot, and William Faulkner were mythopoeic writers in some of their work.

N

naïveté

Artlessness, simplicity, lack of sophistication or of judgment. Naïveté is exhibited in literature by numerous unaffected, unsuspecting, and ingenuous characters, such as the husband (Charles) in Flaubert's *Madame Bovary* or Dr. Will Kennicott in Sinclair Lewis's *Main Street.* Sometimes a naïve (simple) character is used to narrate a short story because implications of the action involved will have increased *irony owing to the teller's lack of understanding; Sherwood Anderson used such a narrator in *I'm a Fool* and *Sophistication,* and Ring Lardner did so in *Haircut.*

narcissism

Excessive admiration of oneself. *Narcissism* is derived from Narcissus, a youth in classical mythology who became infatuated with his own image reflected in a pool. (Eventually, Narcissus wasted away and was transformed into the flower of the same name.) Self-love and inflated *ego (egoism) are evidenced by numerous characters in history, among them Nero, Julius Caesar, and Alexander the Great, and by such strictly literary creations as Becky Sharp in Thackeray's *Vanity Fair* and Heathcliff in Emily Brontë's *Wuthering Heights. Narcissism,* in *psychiatry, refers to sexual excitement stemming from admiration of one's own body.

narration

A *form of discourse the principal purpose of which is to relate an event or series of events. *Narration,* from a Latin word meaning "tell," is also called "narrative," which may be used as an adjective or noun. Narration (or narrative) appears in *history, news stories, *biography, *autobiography, and the like but is usually applied to such *forms of

writing as the *anecdote, *conte, *exemplum, *fable, *fabliau, *fairy tale, *incident, legend, *novel, *novelette,
*short story, and *tale. The primary and basic appeal of
narration is to the emotions of the reader or hearer. See
FICTION, PLOT.

narrative hook

A device used at the beginning of a work of fiction intended to arouse the interest of readers and make them eager
to read further. Beginning *in medias res is a kind of
narrative hook. Other forms are the use of *paradox, of a
startling quotation, the mention of a murder or accident, or
indeed any statement that will excite curiosity which demands satisfaction. Notice how many intriguing questions
are raised in the reader's mind by this beginning of William
Faulkner's story *A Rose for Emily:*

> When Miss Emily Grierson died, our whole town
> went to her funeral: the men through a sort of
> respectful affection for a fallen monument, the
> women mostly out of curiosity to see the inside of
> her house, which no one save an old man-servant—a
> combined gardener and cook—had seen in at least
> ten years.

narrator

One who tells a story, either orally or in writing. In fiction,
a narrator may be the ostensible author of the story. (See
POINT OF VIEW.) Whether a story is told in the first person
or not, a narrator is always implied in a work of fiction in
the person of someone involved in the action or that of the
writer himself. In Conrad's *Youth,* the narrator, Marlow,
tells a group of friends about a series of events that he was
involved in as a young man, but occasionally the account is
interrupted by comment from one of the listeners, presumably the author himself, who becomes a sort of subnarrator.

National Book Awards

An annual event sponsored by American publishers, book-
sellers, and manufacturers to award cash prizes for distinguished books by Americans in the fields of biography, the
novel, nonfiction, and poetry.

nationalism

(1) Devotion to the interests of one's own nation; (2) national spirit; (3) the policy of advocating and advancing the
concerns of one's own nation considered as separate from
the interests of all other nations. A spirit of nationalism is
less boastful and militant than *chauvinism and less emotional than patriotism.

For instance, it required 250 years for Anglo-Saxons and
their Norman conquerors to merge individual identities into

one nation. Their sense of nationalism came into existence when they united in the Hundred Years' War (1337–1453) against France, fought side by side against a common enemy, and, in a newly found spirit of nationalism, proudly began to think of themselves as Englishmen.

naturalism

In literature, an attempt to achieve fidelity to nature by rejecting idealized portrayals of life. *Naturalism* may be further defined as a *technique or manner of presenting an objective view of man with complete accuracy and frankness. Naturalistic writers hold that man's existence is shaped by heredity and environment, over which he has no control and about which he can exercise little if any choice. Novels and plays in this movement, emphasizing the animal nature of man, portray characters engrossed in a brutal struggle for survival. Émile Zola, founder of the French school of naturalism, held that a novelist should dissect and analyze his subjects with dispassionate, scientific accuracy and minuteness.

Among adherents of naturalism in American literature, in at least some of their works, were Theodore Dreiser, Ernest Hemingway, Eugene O'Neill, and William Faulkner. See REALISM.

near rhyme

Corresponding sounds which are not true or exact. For instance, Pope employed near rhyme with *restored* and *word.* See APPROXIMATE RHYME.

necrophilia

A psychiatric term referring to an erotic attraction to corpses. *Necrophilia* is often applied in literary *criticism to writers who are fascinated by the dead and to works in which deceased persons play a prominent role. Ghost stories frequently involve necrophilia. The ghost of Hamlet's father plays a necrophilic role in *Hamlet,* and Banquo does so in *Macbeth.* Edgar Allan Poe, many of whose stories and poems deal with death, declared that "the death, then, of a beautiful woman is . . . the most poetical topic in the world." See METEMPSYCHOSIS.

nectar

In classical mythology, nectar was the life-giving drink of the gods. (See AMBROSIA.) In literature, *nectar* is employed to refer to any delicious drink or to an event, meeting, or conversation that provides pleasure and delight.

née

A term from French, meaning "born," placed after the name of a married woman to provide her maiden name: Madame de Staël, née Necker.

negative capability

A term used by John Keats as a name for the impersonality and objectivity of a writer. Negative capability, which has about the same meaning as *aesthetic distance, applies to the "innate universality" which Keats attributed to Shakespeare, that capacity which the latter had for "being in uncertainties, mysteries, doubts, without any irritable reaching after fact and reason." *Negative capability* is used by some critics to describe qualities in a writer which enable him to keep his own personality entirely apart from what he is relating or discussing.

nemesis

In classical mythology, Nemesis was the goddess of divine retribution (punishment). Spelled with a small letter, *nemesis* applies to (1) a rival or opponent who cannot be overcome or handled; (2) any situation or condition which one cannot change or triumph over; (3) an agent, or an act, of punishment. *Nemesis,* roughly synonymous with *fate, is generally used in literature to suggest that everyone gets his share of good and bad fortune and that, sooner or later, justice will prevail. For instance, in *Macbeth,* Macduff is the nemesis of Macbeth and Lady Macbeth.

neoclassicism

A style of writing developed in the seventeenth and eighteenth centuries that rigidly adhered to *canons of *form derived from classical antiquity. Neoclassicism ("new" *classicism) was notable for emotional restraint, elegance and exactness of *diction, strict observance of the three *unities, common sense, *rationalism, and *logic. The "modern" writers cited under the entry CLASSICISM were neoclassicists. In architecture, *neoclassicism* refers to the use of Greek orders and decorative details, geometric compositions, plain wall surfaces, etc.

neologism

A new word or phrase, a *coinage. *Neologism* also applies to a new doctrine, such as a fresh interpretation of the *Bible or of some other work of literature. See ACRONYM, COINAGE, PORTMANTEAU WORD.

Neoplatonism

A philosophical system originating in the third century A.D., based on *Platonism, Oriental *mysticism, and traces of Christianity. Both *Neoplatonism* and *Platonism* are rather vague terms; generally, they apply to concern with aspirations of the human spirit (see HUMANISM), with the placing of mind over matter, with optimistic but somewhat mysterious approaches to the fundamental problems of man and the universe. Among Neoplatonic literary selections may be mentioned Wordsworth's *Ode on Intimations of Immortality from Recollections of Early Childhood.*

ne plus ultra

A Latin term meaning "no more beyond" and now employed to mean "the highest point," "summit," "the limit of achievement," "greatest degree."

New Criticism

A form of criticism (evaluation) that relies on close and detailed analysis of the language, imagery, and emotional or intellectual meanings of a literary work. New Criticism emphasizes concentrated study and subsequent interpretation of a selection as a selection rather than as a biographical or historical study or as a statement of philosphy, ethics, or sociology. In New Criticism, analysis of the text itself results in reputed discovery of layers of meaning. This approach, first developed at Vanderbilt University, has among its followers such American authors as Allen Tate, Robert Penn Warren, Yvor Winters, and Kenneth Burke. See ANALYSIS, CRITICISM, EXPLICATION.

nihilism

A term derived from a Latin word meaning "nothing," "a thing of no value," *nihilism* means (1) total rejection of established laws and institutions; (2) *anarchy, terrorism, or other revolutionary activity; (3) total and absolute destructiveness. In philosophy, *nihilism* refers to an extreme form of *skepticism that involves denial of any possible objective basis for truth. *Existentialism may be considered a form of nihilism to the degree that it considers traditional values and beliefs unfounded and all human existence aimless, senseless, and useless.

nihil obstat

A Latin term meaning "nothing stands in the way." In the Roman Catholic Church, *nihil obstat* refers to permission to publish a book (after certification that it contains nothing contrary to Catholic faith or morals). See IMPRIMATUR.

nirvana

A place, or a state of mind and body, characterized by being free from (or oblivious of) worry, pain, and the external world. *Nirvana,* derived from a Sanskrit word meaning "a blowing out," a "clearance," in the Buddhist religion involves removal of individual passion, delusion, and hatred; in Hinduism, *nirvana* (often spelled with a capital letter) refers to salvation of the soul through union of the individual

self with Brahma (supreme being, primal source). See ELYSI-
UM.

Nobel prize

An award named after Alfred B. Nobel (1833–1896), Swed-
ish engineer and chemist, who left a large sum of money
(nine million dollars) the interest from which is annually
distributed to persons considered to have contributed out-
standingly to mankind. Nobel prizes are awarded in peace,
physics, chemistry, medicine or physiology, economics, and
literature. English and American winners of the Nobel prize
for literature have included Rudyard Kipling, William Butler Yeats, George Bernard Shaw, Sinclair Lewis, John Galsworthy, Eugene O'Neill, Pearl Buck, T. S. Eliot, William
Faulkner, Bertrand Russell, Winston Churchill, Ernest Hemingway, and John Steinbeck.

noblesse oblige

A French term that means "nobility obliges." The term
refers to the moral obligation of rich or highborn persons to
display charitable, thoughtful, honorable, and considerate
conduct toward people less fortunate. See DE RIGUEUR.

nocturne

A lyric poem that expresses thoughtful feelings considered
appropriate to evening and nighttime. *Nocturne* applies in
music to a *composition with a *mood of twilight or evening. Gray's *Elegy Written in a Country Churchyard* has a
nocturnal feeling. Carl Sandburg's *Nocturne in a Deserted
Brickyard* provides an illustration:

> Stuff of the moon
> Runs on the lapping sand
> Out to the longest shadows . . .
> Fluxions of yellow and dusk on the waters
> Make a wide dreaming pansy of an old pond
>   in the night.

noh

Classic drama of Japan. Noh, often spelled nō, was developed in the fourteenth century from ritual dances associated with ancient Shinto worship. Noh plays are formal,
restrained, and subtle. See KABUKI.

nom de plume

A French phrase meaning "pen name." (See ALLONYM, PEN
NAME, PSEUDONYM.) A less-used phrase, also from French,
nom de guerre means an assumed name under which a person fights or writes. "Mark Twain" was the nom de plume
of Samuel L. Clemens; "George Orwell" was the pen name
of Eric Blair.

nominalism

The doctrine that general or *abstract words do not stand for objectively existing realities, that such terms as *society* and *man* are mere "names." Nominalism in literature is an attempt to stress *concreteness. See GENERAL SEMANTICS, SEMANTICS, WORD.

nonce word

A term coined and used for a particular occasion. *Nonce* means "the present," "now," and so a nonce word is a *coinage, a *neologism, newly designed to fit a specific situation. Lewis Carroll's *jabberwocky is a nonce word. The coinages in James Joyce's *Ulysses* and *Finnegans Wake* are nonce words.

non compos mentis

Not of sound mind, mentally incapable or deficient. See COMPOS MENTIS.

nonfiction

As opposed to *fiction and distinguished from *drama and *poetry, nonfiction is that branch of literature presenting ideas and opinions based upon facts and reality. Considered as nonfiction are such types of writing as *autobiography, *biography, the *essay, and *history. However, most fiction and drama and some poetry contain nonfictional elements; most nonfiction reveals some imaginative (invented) passages.

nonsense verse

A form of light verse which is entertaining because of its rhythmic appeal and absurd or farfetched ideas. See DOGGEREL, JINGLE, LIGHT VERSE, LIMERICK, MACARONIC, NURSERY RHYME. Also, see JABBERWOCKY; this *stanza from Lewis Carroll's *Jabberwocky* will serve to illustrate nonsense verse:

> "And hast thou slain the Jabberwock?
> Come to my arms, my beamish boy!
> O frabjous day! Callooh! Callay!"
> He chortled in his joy.

non sequitur

A Latin phrase meaning "it does not follow." A non sequitur is a conclusion, an *inference, which does not follow from the *premises (*propositions, *assumptions). See LOGIC.

nostalgia

A desire to return in thought or in fact to one's home, to a former time in one's life, to one's friends and family. Nostalgia, derived from Greek words meaning "return home" and "pain," is usually associated with homesickness, with a longing for the past. A major theme of Thomas Wolfe's *You Can't Go Home Again* is nostalgia. Robert Burns's *Auld Lang Syne* ("old long since") is a poem (song) of nostalgia; so too is Thomas Hood's poem "I remember, I remember / The house where I was born." Charles Lamb's *Dream-Children: A Reverie* is an essay filled with nostalgia.

nota bene

A Latin phrase meaning "note well." This term for "take notice" is frequently shortened to N.B.

noumenon

In the philosophy of Immanuel Kant (1724–1804; German thinker), *noumenon* refers to anything which can be the object only of mental intuition and not the result of using one's senses. Sometimes referred to as "the object of pure reason," *noumenon* is in contrast to *phenomenon* (a fact, circumstance, or occurrence that can be observed). These lines from Wordsworth's *The Excursion* are noumenal:

> . . . One in whom persuasion and belief
> Had ripened into faith, and faith become
> A passionate intuition.

novel

A lengthy fictitious prose narrative portraying characters and presenting an organized series of events and settings. A work of *fiction with fewer than 30,000 to 40,000 words is usually considered a *short story, *novelette, or *tale, but the novel has no actual maximum length. Every novel is an account of life; every novel involves *conflict, *characters, *action, *settings, *plot, and *theme. See EPISTOLARY, HISTORICAL NOVEL, PROBLEM NOVEL, POINT OF VIEW, ROMANCE.

novelette

A short *novel. Among short novels are Voltaire's *Candide,* Fitzgerald's *The Great Gatsby,* John Buchan's *The Thirty-nine Steps,* Bram Stoker's *Dracula,* Stevenson's *Dr. Jekyll and Mr. Hyde,* George Eliot's *The Lifted Veil,* Joseph Conrad's *The Secret Sharer,* Virginia Woolf's *Between the Acts,* Melville's *Billy Budd,* and Hemingway's *The Old Man and the Sea.*

novella

An Italian term meaning "a story," *novella* refers to a relatively short prose narrative, comparable in length to a long *short story or a *novelette. Boccaccio's *The Decameron* is a collection of 100 novelle (plural form), pithy tales of varying length that focus upon one dominant event rather than a series of actions. Among celebrated European writers of novelle may be mentioned Goethe and Thomas Mann.

noxious

Morally harmful, pernicious to mental or physical health. *Noxious* is a critical term applied to literature considered unwholesome, hurtful, or decadent. In the eyes of some readers, all *pornography, for instance, is noxious. So, too, is considered some of the work of Oscar Wilde, such as *The Picture of Dorian Gray.* See OBSCENITY.

nuance

A term from French which refers to a subtle shade, or *tone, of expression, *color, and feeling. The nuances of a literary selection are its delicate distinctions of meaning, its subtleties and refinements of *taste and *mood. For instance, Tolstoi proved himself a master of nuance in *War and Peace* when narrating the engagement of Princess Natasha Rostova, her attempted elopement with a scoundrel, and her eventual marriage to Pierre Bezuhov.

numerology

A study of numbers to determine their supposed influence upon one's life, fortunes, future, etc. Numerology is a pseudo-science, but many writers of the past have held that certain numbers possess a mystic and powerful significance. Pythagoras (Greek mathematician and philospher of the sixth century B.C.) held that numbers were influential principles: that 1 was unity and represented deity; 3 was perfect harmony; 6 was justice, etc. With ancient Romans, 2 was the most fatal of numbers; in ecclesiastical symbolism 9 referred to the nine orders of angels. Dante's *Divine Comedy* consists of three books, is written in *terza rima (third rhyme), and describes Hell as consisting of nine circles (3 X 3). Attitudes toward 13 have continued to the present day.

nursery rhyme

A simple poem or song for infants and young children. See LULLABY.

nymphomania

Abnormal and uncontrollable sexual desire in women. (See SATYRIASIS.) Nymphomania, derived from *mania* and *nymph* (a Greek term for *bride*), is a pathological condition but one that appears often in current novels emphasizing sexual situations and drives.

O

obiter dicta (dictum)

Incidental, "in passing" opinions or remarks. *Obiter dictum* (singular) is Latin for "a saying by the way," "an incidental comment." *Obiter dicta* (plural) is used in legal circles to apply to supplementary opinions or statements by a judge that are not essential in a decision and therefore not binding.

obituary

A notice of the death of a person. The expression, derived from a Latin word for "death" and "the dead," is both a noun and an adjective (an *obituary* notice). Obituaries, usually appearing in newspapers, normally include a biographical sketch of the deceased.

objective correlative

A chain of events, or a situation, which makes objective a particular (subjective) emotion. *Objective correlative,* a term first used by T. S. Eliot in a critical study of *Hamlet,* implies an impersonal means of communicating feeling. Eliot wrote, "When the external facts, which must terminate in sensory experience, are given, the emotion is immediately evoked." Eliot held that the emotions which dominated Hamlet are not justified by the facts in the play. The term *objective correlative* is widely and somewhat vaguely used by adherents of the *New Criticism. See AESTHETIC DISTANCE, NEGATIVE CAPABILITY, OBJECTIVITY.

objectivity

(1) A dealing with outward things; (2) reality as it is, or seems to be, apart from one's thoughts and feelings; (3) intentness on objects external to the mind. In literature, objectivity is a quality of impersonality, of freedom from

personal sentiments, beliefs, and emotions. Some of the work of Henry Fielding, Anthony Trollope, and Ernest Hemingway, for example, treats events as external rather than as affected by the reflections and *point of view of the author. See AESTHETIC DISTANCE, NEGATIVE CAPABILITY, OBJECTIVE CORRELATIVE.

obligatory scene

An *episode which is so fully expected by the audience that a dramatist is "obliged" to provide it. In *Ghosts,* by Henrik Ibsen, the audience, aware that Regina and Oswald are half sister and brother, witnesses their growing sexual interest in each other. The episode in which they "discover" their true relationship is an obligatory scene.

oblique

Indirect; not expressly stated or directly explained; not straightforward. *Irony, for example, is an oblique method of writing; and *innuendo, for another example, is an indirect *implication. All *characterization that is accomplished more through the deeds and remarks of persons than through direct explanatory statements by the author is oblique. Although Prince Hal is reckless and impulsive throughout *Henry IV,* Part 2, Shakespeare does not directly say so; instead, he uses oblique methods of characterization, such as the scene in which Prince Hal teases Francis. In the sense that literature is a reflection or mirror of life, all literature is somewhat oblique.

obscenity

Indecency; that which is offensive to modesty or delicacy or may be considered repulsive and disgusting. Defining *obscenity* is less difficult than determining which literary works are obscene and which are not. See BOWDLERIZE; CENSORSHIP; GRUNDY, MRS; PORNOGRAPHY; TABOO.

obscurantism

(1) Deliberate evasion, uncertainty, or obscurity of clarity and meaning; (2) opposition to the increase and spread of knowledge. Derived from a Latin word meaning "dark," *obscurantism* refers to the concealment or confusion of meaning in certain literary works, especially those in which the author appears purposeful and willful in efforts to be ambiguous. Many products of *surrealism and *Theater of the Absurd, for instance, have been called obscurantist. See ESOTERIC.

obsolete diction

Words and phrases which have completely passed out of use. (See ARCHAISM.) An obsolete expression is dead; an obsolescent expression is one that is dying. *Infortune* (for *misfortune*) is obsolete diction; so are *egal* for *equal* and *prevent* for *precede.*

occasional verse

*Poetry (or *doggerel) written for a special occasion, usually to commemorate a social, historical, or literary event. When occasional verse is witty or satiric, it is sometimes called vers de société. Among well-known literary selections written for special occasions are Spenser's *Epithalamion* (celebrating his marriage); Milton's *Lycidas* (on the death of Edward King, the author's friend); Tennyson's *Ode on the Death of the Duke of Wellington;* Kipling's *Recessional* (for Queen Victoria's Diamond Jubilee, 1897). See POET LAUREATE.

occult

An adjective meaning "mysterious," "secret," "hidden from view," and "beyond the range of ordinary knowledge." (See METAPHYSICS.) As a noun, *occult* refers to supernatural affairs and agencies. (See MYTH.) The occult sciences, once so called because they were hidden mysteries, were alchemy, magic, and astronomy. Several of Hawthorne's short stories deal with occult subjects, notably *The Birthmark* and *Rappaccini's Daughter.*

octameter

A verse (line) of poetry consisting of eight feet. (See FOOT, METER.) Octameter, also spelled *octometer,* is rare in poetry; each of these lines from Tennyson's *Locksley Hall* consists of eight feet (trochaic octameter):

> In the spring a livelier iris changes on the
> burnished dove;
> In the spring a young man's fancy lightly
> turns to thoughts of love.

octastich

A group of eight lines of poetry. *Octastich* is made up of *octa* (an element in loan words from Greek and Latin meaning "eight") and *stich* ("row, line, verse"). See OCTAVE, OTTAVA RIMA.

octave

Like *octastich, an octave refers to a *stanza of eight lines, but especially to the first eight lines in an *Italian sonnet. Usually, but not always, the octave of a sonnet asks a question answered in the *sestet (six following lines) or states a condition or generalization which is "resolved" in the sestet. See SONNET.

octavo

The size of a book (about 6 by 9 inches) determined by folding the printed sheets to form eight leaves (sixteen pages). The term *octavo,* which also applies to a *book of this size, is usually abbreviated to 8vo. See FOLIO.

octet

(1) Any group of eight, such as a company of eight singers, or musicians, or dancers; (2) a musical composition for eight voices or eight instruments; (3) an *octave.

ode

Originally, an ode was a poem meant to be sung, but its meaning has been altered to apply to a lyric poem with a dignified *theme that is phrased in a formal, elevated *style. (See COW-LEYAN ODE, HORATIAN, PINDARIC.) Among well-known odes are Shelley's *To a Skylark,* Dryden's *Alexander's Feast,* Gray's *The Bard* and *The Progress of Poesy,* James Russell Lowell's *Ode Recited at the Harvard Commemoration,* and Allen Tate's *Ode on the Confederate Dead.*

Oedipus complex

Sexual desire of a son for his mother. As a psychiatric term, *Oedipus complex* refers to the unresolved desire of a child for sexual gratification through a parent of the opposite sex. This condition involves identification with, and later hatred of, the parent of the same sex, who is considered by the child as a rival. Actually, in *Freudianism, when the boy is sexually attracted to his mother, there is an Oedipus complex; when the girl desires her father, an Electra complex results. (Electra incited her brother to kill their mother in revenge for the latter's murder of their father.)

Oedipus complex is derived from the story of Oedipus, a figure in Greek *legend, who was once a king of Thebes. As prophesied, he unknowingly killed his father and married his mother. Both the Oedipus complex and the Electra complex have been used in modern fiction and drama, notably in the work of Eugene O'Neill and Tennessee Williams.

off rhyme

Approximate but not actual correspondence (identity) of sounds, such as *mirth* and *forth.* See APPROXIMATE RHYME.

offset process

A method of printing. A stone, metal, or paper plate is used to make an inked impression on a rubber surface (blanket or sheet) which transfers it to the paper being printed. The method is called offset because the impression is not made directly on the paper.

Old English

A term referring to the English language as it was spoken and written from about A.D. 450 to about 1150. (See AN-GLO-SAXON.) Contrary to what might be expected from primitive and nomadic tribes such as the Angles, Saxons, and Jutes, Old English had a vocabulary of some 50,000 words and was capable of conveying sophisticated ideas. For instance, a native Old English word, *God*, was combined with *spell* ("talk," "message") into *Godspell* or, in modern English, *gospel*. Old English *godsunu* has become modern *godson*. Old English now appears at least as foreign as Latin or French, but many words are recognizable, such as *hete* ("hate"), *heofon* ("heaven"), *sawol* ("soul"), *fyr* ("fire"), and *weorc* ("work").

old wives' tale
A story, idea, or belief traditionally passed on by old women. The term is used to refer to superstitions or fixed notions that have no basis in fact. The term is also applied to gossipy, long-winded stories. In a letter, the apostle Paul advised his friend, "But refuse profane and old wives' fables and exercise thyself rather unto godliness" (1 Timothy 4:7). Arnold Bennett's *The Old Wives' Tale* (1908) is a lengthy story *about* two sisters, both "old wives," Sophia and Constance Baines.

Olympian
Majestic, aloof, incomparably superior. *Olympian* refers to Mount Olympus, a mountain in Greece and the mythical home of the greater Greek gods. Such writers as Shakespeare and Milton have been referred to as Olympian because of their transcendent genius. In *The Master: Lincoln,* Edwin Arlington Robinson paid this tribute to Abraham Lincoln:

> The saddest among kings of earth,
> Bowed with a galling crown, this man
> Met rancor with a cryptic mirth,
> Laconic—and Olympian.

omnipotence
Unlimited power, supreme authority. In literature, omnipotence has been attributed to Greek and Roman gods and to emperors of Rome, but in recent centuries this condition has usually been allocated only to God, as in Milton's reference to Satan in *Paradise Lost:*

> . . . Him the Almighty Power
> Hurled headlong flaming from the ethereal sky,
> With hideous ruin and combustion, down
> To bottomless perdition, there to dwell
> In adamantine chains and penal fire,
> Who durst defy the Omnipotent to arms.

omniscience
Infinite knowledge; complete awareness or understanding; ability to see everything. Omniscience is exercised by those

authors who tell a story from an omniscient *point of view. With this *technique, a writer is capable of seeing, knowing, and telling whatever he wishes. The author, assuming omniscience for himself, is free to move his characters in time and place, to describe the physical action and private thoughts of characters, to comment upon what happens and to make clear the *theme of his story in whatever ways he chooses. Most of the world's novels and plays considered greatest are told from an omniscient point of view.

one-acter

A play consisting of one act. A one-acter, like a *short story, demands concentration on one *theme as well as *economy in *style, *setting, and plotting. Sir James M. Barrie, George Bernard Shaw, John Galsworthy (England); Gerhart Hauptmann (Germany); Johan August Strindberg (Sweden); and Eugene O'Neill and Paul Green (United States) have written many successful one-act plays.

onomastics

A study of the origin and history of proper names. From a Greek term meaning "names," onomastics is concerned with the *folklore of names, their current application, spellings, pronunciations, and meanings. An example of onomastics is George Stewart's *Names on the Land* (1945, 1957), a historical account of place naming in the United States.

onomatopoeia

The formation and use of words that suggest by their sounds the object or idea being named: *bowwow, bang, buzz, cackle, clatter, hiss, murmur, sizzle, twitter, zoom.* Onomatopoeia is also a figure of speech, the use of "imitative" words for rhetorical effect. In the hands of an accomplished writer, onomatopoeia is a powerful device by which sound is made, in Alexander Pope's words, "an echo to the sense," as he illustrated in *An Essay on Criticism:*

> Soft is the strain when Zephyr gently blows,
> And the smooth stream in smoother numbers flows;
> But when loud surges lash the sounding shore,
> The hoarse, rough verse should like
>   the torrent roar:
> When Ajax strives some rock's vast weight to throw,
> The line too labors, and the words move slow.

ontology

The study and science of being, of existence. Ontology is a branch of *metaphysics that studies the nature of existence as such, distinct from material or spiritual or emotional existence. In *New Criticism, *ontology* is applied to the *structure and *texture of a poem that together yield its complete meaning.

opaque

Obscure, hard to understand, not clear or lucid. An opaque literary selection is difficult to grasp and interpret. The opacity of a selection may be due to some shortcoming of its readers or to its *esoteric qualities. Every great work of literature is to some degree opaque in that it provides a wealth of meanings on different levels, all of them subject to different understandings and interpretations. Millions of readers and viewers have considered *Hamlet* the greatest play of all time; T. S. Eliot thought that it is somewhat opaque (see OBJECTIVE CORRELATIVE).

op. cit.

An abbreviation of the Latin phrase *opere citato* ("in the work cited"). See IBIDEM, LOC. CIT.

opera

A *drama set to music. From Latin and Italian words meaning "work," an opera is an extended dramatic *composition in which parts are sung to instrumental accompaniment. Many operas include arias, choruses, recitatives (declamatory passages), and ballet. Although opera is musical drama, it is more serious, artistic, and dignified than *musical comedy, *mummery, and *vaudeville.

opéra bouffe

A French term for "comic opera," "a farcical musical drama," an "operatic *extravaganza." This form, apparently developed from *vaudeville music, was a forerunner of the comic operas of Gilbert and Sullivan.

operetta

A short, amusing, lighthearted *opera. An operetta, a diminutive (smaller form) of opera, emphasizes music and *spectacle and contains some spoken dialogue as incidental. Except for minor differences in staging, an operetta and an opéra bouffe are identical.

opprobrium

Disgrace or reproach brought about by conduct considered shameful. *Opprobrium* is a *synonym for *infamy* and *strong condemnation*. Daniel Webster suffered opprobrium when he championed the Compromise of 1850 in his Seventh of March speech. Whittier heaped opprobrium upon Webster in his poem *Ichabod:*

> All else is gone; from those great eyes
> The soul has fled:
> When faith is lost, when honor dies,
> The man is dead!

oral, verbal

These words, sometimes confused by writers and speakers, are closely related but not synonymous. *Oral* means "uttered by the mouth," "spoken," whereas *verbal* means "in the form of words" whether written or spoken. See VERBAL, ORAL.

oral transmission

The spreading or passing on of material by word of mouth. The term is applied especially to the *ballad, the *epic, and *folklore, some of which, in the opinion of some scholars, were originally made known to audiences only by recitation and singing and were handed down to succeeding generations through memory rather than in written form. The theory of oral transmission is that traditional material (not only the *forms just mentioned but also *folktales, *fables, *proverbs, *old wives' tales, and *songs) were first the property of the so-called common people who repeated (or sang) such items, consciously or unconsciously altered them, and taught them to their children from one generation to the next.

oration

A formal speech delivered on a special occasion. An oration, characterized by elevated *style and *diction and by studied delivery, is an eloquent address suitable for an anniversary celebration, political controversy, a funeral, and academic exercises. The most famous oration in literature may be Mark Antony's speech in *Julius Caesar* (act 3, scene 2): "Friends, Romans, countrymen, lend me your ears . . . ." Other orations are Demosthenes's *Philippic against the ruler of Macedon; Cicero's *diatribes against Catiline; Daniel Webster's Seventh of March speech (see OPPROBRIUM); Abraham Lincoln's Gettysburg Address.

order

Succession or sequence; the disposition of items following one another in time, space, or *logic. Every literary selection reveals some kind of order, *form, or underlying *structure. Sometimes, order is determined by *conventions; for example, a Petrarchan *sonnet must be ordered into an *octave and *sestet, with a fixed *rhyme scheme. A *tragedy may be ordered in its story arrangement by classic divisions into *acts with specific roles for each part.

In all writing, a plan of some sort reveals that the author has brought order (authoritative direction) to his materials by the use of *deduction or *induction, by proceeding from the known to the unknown, by *classification and division, by *cause and effect, by *comparison and contrast, by *analogy, or by some other means that provides an understandable arrangement of thought and action. See ORGANIZATION.

organization

Forming coordinated and interdependent parts into a whole; giving organic character and *structure to a literary selection. The organization of all *fiction is largely determined by *plot. The organization of *drama depends upon its division into *acts and *scenes. The organization of *poetry is affected by its *meter, *rhyme scheme, arrangement in *stanzas, etc. The patterns of organization in essays, biography, articles, etc., include chronology (time sequence), space (see POINT OF VIEW), similarity or contrast, *analysis, and *logic.

Every effective work of literature possesses and reveals some kind of *order and organization, but the organic form of any selection apparently has developed from a conception in the thought, personality, and feelings of its author as opposed to dependence upon a fixed and mechanical structure dictated by *convention. For this reason, no two novels or lyric poems or short stories or plays ever reveal precisely the same organization.

Oriental theater

Drama as it has originated and developed in the East, particularly in Japan and China. Dramatic productions of the Orient, stylized and symbolic, differ greatly from European and American plays in *plot, *characterization, stage *settings, and the like. Oriental drama resembles *pantomime and ballet more than Occidental *comedy or *tragedy. See CHINOISERIE, KABUKI, NOH.

originality

In literature, *originality* applies to the ability to think and express oneself in an independent way. Originality is a matter of creative ability, of individuality, of providing a unique approach to a given subject. Only a few geniuses in literature have conceived wholly fresh ideas and completely novel ways of conveying them, but every author worth reading has revealed some capacity for independent thought, individual insight, and constructive imagination. Goethe has provided an illuminating comment on originality:

> The most original authors of modern times are such not because they create anything new but only because they are able to say things in a manner as if they had never been said before.

orthodoxy

Belief in, and practice of, opinions, doctrines, and customs generally approved and held to be sound and correct. Orthodoxy applies particularly to theological and religious ideas, but it also has bearing upon the attitudes of writers concerning subject matter, *style, and the purposes of literature. Orthodoxy in literature varies from generation to

generation so that, for example, what was considered orthodox in *Victorian times was decidedly unorthodox fifty years
later. Also, a writer may reveal orthodoxy in *form and an
almost total lack of it in subject matter or, conversely, may
express "accepted, approved, and conventional" thoughts in
unorthodox style, such as *free verse or *interior monologue. See HETERODOXY.

orthoepy

A term from Greek meaning "correctness of diction." In English, *orthoepy* means the study of correct pronunciation.

orthography

Correct spelling; the art or practice of writing words with the
proper letters, according to accepted usage. *Orthography* is
also a term in *grammar which generally applies to the use of
letters of the alphabet.

o tempora, o mores

A Latin phrase meaning "oh times, oh customs."

otiose

An adjective applied to writing that is (1) verbose, wordy, long-
winded; (2) leisured; (3) rambling; (4) futile, useless. *Otiose,*
from a Latin word meaning "leisure," is usually applied to writing or speech that is worthless and pointless.

ottava rima

A *stanza of eight iambic pentameter lines rhyming *abababcc.*
Ottava rima has been used by many authors, including Spenser,
Milton, Keats, and Byron. This is ottava rima, the second stanza
of W. B. Yeats's *Sailing to Byzantium:*

> An aged man is but a paltry thing,
> A tattered coat upon a stick, unless
> Soul clap its hands and sing, and louder sing
> For every tatter in its mortal dress,
> Nor is there singing school but studying
> Monuments of its own magnificence;
> And therefore I have sailed the seas and come
> To the holy city of Byzantium.

outline

(1) A general sketch, report, or account that indicates only
the main features of a selection, book, or project; (2) the
arrangement of clusters of related ideas in a sequence that
will reveal the *order and *organization of a written *composition or a speech. Every literary work of any distinction
is so ordered and organized that an outline can be made of
its contents and structure.

overtone

In music, an overtone is a sound frequency higher than the

fundamental *tone of a passage. In literature, *overtone* is related to *connotation—the additional or associated meaning of a word that is "over" or "above" its exact meaning. Also, a passage or scene in a novel, for example, may have overtones that add something of significance to the literal account. For instance, every *incident involving Popeye, the cruel killer in Faulkner's *Sanctuary,* has overtones conveying to readers the idea that this sadistic monster is a *symbol of the ruthlessness and materialism that destroyed the antebellum social order of the South.

Oxford Movement

A revolt beginning in 1833 at Oxford University against the *rationalism and *materialism which had developed in the Church of England. Followers of this movement attempted to combat *skepticism and to restore to church worship the beauty, purity, and dignity of earlier times.

In 1921, an organization also founded at Oxford and known as the Oxford Group began advocating absolute *morality in public and private life. In 1938, this movement came to be known as Moral Re-Armament, a scheme for world betterment through personal and national concepts of ethical behavior.

oxymoron

A figure of speech in which two contradictory words or phrases are combined to produce a rhetorical effect by means of a concise paradox. For example, *sophomore* comes from two Greek words meaning "wise" and "foolish." The phrase *eloquent silence* is an oxymoron. These lines from Tennyson's *Lancelot and Elaine* contain several oxymora:

> The shackles of an old love straighten'd him,
> His honour rooted in dishonour stood,
> And faith unfaithful kept him falsely true.

See ANTITHESIS.

P

pace

Rate of movement; tempo. A literary selection, such as a *novel, is said to have a slow pace if it contains *digressions, if it has substantial amounts of *exposition and *description, and if its *incidents do not follow in rapid succession. An *adventure story, *fairy tale, *ballad, or *detective story is likely to move at a fast pace. With rare exceptions, every outstanding work of narrative literature varies its pace to accommodate differing *moods and *actions.

paean

(1) A song of joy, praise, or triumph; (2) a *hymn of thanksgiving. Paean, derived from the name of a legendary Greek physician to *Olympian gods, originally referred to a song of healing or to an *incantation of some sort, but later the term was applied to songs before battle or on other momentous occasions. Sophocles's *Antigone* contains numerous paeans, notably the cry of exultation beginning "Wonders are many, and none is more wonderful than man."

paeon

A *foot consisting of one long (stressed) syllable and three short (unstressed) ones in any order of appearance. Such a foot is unsuited to English, but Gerard Manley Hopkins used paeons of various kinds in his poem *The Windhover*. In this poem, Hopkins's reference to a falcon as "dapple-dawn-drawn" is a paeon in which an accented syllable is followed by three unaccented syllables.

paganism

The beliefs and practices of irreligious or hedonistic persons. (See HEDONISM.) *Paganism* also refers to the traditions and customs of those who profess a polytheistic ("many gods") religion, as the ancient Greeks and Romans did. Matthew Arnold wrote, "the Renascence [Renaissance] is . . . a return toward the pagan spirit . . . toward the life of the senses." Derived from a Latin term meaning "village" or "rural district," *pagan* was originally applied to people living remote from centers of civilization who had not heard of Christianity. In current use, *paganism* applies to indifference to things of the spirit and to delight in material possessions and pleasures.

page

(1) One side of a leaf of something written or printed, such as a *book, *manuscript, or *letter; (2) a single sheet of paper; (3) a noteworthy event or period, as "a forlorn page in American history"; (4) a young man in attendance on a person of rank; (5) in *medieval times, a lad in training for knighthood.

pageant

(1) An elaborate public *spectacle designed to celebrate a historical event; (2) a costumed procession or *tableau; (3) a scaffold or stage on which plays were performed in the *Middle Ages; (4) anything comparable to a spectacle or procession in splendor, colorful variety, and grandeur. In modern times, *pageant* is applied to any elaborate outdoor performance, march, or procession. See MUMMERY, SPECTACLE.

page proof

An impression of typeset matter taken from each *page and *proofread as a final check. On page proof, galley corrections (see AUTHOR'S PROOF) have been made and illustrations and *footnotes have been arranged in their proper places. See FOUNDRY PROOF, PROOF.

paleography

The study of ancient writings. Derived from Greek words meaning "old" and "writing," paleography is a method of determining the date, origin, and authenticity of *manuscripts through a study of writing materials, styles of handwriting, inks, etc.

palilogy

Repetition of a word or phrase for the purpose of emphasizing it. *Palilogy,* from a Greek term meaning "speaking over again," is illustrated in this statement from the *Bible (Isaiah 38:19): "The living, the living, he shall praise thee."

palimpsest

A *parchment or other writing material from which the text has been erased or removed to make room for new writing. *Palimpsest,* from Greek words meaning "scraped again," is a term appearing often in the science of *paleography. See MANUSCRIPT.

palindrome

A word, sentence, or verse reading the same backward as forward: "civic"; "Madam, I'm Adam"; "Able was I ere I saw Elba." (See ACRONYM, ANAGRAM.) A palindrome is a word stunt not calculated to contribute to literature, but early in the eighteenth century an obscure English poet did write a revealing line: "Lewd did I live & evil I did dwel'."

palinode

A piece of writing that retracts something written earlier; a *recantation. A famous palinode is Chaucer's *Legend of Good Women,* in which the author "takes back" what he had earlier said about the unfaithfulness of women in poems such as *Troilus and Criseyde.*

pamphlet

A complete, unbound publication of less than 100 pages stitched or stapled together; a short *essay or *treatise, usually a controversial *tract, on some topic of contemporary interest. A famous pamphlet was John Milton's *Areopagitica,* an essay advocating freedom of the press. Thomas Paine's *Common Sense* was a pamphlet setting forth arguments for American independence from England. *The Federalist* (1787–1788) appeared as a series of eighty-five pamphlets written in support of the United States Constitution.

panache

Verve, swagger, flare. *Panache* is used in literature to describe an author's or character's flamboyant manner and grand style. Heroic and adventurous persons who act with self-confidence and assurance exhibit panache. George Bernard Shaw based much of his career upon panache; in other ways and with differing results so did F. Scott Fitzgerald, Thomas Wolfe, and Ernest Hemingway.

panegyric

An *oration, dignified speech, or written *composition praising someone or some achievement. A panegyric is a formal and elaborate commendation. (See ENCOMIUM, EULOGY.) The term *panegyric* has come to mean excessive flattery, such as that in a *blurb for a literary work or in the nominating speeches of politicians.

panel discussion

An organized exchange of ideas delivered before an *audience. In a panel discussion, a group of experts discusses a selected topic. In this phrase, *panel* refers to the group chosen to speak, a selection made from the general public.

Such discussions occur frequently on *television and radio programs.

pangram

An exercise (clause, *sentence, *composition) containing all the letters of the alphabet. *Pangram* comes from Greek words meaning "all" and "letters." See ALPHABET VERSE, LIPOGRAM.

panning

Photographing or televising while rotating a camera. In the process of panning, a camera is moved on its horizontal or vertical axis so as to keep a moving person or object in view or to photograph a *panorama.

panorama

(1) A wide view of an extensive area in all directions; (2) an extended pictorial representation of a landscape or other scene; (3) a continuously passing or changing scene; (4) a comprehensive survey.

Each of these four somewhat different meanings of *panorama* is embraced in the phrase *panoramic method,* which applies to (1) fiction in which plentiful *descriptions of place and person are given directly by the author and (2) any literary work that provides a sweeping, inclusive view of an age, *epoch, or event. Joseph Fielding and Sir Walter Scott provided much direct description in all their novels. *A Tale of Two Cities* (Dickens) and *War and Peace* (Tolstoi) are panoramic historical novels.

pantheism

The doctrine and belief that God is the entire universe or, put another way, that every part of the universe is a manifestation of God. *Pantheism* refers to any philosophical or religious concept that identifies God and the universe. Goethe, Wordsworth, and Emerson wrote several poems about pantheism; the following lines from Wordsworth's *Lines Composed a Few Miles Above Tintern Abbey* provide a poetic definition and explanation:

> ... And I have felt
> A presence that disturbs me with the joy
> Of elevated thoughts; a sense sublime
> Of something far more deeply interfused,
> Whose dwelling is the light of setting suns,
> And the round ocean and the living air,
> And the blue sky, and in the mind of man;
> A motion and a spirit, that impels
> All thinking things, all objects of all thought,
> And rolls through all things.

pantomime

(1) A play or entertainment in which performers express ideas and actions by movements only; (2) the art and *technique of conveying emotions or feelings by mute gestures. The name *pantomime* was originally given to ancient Roman actors in a *dumb show but later was attached to a performance itself, such as that in which a *harlequin appears. Pantomime appears in silent motion pictures, in Christmas entertainments and other *pageants, in *puppetry, and in stage plays when, at intervals, no *dialogue is spoken. See CHARADE, COMMEDIA DELL'ARTE, MIME.

pantoum

A Malay verse form consisting of an indefinite number of *quatrains (four-line *stanzas), with the second and fourth lines of each quatrain repeated as the first and third lines of the following stanza. Because the form results in rigidity and monotony, no outstanding English poetry is written in pantoum form, but the French writer Victor Hugo used it successfully in *Les orientales* early in the nineteenth century.

papier-mâché

A substance made of pulped paper or paper pulp mixed with glue and other materials, molded when moist to form various objects, and becoming hard and strong when dry. A term from French, *papier-mâché* as an adjective has come to mean "easily destroyed," "quickly discredited"; the term is sometimes applied to literary works considered false, pretentious, unsound, or illusory.

parabasis

A choral *ode in ancient Greek drama that was addressed to the audience. A parabasis was independent of the *action of the play itself.

parable

A story designed to convey some religious principle, moral lesson, or general truth. A parable always teaches by comparison with actual events (the situation that called forth the parable for illustration). In this sense, a parable is an *allegory and thus differs from some *apologues and *fables. Well-known examples of parables are those of the Biblical prodigal son and the good Samaritan.

paradigm

An example, a pattern. In *linguistics, *paradigm* refers to a set of forms, all of which contain a particular element, and to a display in fixed arrangement of such a set: *man, man's, men, men's; girl, girl's, girls, girls'*. In literature, *paradigm* is occasionally used as a *synonym for *model, ideal, standard,* and *paragon.* See PROTOTYPE.

paradox

(1) A statement apparently self-contradictory or absurd but really containing a possible truth; (2) a self-contradictory, false *proposition; (3) an opinion or statement contrary to generally accepted ideas. Shakespeare employed a paradox when he wrote, "Cowards die many times before their deaths." Wordsworth's comment "The child is father of the man" is a paradox. See EPIGRAM, HYPALLAGE, OXYMORON.

paragoge

The addition of a sound or group of sounds at the end of a word. Paragoge is illustrated in *righto* (for *right*), *boughten* (for *bought*), *lovèd* (for *loved*).

paragraph

A group of statements, of *sentences, developing a topic or idea; a distinct part of a *composition dealing with a particular subject. *Paragraph* sometimes refers to a note, item, or brief article in a newspaper. Clearly formed and developed paragraphs are an integral part of all effective prose; in poetry, *stanzas are a kind of paragraph.

paraleipsis

Also spelled *paralepsis* or *paralipsis, paraleipsis* is the suggestion, by abbreviated treatment, that much of significance is being omitted. Paraleipsis (from Greek terms meaning "leaving to one side") is illustrated by such phrases as "not to mention other . . . ," "overlooking," "and so forth."

parallelism

Arrangement of the parts of a *composition so that elements (parts) of equal importance are balanced in similar constructions. Such structural order applies to words, phrases, clauses, sentences, paragraphs, and complete units of compositions. From a Greek word meaning "beside one another," parallelism is a rhetorical device that has been used in all known literature of every *genre. The technique may be illustrated in this quotation from Psalm 19: "Day unto day uttereth speech, and night unto night showeth knowledge." See ANAPHORA, ANTITHESIS, BALANCED SENTENCE, ORDER.

paraphrase

Restatement of a passage giving the meaning in another form; rewording. From Greek terms meaning "beside" and "speech," paraphrase usually involves expanding the original text so as to make it clear. Many modern critics object to paraphrasing, but the activity is essential for everyone who wishes to absorb what he reads. Here, for example, is a paraphrase of Keats's *sonnet *On First Looking into Chapman's Homer:*

I have read widely in the great classics of literature and have noted many examples of superb poetry. I had often been told of the work of Homer and the poetry which he had created, but I never really understood or appreciated its beauty and power until I read Chapman's translation. Then I felt as awed as some astronomer who unexpectedly discovers a new planet, or as surprised and speechless as Cortez [Balboa] and his followers were when they saw the Pacific Ocean for the first time, from Panama.

parataxis

Placing together words, phrases, or clauses without connecting words: "I came, I saw, I conquered." *Parataxis* is derived from Greek terms meaning "arranging in order for battle," possibly a fitting origin for words in parataxis in the marriage ceremony: " . . . from this day forward, for better for worse, for richer for poorer. . . . "

parchment

The skin of sheep or goats prepared for use as material on which to write. *Parchment* is derived from the name of a city in Asia Minor where it was first used in pre-Christian times as a substitute for papyrus (thin strips of a plant so named, prepared for writing). See PALEOGRAPHY, VELLUM.

parenthesis

(1) A word, phrase, or clause inserted into a statement which is grammatically complete without it; (2) either or both of a pair of signs used to mark off explanatory or qualifying remarks. A parenthetic (or parenthetical) remark is one that interrupts a main statement but does not affect basic meaning. *Parenthesis,* from a Greek word meaning "put in beside," is often used to suggest an *interlude or interval. When one "adds a parenthesis," one makes an additional comment that does not materially alter what he has already said or written. Henry James, James Joyce, and William Faulkner have made extensive use of parenthetical material.

pari passu

A Latin phrase that means "with equal pace or progress." The phrase is used in English to suggest "side by side," "fairly," "without partiality."

parlance

A manner or way of speaking. *Parlance* is an approximate *synonym for *idiom and *vernacular: legal parlance, mountaineer parlance, etc. *Parlance,* an *archaism for *talk* and

parley, is sometimes used to refer to a formal discussion: dip-
lomatic parlance.

parlous

(1) An archaic word for *difficult, dangerous;* (2) clever,
shrewd. *Parlous* is frequently used as a syncopated variant of
perilous (these parlous times).

Parnassus

A mountain in central Greece, famed as the home of Apollo and
the Muses. *Parnassus* is sometimes used to refer to the world
of poetry and poets and to any center of artistic activity. It was
to the Parnassian world of literature that Dr. Johnson referred
in *The Rambler:* "Parnassus has its flowers of transient fragrance, as well as its oaks of towering height, and its laurels of
eternal verdure."

parody

Any humorous, satirical, or *burlesque imitation of a person,
event, or serious work of literature. Parody is designed to ridicule in nonsensical fashion or to criticize by clever duplication.
(See BURLESQUE, CARICATURE, LAMPOON, TRAVESTY.) Here is a
parody of Walt Whitman by a minor American poet, Bayard
Taylor:

> Everywhere, everywhere, following me;
> Taking me by the buttonhole, pulling off my boots,
>   hustling me with the elbows;
> Sitting down with me to clams and the
>   chowder-kettle;
> Plunging naked at my side into the sleek,
>   irascible surges;
> Soothing me with the strain that I neither
>   permit nor prohibit;
> Flocking this way and that, reverent, eager,
>   orotund, irrepressible;
> Denser than sycamore leaves when the
>   north-winds are scouring Paumanok;
> What can I do to restrain them? Nothing,
>   verily nothing.

paronomasia

An *archaism for *pun; the use of a word in different
senses or of words similar in sound to achieve *humor or a
double meaning. In John Donne's *Hymn to God the Father,*
paronomasia occurs in the use of *Son (sun)* and *done
(Donne):*

> . . . Swear by Thyself that at my death Thy Son
> Shall shine as he shines now and heretofore;
> And, having done that, thou hast done;
> I fear no more.

parrhesia

Boldness of speech; freedom of expression. Parrhesia, a kind of blunt frankness, is common in modern literature, especially in the use of plain talk for the physiological and sexual activities of men and women. See EUPHEMISM.

parsing

Describing a word (or series of words) grammatically. Parsing consists of telling the part of speech of a word, its forms, and its relations to other words. See CONJUGATION, DECLENSION.

passim

A Latin term meaning "here and there," "in various passages." *Passim* is used in *footnotes to indicate the *source and repetition of an idea or phrase scattered throughout a written work.

passion

(1) Any powerful, compelling feeling or emotion, such as love, desire, hate, fear, grief; (2) strong feeling, fondness, or enthusiasm for something; (3) strong sexual desire, lust. These lines from Robert Browning illustrate the meaning of *passion* as an intense emotion or mental agitation:

    ...Only I discern
    Infinite passion, and the pain
    Of finite hearts that yearn.

Hawthorne's comment in *The Scarlet Letter* (referring to Hester Prynne) illustrates all three of the meanings of *passion* listed above: "Let men tremble to win the hand of woman, unless they win along with it the utmost passion of her heart."

passion play

A dramatic presentation of the sufferings of Christ on the Cross or his anguish subsequent to the Last Supper. In Europe during *medieval times, many *mystery plays were called passion plays. A *drama dealing with the life, trial, crucifixion, and resurrection of Christ has been presented at intervals since the seventeenth century at Oberammergau, Germany.

pastiche

A literary or musical composition made up of scraps, parts, or *motifs of works from different sources. A pastiche is a medley, an incongruous combination of materials and forms, a hodgepodge. See CENTO, COLLAGE, PARODY.

pastoral

(1) A poem or other artistic *composition dealing with the life of shepherds or with simple rural existence; (2) a picture or work of art representing the life of shepherds; (3) simplicity, charm, and serenity such as those attributed to country life. *Pastoral,* from the Latin word *pastor* ("shepherd"), applies to any literary *convention that places kindly rural people in nature-centered activities. Milton's *Lycidas,* Spenser's *The Shep-*

heardes Calender, and Arnold's *Thyrsis* have pastoral qualities. (See BUCOLIC, ECLOGUE, GEORGIC.) A *pastorale* is a piece
of music (*opera, cantata) suggestive of country life. Pastoral
*drama, pastoral *elegies, and pastoral *romances are different
kinds of *compositions, each with rural settings and characters.

pastourelle
A lyrical debate in which a suitor of high rank (knight, scholar)
woos a shepherdess. Pastourelle, a French word implying a
dance movement, always follows the traditions of *courtly love
except that the maiden invariably remains virtuous regardless
of the outcome of this wooing game.

paternoster
The Lord's Prayer in Latin. *Pater noster* is Latin for "our father." The term applies to a recitation of this prayer as an act
of worship and to a certain bead in a rosary which indicates that
the Lord's Prayer should be said. *Paternoster* is now applied to
any statement or recital of words used as a prayer.

pathetic fallacy
Crediting inanimate objects with the emotions and traits of
human beings. The phrase was coined by John Ruskin (1819–
1900), an English author, who quoted the following lines from
a nineteenth-century English poem and then wrote:

> They rowed her in across the rolling foam—
> The cruel, crawling foam.
>
> The foam is not cruel, neither does it crawl. The
> state of mind which attributes to it these characters
> of a living creature is one in which the reason is
> unhinged by grief. All violent feelings have the
> same effect. They produce in us a falseness in all
> our impressions of external things, which I would
> generally characterize as the "pathetic fallacy."

Poetry and prose are filled with examples of what may be
called false emotionalism and impassioned *metaphors: cruel
sea, smiling skies, laughing waters, etc. Sense-making or not, the
pathetic fallacy can produce beautiful effects, as in Coleridge's
lines: "The one red leaf, the last of its clan / That dances as often
as dance it can." See BATHOS, PATHOS.

pathos
From a Greek word meaning "suffering," *pathos* refers to that
ability or power in literature (and other arts) to call forth feelings of pity, compassion, and sadness. In *King Lear,* Cordelia's
plight involves pathos, and she is therefore a pathetic figure, as
Ophelia in *Hamlet* and Little Nell in Dickens's *The Old Curiosity Shop* are. See BATHOS, EMPATHY, PATHETIC FALLACY.

patois
Rural or provincial forms of speech; the *dialect of common

people as distinguished from literary language. *Patois,* a term from French, is often used to refer to a mixture of two or more languages or is employed as a *synonym for *argot, *cant, or *jargon. See DIALECT.

patron

One who supports an artist (writer, musician, etc.), institution, charity, or the like with money, gifts, or endorsements. Patrons have provided influential and material support to many writers of the past and present.

patronym

From Greek words meaning "father" and "name," *patronym* refers to a family name formed with a *suffix or a *prefix to indicate descent (relationship). *Williamson* (son of William) is a patronym or patronymic word, as are *Macdonald* (son of Donald), *Fitzgerald* (son of Gerald), *Petrovich* (son of Peter), and O'Reilly (decendant of Reilly).

pattern

(1) A model, an *archetype, a guide; (2) a combination of qualities and tendencies that form a consistent and characteristic arrangement. For example, the five-act plays of ancient Greece and Rome provided a pattern for *Renaissance writers many centuries later. In the second meaning of *pattern,* the development of *action in an Elizabethan tragedy was arranged in a consistent and distinct order. In poetry, for another example, *pattern* is the verse form expressed through the sounds and movements of words, as well as their sense. See FORMULA, STRUCTURE.

patter song

A comic song depending upon rapid delivery. Patter songs, which appear often in Gilbert and Sullivan *operettas, depend upon clever wording and tricky musical phrasing, as in these lines from *H.M.S. Pinafore:*

> And so do his sisters, and his cousins,
>   and his aunts!
> His sisters and his cousins,
> Whom he reckons up by dozens,
> And his aunts!

pedagese

Educators' *gobbledygook; the *diction of some schoolmasters and professors. Pedagese is inflated language filled with *bombast and *jargon, found in the writings and speeches of professional educators and social scientists.

pedantry

Display of learning; slavish attention to rules and details; rigid adherence to book knowledge at the expense of common sense. *Pedantry* or *pedantic* is applied to writing that contains many *allusions, foreign phrases, quotations, and the like. In Shakespeare's *Love's Labour's Lost,* Holofernes, the village schoolmaster, is an incurable pedant who prides himself on the precision of his pronunciation and the excellence of his Latin. See PRECIOSITY.

Pegasus

In classical mythology, Pegasus was a winged horse reputedly sprung from Medusa's body at her death. The name has long been associated with poetry and poetic inspiration, perhaps because Pegasus is supposed to have opened the inspiring fountain of the *Muses with a stroke of its hoof. A well-known *anthology is entitled *The Winged Horse Anthology.* Poets have sometimes called on Pegasus as a *symbol and *source of poetic aid instead of on the Muses. See DIVINE AFFLATUS.

pejorative

Having a disparaging, deprecatory, belittling effect or force; sharply critical. From a Latin term meaning "made worse," *pejorative* appears often in *criticism as an adjective finding fault with, discrediting, or lowering the value of literary selections being reviewed. For instance, a pejorative term for *poet* is *poetaster* (an inferior poet). To speak of a novel as *contrived* is to speak pejoratively.

pen name

A *pseudonym; a *nom de plume; a name used by an author instead of his real name. The pen name of William Sidney Porter was O. Henry.

penny dreadful

A sensational novel of crime, adventure, or violence. The term is an *archaism even in England for cheap and morbid *melodrama. See DIME NOVEL, PULP MAGAZINE.

pentameter

A line of five metrical feet. (See METER.) Pentameter, from Greek words meaning "five" and "measure," is more widely used in poetry in English than any other length of line.

pentastich

A *stanza consisting of five lines. *Pentastich* is a *synonym of *cinquain. This song from Tennyson's *The Princess* is a pentastich:

> Dear as remembered kisses after death,
> And sweet as those by hopeless fancy feigned
> On lips that are for others; deep as love,
> Deep as first love, and wild with all regret;
> O Death in Life, the days that are no more!

penultimate

An adjective meaning "next to the last." The penultimate word in the preceding sentence is *the;* the penultimate syllable in *penultimate* is *ti.*

perfect rhyme

The identity of *sound in words pronounced the same or in which stressed vowels and following consonants are the same: *Pain, pane; rein, reign; bough, bow; line, fine.* See RHYME.

periodical

A publication issued at regularly recurring intervals. *Periodical* derives its name from *periodic* (recurring at intervals) and is applied to *magazines and *journals but not ordinarily to newspapers.

periodic sentence

A sentence that is not grammatically complete until the end, or nearly the end, of the sentence is reached. Writers often produce an effect of *suspense by holding back the termination of a main clause, as in this sentence by Bret Harte:

> And pulseless and cold, with a Derringer by his side and a bullet in his heart, though still calm as in life, beneath the snow lay he who was at once the strongest and yet the weakest of the outcasts of Poker Flat.

peripety

A sudden turn of events. *Peripety,* also spelled *peripeteia,* as in the original Greek, is a reversal of fortune for the *protagonist in *drama or *fiction. Aristotle gives as an example of peripety the scene in Sophocles's *Oedipus Rex* in which the First Messenger, believing he will free Oedipus from fear, does the exact opposite: the parents who have died, the messenger reports, were really Oedipus's foster parents. See ACTION, CATASTROPHE, CLIMAX, CRISIS.

periphrasis

A roundabout way of speaking or writing; *circumlocution; an indirect or abstract form of wordiness. Periphrasis, from Greek words meaning "about" and "speech," is illustrated by the use of "the answer is in the negative" for a simple "no." Examples of periphrasis appear in this excerpt from a letter to David Copperfield written by Micawber:

> Under these circumstances, alike humiliating to endure, humiliating to contemplate, and humiliating to relate, I have discharged the pecuniary liability contracted at this establishment, by giving a note of hand, made payable fourteen days after date, at my residence, Pentonville, London.

See CONCISENESS, GOBBLEDYGOOK, JARGON, PLEONASM, TAUTOLOGY.

peroration

The concluding part of a speech (or *composition) in which the speaker (or writer) sums up principal points and urges them upon his listeners (or readers) with force and earnestness. *Peroration* is usually applied to the rhetorical performance that ends a public address. See ELOCUTION, ELOQUENCE, ORATION.

per se

A phrase from Latin meaning "intrinsically," "by its very nature," "of, for, or in itself."

persiflage

Light, bantering talk; flippancy; raillery. A term from French, *persiflage* refers to the kind of jesting that appears in much of the dialogue in plays by such writers as Oscar Wilde and Noel Coward. For example, these comments in Wilde's *Lady Windermere's Fan* are persiflage:

> Nowadays we are all of us so hard up that the only pleasant things to pay are compliments. They're the only things we *can* pay.

> In this world there are only two tragedies. One is not getting what one wants, and the other is getting it.

persona

An invented person; a character in *drama or *fiction. *Persona,* a Latin word meaning "mask," is used in *Jungian psychology to refer to one's "public personality"—the façade or mask presented to the world but not representative of inner feelings and emotions. (See DRAMATIS PERSONAE.) In literary criticism, *persona* is sometimes used to refer to a person figuring in, for example, a poem, someone who may or may not represent the author himself.

personal essay

An informal *composition employing an intimate *style and an urbane, relaxed, conversational manner to deal with subject matter that at least in part is *autobiographical. See ESSAY, FAMILIAR ESSAY, INFORMAL ESSAY.

personification

A figure of speech in which *abstractions, animals, ideas, and inanimate objects are endowed with human form, character, traits, or sensibilities. In personification, an entirely imaginary creature or person also may be conceived of as representing an idea or object. A kind of *metaphor, personification is a frequent resource in poetry and occasionally appears in other types of writing as well. An exquisite example of personification appears in Keats's *Ode on a Grecian Urn,* in which a vase is referred to as a woodland recorder of events:

Sylvan historian, who canst thus express
A flowery tale more sweetly than our rhyme.

See ALLEGORY, APOSTROPHE, PATHETIC FALLACY, PROSO-
POPOEIA.

perspective

A word of several meanings, *perspective,* in literature, usually refers to an author's mental view, his faculty for seeing
all pertinent data (action, ideas, characters, etc.) in a meaningful relation. From Latin words meaning "to see
through," *perspective* applies to the state of one's ideas,
one's *point of view. For instance, Thomas Hardy had a
perspective on life that was fatalistic, gloomy, and pessimistic; Hemingway's perspective was that life is a combat between strength and weakness; Carl Sandburg's perspective
was a mixture of tolerance, humanitarianism, and anger.

persuasion

A form of *argumentation that is designed to convince,
arouse, attain a specific goal. Persuasion attempts to prevail
on listeners or readers to do something, to react positively,
and to bring such conviction that the recipient will think,
believe, and be moved to respond actively. Persuasion may
make use of the other *forms of discourse, but it usually
combines an appeal to emotions with an appeal to the
intellect. A common form of persuasion is the *oration (such
as Winston Churchill's speeches to the British people during
World War II) and the *pamphlet (such as the *tracts which
John Milton wrote advocating that divorce be granted on
grounds of incompatibility).

Petrarchan

A reference to Petrarch (1304–1374), an Italian scholar and
poet. *Petrarchan* is specifically applied to a form of the
*sonnet divided into an *octave and *sestet. (See ITALIAN
SONNET.) A Petrarchan *conceit is an exceptionally elaborate
and exaggerated comparison. (See CONCEIT.) Petrarchism, a
style introduced by the poet in his sonnets, is notable for its
formal perfection, grammatical complexity, and elaborate
*figurative language.

Philippic

A speech filled with angry accusations, denunciations, and
*invective. *Philippic* is a term derived from the orations of
Demosthenes (a fourth-century-B.C. Athenian statesman and
orator) that attacked King Philip II of Macedon (an ancient
country in the Balkan Peninsula) as an enemy of Greece.
See ORATION.

Philistine

A person indifferent to culture and refinement; a commonplace, conventional individual. *Philistine* was the name of one of the inhabitants of ancient Philistia, a country at constant war with the Israelites. Philistines were considered barbaric (see BARBARISM), rude, warlike, and uncouth. In an essay (*Sweetness and Light*) Matthew Arnold a century ago called persons hostile to culture and devoted to material prosperity Philistines. The word *Philistinism* now means an obsession with wealth and a contempt for "art, beauty, culture, or spiritual things."

philology

The scientific study of *language and *literature. Philology is often restricted to a study of the *language* of written records in order to determine their original forms, meanings, and authenticity. In this sense, a philologist is a specialist in *linguistics.

philosophy

Investigation of the principles and truths of knowledge, being, and conduct. *Philosophy,* from Greek words meaning "love of wisdom," is a broad term impossible to define fully and accurately, but it does involve critical (analytical) study of the basic principles, concepts, and tenets of various fields of knowledge, including *aesthetics, *epistemology, *logic, and *metaphysics. The term *natural philosophy* was once applied to the physical sciences, *moral philosophy* to the social sciences, and *metaphysical philosophy* to all other known branches of knowledge. In general terms, a philosopher is one who regulates his life, judgments, and speech in the light of reason; a philosophical person is one who tries to be rationally and sensibly calm and thoughtful at all times. See CYNICISM, HEDONISM, STOICISM.

philter (philtre)

A drug supposed to cause a person taking it to fall in love. *Philter,* from a Greek word meaning "to love," also applies to a magic draught or charm used for any purpose. In *Othello* (act 1, scene 2), speaking of Desdemona, Brabantio says to Othello:

> Damn'd as thou art, thou hast enchanted her;
> For I'll refer me to all things of sense,
> If she in chains of magic were not bound . . .
> . . . thou hast practiced on her with foul charms,
> Abus'd her delicate youth with drugs or minerals
> That weaken motion.

phoneme

A basic unit of *sound. A phoneme may be illustrated by the difference in sound and meaning of *pit* and *bit.* In *linguistics, a phoneme is any one of a small set of units by which *morphemes, *words, and *sentences are represented. See ALLOPHONE.

phonetics

The study and science of speech sounds: their production, transmission, and reception. Phonetics also involves the analysis, transcription, and classification of the *sounds of speech.

phonics

A method of teaching reading and pronunciation based upon the phonetic (sound) interpretation of spelling. (See PHONEME, PHONETICS.) *Phonics,* an *obsolete term for *phonetics,* is considered a singular (not plural) noun.

photocomposition

The technique of setting *type by means of a photocomposer. In photocomposition, as in *Linotype composition, a keyboard is manipulated by an operator "setting" from *copy, but each line of characters is photographed rather than produced directly (as in Linotype) in metal.

photogravure

Any of several processes for making an *intaglio plate from a photograph: an engraving is formed on a metal plate from which ink reproductions can be made. See GRAVURE, PRINTING.

phraseology

Manner of speaking, style of oral or written expression. *Phraseology* also refers to the language characteristic of a profession or group (legal phraseology) and is thus related to *argot and *jargon. One's phraseology is one's "way of saying or writing" whatever he wishes to communicate. See DICTION.

picaresque

A term applied to fiction in which adventures of a *rogue are narrated in humorous or satiric scenes. *Picaresque,* from a Spanish word meaning "knave" or "rascal," applies to *novels and *tales that depict in realistic detail the everyday lives of common people. A typical picaresque novel presents the life story of a rogue who makes his way more through his cunning than through hard work. *Gil Blas* is the best-known picaresque story in French; Defoe's *Moll Flanders* is the most famous in English.

pidgin

An auxiliary language; a form of oral communication between speakers of different languages. (See LINGUA FRANCA.) The word *pidgin,* possibly a corruption by Chinese of the word *business,* appears in the phrase *pidgin English,* a *jargon used in Chinese ports and elsewhere in the Far East.

pièce de résistance

A term from French referring to the principal dish of a meal or the main event, incident, or article of a series or group.

pied-à-terre

A small dwelling for temporary use. *Pied-à-terre*, a term from French literally meaning "foot on ground," usually refers to one's second home, especially a small apartment in a city maintained by a resident whose principal domicile is in the country or abroad.

Pindaric

A reference to Pindar, a fifth-century-B.C. Greek poet. Specifically, *Pindaric* refers to a form of *ode consisting of several divisions, each of which is composed of a *strophe and *antistrophe of identical form and a contrasting *epode. A Pindaric ode is also called "regular." (See COWLEYAN ODE, ODE.) A well-known Pindaric ode is John Dryden's *Alexander's Feast*.

pique

Irritation, resentment; a word from French.

pirated edition

An unauthorized *edition of a literary work. A pirated edition is usually a work stolen from one country and published in another. Every pirated work today is an infringement of *copyright, but before the establishment of international copyright conventions, publications often appeared in foreign countries without permission; for example, numerous eighteenth- and nineteenth-century English novels appeared in the United States in pirated editions.

pitch

Variations from high to low in the *sounds of an utterance. Depending upon the relative rapidity of the vibrations by which it is produced, *pitch* refers to the degree of height or depth of a vocal or musical tone. See INTONATION.

placebo

(1) Vespers of the office for the dead in *rituals of the Roman Catholic Church; (2) a substance given merely to satisfy a patient who supposes it to have medicinal value. *Placebo* is a term sometimes conferred upon light *novels, *Western and *mystery stories, and similar literary fare that is harmless in itself but usually without genuine value.

plagiarism

Literary theft. Plagiarism is taking or closely imitating the language and thoughts of another author and representing them as one's own. Plagiarism, from a Latin word meaning "kidnapper," ranges from inept *paraphrasing to outright theft. "Borrowing," wrote John Milton, "if it be not bettered by the borrower, among good authors is accounted plagiarie" [plagiarism]. See GHOST WRITER.

plainsong
Any simple, unadorned melody. In the *Oxford Dictionary of Music, plainsong* rhythm is referred to as "the free rhythm of speech, arising from the unmetrical nature of the words to be recited in unison—psalms, prayers, and the like." See CHANT.

plaint
A complaint; a poem expressing grief or sorrow. See COM-PLAINT, KEENING, LAMENT.

plangent
An adjective meaning "resounding loudly," "beating or dash-ing." *Plangent* has been used to describe the sound of bells and the sound and movement of waves. One English writer has referred to the "long, plangent ripple of the harp strings," and another has mentioned "plangent organ music."

platitude
A flat, dull, or trite remark. Derived from a French word mean-ing "flat," *platitude* is usually applied to statements made as though they were important. See BANALITY, BROMIDE, CLICHÉ, HACKNEYED, TRITENESS, TRUISM.

platonic
Entirely spiritual, free from sensual desire. The phrase *platonic love* refers to affection without sexual desire. Platonic criticism seeks the values of a literary work in its *extrinsic (external) qualities rather than in the work itself. See ARIS-TOTELIAN.

Platonism
The doctrines and teachings of Plato (427–347 B.C.), Greek philosopher, whose primary concern was with aspirations of the human spirit, with man's possibilities and destinies. In the *Dialogues,* Plato repeatedly urged mankind to seek and express ideas of justice, love, courage, friendship, and virtu-ous living. Platonism contends that physical objects are short-lived representations of unchanging ideas and that ideas alone provide true knowledge. Platonism also implies the immortality of the soul, which through a series of incar-nations (rebirths), has the power and ability to recall ideas and *images from one life to the next.

Platonism has had great appeal for many writers through the centuries, including Spenser (*Hymn in Honor of Beauty*), Ralph Waldo Emerson (essays and poems), and William Words-worth *(Ode on Intimations of Immortality from Recollec-tions of Early Childhood).*

plausibility

A term applied to characters, ideas, and events that are believable, that seem worthy of approval and acceptance. *Plausibility* refers to the appearance of truth; a plausible *characterization, *incident, conversation, or suggestion appears reasonable but is not necessarily entirely true or accurate. All worthy literary artists seek to produce work that is credible, no matter how imaginative it may be. See BELIEF, SUSPENSION OF DISBELIEF, VERISIMILITUDE.

play

A literary *composition in dramatic form intended to be presented on a stage by actors who assume identities, speak *dialogue, and perform *actions devised by an author. See DRAMA.

play-within-a-play

A segment of dramatized action (a miniature *drama) that is presented within the framework of a larger and longer *play. The principal *plots of such plays as Shakespeare's *The Taming of the Shrew* and Francis Beaumont's *The Knight of the Burning Pestle* are set within the framework of a play-within-a-play. A well-known example of this *form is the performance arranged for King Claudius in act 3, scene 2, of *Hamlet.* See FRAME STORY.

pleonasm

The use of more words than are necessary to express an idea. Pleonasm, from a Greek term meaning "to be or to have more than enough," may consist of needless repetition or the use of unnecessary words. See CONCISENESS, DEADWOOD, TAUTOLOGY, VERBIAGE.

plot

A plan or scheme to accomplish a *purpose. In literature, *plot* refers to the arrangement of events to achieve an intended effect. A plot is a series of carefully devised and interrelated *actions that progresses through a struggle of opposing forces (*conflict) to a *climax and a *denouement. A plot is different from a *story or story line (the order of events as they occur). This distinction has been made clear by E. M. Forster, the English novelist:

> We have defined a story as a narrative of events arranged in their time sequence. A plot is also a narrative of events, the emphasis falling on a causality [see CAUSE AND EFFECT]. "The king died and then the queen died" is a story. "The king died, and then the queen died of grief" is a plot.

plurisignation

The result of using words with multiple meanings and thus producing differing lines of thought and understanding. (See AMBIGUITY.) Plurisignation, from Latin words meaning "several distinguishing marks," is a standard means of achieving *irony. See DOUBLE ENTENDRE, OXYMORON, PARADOX.

poem

A *composition in *verse that is characterized by a highly developed artistic *form, the use of *rhythm, and the employment of heightened language to express an imaginative interpretation of a situation or idea. See POETRY, VERSE.

poesy

An *archaism for *poetry. *Poesy* refers to the *techniques and art of poetic *composition in general. In *The Defence of Poesy* (1595), Sir Philip Sidney defended poetry (and all imaginative literature) against its attackers.

poetaster

An inferior poet. A poetaster is a versifier, a dabbler, a *dilettante in verse. The *suffix *-aster* is a Latin term denoting anything that merely apes the true thing or that imperfectly resembles it.

poète maudit

A term from French meaning "poet accursed," "a miserable poet." A poet who considers himself surrounded, as Shelley did, by "a hellish society of men," feels that he is an outcast and that his imaginative powers and sensitivity are a *curse rather than a blessing.

poetic diction

Words selected for their supposedly poetic quality; *diction somewhat different from that of ordinary speech and *prose. In his *Poetics,* Aristotle wrote that poets should use *metaphors, unusual words, and various stylistic ornaments. Just what is—or should be—considered poetic diction has been argued for centuries, but since early in the nineteenth century, such words as *whilom, oft, perchance, thrice, eftsoons,* etc., have appeared less and less frequently. Wordsworth once announced his intention of "fitting to metrical arrangement a selection of the *real language* of men in a state of vivid sensation." Poets of the twentieth century have generally denied differences between the language of poetry and that of prose or speech; current tendencies are to permit in poetry the widest possible range in vocabulary.

poetic justice

An ideal distribution of rewards and punishments. The phrase was first used in the seventeenth century to express the notion that in literature (as not always in life) the good should be rewarded and the evil punished. The word *poetic* does not imply that the concept refers only to poetry; rather it refers to the Greek term from which *poetic* was derived: "a maker," that is, any writer of verse or prose. As generally understood, poetic justice applies to the logical and thoroughly motivated outcome of a play, novel, or narrative poem, even though evil seems temporarily rewarded and good meets with defeat or disaster. In *The Dunciad,* Pope wrote:

> Poetic Justice, with her lifted scale,
> Where, in nice balance, truth with gold she
> weighs,
> And solid pudding against empty praise.

poetic license

Liberty taken by a writer (poet, novelist, dramatist, essayist, etc.) to produce a desired effect by deviating from conventional *form, established rules, and even fact and *logic. For example, any writer (and especially a poet) may claim the "license" to depart from normal word order (see INVERSION), to employ *archaisms, to use—and overuse—*figurative language, to employ *cadence and *rhythm to degrees not found in ordinary speech, etc. The greatest poets do not permit liberty to become license and rarely indulge in breaches of idiom, grammar, and pronunciation (for the sake of *rhyme).

poetic prose

Ordinary spoken and written language (*prose) that makes use of *cadence, *rhythm, *figurative language, or other devices ordinarily associated with *poetry. (See POLYPHONIC PROSE.) Novelists, essayists, and short-story writers occasionally use a short passage of poetic prose to achieve a special effect. Such *composition is somewhat rarer now than it was in earlier centuries, but it occasionally appears in current or recent literature. Note, for example, the cadence and rhythm, the *diction, and the word repetition in this opening paragraph from Ernest Hemingway's *In Another Country:*

> In the fall the war was always there, but we did not go to it any more. It was cold in the fall in Milan and the dark came very early. Then the electric lights came on, and it was pleasant along the streets looking in the windows. There was much game hanging outside the shops, and the snow powdered in the fur of the foxes and the wind blew their tails. The deer hung stiff and heavy and empty, and small birds blew in the wind and the wind turned their feathers. It was a cold fall and the wind came down from the mountains.

poetics

(1) Literary *criticism dealing with *poetry; (2) a *treatise

(treatment) of poetry; (3) the study of *prosody (meter, versification). *Poetics* is an *archaism, a disused term for the art and *technique of poetry. (See POESY.) However, Aristotle's *Poetics,* possibly the most influential work ever written on poetry, has remained a *bible for critics and writers for more than twenty centuries.

poet laureate

A poet appointed for life as an officer of the royal household in Great Britain. A poet laureate was formerly expected to compose verse for state occasions, but for a century now the title has been largely a mark of distinction for a writer recognized as eminent or representative. (See LAUREATE.) The first poet laureate officially recognized in England was Ben Jonson (1573–1637), but the specific title was first given to John Dryden (1631–1700). Among poets laureate have been Wordsworth, Tennyson, Alfred Austin, Robert Bridges, and John Masefield.

poetry

(1) Literary work in metrical form or patterned language; (2) the art of rhythmical *composition, written or spoken, designed to produce pleasure through beautiful, elevated, imaginative, or profound thoughts. Poetry cannot really be defined because it involves many differing aspects of subject matter, form, and effect; here are a few of many thousands of attempts to explain what poetry is and does:

> Poetry is the record of the best and happiest moments of the best and happiest minds.
>
> Shelley

> Poetry ... a criticism of life under the conditions fixed for such a criticism by the laws of poetic truth and beauty.
>
> Matthew Arnold

> Poetry is the imaginative expression of strong feeling, usually rhythmical ... the spontaneous overflow of powerful feelings recollected in tranquillity.
>
> Wordsworth

> ... the poetry of words [is] the rhythmical creation of beauty. Its sole arbiter is taste. ... Unless incidentally, it has no concern whatever either with duty or with truth.
>
> Poe

> Poetry is language that tells us, through a more or less emotional reaction, something that cannot be said.
>
> Edwin Arlington Robinson

> ... the rhythmic, inevitably narrative, movement from an overclothed blindness to a naked vision.
>
> Dylan Thomas

All poetry may be called verse, but not all *verse is poetry. Like poetry, verse is patterned language. These lines consist of words arranged in a *pattern:

Here lies the body of Jonathan Blank:
He dropped a match in a gasoline tank.

Such verse is metrical and rhythmical, but it is not poetry because it does not contain the high and genuine thought, the imagination, and the deep emotion of true poetry. See DOGGEREL.

point of view

(1) A specified position or method of consideration and appraisal; (2) an attitude, judgment, or opinion. In literature, *point of view* has several special meanings: (1) *physical* point of view has to do with the position in time and space from which a writer approaches, views, and describes his material; (2) *mental* point of view involves an author's feeling and attitude toward his subject; (3) *personal* point of view concerns the relation through which a writer narrates or discusses a subject, whether first, second, or third person.

In *personal* point of view, several arrangements are possible. If a writer assumes the point of view of a character, he becomes an "author participant" and usually writes in the first person. This is the point of view of Defoe's Robinson Crusoe, who, as author, relates what happened to him and reveals his own feelings in his own words. If the writer adopts the point of view of a minor character, he becomes an "author observant" who sits on the sidelines and reports the story. In several of Conrad's stories (for example, *Heart of Darkness*), the narrator observes more than he participates. When an author selects an impersonal point of view and detaches himself completely, he becomes Godlike, an "author omniscient." He sees all, hears all, knows all; his all-seeing eye can focus wherever he pleases; he can see into the minds of characters, and even report everyone's innermost thoughts. Thackeray's *Vanity Fair* is written from an omniscient point of view. See OMNISCIENCE.

In lengthy works of fiction, writers sometimes employ combinations of these methods (points of view).

polarization

This term from science has been extended to mean concentration of interests or forces upon two contrasting or conflicting opinions. *Polarization* implies the presence or manifestation of two opposite attitudes, principles, tendencies, or *points of view. The question of slavery polarized the United States in the 1850s and 1860s. The contrasting views of romantic and realistic novelists constitute a type of polarization. Attitudes toward war and peace have been polarizing influences for many centuries.

polemics
The art and practice of *argumentation; controversy; debate. *Polemics,* from a Greek word meaning "hostile" or "opposed," especially applies to arguments in church circles designed to refute errors of belief (see ORTHODOXY). Noted polemicists in literature include John Milton, Jonathan Swift, Martin Luther, Jean-Jacques Rousseau, John Calvin, Patrick Henry, John C. Calhoun, Upton Sinclair, Lewis Mumford, and Norman Mailer.

poltergeist
A ghost or spirit. A poltergeist, from German words meaning "noise ghost," purportedly indicates its mischievous presence by knockings, rappings, and other noises. See APPARITION.

polyphonic prose
Prose which exhibits such devices of poetry as *alliteration, *assonance, *cadence, and *rhythm. *Polyphonic* is derived from Greek words meaning "many-voiced." See POETIC PROSE.

polysyllabication
Words of three, four, or more syllables. (See FINE WRITING, PEDAGESE, PEDANTRY.) Polysyllabic rhyme is the rhyming of the last three or more syllables of two words (*mechanical, tyrannical*). Polysyllabic humor consists of using long words for amusing effects: *terminological inexactitude* for *lie.* Charles Dickens used polysyllabic humor in much of his work.

popular ballad
An uncomplicated, short, story-telling *poem intended for oral recitation or singing. (See BALLAD, FOLK BALLAD.) One scholar (F. B. Gummere) has said of the popular ballad that it is "impersonal in material, probably connected in its origins with the communal dance, but submitted to a process of oral tradition among people who are free from literary influences and fairly homogeneous in character." In certain sections of the United States, especially in the southern Appalachian Mountains, popular ballads that originated in England and Scotland are still known and sung. See ORAL TRANSMISSION.

pornography
Obscene literature, art, or photography. The term is derived from Greek elements meaning "writing about harlots." Pornography is as old as writing, but little of it possesses literary merit. See CENSORSHIP, OBSCENITY, VULGARITY.

portentous
Significant, momentous. In literature, *portentous* is usually applied to events that are ominously indicative of future happenings or to occurrences that are amazing, marvelous, and either prodigious or threatening. The encounter of Macbeth and the witches was a portentous event. Also portentous was the seduc-

tion of Roberta Alden by Clyde Griffiths in Theodore Dreiser's *An American Tragedy.*

portmanteau word

A term made by putting together parts of other words. (See COINAGE, NEOLOGISM.) *Portmanteau,* from French words meaning "to carry" and "cloak," is the English name of a trunk or suitcase that opens into two halves. Lewis Carroll, who applied the term *portmanteau word* to expressions he invented, had in mind "two meanings packed up into one word," as Humpty Dumpty explained to Alice in *Through the Looking-Glass.* Portmanteau words concocted by Lewis Carroll included *slithy* (*lithe* and *slimy*) and *frumious* (*fuming* and *furious*). In *Finnegans Wake,* James Joyce used numerous portmanteau words, such as *bisexcycle* and *ordinailed ungles.*

portrayal

(1) Graphic *description; (2) dramatic representation. *Portrayal,* which comes from Latin words meaning "to draw forth," "to depict," refers to the portrait (*characterization) of individuals presented in literary selections and also to the performance of an actor who plays (interprets) the role of a stage character.

positivism

A philosophical system concerned with facts only, excluding speculation about ultimate causes. Positivism concentrates on man and his human condition and ignores spirituality, theology, and *metaphysics. (See HUMANISM, to which positivism is closely related.) A leading positivist in English literature was John Stuart Mill.

post hoc

A Latin phrase meaning "after this," "afterward." The expression in full is *post hoc, ergo propter hoc,* meaning "after this, therefore because of it." The phrase refers to an error in thinking: accepting as a cause something that occurred earlier in time but may have no bearing upon the present situation. See LOGIC.

potboiler

A mediocre literary work produced solely for financial gain; a task performed to keep the pot boiling, that is, to eat. See GRUB STREET, HACK.

potpourri

A mixture of unrelated objects, extracts, or subjects. *Potpourri* is derived from two French words meaning "rotten pot," a phrase in turn from Spanish words meaning "a highly seasoned stew." A potpourri is a collection of miscellaneous literary extracts or items. See CHRESTOMATHY, COMMONPLACE BOOK, FARRAGO.

poulter's measure

A rarely used metrical pattern consisting of a *couplet with one
line in iambic *hexameter (six feet) and one line in iambic
*heptameter (seven feet). The term was derived from a former
practice of poulterers (dealers in chickens and eggs) of giving
twelve eggs in the first dozen bought and fourteen in the second. This *couplet from an obscure poem by a minor poet
illustrates the pattern:

> There is / beyond / the Alps, / a town /
> of an/cient fame,
> Whose bright / renown / yet shin/eth clear, /
> Veron/a men / it name.

pragmatism

A philosophical movement emphasizing practical consequences and values. Pragmatism stresses utility and practicality. A major advocate of pragmatism (which in Greek meant
"deed" or "business") was the American psychologist and
philosopher William James, who wrote, "The 'whole meaning'
of a conception expresses itself in practical consequences,
consequences either in the shape of conduct to be recommend-
ed, or in that of experience to be expected." James, John
Dewey, and many other pragmatists have held that living is
more important than logical thinking and that thought should
aim not so much at discovering final truths as at satisfying practical ends. Pragmatism has been influential in the development
of *realism in modern literature throughout the world.

preamble

An introductory statement; a *preface; an *introduction.
Preamble, from Latin words meaning "walking before," applies to any introductory portion of a written *document that
states the reasons for, and explains the purpose of, what follows.
The best-known preamble in the United States is that which
sets forth the principles of American government: "We the
people of the United States, in order to form a more perfect
Union. . . . "

precept

A direction or commandment given as a rule of conduct. A
precept is a *maxim, a concise, practical bit of advice concerning moral or ethical behavior. Polonius's suggestion to his son
Laertes in *Hamlet* is a precept: "Neither a borrower nor a
lender be." Benjamin Franklin wrote scores of precepts, such
as "Never leave that till tomorrow which you can do today";
"Keep thy shop and thy shop will keep thee"; "Eat not to dullness; drink not to elevation." See ADAGE.

preciosity

Excessive refinement in *language, *taste, or *style. Preciosity, a term applied to consciously fastidious work, is a kind of *fine writing; *Euphuism is also roughly synonymous. These lines from Pope's *The Rape of the Lock,* exhibit preciosity for the purpose of ridiculing it (see BURLESQUE, MOCK EPIC, MOCK HEROIC):

> From silver spouts the grateful liquors glide,
> While China's earth receives the smoking tide.

(Hot coffee is poured from silver pots into china cups.) See PURPLE PROSE.

précis

A short *summary of the essential ideas of a larger *composition. A précis (the form is both singular and plural) is the basic thought of a passage, reproduced in miniature and retaining something of the *mood and *tone of the original. (See ABRIDGMENT.) This statement by Henry Fielding is followed by a précis:

> But as for the bulk of mankind, they are clearly devoid of any degree of taste. It is a quality in which they advance very little beyond a state of infancy. The first thing a child is fond of in a book is a picture, the second is a story, and the third a jest. Here then is the true Pons Asinorum which very few readers ever get over. (69 words)

> Most people lack taste; they remain childlike. Readers, like children, rarely ever get over the "bridge of asses" constituted by pictures, stories, and jokes. (24 words)

predestination

*Fate, destiny, determination in advance. *Predestination,* from Latin words meaning "to appoint beforehand," is usually applied to the belief that events are decreed by God before they occur. *Calvinism held that God predestined certain souls (persons) as "elect" and therefore chosen to go to heaven, others as "damned" and headed for hell. See DETERMINISM, FORESHADOWING, NATURALISM.

preface

A preliminary statement, an introductory part of a longer work. *Preface,* from Latin meaning "a saying before," is usually applied to introductory remarks by the author or editor of a book, mentioning *purpose and scope and offering thanks to others for assistance rendered. See EXORDIUM, FOREWORD, INTRODUCTION, PREAMBLE, PROLEGOMENON, PROLOGUE, PROTASIS.

prefix

An *affix; an element (usually a *syllable) placed before another word or part of a word. Every prefix added to a *word, *stem, or *combining form qualifies or adds to meaning. Knowledge of the existence and meanings of some of the hundreds of prefixes in English words is of enormous value to readers in quickly getting at the sense of unfamiliar words. Following is a list of fifty common prefixes (some of which may be called *combining forms) together with one or more of several approximate meanings for each and suggested illustrative words:

a-	not	amoral, anonymous
ad-	to, against	adverse, adjective
ambi-	around, both	ambiguous, ambidextrous
ante-	before	antedate, anteroom
anti-	opposite	antisocial, antiwar
audio-	hearing	audio-visual, audition
auto-	self, same	autograph, autobiography
bene-	well, good	beneficial, benefit
bi-	two, twice	biannual, bifocal
bio-	life	biography, biology
circum-	about, around	circumstance, circumflex
co-	complement of	comaker, cosigner
col-	together	collateral, collection
com-	in association	combine, compare
cross-	against	crosscut, crosstown
de-	away, down, from	demerit, degrade
dis-	apart, not, away	disbar, disability
ec- (ex-)	from, out of	eccentric, eclectic
en- (em-)	in, on, into	enact, empower
epi-	upon, before	epigram, epilogue
ex-	out of, from	exclaim, excommunicate
extra-	beyond, without	extrajudicial, extrasensory
hemi-	half	hemisphere, hemiplegia
hyper-	beyond the ordinary	hypercritical, hypersensitive
il-	not	illogical, illegitimate
im-	opposed, negative	immoral, imbalance
inter-	among, between	interdepartmental, intercollegiate
intra-	within	intramural, intravenous
ir-	not, opposed	irreligious, irreducible
meta-	along with, among	metaphysics, metamorphism
mono-	one, alone	monochrome, monologue
neo-	new, recent	neophyte, neolithic
non-	not	nonpayment, noninterference
para-	beside	paragraph, parachute
per-	through, thoroughly	pervert, perfect
peri-	about, beyond	perimeter, perigee
poly-	many	polygon, polysyllable
post-	behind, after	postscript, postgraduate

pro-	for, forward	proclivity, proceed
pseudo-	false	pseudoclassic, pseudonym
re-	backward, again	revert, return
retro-	backward	retrogress, retroactive
semi-	half	semidetached, semicolon
sub-	under, from below	subterranean, sublime
super-	above, beyond	supernatural, supersensitive
syn-	together, with	synthesis, syndrome
tel- (tele-)	distant	telegraph, telecast
trans-	across, beyond	transcend, transmit
ultra-	beyond, in excess of	ultrared, ultrasonic
un-	not, reverse of	unfair, unbend

prelude

A preliminary; in literature, a brief poem preparatory to a longer one. In music, a prelude is a short, independent *composition for instruments. James Russell Lowell's lengthy verse *parable *The Vision of Sir Launfal* is in two extended parts, each with a prelude. See EPILOGUE, PROLOGUE.

premise

A *proposition (statement) supporting, or helping to support, a conclusion. A premise is an assumption, a basis on which reasoning proceeds. (See LOGIC, SYLLOGISM.) For example, in writing *A Connecticut Yankee in King Arthur's Court,* Mark Twain started with the premise that knighthood and medieval chivalry are forms of childish *barbarism. His novel satirically exposes the abuses of *feudalism and reveals his own conclusions about democracy.

Pre-Raphaelite

One of a group of young English writers and artists who, about 1850, united to resist *conventions in literature and art and sought to revive the style and spirit of Italian artists before the time of Raphael (1483–1520). Pre-Raphaelite poetry, such as that of Dante Gabriel Rossetti and William Morris, exhibits sensuousness, archaic *diction, *symbolism, and elaborate attention to the physical details of nature.

presentiment

An impression or feeling of something about to happen. *Presentiment,* a noun, is closely related to *portentous.* See FORESHADOWING.

preternatural

Exceptional, abnormal, out of the ordinary course of nature. A *popular ballad or *fairy tale usually involves preternatural happenings. See SUPERNATURALISM.

prima facie

At first view, at first appearance. *Prima facie,* a Latin

phrase, is used to mean plain, clear, self-evident, or obvious. In law, prima facie evidence, unless rebutted, is grounds for belief sufficient to establish a fact.

primary source

A source is any place or thing from which something comes or is obtained. A primary source is one that is of first, direct, and immediate importance. In literary scholarship, a primary source refers to a person with firsthand knowledge, a manuscript written at the time or on the scene of the subject being studied, a recorded contemporary conversation, etc. For example, a primary source for a biographer of Thomas Jefferson would be written comments about him by such contemporaries as George Washington and Benjamin Franklin. See SECONDARY SOURCE.

primer

An elementary book; an introductory book of first principles. *Primer* was originally a name for prayer books or religious manuals; the first book printed in the American colonies was such a primer, *The Bay Psalm Book* (1640). See ABECEDARIUM.

primeval

A term referring to the first age, or ages, of the world. *Primeval* applies to any form of existence or life from the beginnings and thus has the meaning of "first formed." In *Evangeline,* Longfellow refers to "the forest primeval," and, in an introduction to a historical work on America *(Pioneers of France in the New World),* Francis Parkman wrote:

> A boundless vision grows upon us: an untamed continent; vast wastes of forest verdure; mountains silent in primeval sleep; river, lake, and glimmering pool; wilderness oceans mingling with the sky.

primitivism

Belief that the qualities of early cultures are superior to those of contemporary civilization. The doctrine of primitivism flourished in eighteenth- and early nineteenth-century France and England. Rousseau attacked French life and society as artificial and corrupt and urged a return to nature; Wordsworth and William Blake in England exhibited strong traces of primitivism in their poetry. A concept of the noble savage produced an idealized American Indian, depicted many times in the *Leatherstocking Tales* of James Fenimore Cooper. Elements of primitivism, related to the natural goodness of man and the "essential" evils of civilization, have persisted up to the present. See REALISM, ROMANTICISM.

primus inter pares

A Latin term meaning "first among equals." The president of a republic, such as the United States, may be referred to as *primus inter pares.*

printing

The *technique, or art, of causing an *image to be transferred to a surface regardless of the method used. These methods carry different names (relief, letterpress, intaglio, planographic, stencil) depending upon the type of printing plate or other material containing the image to be printed, the way of forming the image on the plate or material, and the method by which the image is transferred to a surface. See BAS-RELIEF, BLOCK PRINTING, GRAVURE, LETTERPRESS, OFFSET PROCESS, TYPOGRAPHY, XEROGRAPHY.

probability

In literature, *probability* refers to the likelihood of *belief. See CHARACTERIZATION, CREDIBILITY, MOTIVATION, PLAUSIBILITY, VERISIMILITUDE.

problem novel, play

In all narrative literary works, a problem deals with the choices of action open to characters involved or to society at large. Thus a problem novel or problem play depicts characters in a state of *conflict, a statement true of every worthwhile piece of fiction or drama. In a narrower sense, a problem novel or play suggests a thesis. *Uncle Tom's Cabin* is a problem novel not only because of conflicts faced by its characters but also because its *purpose was to reveal the injustices of slavery. Arthur Miller's *Death of a Salesman* deals with problems faced by Willy Loman, his wife, and his sons, but it is a problem play in that it is concerned with what the author considers false values in society. Other problem novels and plays which both develop conflict and reveal a thesis are Remarque's *All Quiet on the Western Front,* Steinbeck's *The Grapes of Wrath,* Galsworthy's *Justice,* and Clifford Odets's *Waiting for Lefty.* See PROPAGANDA, THEME, THESIS.

prochronism

A chronological error; a detail in literature that precedes its occurrence in history. *Prochronism* is a synonym of *anachronism and of one of the meanings of *prolepsis.

Procrustean

A reference to Procrustes, a robber who, in classical mythology, stretched or cut off the limbs of victims to make them conform to the length of his bed. *Procrustean* suggests any attempt to shape men's thinking by arbitrary or violent means. The brainwashing of military or political prisoners described in several novels of recent years is Procrustean.

proem

A brief introduction. A proem is closely related in meaning to
*preface and *preamble but is usually applied only to an intro-
ductory discourse of a longer poem.

profanity

Originally, *profanity* applied to irreverence or contempt for
sacred ideas and principles. The term now usually refers to
*language that is considered vulgar, coarse, obscene, or blas-
phemous. See VULGARITY.

profile

A term generally referring to an outlined view, especially the
human face viewed from one side. In literature, profile is a form
of writing which combines biographical material with character
interpretation. A profile offers a *silhouette, a partial view,
rather than a rounded portrait of a subject and bears somewhat
the relation to a full-length *biography that a *short story does
to a *novel. See PSYCHOGRAPH.

prolegomenon

A preliminary discussion, an introductory essay. *Prolegomenon*
is a synonym for *prologue, especially one that is learned and
lengthy.

prolepsis

A figure of speech in which an expected event is referred to as
though it had already occurred: Hamlet, wounded, exclaims,
"Horatio, I am dead." Prolepsis is also a rhetorical device in
*argumentation: anticipating and answering an opponent's ob-
jections. The term additionally may refer to the assigning of an
event or person to a period earlier than the actual one and in
this meaning is a synonym of *anachronism and *prochronism.

proletarian

A reference to the proletariat, that is, unpropertied classes who
must sell their labor to survive. *Proletarian* is derived from a
Latin term naming a Roman citizen who contributed to the
state only through bearing children (*proles*). A proletarian novel or play is one that portrays distressing social and economic
conditions among working classes. See PROPAGANDA; SOCIO-
LOGICAL NOVEL, PLAY; THESIS.

prolixity

The use of excessive detail; a characteristic of writing that extends to tedious and unnecessary length. Prolixity is a synonym
of *verbosity. See CONCISENESS.

prologue

The opening section of a longer work. In ancient Greek tragedy, a prologue was the part of a *play that set forth the subject

of the *drama before the *chorus entered. The term is now used to refer to the *preface or introductory part of a *novel, long *poem, or play. In his Prologue to *The Canterbury Tales,* Chaucer provides a background and *setting for what is to follow as well as detailed *sketches of the characters who are to appear. The first part of Shakespeare's *Henry IV* opens with an explanatory speech; the second part begins with a prologue called an induction. See EPILOGUE.

prompt copy, prompter

A prompt copy is the script (text) of a play containing notes and *cues. Also called a prompt book, such a copy is used by the director or stage manager or a prompter, who follows a play in progress, repeating missed cues and supplying actors with forgotten lines.

proof

A term of several meanings, in literature *proof* usually refers to (1) *evidence sufficient to establish something as true or to produce belief in an action or character; (2) a trial impression from a printing surface taken for inspection and correction. See FOUNDRY PROOF.

proofreaders' marks

	Delete		*lc*	lowercase Word
	Delete and close up		*cap*	Capital letter
□	Quad (one cm) space		*sc*	SMALL CAPITAL LETTER
⊔	Move down		*bf*	**Boldface type**
⊓	Move up		*ital*	*Italic type*
⊏	Move to left		*rom*	Roman type
⊐	Move to right		*wf*	Wrong font
eq #	Equalize spacing between words		#	Insert space
×	Broken letter		⌒	Close up
⁋	Begin a new paragraph		♻	Turn letter
no ⁋	No new paragraph		⊙	Period
stet	Let type stand as set		⌃	Comma
?	Verify or supply information		⌄	Apostrophe
tr	Transpose letters or marked words		⌄/⌄	Quotation marks
sp	Spell out (abbrev) or (2)		;/	Semicolon
⌣	Push space down		⊙	Colon
=	Straighten type		?/	Question mark
‖	Align type		!/	Exclamation mark
run in	Run in material on same line		=/	Hyphen
bu	Change (x/y) to built-up fraction		⊥/⊥	En dash
sh	Change x/y to shilling fraction		⊥/⊥	Em dash
⌃	Set 5 as subscript		⊥	Two-em dash
⌄	Set 5 as exponent		(/)/ ( )	Parentheses
			[/]/ [ ]	Brackets

proofreading

The close reading of printer's *proof and *copy in order to detect and mark errors to be corrected.

prop

An item of furniture, an ornament, or a decoration in a

stage *setting; any object handled or used by an actor in a performance. *Prop,* an abbreviation of *property,* refers to any physical object used in a stage presentation other than the stage itself, costumes of the actors, and lighting effects.

propaganda

Information, ideas, or rumors spread to help or harm a person, group, movement, belief, institution, or nation. The term *propaganda* originally referred to a committee of cardinals established early in the seventeenth century by the Roman Catholic Church with supervision over the training of priests for work in foreign missions. *Propaganda* is now applied to any literary work, scheme, or association for influencing opinion in political, social, religious, ethical, economic, or other matters. A propaganda (or propagandistic) *play or *novel seeks to advance particular doctrines or principles, such as, for instance, the novels of Upton Sinclair in their advocacy of socialism. Propaganda is attacked by most critics and general readers because it is an attempt to influence opinions and actions deliberately, but by this definition all education and most literature are propagandistic. See PROBLEM NOVEL, PLAY; SOCIOLOGICAL NOVEL, PLAY; THESIS.

proportion

In literature, *proportion* refers to the relation between parts of a *composition. In writing, *proportion* is usually applied to the length and emphasis of *paragraphs, chapters, and main parts of a work. See COHERENCE, ORGANIZATION, SYMMETRY.

proposition

(1) A plan, scheme, or suggestion; (2) a statement of the subject of an argument (see ARGUMENTATION, PERSUASION); (3) a statement in which something is affirmed or denied, that is, a *premise. The first of these three definitions is illustrated in this remark by Celia in Shakespeare's *As You Like It:* "It is as easy to count atomies [specks in a sunbeam] as to resolve the propositions of a lover." The second definition is explained in Francis Bacon's remark in his essay *Of Cunning:* "It is a good point . . . for a man to shape the answer he would have in his own words and propositions." The beginning of Abraham Lincoln's Gettysburg Address illustrates the third definition: "Fourscore and seven years ago our fathers brought forth on this continent a new nation, conceived in liberty, and dedicated to the proposition that all men are created equal."

proscenium

That part of the stage in a modern theater which lies between the orchestra and the curtain. A proscenium arch is a decorative structure that separates a stage from an auditorium. *Proscenium* is often used as a *synonym for the stage itself. See APRON.

prose

The ordinary form of spoken and written language. The term *prose* applies to all expression in language that does not have a regular rhythmic pattern. Coleridge offered a helpful definition: "I wish our clever young poets would remember my homely definitions of prose and poetry: that is, prose—words in their best order; poetry—the best words in their best order." A surprised character in Molière's *Bourgeois Gentleman* remarks, "Good Heavens! For more than forty years I have been speaking prose without knowing it." See POETIC PROSE, POLYPHONIC PROSE.

prosody

The science and study of *versification. The term *prosody*, from Greek words meaning "modulation of voice" and "song sung to music," involves such topics as *accent, *meter, *rhyme, *rhythm, and *stanza form. See SCANSION.

prosopopoeia

Representation of an imaginary, absent, or dead person as acting or speaking. *Prosopopoeia* is a *synonym for *personification.

prospectus

A plan or detailed *sketch for a proposed literary work. *Prospectus,* from Latin words meaning "to look forward," usually involves a statement about the contents and scope of a proposal. See OUTLINE.

prosthesis

The addition of one or more sounds or syllables to a word. Prosthesis, which in Greek means "addition," is illustrated in the final word of this line from Keats's *The Eve of St. Agnes:* "The owl for all his feathers was a-cold."

protagonist

The leading character of a *drama, *novel, or other literary work. *Protagonist* in Greek meant "first combatant"; such a person is not always the *hero of a work, but he is always the principal and central character. The rival of a protagonist is an *antagonist. In Maugham's *Of Human Bondage,* Philip Carey, the clubfooted orphan, is the protagonist; in Hemingway's *The Old Man and the Sea,* Santiago, an old Cuban fisherman, is the protagonist. See AGON, DEUTERAGONIST, TRITAGONIST.

protasis

(1) The clause expressing the condition in a conditional sentence: "*If you decide to leave,* then I will, too." See APODOSIS. (2) The first part of an ancient (classical) drama in which characters are introduced and the subject of the play is proposed. (See PROLOGUE.) *Protasis,* a Greek word mean-

ing "a stretching forward," is related to *catastasis and *epitasis.

prototype

The original or model on which something is formed or based; someone or something that serves to illustrate the typical qualities of a class. *Prototype,* from a Greek word meaning "original," is closely related to *archetype. For instance, Ananias, a liar mentioned in the Bible (Acts 5), is a prototype of all persons who tell lies; the bragging soldier (*miles gloriosus) of ancient drama was the prototype of all cowardly braggarts in literature, including Shakespeare's Falstaff.

proverb

A short saying, usually of unknown or ancient origin, that expresses some useful thought or commonplace truth. In the Bible, a proverb is a profound saying or maxim that requires interpretation. Proverbs are usually expressed in simple, homely language that is sometimes allegorical or symbolic: "A stitch in time saves nine." (See ADAGE, APHORISM, APOTHEGM, GNOMIC, MAXIM, SAW, SAYING.) A student of proverbs goes by the awesome name of paroemiologist.

provincialism

(1) A word, expression, or pronunciation peculiar to a section or province. See LOCALISM. (2) Narrowness of mind or ignorance resulting from sheltered life without exposure to cultural or intellectual activity. Most of the characters in Thomas Hardy's novels employ provincialisms in their speech and reflect provincialism in their lives. See LOCAL COLOR, REGIONALISM.

psalm

A sacred *song or *hymn. From a Greek term meaning "song sung to the harp," *psalm* refers especially to the songs of praise included in the Old Testament book of the Bible called *Psalms.* Longfellow's *A Psalm of Life* is an optimistic call to action that contains such memorable lines as:

Trust no future, howe'er pleasant!
Let the dead Past bury its dead!
Act—act in the living Present!
Heart within, and God o'erhead!

Lives of great men all remind us
We can make our lives sublime,
And, departing, leave behind us
Footprints on the sands of time.

pseudepigrapha

A collective term for writings bearing a false title and for books credited to someone other than the real author. *Pseudepigrapha* applies especially to spurious Biblical works that do not belong among the canonical (see CANON) books and the Apocrypha (see APOCRYPHAL).

pseudonym

A fictitious name used to conceal identity. When a pseudonym is assumed by an author, it is also a *nom de plume and *pen name. Voltaire was the pseudonym of François Marie Arouet; Charlotte Brontë wrote under the pseudonym of Currer Bell.

psyche

(1) The spirit, mind, or soul of man; (2) the mental (psychological) structure of a person, viewed as a moving force in his life. *Psyche,* which in Greek means "breath," in classical mythology was considered a *personification of the soul in the form of a beautiful girl who was loved by Eros (Cupid). (A classic account of this love story appears in Walter Pater's *Marius the Epicurean,* a philosophical *romance.) In literature, psyche is generally understood to be the animating principle or directing force in one's behavior.

psychedelic

An adjective applied to a mental state of calm and tranquillity. *Psychedelic* also refers to pleasurable sense perceptions and *hallucinations. A psychedelic drug, such as mescaline or LSD, is one that fosters a trancelike state.

psychiatry

The science and practice of treating mental diseases. Psychiatry has played an important role in literature since the beginning of the twentieth century, notably in the works of such American dramatists as Eugene O'Neill and Tennessee Williams. (See FREUDIANISM, JUNGIAN.) Mental diseases themselves, however, have appeared in literary works for many centuries; psychiatrists have debated the mental disturbances of such characters in literature as Oedipus, Antigone, King Lear, Hamlet, Othello, Julius Caesar, Nero, Cromwell, and Napoleon.

psychoanalysis

(1) A technical procedure for investigating unconscious mental processes; (2) a systematic *structure of theories concerning the relation of conscious and unconscious emotional processes. *Psychoanalysis* applies to professional (medical) investigation, diagnosis, and treatment, but the *implications of this method are apparent in scores of plays, novels, and short stories. Stevenson's *Dr. Jekyll and Mr. Hyde,* Hawthorne's *Ethan Brand,* and Poe's *The Fall of the House of Usher* are three of scores of short stories alone that have been termed psychoanalytical in form and development.

psychograph
A psychologically oriented *biography or *profile. The term was first applied by the American biographer Gamaliel Bradford (1863–1932) to the "soul pictures" he wrote of 115 famous men and women in a series of books. Bradford defined psychography as "the condensed, essential, artistic presentation of character . . . it seeks to extract what is essential, what is permanent, and so vitally characteristic." See CHARACTER SKETCH, PROFILE.

psychological novel
A narrative that focuses on the emotional lives of its characters and explores their varied levels of mental activity. A psychological novel concentrates less on *what* happens than on the *why* and *wherefore* of *action. Such a narrative emphasizes "interior" characterization and the motives that result in "external" action. In a sense, a psychological novel is an interpretation of "inner" or "invisible" lives. Thus, the stories in Chaucer's *Canterbury Tales* are psychological, and so are the great tragedies of Shakespeare. Dickens, Thackeray, Henry James, Hardy, and Conrad wrote psychological novels as well, but the term is more often applied to twentieth-century works that use such devices as *interior monologue and *stream of consciousness *techniques.

puissance
A literary term meaning power, force, or might. *Puissance,* from a Latin word for "strength" or "ability," is now an *archaism.

Pulitzer prize
One of a group of annual awards established by Joseph Pulitzer, a Hungarian-born American newspaper owner and editor. Pulitzer prizes were designed for the "encouragement of public service, public morals, American literature, and the advancement of education." Since 1918, they have been awarded to Americans for novels, plays, poetry, biographies, histories, newspaper reporting, editorial writing, cartooning, news photography, and, since 1962, general nonfiction.

pulp magazine
A *periodical containing lurid or sensational stories or articles, printed on low-quality paper made of wood pulp. See CONFESSION, SLICK MAGAZINE, WESTERN STORY.

pulp writer
A person who writes for *pulp magazines. See GRUB STREET, HACK.

pun
A play on words; the humorous use of a word emphasizing different meanings or applications. (See EQUIVOQUE, PARONO-

MASIA.) The pun has often been called "the lowest form of wit"; one English writer (John Dennis) remarked that the maker of a bad pun would not hesitate "to pick a pocket," and Charles Lamb scornfully wrote, "A pun is a pistol let off at the ear, not a feather to tickle the intellect." Puns, however, have appeared in literature since the time of Homer (eighth century B.C.). An effective pun appears in these lines by a nineteenth-century versifier, Anita Owen:

> O dreamy eyes,
> They tell sweet lies of Paradise;
> And in those eyes the lovelight lies
> And lies—and lies—and lies!

puppetry

The art of making artificial figures perform on a miniature stage; *mummery. Puppetry, derived from a Latin word for *doll*, involves the manipulation of small figures representing persons or animals through the use of rods, wires, strings, or fingers. A puppet show is a dramatic performance, such as a Punch-and-Judy show, in which characters are made to act while the manipulator (or someone else) speaks words.

purgation

The act of cleansing. For comment on the purposes and effects of purgation in literature, see CATHARSIS.

purist

One who strictly observes purity in language and insists that others do likewise. A purist overstresses minute points of *diction, pronunciation, grammar, etc., and is likely to use bookish English on all occasions. See PEDANTRY.

Another application of *purist* is to a person who feels that foreign words should be excluded from English and that the language should be "unmixed and unmangled with the borrowings of other tongues." Wordsworth attempted in many poems to use simple words drawn from actual speech; Edna St. Vincent Millay tried to write a long poem, *The King's Henchman,* using only words of Anglo-Saxon derivation. Most linguists agree that the English language will continue to enrich itself just as it has done for a thousand years. When Spenser in *The Faerie Queene* referred to Chaucer as a "well of English undefiled," he was a patriotic purist, but he was writing nonsense.

Puritanism

The principles and practices of Puritans, a class of English Protestants within the Church of England who, in the sixteenth century, began demands for reform in doctrine and worship. In the seventeenth century, Puritanism became a powerful political party. (See CALVINISM.) The Puritans who came to the New World on the *Mayflower* wished to set up a form of government in which their ideas of "purified" religion could prevail.

Puritanism has come to imply strictness in moral and religious matters. A puritanical person is considered rigidly austere. Although Puritanism is a *pejorative term, what James Russell Lowell said should be remembered: "Puritanism, believing itself quick with the seed of religious liberty, laid, without knowing it, the egg of democracy."

purple prose

Writing filled with exaggerated literary devices and marked by ornate diction and structure. Purple prose (so called because *purple* implies *regal* or *princely*) makes excessive use of *parallelism, imagery, figurative language, *poetic diction, *cadence, and *polysyllabication. Such writing is sometimes referred to as "purple patch," because it stands out from the passages around it. See FINE WRITING, PRECIOSITY.

purpose

The intended or desired result wished by an author; the end, aim, or goal in the mind of a writer before, during, and after the *composition of a literary work. All writing should have as a central *purpose the communication of ideas and feelings. Effective literary selections never deviate from this central purpose and never fail to achieve the precise effects planned by their authors. See CONTROLLING IMAGE, DOMINANT IMPRESSION, PERSPECTIVE.

putative

Reputed, supposed. From a Latin word meaning "to think," *putative* is often used to mean "commonly regarded as such." The putative and actual authors of *The Federalist,* a series of eighty-five essays supporting the United States Constitution, were John Jay, James Madison, and Alexander Hamilton. The putative author of *Gulliver's Travels* was Lemuel Gulliver; the actual author was Jonathan Swift.

pyrrhic

(1) A metrical foot of two short (unaccented) syllables. Common in classical poetry (Greek and Latin), the pyrrhic foot is unusual in English verse; in fact, a pyrrhic may be considered a double *anacrusis. See DIBRACH. (2) An ancient Greek warlike dance in which the motions of combat were imitated. The war dances of North American Indians were pyrrhic in nature. (3) An adjective applying to a victory won at too great a cost. (Pyrrhus, king of Epirus, won a notable battle with the Romans in the third century B.C. but lost so many of his men that he allegedly said, "One more such victory and we are lost.")

Q.E.D.

An abbreviation of the Latin words *quod erat demonstrandum* ("which was to be shown or demonstrated"). The term appears in *argumentation, *logic, and mathematical proofs.

quadrivium

During the *Middle Ages, the four subjects leading to a Master of Arts degree: arithmetic, astronomy, geometry, and music. (See SEVEN LIBERAL ARTS.) *Quadrivium* is a Latin word meaning "place where four ways meet," that is, a crossroads.

quantitative verse

Metrical language whose underlying *rhythm is determined by the duration of *sound in utterance. Quantitative verse makes use of the quantity of time allowed or required for the pronunciation of a word and is common in Greek, Latin, Hebraic, and Japanese poetry. English verse is "qualitative" in that it largely relies on *accent, *rhythm, and *meter. However, English poetry does have some quantitative values: see, for example, the quotation from Coleridge under the entry FOOT.

quarto

A book size of about 9 ½ by 12 inches, determined by folding printed sheets twice to form four leaves (eight pages). *Quarto* is often abbreviated as 4to. See FOLIO, OCTAVO.

quatorzain

A poem of fourteen lines. A quatorzain does not follow all the forms prescribed by a *sonnet pattern. Every well-known *rondel in English is a quatorzain.

quatrain

A *stanza or *poem of four lines. The quatrain is the most common stanzaic form of poetry written in English. This quatrain, with a typical *rhyme scheme of *abab,* is by William Savage Landor:

> I strove with none; for none was worth
>   my strife,
> Nature I loved, and, next to Nature, Art;
> I warmed both hands before the fire of life;
> It sinks, and I am ready to depart.

quem quaeritis

A Latin term meaning "whom do you seek?" The expression is applied to the earliest known form of liturgical drama; it is based on the visit to Christ's tomb by three women who discovered that the tomb was empty. An angel, guarding the sepulcher, asked, "Whom do you seek?" When told that Christ had risen, the women departed joyfully. See LITURGICAL DRAMA, MYSTERY PLAY.

quibble

(1) Petty or minor objections and criticism; (2) the use of ambiguous or irrelevant language to evade a point at issue; (3) a play on words, a *pun. Derived from *quip* or *gibe,* *quibble* always involves a misleading or unfair verbal device of some sort.

quidnunc

A two-word Latin term meaning "what now?" As one word, *quidnunc* refers to a gossip, a busybody, a person who is eager to know the latest news (what now?).

quién sabe

A Spanish expression meaning "who knows?"

quintain

A *stanza of five lines. (See CINQUAIN, PENTASTICH, TANKA.) Poe's *To Helen* consists of three quintains, of which this is the second:

> On desperate seas long wont to roam,
> Thy hyacinth hair, thy classic face,
> Thy Naiad airs have brought me home
> To the glory that was Greece
> And the grandeur that was Rome.

quintessence

(1) The most perfect form of something; (2) the pure and concentrated *essence (inner being) of a substance. (*Quintessence* literally means "fifth essence"; in ancient and medieval philosophy, the first four essences were air, earth, fire, and water. See

HUMORS.) Some of the poems of Keats and Shelley, for instance, have been referred to as the quintessence of poetic beauty; Shakespeare has been called the quintessential dramatist and poet of all time.

quip

A witty saying; a sharp, sarcastic remark. A quip can be cutting or jesting, but it always conveys *humor or *wit. When a quip reaches written form, it is likely to be called an *aphorism, *apothegm, or *epigram.

quire

(1) A set of twenty-four sheets of paper; (2) a section of printed leaves in proper sequence for binding. (See BINDING.) *Quire* is derived from a Latin term meaning "set of four sheets" or "four each."

quod vide

A Latin term meaning "which see." In most speech and writing the phrase is abbreviated to q.v.

quoin

In *printing, *quoin* is the term for a wedge of wood or metal used to fasten (secure) *type in a *chase (rectangular iron frame).

R

Rabelaisian

An adjective applied to literary selections characterized by coarse, broad *humor and keen *satire. *Rabelaisian* is derived from the name of François Rabelais (1490–1553), a French satirist who, in *Gargantua and Pantagruel,* revolted against medieval moral *conventions and wrote with gross humor, mocking and irreverent satire, and sensual detail. Jonathan Swift and Laurence Sterne have been called Rabelaisian, but the *epithet is not entirely accurate: each of these English writers combined depth of *purpose with genuine insight, as did Rabelais, but without his disregard for propriety and without his exuberant, indecent fun.

radicalism

The holding or following of extreme views and principles; extremism; advocacy of fundamental economic, social, and political reforms by direct and often uncompromising methods. Radicalism, from a Latin term meaning "having roots," emphasizes going to the base, or bottom, of matters and thus often seems immoderate and intemperate in its thoroughness and completeness. In literature, *radicalism* applies to the opinions and attitudes of writers and also to the *forms and *techniques which they use. *Anarchy is a type of *radicalism;* so, too, are *dadaism, *imagism, and *surrealism.

raillery

Good-humored ridicule, banter. *Raillery,* a French term, is applicable to such light, playful, teasing remarks as appear in *vers de société and in comedies by Oscar Wilde, George Bernard Shaw, and Noel Coward. See PERSIFLAGE.

raison d'être

A French phrase meaning "reason for being," "justification for existence." The term may be applied to the *motivation, *purpose, or central goal of *characters in literature. When Keats wrote "Beauty is truth, truth beauty" and then suggested that this knowledge was sufficient, he was explaining their "reason for being." As a somewhat more rational ground for existence, the Preamble to the Constitution of the United States sets forth the raison d'être for the articles that follow.

random

Proceeding, made, or occurring without definite reason, purpose, or aim. Certain *personal essays may appear to be a more or less random collection of haphazard, stray, aimless, or casual remarks, but this appearance is deceptive. No worthwhile literary selection is ever random in either *structure or *contents, despite outward *evidence.

ratiocination

The process of logical reasoning. Ratiocination is a systematic method of thinking with order and precision, proceeding from careful examination of data to exactly phrased conclusions. (See DEDUCTION, INDUCTION.) The word was given literary significance by Edgar Allan Poe, who wrote several stories that he called ratiocinative, among them *The Purloined Letter, The Gold Bug,* and *The Mystery of Marie Roget. Ratiocination* signifies a kind of writing which solves, through logical thought processes, some sort of *enigma. See DETECTIVE STORY.

rationalism

Acceptance of reason (intellect) as the supreme authority in matters of belief, conduct, and opinion. Rationalism is a doctrine in *philosophy which holds that reason alone is a *source of knowledge, entirely independent of experience. It is also a theological doctrine that the human mind, unaided by divine revelations, is an adequate or sole guide to religious truths. This concept of the supremacy of the intellect made rationalism an ally of *neoclassicism and an opponent of *Calvinism, *mysticism, and *Puritanism. See DEISM, HUMANISM, PRIMITIVISM.

reader identification

The process by which a reader associates with himself the feelings and responses of *characters in literature; transference to the reader of the emotions of literary characters; complete acceptance by a reader of the *theme and *thesis of a literary work. See EMPATHY, SYMPATHY. For further comment on reader identification, see BELIEF, IDENTIFICATION.

realism

(1) A theory of writing in which the familiar, ordinary aspects of life are depicted in a matter-of-fact, straightforward manner

designed to reflect life as it actually is; (2) treatment of subject matter in a way that presents careful descriptions of everyday life, often the lives of so-called middle or lower classes.

Realism, which refers to both the content and *technique of literary creation, has been evident in literature from its very beginnings. For example, the English novelist and essayist C. S. Lewis has referred to

> ... the dragon "sniffing along the stone" in *Beowulf;* Layamon's Arthur, who, on hearing that he was king, sat very quiet and "one time he was red and one time he was pale"; the pinnacles in *Gawain* that looked as if they were "pared out of paper"; Jonah going into the whale's mouth "like a mote at a minster door"; ... Falstaff on his death-bed "plucking" at the sheet ...

Although realism has always suggested accuracy of speech and detail, thorough background information, and a concern for *verisimilitude, the term took an added meaning during the nineteenth and early twentieth centuries on the Continent and in England and the United States: emphasis on photographic details, probing analysis of "things as they really are," the frustrations of characters in atmospheres of depravity, decay, or sordidness. *Realism* has been, and remains, a somewhat elusive, vague term, but it is fair to say that varied aspects of "realistic" subject matter and treatment have appeared in numerous plays, poems, and short stories of modern times and in novels by such writers as Daniel Defoe, Henry Fielding, Thackeray, Dickens, Balzac, Zola, Tolstoi, Mark Twain, William Dean Howells, John Galsworthy, Sinclair Lewis, and John O'Hara. See DETERMINISM, MIMETIC, NATURALISM, PRAGMATISM, VERISIMILITUDE.

ream

A quantity of paper, now most often considered to be 500 sheets. Some paper manufacturers and printers estimate a ream as twenty *quires (480 sheets); a printer's ream, or perfect ream, consists of 516 sheets.

Reason, Age of

See AGE OF REASON, ENLIGHTENMENT.

rebus

Representation of a word or phrase by pictures or *symbols. *Rebus,* from a Latin word meaning "by things" (that is, not by words), is a kind of picture writing that uses actual drawings to represent ideas (pictures of a bull and a horn represent a loudspeaker or bullhorn). Words alone may constitute another kind of rebus: two gates and a head are a rebus for Gateshead. In *The Alchemist,* Ben Jonson used a rebus to give the name of a tobacco shop proprietor (Abel

Drugger), the first line of which is "He first shall have a bell—that's Abel."

rebuttal

A reply; a rejoinder; a refutation by argument or *evidence. *Rebuttal,* a term used in *argumentation, or *forensics, signifies comment (speech or writing) designed to oppose or nullify arguments presented by someone else. *Rebuttal* is also used as a term for the final summing up of answers to the arguments of opponents.

recantation

Withdrawal or disavowal of earlier opinions or actions. From Latin words meaning "to sing back," "to sing again," a recantation is a repudiation, a formal "taking back" of a previous deed or statement. (See PALINODE.) Late in life, Boccaccio agreed to "direct the mind toward eternal things" and wrote a recantation of such "delights of the temporal" as his bawdy work *The Decameron.*

Received Pronunciation

A term, also given as Received Standard, which refers to the form of educated English spoken in southern England, specifically that in English public schools and at Oxford and Cambridge Universities. Such pronunciation is recognized as "conforming to a standard, as being in accordance with common practice."

recherche what?

A term from French meaning "quest," "inquiry," or "careful search." An autobiographical novel is sometimes referred to as research into the author's past (*recherche du temps perdu*—a retelling of lost time).

recondite

Profound, difficult, abstruse. A recondite subject or literary work involves a topic beyond ordinary understanding or knowledge. See ESOTERIC.

recto

A Latin word meaning "right." The term is used to refer to a right-hand page of a *book and to the front of a leaf (as opposed to *verso). In a book with numbered pages, recto pages always have the odd numbers.

redaction

Editing or revising a work for publication. Redaction also may involve digesting a longer work. (See ABRIDGMENT.) Sir Thomas Malory's *Morte d'Arthur,* a compilation, *translation, and *abridgment of *Arthurian romances, is a redaction.

reductio ad absurdum

A Latin phrase meaning "reduction to an absurdity." The phrase is a method of *argumentation that reveals the falsity of a *proposition by showing the foolish conclusion to which it would logically lead. In *A Modest Proposal,* Swift proceeds with rigorous logic to deduce arguments from a shocking *premise so quietly assumed that readers are disposed to assent before becoming aware of what their assent implies. The outcome is ghastly rather than "absurd," but the original premise is "reduced" to an impossible conclusion.

redundancy

Superfluous repetition or overlapping of words and phrases. Redundancy is a characteristic of literary *style marked by *pleonasm and *verbiage. The senility of Polonius (in Shakespeare's *Hamlet*) is repeatedly shown by the redundancy of his speech, as, for example:

> That he is mad, 'tis true; 'tis true 'tis pity;
> And pity 'tis 'tis true; a foolish figure!
> But farewell it, for I will use no art.
> Mad let us grant him then; and now remains
> That we find out the cause of this effect,
> Or rather say, the cause of this defect,
> For this effect defective comes by cause;
> Thus it remains, and the remainder thus.

referent

The word, term, object, or event to which a *symbol or another term applies (refers). (See GENERAL SEMANTICS, WORD.) In *logic, a referent is the first term in a *proposition to which succeeding terms relate. See PREMISE, SYLLOGISM.

reformation

The act of amending or improving what is unsatisfactory, wrong, or corrupt. Spelled with an *uppercase letter, *Reformation* applies to the sixteenth-century religious movement which had for its object reform within the Roman Catholic Church and led to the establishment of Protestant churches. The Reformation was a dual movement: it was a Protestant revolution and also a reformation within the Catholic Church which led to the reduction of abuses, establishment of schools, and firmer discipline for the clergy. In *The Magic Mountain,* Thomas Mann wrote, "The invention of printing and the Reformation are and remain the two outstanding services of central Europe to the cause of humanity." In his first inaugural address, Thomas Jefferson listed the principles which had guided the steps of the newly created United States "through an age of revolution and reformation."

refrain

A phrase or verse (line) recurring at intervals in a *poem or *song, usually at the end of a *stanza. A refrain may help to establish the *meter of a poem, indicate its *tone, or reestablish its *atmosphere. A refrain may also be a nonsense line (such as "With a hay, and a ho, and a hey nonino" in Shakespeare's *As You Like It*) or a word or phrase that takes on added significance each time it appears (like the word "Nevermore" in Poe's poem *The Raven*). See INCREMENTAL REPETITION, REPETEND.

refutation

The act of proving (or attempting to prove) that an opinion or accusation is false or erroneous. Refutation, from Latin words meaning "checked" or "resisted," plays an important part in *calumny, *censorship, *libel, and *slander.

regionalism

(1) Representation in literature of a particular section or area; (2) fidelity in writing to a specific geographical region, accurately reproducing its speech, manners, customs, folklore, beliefs, dress, and history. See LOCAL COLOR.

Regionalism is an element in nearly all literature, since most selections involve a *locale or *setting; the term, however, is usually applied to writings in which locale is thought of as a subject interesting in itself. The Wessex novels of Thomas Hardy are regional literature. The poetry of Robinson Jeffers is filled with *allusions to California and the Pacific; Yevgeny Alexandrovich Yevtushenko's poems deal exclusively with his home area in Russia and the emotions of his neighbors; Dylan Thomas's poetry is loaded with references to his native Wales. Such novelists as Willa Cather, Ellen Glasgow, Thomas Wolfe, and William Faulkner have exhibited regionalism in much of their work. For most literary craftsmen, the impetus, ideas, and imagery of their writing spring from the land and the people closest to them.

relique

An *archaism for *relic* (a surviving memorial). A relique is a lingering trace of something or an object that has interest because of its age or association with the past. Thomas Percy, an English student of *antiquarianism, collected old poetry (sonnets, ballads, songs, romances) and called the resulting book *Reliques of Ancient English Poetry* (1765).

remainder

A copy of a book remaining in a publisher's stock when its sale has practically ceased. Remainders are often disposed of at reduced prices to dealers who retail such copies to buyers.

Renaissance

The activity, spirit, and time of the revival of art, learning, and literature in Europe extending over a period of 300 years (about

1350 to 1650). *Renaissance,* also spelled *Renascence,* means "rebirth," but the Renaissance was less a rebirth than an *epoch which marked a transition from the medieval to the modern world. In literature, the period was notable for a revival of interest in the *humanities and a rediscovery of *classic works of Greek and Roman origin. The Renaissance, however, was a many-pronged *era that included vigorous new trends in art, science, religion, and politics. Also, the Renaissance ushered in the growth of cities and commerce, as well as increased travel throughout Europe and resolute and determined colonization in the New World. Intellectually and socially, the period witnessed increased emphasis on the importance of human lives as contrasted with the subordination of individuals during feudal times. See ELIZABETHAN, FEUDALISM, HUMANISM.

repartee

Conversation full of quick, witty replies. Repartee, a term from French, appears often in the plays of Wilde, Shaw, Noel Coward, and William Saroyan and in *fiction by such writers as Raymond Chandler, James Thurber, and Peter De Vries. See PERSIFLAGE, QUIP, RAILLERY, STICHOMYTHIA.

repertoire

A store or stock of items available. In literature, *repertoire* refers to the list (or inventory) of plays which a company of actors is prepared to perform. Both *repertoire* and *repertory* are terms sometimes applied to the collected works of an author and to the kinds of personal experience and collected data which a writer can use, upon demand, in his work.

repetend

A word or phrase repeated at irregular intervals in a poem. A repetend resembles a *refrain except that it may only partially repeat and may appear anywhere in a selection. The following lines from Poe's *Ulalume* contain several repetends:

> The skies they were ashen and sober;
> The leaves they were crispèd and sere—
> The leaves they were withering and sere.

The repetend is only one of several devices in poetry based on repetition; others are *alliteration, *anaphora, *assonance, *consonance, *meter, refrain, and *rhythm.

report

An account or statement describing in detail a situation or an event. A report is usually based on observation, inquiry, or both. Many *articles and *columns and most *nonfiction generally consist of reports or contain reports as a part of their *contents.

reportage

(1) The act or *technique of reporting news; (2) reported news;

(3) a written account, a *report. *Reportage,* a term from French, is used most often in newspaper circles, but the technique itself has been employed in such full-length works as Defoe's partly fictional *A Journal of the Plague Year* and Truman Capote's *In Cold Blood.*

requiem

Any *chant, *dirge, *hymn, or musical service for the dead. *Requiem,* which means "rest," is the first word in the Roman Catholic Requiem mass, a service dedicated to asking repose for the souls of the dead. At the funeral of Ophelia (in *Hamlet*), the priest, who suspects that she was a suicide, exclaims:

> We should profane the service of the dead
> To sing sage requiem and such rest to her
> As to peace-parted souls.

Stevenson's *Requiem* is a buoyant poem containing these lines:

> Under the wide and starry sky,
> Dig the grave and let me lie.
> Glad did I live and gladly die,
> And I laid me down with a will.

requiescat in pace

A Latin term meaning "May he (or she) rest in peace." A requiescat is a wish or prayer for the repose of the dead.

research

Systematic and thorough investigation. Research, meaning to "seek again," involves diligent inquiry into a subject in order to make certain precisely what the available and applicable facts and theories concerning it are.

residuum

The remainder of something. *Residuum* applies to that which remains after a part is taken or in some manner disposed of. The term is used in legal *jargon to refer to the part of an estate that remains after all debts are settled and bequests made; *residuum* also applies to that part of an author's work that is considered permanently appealing, or *classic.

resolution

(1) The events following the *climax of a *play or *story (see ACT, FALLING ACTION); (2) determination, resolve, or *purpose such as, for instance, the plan announced by Wordsworth and Coleridge in their Preface to the *Lyrical Ballads* to revolt against what they considered the artificial literature of their day; (3) a formal expression of opinion by an organization, club, legislature, etc., such as the Declaration of Independence.

restoration

The act of renewal, revival, or reestablishment, such as the return of something to a former, original, or unimpaired state:

the restoration of colonial Williamsburg. In literature, the *Restoration* refers to the return of Charles II to the English throne in 1660; the Restoration age in English literature is commonly considered the years from 1660 to the revolution in 1688, when Parliament regained power.

résumé

A summing up; a *summary. (See ABRIDGMENT, ABSTRACT, EPITOME.) *Résumé,* a French term meaning "resumed," is also applied to a brief account of personal, educational, and professional experience and qualifications, such as that of an applicant for work.

revenge tragedy

A form of *drama popular in *Elizabethan England. The typical revenge (exacting punishment, "getting even") tragedy emphasized bloodshed, violence, and lurid incidents involving incest, adultery, ghosts, suicide, dead bodies, etc. The *theme of a revenge tragedy usually involved the revenge of a son for his father (*Hamlet*) or a father for his son (Thomas Kyd's *The Spanish Tragedy*).

review

A critical article or report on a recent *book, *play, *poem, *opera, motion picture, etc. A review typically announces a work or performance, discusses its subject, and comments on its merits or faults. See BOOK REVIEW, CRITICISM, CRITIQUE.

revue

A form of theatrical entertainment. A revue, a French term for *review,* consists of a variety of dances, choruses, songs, and skits. A typical revue parodies or satirizes current fads, recent events, and persons in the public eye; it normally has no real *plot but is lavish in its stage settings, scenery, costuming, etc.

rhetoric

The theory and principles concerned with effective use of language, both written and oral. To the ancient Greeks, rhetoric was essential for *argumentation and oratory (the Greek word *rhetor* means "orator"), and it eventually became one of the *seven liberal arts. (See TRIVIUM.) According to *Aristotelian theory, rhetoric was a way of organizing material for the presentation of truth, but Socrates (and many later thinkers) have considered it a superficial art, that of "making great matters small and small things great." In modern times, *rhetoric* has come to mean the art or science of literary uses of language. It is concerned with the effectiveness and general appeal of communication and with methods of achieving literary quality and vigor. Rhetoric is only loosely connected with specific details of mechanics, grammar, etc. See ARGUMENTATION, EFFECTIVENESS, ELOCUTION, ELOQUENCE, PERSUASION.

rhetorical question

A question asked solely to produce an effect or to make a statement but not expected to receive an answer. The purpose of such a question, to which the answer is obvious, is usually to make a deeper impression upon the hearer (or reader) than a direct statement would. James Russell Lowell's line in *The Vision of Sir Launfal* is a rhetorical question: "And what is so rare as a day in June?" Shakespeare uses a series of rhetorical questions in this speech by Shylock in *The Merchant of Venice:*

> Hath not a Jew eyes? Hath not a Jew hands, organs, dimensions, senses, affections, passions; fed with the same food, hurt with the same weapons, subject to the same diseases, heal'd by the same means, warm'd and cooled by the same winter and summer, as a Christian is? If you prick us, do we not bleed? If you tickle us, do we not laugh? If you poison us, do we not die? And if you wrong us, shall we not revenge?

rhyme

Similarity or identity of *sound in words. Two words rhyme (or rime) when their accented vowels and all succeeding sounds are identical: *rain, stain; skating, dating; emotion, demotion; fascinate, deracinate.* Rhyme is more than an ornament in *poetry. It provides pleasing sense impressions; it helps to establish stanzaic form; it is an aid in memorizing; it contributes to the *unity of a poem. For comment on the many different kinds of rhyme in poetry, see DOUBLE RHYME, END RHYME, EYE RHYME, FEMININE RHYME, HALF RHYME, HEAD RHYME, IMPERFECT RHYME, INTERNAL RHYME, LEONINE VERSE, MASCULINE ENDING, PERFECT RHYME, RHYME ROYAL.

rhyme royal

A form of verse (also spelled *rime royal*) consisting of seven-line *stanzas of iambic *pentameter in a fixed *rhyme scheme (*ababbcc*). Its introducer, Geoffrey Chaucer (1340–1400), used this form in many of his poems. This stanza from Wordsworth's *Resolution and Independence* is in rhyme royal:

> There was a roaring in the wind all night:
> The rain came heavily and fell in floods;
> But now the sun is rising calm and bright.
> The birds are singing in the distant woods;
> Over his own sweet voice the stockdove broods;
> The jay makes answer as the magpie chatters;
> And the air is filled with pleasant noise of waters.

rhyme scheme

The *pattern of rhymes used in a *poem, usually marked by letters to indicate correspondences. The four-line *stanza, or *quatrain, is usually written so that the first line rhymes with the third and the second with the fourth; this rhyme scheme is noted as *abab.* In an *English sonnet, the fourteen lines have a rhyme scheme of *abab, cdcd, efef, gg.*

rhythm

Uniform recurrence (repetition) of beat or *accent; the measured flow of words in *verse or *prose. Rhythm in verse is most often established by a combination of accent and number of syllables. (See METER.) In prose, rhythm is marked by variety of movement; among contributors to prose rhythm are *balanced sentences, variety in sentence structure and length, transitional devices, and *euphony. (See CADENCE, POLYPHONIC PROSE.) An example of rhythmic prose is provided under the entry POETIC PROSE. Also, see SPRUNG RHYTHM.

riddle

A puzzling problem or question; an enigmatic (see ENIGMA) saying or speech; a statement or query so phrased as to require ingenuity in discovering its meaning. Riddles were a popular literary *form during the Middle Ages and are still prevalent in *conundrums and in certain kinds of *wisecracks. (See CHARADE, REBUS.) The most famous riddle in all history and literature is that of the Sphinx: "What goes on four feet, on two feet, and three / But the more feet it goes on, the weaker is he? " Oedipus, a king of Thebes (see OEDIPUS COMPLEX), solved the riddle: a man, who as an infant crawls upon all fours and as an adult walks erect on his own two feet, in old age supports his tottering legs with a staff (stick).

ridicule

Speech, writing, or action intended to cause contemptuous laughter at a person; derision; scornful or mocking language. Ridicule, from a Latin word meaning "to laugh," is a method of making fun of a person, idea, or institution; as such, it is an element in much *burlesque, *caricature, *satire, and *travesty.

riding rhyme

A little-used *synonym for the *heroic couplet; presumably so named because it is the *meter used in certain poems involving riders on horseback, such as Chaucer's *The Canterbury Tales.*

rime riche

A term from French meaning "rich rhyme," *rime riche* is an approximate *synonym for *identical rhyme and *perfect rhyme. *Loaded* and *unloaded* are an example of rime riche.

rising action

That part of a *plot involving *complication and *conflict and leading up to a *climax, or turning point, in a play (or novel). In much classical and Elizabethan drama, rising action largely occurred in the first two acts of a five-act production. See ACT.

ritornello

An Italian term for (1) an orchestral *interlude between arias, scenes, or acts in an *opera; (2) a line or group of lines repeated at intervals in a poem. See REFRAIN, REPETEND.

ritual

Observance of set forms; the conduct of a formal ceremony which has become traditional. Literature is filled with accounts of rituals such as human sacrifices, feasts, dances, coronations, and religious ceremonies. The lighting of a bonfire (chapter 3, Hardy's *Return of the Native*) is a ritual observed by the inhabitants of Egdon Heath. It is a ritual when, in Hawthorne's *Scarlet Letter,* Hester Prynne is led from prison to the marketplace and is subjected to public scorn. Ritual also involves prescribed codes of social behavior, such as shaking hands or removing one's hat upon entering a house, etc.

Robin Hood theme

A *pattern, or *formula, of action in which poor or disadvantaged persons achieve success through the aid of some benefactor or outside agency. The expression derives its name from the legendary English outlaw who robbed the rich to give to the poor and who was a model of generosity, courage, and justice. The Robin Hood theme is a variant version of the Cinderella story, in which a drudge is helped by a good fairy to win a prince and thus "live happily ever after."

rococo

A word of several meanings in architecture and art, *rococo* in literature is usually applied to *style that is ornate, overly decorated, and pretentious. Several of Swinburne's poems have been termed rococo, and so have Pope's *The Rape of the Lock* and Wilde's *The Ballad of Reading Gaol.*

rodomontade

A French term meaning "boasting," "bragging." The word is derived from the name of a boastful king in Ariosto's *Orlando Furioso,* an Italian *epic. (See BRAGGADOCIO.) Falstaff's description of his fight with highwaymen (Shakespeare's *Henry IV,* Part 1, act 2, scene 2) is rodomontade.

Rogers, Bruce
An American book designer and printer (1870–1957).

rogue
(1) A dishonest person, a scoundrel; (2) a playfully mischievous person, a scamp; (3) a tramp or vagabond. All three kinds of rogue appear in *picaresque novels. Robin Hood (see ROBIN HOOD THEME) has been called the most appealing rogue in legend and literature.

roman à clef
A French phrase for a *novel that represents actual historical characters and events in the form of fiction. With the literal meaning of "novels with a key," romans à clef include such titles as Aldous Huxley's *Point Counter Point,* Ernest Hemingway's *The Sun Also Rises,* Somerset Maugham's *Cakes and Ale,* and Robert Penn Warren's *All the King's Men.*

roman à thèse
A French term for a novel with a *thesis. See PROBLEM NOVEL, PLAY; PROPAGANDA.

romance
A term originally referring to a *medieval narrative in prose or verse dealing with heroic persons and events. *Romance* now applies to any fictional account of heroic achievements, colorful scenes, passionate love, or supernatural experiences. A romance is sometimes considered a fanciful or extravagant story or daydream. Sir Walter Scott was a notable writer of romances of a traditional sort, but the term is currently applied most often to "romantic fiction" or to a love affair.

Romanesque
A term with varied meanings in architecture, painting, and sculpture, *Romanesque* applies in literature to fanciful or extravagant narration, such as love stories and *fables.

roman-fleuve
A French phrase for a novel in which generations of members of a family are told about in long and leisurely narrative. A well-known series of romans-fleuves (stream novels) is John Galsworthy's *The Forsyte Saga.*

roman policier
A French term ("police novel") for detective story. A well-known writer of the roman policier, Georges Simenon, has importantly influenced detective fiction with his twentieth-century sleuth Inspector Maigret. See DETECTIVE STORY, WHODUNIT.

romanticism
The term *romanticism* cannot be precisely applied to a specific state of mind, *point of view, or literary *technique. As a

movement, it arose so gradually in so many different aspects in so many parts of Europe that a satisfactory definition is impossible. In France, Victor Hugo (1802–1885) emphasized as a controlling idea in romanticism the "liberalism of literature," the freeing of an artist from restraints and rules imposed by classicists and the encouragement of revolutionary political ideas. In Germany, Heinrich Heine (1797–1856) thought the dominant aspect of romanticism was its revival of the past (medievalism) in letters, art, and life. A later English writer (Walter Pater, 1839–1894) suggested that the adding of strangeness to beauty constituted the romantic spirit of the age. Other writers have insisted that the so-called romantic mood is a desire to escape from reality, especially unpleasant reality. This widespread movement of the eighteenth and nineteenth centuries exhibited each of these characteristics.

Specifically, romanticism may be called a literary attitude in which imagination is considered more important than formal rules and reason (*classicism) and than a sense of fact (*realism).

Romanticism as applied to the social, political, and literary revolution that swept through Western Europe and culminated in England from 1798 to 1832 had psychological implications and suggests changes in attitude toward the human experience from which literature is derived. Among these changes were increasing emphasis on the individual as opposed to social *convention and *tradition; emphasis on mystery and the supernatural—strangeness and wonder as opposed to common sense, the infinite as opposed to the finite; emphasis on the imaginative and emotional as opposed to the rational—an appeal to the heart rather than the head.

In effect, romanticism is a literary and philosophical theory which tends to place the individual at the center of life and experience and represents a shift from *objectivity to *subjectivity. These concepts of romanticism have contributed significantly to the establishment of the modern democratic world.

Romany

(1) A gypsy, a nomadic person whose ancestors migrated from India and settled in various parts of Asia, Europe, and North America; (2) the language of gypsies, a *dialect form of Indic. As an adjective, *Romany* refers to the customs, habits, and traditions of gypsies, about whom George Borrow, a nineteenth-century English traveler and author, wrote extensively.

rondeau

A short poem, the name of which is derived from a French word meaning "little circle." A rondeau typically consists of fifteen (or thirteen or ten) lines using only two rhymes. Austin Dobson's *With Pipe and Flute* is a rondeau:

With pipe and flute the rustic Pan
Of old made music sweet for man;
And wonder hushed the warbling bird,
And closer drew the calm-eyed herd,
The rolling river slowlier ran.

Ah! would,—ah! would, a little span,
Some air of Arcady could fan
This age of ours, too seldom stirred
With pipe and flute!

But now for gold we plot and plan;
And from Beersheba unto Dan
Apollo's self might pass unheard,
Or find the night-jar's note preferred—
Not so it fared when time began
With pipe and flute!

rondel

A short poem resembling the *rondeau. A rondel is usually a group of *stanzas totaling fourteen lines running on two rhymes; the first two lines are repeated at the middle of the poem and again at the end. The rondel differs from the rondeau only in number of lines and the use of complete, not partial, lines for the *refrain.

root (stem)

A morpheme (meaningful part of a word) to which an *affix (a prefix or suffix) may be added. Such an element is variously called a stem, base, or root. For example, *ten,* the root of Latin *tendere,* appears in such words as *intense* and *tension.* See COMBINING FORM, MORPHEME, PREFIX, SUFFIX.

rotogravure

A process by which text (words) and pictures are printed from a copper cylinder etched from plates. See GRAVURE, PHOTOGRAVURE.

round

(1) An adjective applying to an adequately developed character; see FLAT CHARACTER, ROUND CHARACTER. (2) A dance with movement in a circle or ring. (3) A musical composition in which several voices follow each other in singing lines at equally spaced time intervals. For instance, "Three Blind Mice" is often sung as a round.

round character

A person in a literary selection who is so fully described as to be recognizable, understandable, and individually different from all others appearing in the same selection. E. M. Forster said, "The test of a round character is whether it is capable of surprising in a convincing way," by which he meant that such a person is not a *stock character or a

mere *type. See CHARACTER, CHARACTERIZATION, FLAT CHAR-
ACTER, FOIL.

roundel

A poem in the *pattern of a *rondeau but consisting of
eleven lines. Like the rondeau and the *rondel, the roundel
uses only two rhymes and a twice-repeated refrain.

roundelay

A term used as a label for such fixed forms as the *rondeau,
*rondel, and *roundel. *Roundelay* may mean the musical
background (setting) for a poem in fixed form and also a
round dance itself.

Round Table

The famous table, made round to avoid quarrels as to
precedence, about which King Arthur and his knights gath-
ered. (See ARTHURIAN, KNIGHTS OF THE ROUND TABLE.)
Round table also refers to a discussion, or conference, in
which each person has equal status and equal time to present his views. See PANEL DISCUSSION.

royalty

In publishing, a predetermined portion of the income from
a work paid to its author, editor, or composer. The term,
from a Latin word meaning "kingly," is here applied in the
sense of a "prerogative" or "right."

R.S.V.P.

An abbreviation of the French words *répondez s'il vous
plaît* ("please reply"). In English, the abbreviation appears on
formal invitations to indicate "the favor of a reply is requested."

Rubaiyat

From an Arabic word, *rubaiyat* means *quatrain (four-line
*stanza). The term is nearly always used in a title, *The Ru-
baiyat of Omar Khayyam,* a translation by Edward Fitzgerald
of lines by the eleventh-century Persian poet and astronomer.
Two of the best-known quatrains from *The Rubaiyat* are
these:

> A Book of Verses underneath the Bough,
> A Jug of Wine, a Loaf of Bread—and Thou
> Beside me singing in the Wilderness—
> Oh, Wilderness were Paradise enow!

> The Moving Finger writes; and having writ,
> Moves on; nor all your Piety nor Wit
> Shall lure it back to cancel half a Line,
> Nor all your Tears wash out a Word of it.

rubric

A title, heading, or direction (in a *manuscript or *book) that is
written or printed in red or otherwise distinguished from the

remainder of the text. *Rubric,* from Latin for *red,* also applies to a direction for religious services inserted in a liturgical book. See MARGINALIA.

rune

(1) An *aphorism, *poem, or *saying with mystical meaning; a *riddle. (2) One of the characters of an ancient Germanic alphabet. The Norse god Odin was said to have lost his sanity because of a rune sent him by a maiden rejecting his love. The *Anglo-Saxon poet Cynewulf (ninth century) inserted runic characters into some of his verses.

running head

In bookmaking and *printing, *a running head* is a descriptive word, phrase, title, or the like that is repeated at the top of each *page of a *book, *periodical, etc.

run-on line

A verse (one line) of poetry having a thought that carries over to the next line without a pause. There is no grammatical or sense break until the end of the fourth line in this *quatrain from Tennyson's *In Memoriam:*

> And gathering freshlier overhead
> Rocked the full-foliaged elms, and swung
> The heavy-folded rose, and flung
> The lilies to and fro, and said . . .

See END-STOPPED LINE, ENJAMBEMENT.

S

saga

A lengthy narrative or *legend about heroic events. *Saga,* derived from an Icelandic word meaning *saw (saying), applies particularly to any Scandinavian story of medieval times dealing with the adventures of persons of lofty rank. *Saga* now refers to any traditional legend, *myth, or *tale involving extraordinary, marvelous, or detailed experiences and achievements; Longfellow adapted material from Icelandic sources for his *Saga of King Olaf;* Galsworthy's "saga novel" is entitled *The Forsyte Saga.* See ROMAN-FLEUVE.

salamander

In literature, *salamander* usually refers to a mythical being, especially a large lizard or other reptile, thought to be able to live in fire. Pope wrote, in *The Rape of the Lock,* "The sprites of fiery termagants in flame / Mount up and take a salamander's name." In Shakespeare's *Henry IV,* Part 1, Falstaff refers to a character's nose, made heavy-veined and red from alcohol, as a salamander.

salon

A French term meaning a drawing room or reception room. The term usually refers to an assembly of guests in such a room, especially a group of leaders in art, literature, politics, or society.

sans serif

A printing term meaning "without serifs," that is, type exhibiting letters without finishing strokes (or lines) projecting from the ends of main strokes. See SERIF.

Sapphic

A term referring to Sappho, a Greek poetess born on the

island of Lesbos (Mytilene) in the seventh century B.C. (See LESBIAN.) *Sapphics* is a name applied to four-line *stanzas in a *meter used by Sappho and imitated by the English poet Swinburne in a volume entitled *Sapphics*. A Sapphic verse (line) consists of eleven syllables (see HENDECASYLLABIC) as in this excerpt from a stanza by Swinburne: "Softly touched mine eyelids and lips; and I too." A Sapphic ode is virtually the same as a *Horatian ode.

sarcasm

A form of *irony; bitter and often harsh derision. Sarcasm consists of sneering or cutting remarks; it is always personal, always jeering, and always intended to hurt. Byron's comment on Robert Southey, another English poet, is filled with sarcastic remarks, such as

> He first sank to the bottom—like his work,
> But soon rose to the surface—like himself;
> For all corrupted things are buoyed like corks,
> By their own rottenness. . . .

sardonic

An adjective meaning sneering, scornful, disdainful. A sardonic person, such as Damon Wildeve in Hardy's *The Return of the Native,* is contemptuous of others and biting in his comments about them. See CYNICISM, SARCASM.

Sassenach

A term for "Englishman," Irish in origin, that is usually used disparagingly by *Gaelic persons residing in the British Isles. See ANGLO-SAXON.

satanic

Wicked, diabolical, devillike, evil. The phrase *satanic school* has been applied to a group of nineteenth-century English poets (among them Shelley and Byron) who led somewhat irregular lives and departed from *orthodoxy in many of their opinions. The satanic school of *biography includes writers who not only deal with externals but try to get inside their subjects—inside their minds and even their subconscious. A satanic biographer (such as Lytton Strachey was) attempts to view his subject with detachment, *irony, and probing insistence.

satire

The ridiculing of folly, stupidity, or vice; the use of *irony, *sarcasm, or *ridicule for exposing or denouncing the frailties and faults of mankind. Satire is a literary manner, or *technique, that blends *humor and *wit with a critical attitude toward human activities and institutions. *Satire* is a general term, one usually considered to involve both moral judgment and a desire to help improve a custom, belief, or tradition. (See BURLESQUE, CARICATURE, INVECTIVE, LAMPOON, PARODY.)

*Horatian satire is gentle, chiding, and corrective; *Juvenalian satire is savage and bitter; modern satire is genial (Mark Twain), witty (George Bernard Shaw), or fun-provoking (E. B. White, James Thurber). Outstanding satirists of the past and present are Aristophanes, Juvenal, Horace, Molière, Dryden, Pope, Swift, Thackeray, Evelyn Waugh, Aldous Huxley, Sinclair Lewis, John P. Marquand, Philip Roth, and John Cheever.

satyriasis

Abnormal, uncontrollable sexual desire in men. (See NYMPHOMANIA.) *Satyriasis* is derived from *satyr,* one of a group of mythological woodland deities, part human and part *goat noted for their riotousness and lust. A satyromaniac is a lecher; a satyr play is an ancient Greek drama, a ribald *burlesque presenting a chorus of satyrs. Euripides's *Cyclops* is a satyr play.

saw

A wise *saying, a homely but sentententious remark ("Beauty's but skin deep"). (See MAXIM, PROVERB.) In *As You Like It,* when describing the seven ages of man, Shakespeare referred to the justice

> In fair round belly with good capon lined,
> With eyes severe and beard of formal cut,
> Full of wise saws and modern instances [examples].

saying

A general term for any expression or utterance, especially one that reveals a general truth. Among kinds of sayings are the *adage, *aphorism, *apothegm, *epigram, *maxim, *motto, and *proverb.

scansion

The metrical *analysis of poetry; the division of a line of poetry into feet by indicating *accents and counting *syllables. Scansion is a method of studying the mechanical elements by means of which the poet has secured rhythmical effects. Scansion involves consideration of the *foot, length of line (*meter), and *rhyme scheme of a group of poetic verses. Scansion of the first five lines of Keats's *Endymion* is as follows:

> A thing / of beau/ty is / a joy / forever: *a*
> Its love/liness / increas/es; it / will never   *a*
> Pass in/to noth/ingness; / but still / will keep *b*
> A bow/er qui/et for / us, and / a sleep   *b*
> Full of / sweet dreams, / and health, /
>   and qui/et breathing.   *c*

scatology

Obscene literature. *Scatology,* derived from a Greek word meaning "dung," is closely related to *pornography; in science, the term refers to a study of fossil excrement.

scenario

An *outline of the *plot of a dramatic work, providing particulars about *characters, *settings, and *situations. *Scenario* is most often used as a name for a detailed script of a motion picture: a treatment setting forth action in the sequence it is to follow, detailed descriptions of scenes and characters, actual words (text) to be spoken or shown on the screen, etc. The *plot of a film or *television production is sometimes loosely called its scenario.

scene

(1) The place where some act or event occurs; (2) an *incident or *situation in real life; (3) a division of an *act of a *play; (4) a unit of dramatic action in which a single point is made or one effect obtained.

schematic

A diagram, plan, arrangement, or drawing. A blueprint is a schematic for a building; a *scenario is a schematic for a motion picture or play.

schizophrenia

An emotional disorder marked by withdrawn, bizarre behavior and by intellectual and emotional lack of control and deterioration. Schizophrenia has appeared more and more often in plays and novels since the advent of *Freudianism and *Jungian psychology, notably in the work of Eugene O'Neill, Tennessee Williams, Edward Albee, and William Faulkner. Students and theorists have attributed schizophrenic symptoms to many characters in literature, including Oedipus and Hamlet.

scholasticism

A term now used to mean narrow and unyielding adherence to traditional methods, doctrines, and teachings. (See DIDACTICISM, PEDANTRY, PRECIOSITY.) In literary history, *scholasticism* is used to refer to a system of philosophical and theological teachings predominant in the *Middle Ages. The doctrines of Schoolmen (Abelard, Albertus Magnus, Aquinas, Duns Scotus, et al.) were basically an attempt to reconcile the statements of Aristotle and Plato with Roman Catholic faith and practice. See NOMINALISM.

scholiast

An ancient commentator on the classics. A scholiast wrote *marginalia explaining the *grammar and meaning of passages in *medieval manuscripts that were based on Greek and Latin texts.

schoolgirl style

A manner of writing characterized by *exaggeration, gushiness, and an overuse of intensives. *Counterwords, *hyperbole, and *random punctuation also are hallmarks of schoolgirl style.

science fiction

Narrative which draws imaginatively on scientific knowledge, theory, and speculation in its *plot, *theme, and *setting. Science fiction is a form of *fantasy in which *hypotheses form the basis, by logical *extrapolation, of space travel, adventures on other planets, etc. The form has been in existence since at least the second century: Lucian, a Greek writer, created a *hero who traveled to the moon. Jules Verne (*Twenty Thousand Leagues under the Sea*) wrote science fiction more than a century ago.

scintilla

From the Latin word for *spark, scintilla* means "a trace," "a tiny particle." One scholar has written, for example, that there is not a scintilla of genuine evidence that Francis Bacon wrote any of the plays attributed to William Shakespeare.

scop

An *Anglo-Saxon poet. A scop was a sort of *bard to the court, although he may have wandered about the countryside like a *gleeman. A scop drew his stories from *traditions and *legends of early Germanic peoples and from Biblical accounts.

Scotticism

A *word or *idiom peculiar to, or characteristic of, the *dialect of English spoken in Scotland. The poems of Robert Burns, for example, are filled with Scotticisms: *frae* ("from"), *haet* ("hate"), *wale* ("choose"), etc.

screen play

A motion picture; the *scenario of a motion picture; an *adaptation of a stage *play, *short story, or *novel for a motion picture.

scurrility

Writing or speech that is abusive, coarse, or obscene. *Scurrility* applies to oral or written statements that are derisive, offensive, and insulting. Walt Whitman was the object of scurrilous attacks upon his beliefs, morals, and writings. See CALUMNY, LIBEL, SLANDER.

secondary source

A *source of information that is not primary or original; facts or opinions that are not firsthand and direct. (See PRIMARY SOURCE.) A secondary source of information about a writer would be an encyclopedia article concerning him; a primary source would be facts in a *Who's Who* sketch prepared (or approved) by the author himself.

sectarian
Narrowly limited or confined in interest, purpose, scope, etc. *Sectarian,* derived from *sect* (a party or group united in belief or organization), is usually applied to the special interests of political parties or religious bodies.

segue
A verb derived from a Latin word for *follow, segue* means to continue at once with the next *composition or section (in music) or the next scene (*television, motion pictures). The term is used in the sense of continuing a performance, or presentation, without a break and in the manner or style of the preceding action or section.

semantics
The study of meaning; a branch of *linguistics that deals with the meanings of words and with historical changes in those meanings. Semantics may also be thought of as the relations between signs (words, *symbols) and the mental and physical actions called forth by their meanings. See GENERAL SEMANTICS, SEMIOTICS, WORD.

semblance
(1) An assumed or unreal appearance; (2) outward aspect or appearance; (3) likeness, image, copy; (4) an *apparition, *spectral appearance. *Semblance,* from a French word meaning "to seem," appears in literature in each of the meanings indicated; for example, Dr. Almus Pickenbaugh in Sinclair Lewis's *Arrowsmith* provides a semblance of medical competence and dedication but actually is a fake; the ghost of Hamlet's father is an apparition, a semblance; the musical play *My Fair Lady* provides a semblance of the drama from which it was derived, Shaw's *Pygmalion;* there is not a semblance of genuine kindness or understanding in William Carey, uncle of the *hero in Maugham's *Of Human Bondage.*

seminal
Highly original and thus influencing the development of future events. The work of a seminal writer, such as Bacon, Shakespeare, Wordsworth, or Mark Twain, possesses the "seeds" of growth and causes changes and developments in the thoughts and attitudes of others, readers and authors alike.

semiotics
The study of *symbols and signs. From a Greek word meaning "sign," *semiotics* involves a general theory of symbolism including semantics (word meanings), syntactics (structural relations among symbols), and pragmatics (the relation between behavior and symbols). (See GENERAL SEMANTICS, LINGUISTICS,

SEMANTICS, SYMBOLISM.) The adjective *semiotic* is used in medical *jargon to refer to symptoms of illness.

Senecan

A reference to Lucius Seneca, a first-century Roman philosopher and writer of tragedies. Seneca's plays, modeled on those of Euripides, had a profound effect upon *Renaissance playwrights in their subject matter and use of dramatic *conventions. Senecan tragedy invariably appeared in five *acts, dealt with powerfully conflicting emotions, resulted in *catastrophe, and employed much *bombast. See REVENGE TRAGEDY.

sensibility

Capacity for feeling or sensation; responsiveness to sensory stimuli. *Sensibility* implies quickness and acuteness of apprehension or feeling and, in general, indicates emotionalism rather than *rationalism. As a *synonym for "keen consciousness" or "appreciation," *sensibility* is closely related to *empathy. (See SYMPATHY.) Laurence Sterne's *Tristram Shandy* is a novel of sensibility; Jane Austen's *Sense and Sensibility* (1811) is a narrative contrasting rationalism and this form of emotionalism. Aldous Huxley has written:

> Experience is not a matter of actually having swum the Hellespont, or danced with dervishes, or slept in a dosshouse. It is a matter of sensibility and intuition, of seeing and hearing the significant things, of paying attention at the right moments, of understanding. . . .

sensory words

Phrases and expressions which have an appeal to the senses as well as the mind. Words are sensory when they make an impression on one of the five senses (hearing, etc.). See ALLITERATION, FIGURES OF SPEECH, ONOMATOPOEIA.

sensual, sensuous

Sensual refers, usually unfavorably, to enjoyments and delights derived from the senses and ordinarily implies coarseness, grossness, and lewdness. Falstaff, for instance, took a sensual delight in eating and drinking. *Sensuous* refers, often favorably, to what is experienced through the senses; for example, one enjoys such a sensuous poem as Keats's *The Eve of St. Agnes*.

sentence

A group of words conveying to the listener (or reader) a sense of complete meaning; a group of words containing a subject and predicate and expressing a complete thought; a stretch of prose (or poetry, for that matter) which a competent writer punctuates by beginning with a capital letter and ending with a terminal mark (period, etc.). No fully satisfactory definition of a sentence is possible, but general agreement exists that an effective sentence is perhaps the greatest invention of the human intellect. See LOOSE SENTENCE, PERIODIC SENTENCE.

sententia

A wise saying; a philosophical statement. *Sententia* is a *synonym for *maxim. Sententiae (plural) are usually formal and judicial; use of them results in a sententious style—one containing pithy sayings and moralizing comments.

sentimentalism

Excessive indulgence in sentiment or emotionalism; predominance of feeling over reason and intellect. Sentimentalism in literature is "emotion run wild," with emphasis on feeling rather than on events and circumstances which produced the feeling. Sentimentalism produces a reaction of sentimentality: a quick, too-ready reaction to emotion. Dickens carefully aroused for readers sensations of pity in *The Old Curiosity Shop,* but as Little Nell uncomplainingly fades away into death, sentimentality takes over rather than a more sensible reaction toward the forces that have undermined the orphan's chances for happiness.

septenary

An adjective referring to the number seven. As a noun, *septenary* means a period of seven years, the number seven, and a line of poetry containing seven feet. See FOURTEENER, HEPTAMETER.

septet

Any group of seven persons or objects; a company of seven vocalists or musicians; a poem or *stanza of seven lines. See RHYME ROYAL.

Septuagint

The oldest Greek version of the Old Testament. The Septuagint, from Latin words meaning "seven decades" or "seventy," was prepared (translated and completed) during the third, fourth, and fifth centuries; it still plays an important role in services of the Greek Orthodox Church.

sequel

(1) A literary work that continues the narrative of a preceding work; (2) a result or consequence; (3) a subsequent course of affairs. *Sequel,* from a Latin word meaning "follow," is used in each of these meanings in literature. Galsworthy's *To Let* (1921) is a sequel to *In Chancery* (1920); these novels are sequels to *The Man of Property* (1906), and the three combined form *The Forsyte Saga.* For comment on *sequel* as "following action" or "consequence," see ACTION, CAUSE AND EFFECT, PLOT.

sequential

Following, consequent, subsequent. *Sequential* is derived from *sequence* (the following of one thing after another). The *action in every worthwhile literary selection is sequential because *incidents have a planned *organization that follows the *purpose of the author. See COHERENCE.

serenade

A performance of vocal or instrumental music as a tribute to someone or to some institution. A serenade is usually a song sung by a gallant under his lady's window (the word is derived from an Italian term meaning "evening song"). Shelley's *Indian Serenade* is a poem imitating such a song. A once well-known serenade is that of a minor American poet, Bayard Taylor, called *Bedouin Song,* a part of which is:

> My steps are nightly driven,
> By the fever in my breast
> To hear from thy lattice breathed
> The word that shall give me rest.
> Open the door of thy heart,
> And open thy chamber door,
> And my kisses shall teach thy lips
> The love that shall fade no more
> Till the sun grows cold,
> And the stars are old,
> And the leaves of the Judgment Book unfold.

serendipity

The ability to make fortunate and desirable discoveries by accident. *Serendipity* was coined by an eighteenth-century English essayist and novelist, Horace Walpole, in a *tale entitled *The Three Princes of Serendip;* the heroes of this fairy story "were always making discoveries, by accidents and sagacity, of things they were not in quest of." The story of Jack and the Beanstalk, a nursery tale found among many races and peoples from Assyrians to Zulus, provides an example of serendipity. The word, perhaps by confusion with *serenity,* is sometimes incorrectly used to mean "happiness" or "contentment."

serial rights

The rights (fees, payments, claims) of an author or composer to anything of his that is published or broadcast in installments. As used in book publishing, "first" *serial rights* refers to the appearance of a *novel, for example, in a *periodical prior to its appearance in book form. "Second" *serial rights* applies to publication in other media after first publication in book form. Although *serial,* from a Latin word meaning "connected," refers to items or events appearing or occurring "at regular intervals," the term no longer necessarily carries the meaning of "installments" in magazine and book publishing circles but rather relates to the *time* and *method* of publication.

serif

A term in printing for a lighter line used to finish off the main stroke of a letter such as at the top and bottom of *N*. The word is derived from a Dutch word meaning "stroke." See SANS SERIF.

sermon

A serious speech, especially one on a moral issue; a talk for the purpose of religious instruction; a carefully prepared discourse (*oration) delivered from a pulpit by a clergyman as part of a church service. (See DIDACTICISM, EXEMPLUM.) In *Don Juan,* Byron wrote, "Let us have wine and women, mirth and laughter, / Sermons and soda-water the day after." In the sense of instruction about personal conduct, Shakespeare used *sermon* in these lines from *As You Like It:*

> And this our life, exempt from public haunt,
> Finds tongues in trees, books in the
>   running brooks,
> Sermons in stones, and good in everything.

sesquipedalian

A term describing someone given to using long words. (See PEDANTRY, POLYSYLLABICATION.) *Sesquipedalian,* composed of Latin terms meaning "a foot and a half," also refers to writing that employs pompous, many-syllabled terms. In Boswell's biography of Samuel Johnson, this remark is made to Johnson, a learned man: "If you were to make little fishes talk, they would talk like whales."

sestet

The last six lines of an *Italian sonnet; any *poem or *stanza of six lines. *Sestet,* also spelled *sextet,* may also refer to a group of six vocalists or instrumentalists. See OCTAVE, PETRARCHAN.

sestina

A poem of six six-line *stanzas and an *envoi of three lines. The sestina is a complicated, difficult verse form involving repetition in each stanza of words arranged in different order from their appearance in preceding stanzas. The form has been used by Dante, Petrarch, Sir Philip Sidney, Swinburne, Kipling, Ezra Pound, and W. H. Auden.

setting

The environment or surroundings of anything. The term is usually applied in literature to the *locale or period in which the *action of a play, novel, motion picture, etc., takes place. In theatrical *jargon, *setting* may also refer to scenery or properties (see PROP). The setting of *Macbeth* is Scotland in the eleventh century; more specifically, the *incidents in the play occur in seven different settings—Forres, Inverness, Dunsinane, the forests (witches' scenes), Duncan's camp, Fife, and England. See LOCAL COLOR, LOCALE, REGIONALISM.

seven deadly sins

According to *medieval theology, the seven deadly (capital, cardinal) sins were pride, anger (wrath), envy, sloth (laziness), lust (lechery), covetousness (avarice), and gluttony. Each of these sins resulted in spiritual death; each could be atoned for only through complete and perfect repentance. These sins were often presented in *allegory and *personification in medieval and *Renaissance times. Dante treated each of them in his poetry; Chaucer's *The Parson's Tale* and Spenser's *The Faerie Queene* deal with these flaws. See SEVEN VIRTUES.

seven liberal arts

The seven subjects (or disciplines) studied in *medieval universities. The three studies of the four-year course leading to a baccalaureate degree were the trivium: *grammar (really Latin grammar), *logic, and *rhetoric (especially speaking, oratory). The four subjects following in a three-year curriculum leading to an advanced degree were the quadrivium: arithmetic, geometry, astronomy, and music. See QUADRIVIUM, TRIVIUM.

seven virtues

In the teachings of *scholasticism, the seven virtues were courage (fortitude), prudence, justice, temperance, faith, hope, and charity (love for one's fellows). These virtues were frequently allegorized and personified (see ALLEGORY, PERSONIFICATION) as, for example, in Spenser's *The Faerie Queene*. Seven was a mystic or magic number to the ancients, as witness the seven ages of the world, seven blessings of heaven, seven heresies, seven gifts of the spirit, seven gods of luck, seven names of God, seven sorrows of Mary, etc. See NUMEROLOGY.

Seven Wonders of the World

The most remarkable structures of the ancient world were considered to be the Egyptian pyramids; the mausoleum at Halicarnassus; the Pharos (lighthouse) at Alexandria; the statue of Zeus by Phidias, at Olympia; the temple of Artemis at Ephesus; the hanging gardens of Babylon; the Colossus of Rhodes. A later list gave the Coliseum at Rome; the catacombs of Alexandria; Stonehenge; the leaning tower of Pisa; the great wall of China; the porcelain tower of Nanking; and the mosque of Santa Sophia at Constantinople.

Shakespearean sonnet

A poem of fourteen lines arranged in three *quatrains and

a *couplet. This *stanza was developed by earlier poets (Wyatt and Surrey) during the first half of the sixteenth century; it is referred to also as an *English sonnet, but the Shakespearean sonnet is so named for its greatest practitioner, who wrote 154 such poems. The following sonnet illustrates the form and reveals the poet's belief in the power of poetry to outlive mankind:

> Shall I compare thee to a summer's day?
> Thou art more lovely and more temperate:
> Rough winds do shake the darling buds of May,
> And summer's lease hath all too short a date:
> Sometime too hot the eye of heaven shines,
> And often is his gold complexion dimmed;
> And every fair from fair sometime declines,
> By chance, or nature's changing course untrimmed;
> But thy eternal summer shall not fade,
> Nor lose possession of that fair thou owest
> Nor shall Death brag thou wander'st in his shade,
> When in eternal lines to time thou growest:
> > So long as men can breathe or eyes can see,
> > So long lives this, and this gives life to thee.

shibboleth

A word or formula used as a test. *Shibboleth* was a word chosen by the Gileadites to distinguish fleeting Ephraimites who could not pronounce the *sh* sound. (The incident is recounted in Judges 12.) *Shibboleth* has been extended in meaning (in Hebrew it meant a "stream" or "ear of corn") beyond the concept of testing to refer to any peculiarity or oddity of behavior, pronunciation, way of dressing, etc., that distinguishes a particular set or class of persons.

shoptalk

Conversation or vocabulary having to do with work, especially a particular field of work; talk about one's occupation, hobby, or primary interest. See ARGOT, CANT, IDIOM.

short measure

A *stanza used for *hymns, consisting of four lines, rhyming *abab* or *abcb*. Short measure (or short meter) is so called because three of the lines in the *quatrain consist of three feet (iambic trimeter). This is a short measure (often abbreviated as S.M.) from a hymn by Isaac Watts:

> There is a dreadful Hell,
> And everlasting pains;
> There sinners must with devils dwell
> In darkness, fire, and chains.

See COMMON MEASURE, LONG MEASURE, MEASURE.

short short story

A brief piece of prose *fiction, more condensed than a

*short story. Such a selection may vary in length from 500 to 1,500 words, a length in which *conflict, *characterization, and *setting must be handled deftly and economically. (See ECONOMY.) A short short story contains every ingredient of a *short story but with heightened *focus and brevity. See VIGNETTE.

short story

A relatively short narrative (under 10,000 words) which is designed to produce a single dominant effect and which contains the elements of *drama. A short story concentrates on a single *character in a single *situation at a single moment. Even if these conditions are not met, a short story still exhibits *unity as its guiding principle. An effective short story consists of a character (or group of characters) presented against a background, or *setting, involved, through mental or physical *action, in a *situation. Dramatic *conflict—the collision of opposing forces—is at the heart of every short story.

Short stories have existed in one form or another throughout history. More than 2,000 years ago, the Old Testament revealed narratives about King David, Joseph, Jonah, and Ruth which were essentially short stories. The *fabliau and the *exemplum were *medieval forms of such narratives. Edgar Allan Poe is considered the father of the modern short story. The *genre has flourished throughout the world for more than a century in the works of Maupassant, Mérimée, Zola, Turgenev, Chekhov, Hawthorne, Stevenson, Hardy, and hundreds of twentieth-century craftsmen.

sibilants

Hissing sounds. In *phonetics, a sibilant is a sound such as those spelled with *s* in thi*s*, ro*s*e, pre*ss*ure, plea*s*ure, etc. Sibilants are produced also by the letters and letter combinations *j*, *z*, *ch*, *sh*, *zh*. See ALLITERATION, ASSONANCE, ONOMATOPOEIA.

sic

A Latin word meaning "thus" or "so." *Sic* is usually written in brackets or parentheses to indicate that a word, phrase, etc., which may seem incorrect or strange has been quoted *verbatim or written intentionally.

sigmatism

Defective pronunciation, or overuse, of *sibilants. *Sigmatism,* from the Greek word for *s*, *sigma,* has long been a problem for poets because *s, z, j, sh, zh,* and *ch* necessarily appear often in English words and frequently sound harsh or hissing. Joseph Addison commented on "the hissing so much noticed by foreigners," and Tennyson referred to his own restricted use of sibilants as "kicking the geese out of the boat." Poe deliberately used sigmatism to achieve a *sensory effect in these lines:

Now each visitor shall confess
The sad valley's restlessness.
Nothing there is motionless—
Nothing save the airs that brood
Over the magic solitude.

signature

A distinguishing figure, letter, or number placed at the foot of the first page of every section of a *book to guide the binder in arranging sections in sequence. The term may also refer to a sheet that, when folded, forms four (or a multiple of four) pages of a book or other publication. In American bookmaking, a signature is usually considered to consist of sixteen or thirty-two pages. See FOLIO.

silhouette

From the name of an eighteenth-century French government official, *silhouette* most often refers to a two-dimensional representation of the *outline of an object. It also is used as a term for the appearance of a dark *image outlined against a lighter background. In *printing, *silhouette* is a verb meaning to remove nonessential background from a *halftone so as to produce an outline effect. In literary criticism, *silhouette* is occasionally used as a *synonym for *sketch (a simply developed composition).

simian

Of or pertaining to a monkey or ape, or such an animal itself. *Simian* may mean "imitating" or "copying," as apes are said to imitate man. More logically, mankind itself is simian in view of the facts of evolution. In *This Simian World,* Clarence Day wrote about the human race:

> . . . what marvelous creatures we are! What fairy story, what tale from the Arabian Nights . . . is a hundredth part as wonderful as this true fairy story of simians?

simile

A *figure of speech in which two things, essentially different but thought to be alike in one or more respects, are compared. In a simile the point of likeness is expressed by *like, as,* or *as if.* (See EPIC SIMILE, METAPHOR.) Similes, which make imaginative comparisons for purposes of explanation or ornament, are essential in all poetry and occur frequently in prose as well. Two similes appear in this quatrain from Robert Burns:

> O, my luve is like a red, red rose
> That's newly sprung in June;
> O, my luve is like the melodie
> That's sweetly played in tune.

similitude

Likeness, resemblance. *Similitude* also has the meaning of

*semblance: Bunyan referred to his *Pilgrim's Progress* as being "delivered under the similitude of a dream." Sometimes, *similitude* is used as a *synonym for *simile. See VERISIMILITUDE.

simpatico

Congenial, sympathetic. *Simpatico* is an Italian word implying suitability, compatibility, and agreeableness. See EMPATHY, SYMPATHY.

simplicity

Freedom from complexity, intricacy, or elaborate division into parts; absence of luxury, ornament, and pretentiousness; plainness, artlessness, naturalness. Because human nature is involved and human motivations are frequently complex, simplicity in literature is nearly always relative. Yet all great writers of the past and present have attempted to avoid such intricacy of *style and complexity of subject matter as to prevent or impede communication from writer to reader. See CLEARNESS, ESOTERIC.

simplistic

An adjective appearing often in literary criticism to mean "oversimplified," "made too easy or plain," "less complicated than should be indicated." *Simplistic* is derived from *simple,* which in turn is taken from Latin words meaning "onefold."

sincerity

Freedom from hypocrisy, false pretense, or deceit; earnestness. In literature, *sincerity* involves correspondence between the ideas and ideals of an author and those presented or implied in his work. Also, *sincerity* refers to the integrity with which a literary selection meets its own demands and attitudes in the avoidance of *sentimentalism, *melodrama, *coincidence, and the like and in attempts to meet the tests of *clearness, communication, and *simplicity.

sine die

A Latin phrase meaning "without fixing a day" (for a future meeting or action). The term is generally used to mean "indefinitely" and "undetermined."

sine qua non

A Latin phrase meaning "without which not." The expression is used to mean "an indispensable condition," "something essential." (Conflict is the sine qua non of every work of genuine *fiction.)

situation

A location or position; a state of affairs. In literature, *situation* is a term used to refer to the group of circumstances in which a *character finds himself and to the *setting and conditions under which a work of *fiction begins its *action. (See PLOT.) The opening situation in *Macbeth* is that of a nobleman (Macbeth) who is expecting a visit from his ruler to the castle in Inverness, Scotland. The situation in Flaubert's *Madame Bovary* is that of a young woman living a life of tedium in a small village as the wife of a mediocre physician.

sixain

A *stanza of six lines. A sixain usually consists of a *quatrain and a *couplet, as in this sixain, which is the fourth stanza of Wordsworth's *I Wandered Lonely as a Cloud:*

For oft, when on my couch I lie
In vacant or in pensive mood,
They flash upon that inward eye
Which is the bliss of solitude.
And then my heart with pleasure fills
And dances with the daffodils.

skald

An ancient Scandinavian poet. A skald (also spelled *scald*) played about the same role as an Anglo-Saxon *scop did.

Skeltonics

Rough, unstressed, and rollicking verses named for their originator, John Skelton (1460–1529), an English poet. Skeltonics resemble *doggerel, have an irregular rhyme scheme, and are composed of lines of varying length. This excerpt from a poem by Skelton will illustrate:

Merry Margaret, as midsummer flower,
Gentle as falcon or hawk of the tower,
With solace and gladness,
Much mirth and no madness,
All good and no badness;
So joyously,
So maidenly,
So womanly,
Her demeaning . . .

skepticism

Doubt, unbelief. Skepticism is an attitude of questioning, testing, probing, and, as such, it has constituted an influential *point of view in literature from the beginnings. In ancient Greece, a society of Skeptics maintained that real knowledge is impossible; skeptics have not wanted for followers in all succeeding centuries. See BELIEF, DISBELIEF, GNOSTIC, ORTHODOXY, SUSPENSION OF DISBELIEF.

sketch

(1) A short, descriptive *essay; (2) a short play or brief

dramatic performance; (3) any simply constructed *composition that presents a single *character, single *scene, or single *incident. (See CHARACTER SKETCH, VAUDEVILLE.) A sketch may also be a rough design, plan, or first draft of a literary work or a brief, hasty *outline of an *article, *essay, or *book. Dickens's *Sketches by Boz* ("Boz" was a *pseudonym sometimes used by Dickens) is a series of comments on life and manners, published at *random in various *periodicals.

slander

A malicious, false, and defamatory statement or report. (See LIBEL.) Legally, slander is defamation or *calumny by *oral utterance rather than in writing, drawings, or pictures. The nineteenth-century English critic John Ruskin slandered some of the paintings of James McNeill Whistler, but he was sued for libel by Whistler only when he wrote and published statements such as: "I have seen, and heard, much of *Cockney impudence before now; but never expected to hear a coxcomb ask two hundred guineas for flinging a pot of paint in the public's face." (Whistler was awarded damages of one farthing, a now-withdrawn English coin, then worth less than one cent.)

slang

A particular kind of *colloquialism or *illiteracy, slang consists of widely used terms having a forced, fantastic, or eccentric meaning. (See ARGOT, CANT.) Slang expresses feeling, usually explosively or grotesquely; it prevents *artificiality; it provides useful shortcuts in expression. Nevertheless, most authors use slang only when writing informally or when characterizing in *dialogue individuals who would normally speak in an inexact, *vernacular way. In *Language,* the Danish philologist Otto Jespersen wrote:

> Slang words are words used in conscious contrast to the natural or normal speech; they can be found in all classes of society in certain moods and on certain occasions when the speaker wants to avoid the natural or normal word because he thinks it too flat or uninteresting.

slant rhyme

A *synonym for *approximate rhyme, usually the substitution of *assonance for real *rhyme. The words *giver* and *never* are an example of slant rhyme.

slapstick

Broad comedy characterized by violent and boisterous *action; *farce combined with horseplay in a comic form. The term derives its name from a stick, or lath, used by *harlequins in *commedia dell'arte and *pantomime. Such a slapstick would make a noise when it was used to strike a fellow actor. So-called comic *sketches in *vaudeville involving pie-in-the-face acts, dunkings, and pratfalls are examples of slapstick *farce.

slice of life

Accurate transcription into *fiction or *drama of a segment of actual *experience. (See TRANCHE DE VIE.) In the slice of life *technique, a novelist or dramatist opens a door for the reader, permits him to see and hear characters, and then closes the door without comment or observation. This method is related to that of *stream of consciousness but with a difference noted by Edith Wharton in *The Writing of Fiction:*

> The stream of consciousness differs from the slice of life in noting down mental as well as physical reactions but resembles it in setting them down just as they come, with a deliberate disregard of their relevance in the particular case, or rather with the assumption that their very unsorted abundance constitutes in itself the author's subject.

The unselective presentation of life—life the way it is, without neat and specific beginning and ending, with extreme *realism—has been an important technique for such writers of *naturalism as Zola, Maupassant, Dreiser, James Joyce, Frank Norris, Eugene O'Neill, and James T. Farrell.

slick magazine

A popular, basically nonliterary *periodical. A slick magazine, or a slick, derives its name from the appearance of the coated (polished) stock on which it is printed. See MASS MEDIA, PULP MAGAZINE.

slogan

A phrase, *motto, or distinctive *saying of any group, party, organization, or person; a *catchword. Slogan was originally a war shout used by Scottish clans, a word derived from a Gaelic term for "army cry." The political cry "Throw the rascals out" is a slogan. In an address, James Bryant Conant, former president of Harvard University, said:

> Slogans are both exciting and comforting, but they are also powerful opiates for the conscience.... Some of mankind's most terrible misdeeds have been committed under the spell of certain magic words or phrases.

slush pile

The stack of unsolicited, unwanted, and often worthless *manuscripts accumulated in the editorial offices of a book or magazine publisher before they are rejected. The phrase gets its name from the meaning of *slush* as silly, emotional, or sentimental talk and writing.

sobriquet

A nickname; a name added to, or substituted for, the proper name of a place or person; a familiar form of a proper name. Justice Byron R. White has a sobriquet of "Whizzer." *Sobriquet,* also spelled *soubriquet,* is a French term. See EPI-THET, EPONYM, KENNING.

society

As used in literature, *society* means human beings generally or, less often, an organized group of persons living as members of a community. Society may also be considered as classes of people grouped according to worldly status. In ecology, *society* refers to an integrated group of social organisms of the same species held together by mutual dependence. Thomas Paine made clear what was, for him, a distinction between *society* (association, community) and *government:* "Society in every state is a blessing, but government, even in its best state, is but a necessary evil."

sociological novel, play

A narrative or dramatic work that deals primarily with social questions and problems, that focuses on environmental and cultural factors more than on personal and psychological characteristics. A sociological work centers principal attention on the *society in which characters live, its effects upon them, and the social forces that control *action. Such a work develops a thesis but is not necessarily an all-out effort in propaganda. In *Middlemarch,* George Eliot made a sociological examination in narrative form of a small town. *Muckraking produced several notable sociological works by writers such as Upton Sinclair and Lincoln Steffens. John Steinbeck, Albert Halper, Erskine Caldwell, and John Dos Passos have written sociological novels; Clifford Odets, Irwin Shaw, and Tennessee Williams have written sociological plays. See PROBLEM NOVEL, PLAY; PROLETARIAN; PROPAGAN-DA; THESIS.

sock

A lightweight shoe worn by ancient Greek and Roman actors in *comedy. See BUSKIN.

Socratic

A term referring to Socrates, a fifth-century-B.C. Athenian philosopher. Socratic irony is a *technique of pretending ignorance with a view toward later defeating one's conversational opponent. (See IRONY.) The Socratic method of discourse or *argumentation involves using questions to develop an idea. The intent of the queries is to get the answerer to form his own opinions or make admissions and concessions that will help to establish a *proposition. In *Paradise Regained,* Milton called Socrates the "wisest of men." Plutarch reported that Socrates considered himself neither an Athenian nor a Greek but a "citizen of the world."

solecism

An error, *impropriety, or inconsistency; a breach of etiquette or manners. Specifically, a solecism is an ungrammatical or substandard use (misuse) of language. The word is derived from the name of a city in Asia Minor where "incorrect" Greek was spoken. See BARBARISM, BONER, ILLITERACY, MALAPROPISM.

soliloquy

A speech delivered by a character in a *play (or other literary composition) while he is alone. A soliloquy is an utterance (discourse) by a person (usually an actor) who is talking to himself or is disregardful of, or oblivious to, any hearers present. *Soliloquy,* derived from a Latin word meaning "talking to oneself," is frequently used in *drama to disclose a character's innermost feelings or to provide information needed by the audience (readers). Shakespeare's most famous soliloquies appear in *Macbeth, Hamlet,* and *Othello.* The device has been used often by Eugene O'Neill, Thornton Wilder, Tennessee Williams, Edward Albee, and Samuel Beckett. See ASIDE, INTERIOR MONOLOGUE, MONOLOGUE, STREAM OF CONSCIOUSNESS.

solipsism

The theory that only the self exists or can be proved to exist. Solipsism, from Latin words meaning "self alone," is an extreme form of *subjectivity and of idealism.

solution

An explanation or answer. *Solution* is a term sometimes used instead of *catastrophe or *denouement to indicate the outcome of a work of *fiction or *drama. That is, a solution (answer) is provided for the *complication developed in the *plot of a *play, *novel, or *short story.

song

A short, metrical composition intended for singing; a *lyric; a *ballad. Derived from words in Icelandic, German, and *Old English meaning "to sing," *song* is most often employed in literature to refer to a lyric poem adapted to expression in music. Shakespeare's plays contain some of the finest songs ever written. They are of various kinds: the *aubade, the *dirge, the *ballad, the *pastoral lyric, etc. Ben Jonson's *Song: to Celia* may be the best-known song in literature:

> Drink to me only with thine eyes,
> And I will pledge with mine;
> Or leave a kiss but in the cup,

And I'll not look for wine.
The thirst that from the soul doth rise
Doth ask a drink divine;
But might I of Jove's nectar sup,
I would not change for thine.

I sent thee late a rosy wreath,
Not so much honoring thee
As giving it a hope, that there
It could not withered be.
But thou thereon didst only breathe,
And sent'st it back to me;
Since when it grows, and smells, I swear,
Not of itself, but thee.

sonnet

A poem of fourteen lines, usually in iambic *pentameter, with *rhymes arranged according to certain definite *patterns (*rhyme schemes). A sonnet usually expresses a single, complete thought, idea, or sentiment. The sonnet (a word adapted from a Latin term for "sound") was developed in Italy early during the *Renaissance and was introduced into England by Thomas Wyatt and the Earl of Surrey (Henry Howard) in the sixteenth century. This *stanza has continued to flourish on both sides of the Atlantic ever since. Wordsworth's *Scorn Not the Sonnet* pays a tribute to this stanzaic form and mentions a few of the world's greatest sonneteers:

Scorn not the Sonnet; Critic, you have frowned,
Mindless of its just honors; with this key
Shakespeare unlocked his heart; the melody
Of this small lute gave ease to Petrarch's wound;
A thousand times this pipe did Tasso sound;
With it Camoëns soothed an exile's grief;
The Sonnet glittered a gay myrtle leaf
Amid the cypress with which Dante crowned
His visionary brow: a glow-worm lamp,
It cheered mild Spenser, called from Faeryland
To struggle through dark ways; and when a damp
Fell round the path of Milton, in his hand
The Thing became a trumpet; whence he blew
Soul-animating strains—alas, too few!

See ENGLISH SONNET, ITALIAN SONNET, OCTAVE, PETRARCHAN, SESTET, VOLTA.

sonnet sequence

A group of *sonnets composed by one person and having a unified *theme or subject. The sonnets of such a sequence, or succession, are usually love poems that reflect the progress (and setbacks) of an attachment and reveal the inward emotions of the writer. Among sonnet sequences are Shakespeare's 154 poems in this form, Sir Philip Sidney's *As-*

trophel and Stella, Spenser's *Amoretti,* Elizabeth Barrett Browning's *Sonnets from the Portuguese,* and groups by Edna St. Vincent Millay and W. H. Auden.

sophistication

Worldly wisdom; knowledge of, and experience with, varied tastes, manners, ideas, and customs. *Sophistication* implies adaptability, adroitness, discernment, and the ability to act knowingly in any *situation. See AFFECTATION, PEDANTRY, SIMPLICITY, SOPHISTRY, SUAVITY, URBANITY.

sophistry

A subtle, tricky method of reasoning. Sophistry is a form of *argumentation that seems plausible but actually is false, deceptive, or superficial. Much of the argument about Hamlet's insanity consists of sophistry. A sophist is one who thinks and argues cleverly and adroitly but not soundly, rationally, and logically. Both *sophistry* and *sophist* refer also to a group of professional teachers in ancient Greece who stressed *skepticism, *subjectivity, and *solipsism.

Sophoclean

A reference to Sophocles, a fifth-century-B.C. Greek dramatist. The influence of Sophocles upon drama, especially upon plays of the *Renaissance period, was profound. A moving tribute to Sophocles has been paid by Edith Hamilton, a renowned scholar of the classics:

> In every way, Sophocles is the embodiment of what we know as Greek, so much so that all definitions of the Greek spirit and Greek art are first of all definitions of his spirit and his art. He has imposed himself upon the world as the quintessential Greek . . . he is direct, lucid, simple, reasonable . . . a great tragedian, a supremely gifted poet, and yet a detached observer of life.

sophrosyne

Moderation, discretion. The term, from a Greek word meaning "prudent," refers to the quality of restraint, *understatement, and *simplicity admired by such classical Greeks as Sophocles. (See CLASSICISM, CLEARNESS, ORDER.) Reporting a murder or rape, for example, rather than presenting it onstage is an illustration of sophrosyne.

sorites

A chain of syllogisms. Sorites is a form of *argumentation consisting of several *premises and one conclusion, each conclusion being a premise of the next syllogism. Piled up (or heaped) *propositions, like those in the Declaration of Independence, constitute a form of sorites. Hamlet's *soliloquy "To be, or not to be" is an approximation of sorites. A fifth-century-B.C.

Athenian statesman, Themistocles, "proved" that his baby
boy ruled the entire world by this sorites:
> My infant son rules his mother.
> His mother rules me.
> I rule the Athenians.
> The Athenians rule the Greeks.
> The Greeks rule Europe.
> Europe rules the world.

sortilege

The drawing of lots in an attempt to determine a course of
action or to foretell future events. (See AUGURY, HARUSPEX.)
Sortilege is a form of divination, magic, or sorcery. Sortilege
occurs often in *fairy tales and occasionally in stories about
the *Knights of the Round Table when a particular warrior
is chosen by lot to go on a dangerous mission.

sound

Any auditory effect. In literature, *sound* usually refers to
"speech sound," any of the set of distinctive sounds of a
*language. (See PHONEME, PHONETICS.) The sounds of words
are of enormous importance in literature, especially in poetry. See ACCENT, ALLITERATION, ASSONANCE, CACOPHONY,
CONSONANCE, DISSONANCE, EUPHONY, ONOMATOPOEIA, RHYME,
SENSORY WORDS, SYNESTHESIA.

source

In literature, *source* refers to any *book, *manuscript, person, or statement supplying information for use by a writer.
(See PRIMARY SOURCE, SECONDARY SOURCE.) The term *source*
also designates the origin of literary works, artistic forms, or
philosophical ideas. In this sense, the *Petrarchan sonnet is
the source of the *English sonnet; *dadaism is a source of
*surrealism; the principal source of Shakespeare's *Macbeth*
was Holinshed's *Chronicles of England, Scotland, and Ireland*

space order

One of the more common methods used in planning the
*organization of a literary *composition. When using space
order, a writer chooses some point in space or geography
from which his description of a *setting moves: near to
remote, left to right, points of the compass, etc. (See OR-
DER.) In his famous description of Eustacia Vye in chapter 7
of *The Return of the Native,* Hardy proceeds from comment
on "the queen of night's" hair to her eyes and then to her
mouth.

spectacle

Anything presented to the sight or view, especially something striking, unusual, or impressive. In literature, *spectacle*
usually refers to a display on a large scale. In a novel or

narrative poem, description of a spectacle is sometimes called a set piece, a passage more or less extraneous to the *plot and introduced to supply *color, background, or glamour. In Thackeray's *Vanity Fair,* the lavish ball given on the eve of Napoleon's entry into Belgium is a spectacle.

spectral

Ghostly, resembling a specter or phantom. (See APPARITION.) *Spectral* is also used in literature to suggest "spiritual" and "unworldly." William Blake was speaking of spectral activity in the sense of both "ghostly" and "spiritual" when he wrote:

My spectre around me night and day
Like a wild beast guards my way.
My emanation far within
Weeps incessantly for my sin.

spectrum

A broad range of varied but related objects or ideas. *Spectrum* has several specific meanings in physics and astronomy, but in literature it usually refers to a group of items (opinions, concepts, beliefs, etc.), the individual features of which tend to overlap so as to form a continuous series, or sequence. In the sense of "range," or "scope," reference can be made to the spectrum of an author's ideas or works. For example, Robert Louis Stevenson is said to have "run the spectrum" from *lullabies to psychological fiction of horror and terror.

Spenserian stanza

A stanzaic *pattern consisting of eight lines in iambic *pentameter followed by a line of iambic *hexameter. The *rhyme scheme is *ababbcbcc.* This form derives its name from Edmund Spenser (1522–1599), the English poet who created this pattern for *The Faerie Queene.* Others who have used the Spenserian stanza include Robert Burns (*The Cotter's Saturday Night*), Shelley (*Adonais*), Keats (*The Eve of St. Agnes*), and Byron (*Childe Harold*).

spondee

A *foot of two *syllables, both of which are accented (long): *fourteen, blue-green.* Spondees in English are usually composed of two words of one syllable each (*one, two*). In this line of iambic pentameter from Milton's *Paradise Lost,* the first three feet are spondaic:

Rocks, caves, / lakes, fens, / bogs, dens, /
and shades / of death . . .

See FOOT, METER, SCANSION.

spoonerism

The transposition of initial or other *sounds of words. *Spoonerism* is derived from the name of an English clergyman and Oxford don, W. A. Spooner, noted for such accidental interchange of sounds. Examples attributed to Spooner: "beery wenches"(for "weary benches"); "you have deliberately tasted two worms" (for "wasted two terms"); and "you can leave Oxford by the town drain" (for "down train"). See METATHESIS.

sprung rhythm

A term coined by the nineteenth-century English poet Gerard Manley Hopkins to designate a system of *prosody with the *accent falling on the first *syllable of every *foot; a varying number of unaccented syllables may follow the accented one, but all feet are given equal time length in pronouncing. The result of such varying feet is unusual metrical irregularity, but Hopkins claimed that sprung rhythm is found in most speech and in prose and music. The device can be illustrated with lines from Hopkins's own poetry. The first line of *The Windhover* is in regular iambic *pentameter:

Ĭ caūght / thĭs mōrn/ĭng mōrn/ĭng's mĭn̄/ĭŏn, kīng-

The first line of *The Starlight Night* contains the same number of feet and of accented syllables, but the rhythm (*meter) is sprung:

Loōk ăt thĕ / stārs! / Loōk, / loōk ŭp ăt thĕ / skīes!

stage directions

Instructions written into the *prompt copy (script) of a play, indicating stage actions, scenery, production requirements, lighting, movements of performers, sound effects, costuming, etc. Stage directions may vary from a single word such as *Exit* to lengthy and detailed explanations, such as those in various plays by George Bernard Shaw and Tennessee Williams.

stage whisper

A loud whisper (hushed sound) on a stage, meant to be heard by the audience but not by other characters on the stage. See ASIDE.

staging

A general term in *lingo of the theater for the act, process, and manner of presenting a play on the stage. See DRAMATURGY.

Stanislavski method

A naturalistic, individualized style of acting named after the Russian stage director, actor, and producer Konstantin Stanislavski (1863–1938). See METHOD ACTING.

stanza

The arrangement of lines of verse in a *pattern. A stanza has a fixed number of verses (lines), a prevailing kind of *meter, and a consistent *rhyme scheme. Such a group of lines forms a division of a poem or constitutes a selection in its entirety. The more common forms of stanza (stanzaic patterns) are the *couplet, *tercet, *quatrain, *rhyme royal, *ottava rima, *Spenserian stanza, and *sonnet. Also, see BALLADE, BALLAD STANZA, CHAUCERIAN STANZA, CINQUAIN, CLOSED COUPLET, COWLEYAN ODE, HAIKU, HEROIC COUPLET, HORATIAN, LIMERICK, OCTAVE, ODE, PINDARIC, RONDEAU, RONDEL, ROUNDEL, SESTET, SESTINA, TANKA, VILLANELLE.

stasima

Choral odes in ancient Greek drama. A stasimon, a single ode, was divided into a *strophe and *antistrophe. The last of the stasima in a Greek tragedy was sung just before the *exodus. In Greek, the word *stasimon* means "stationary."

stasis

The state of equilibrium or inactivity caused by opposing equal forces. *Stasis* is derived from Greek words meaning "state of standing." Two characters in a *novel, for example, who are in conflict with each other may be in stasis until some *act or *action alters their "static" condition.

static character

A figure (*character) in a *novel, *play, or *short story who changes little, or not at all, during the progress of action. See CHARACTERIZATION, FLAT CHARACTER.

status quo

A Latin term meaning "state in which." The phrase in English means "the existing condition," "things as they are."

status symbol

An object, habit, custom, or possession by which the social or economic state or condition of the possessor may be judged. A status *symbol is usually something designed or acquired to display or reflect a socioeconomic position higher than the possessor has actually attained.

stave

A line of *verse; a *stanza; a group of lines for musical notation.

stem (root)

The underlying form of a word to which *affixes are added to form a word or change its meaning. See COMBINING FORM, MORPHEME, ROOT.

stereotype

(1) A printing term referring to a method of making metal plates for *printing; (2) a simplified, standardized conception

(*image, belief, habit) with a special meaning and appeal for members of a group; (3) a set form or *convention. In literature, *stereotype* may refer to a *cliché (a worn-out expression); to a *stock character, situation, or response; to a fixed and firmly held custom or *tradition. A *formula story, for example, is a stereotype. A literary *convention is usually a stereotyped *technique or *pattern. A *flat character is a stereotype. In short, *stereotype* may be applied to anything in literature which is fixed and settled (but not necessarily lifeless, stale, and dull).

stet

A verb derived from the Latin verb *stare* ("to stand") and meaning "let it stand" (do not alter). It is used in the editing and *printing of *manuscript material as a direction to retain material previously canceled or to set in type precisely what is shown in the manuscript.

stichomythia

Originally, *stichomythia* referred to *dialogue in a Greek *play in which characters engaged in one-line exchanges. The term has been broadened in meaning to include all *repartee and *oral fencing matches between *characters in plays or other *genres. Hamlet and his mother engage in stichomythia in the scene during which Polonius is killed (act 3, scene 4). The King and Queen engage in prolonged stichomythia in Shakespeare's *Richard III* (act 4, scene 4). A modern example appears in T. S. Eliot's *Murder in the Cathedral* when Thomas à Becket is addressed in four harsh lines:

First Knight: Absolve all those you have excommunicated.
Second Knight: Resign the powers you have arrogated.
Third Knight: Restore to the King the money you appropriated.
First Knight: Renew the obedience you have violated.

stock character

A familiar figure belonging by custom and *tradition to certain types of writing. The *hero and *villain of *melodrama are stock characters (that is, kept regularly on hand). The court *fool, the braggart soldier (*miles gloriosus), the wicked witch, the country bumpkin, the hard-nosed detective, the *confidant (confidante), and the *nymphomaniac are stock characters in various forms of literature and pseudoliterature. See FLAT CHARACTER.

stock response

A reaction by readers or spectators which follows a standard, predictable *pattern. An uncritical, unsophisticated response is cheering the *hero or hissing the *villain.

Traditional *symbols representing mother love, filial devotion, the home, the flag, etc., receive stock responses of veneration. Terror is a stock response to the perils faced by a brave hero or frail heroine. Genuine literary artists strive to provide solid reasons for responses desired. See SENTIMENTALISM, SINCERITY.

stock situation

A recurring *pattern, *incident, or *situation in *fiction and *drama. Mistaken identity is a stock situation, and so are such patterns as "boy meets girl, boy loses girl, boy gets girl"; rags to riches; revenge; the love triangle; and man against the elements. Some stock situations are fundamental rather than contrived; they are *archetypal in that they reecho human views and predicaments. When such situations are treated as *stereotypes, they constitute *formula writing.

stoicism

Repression of emotion, indifference to pain and pleasure. *Stoicism* is derived from the philosophy of a group of fourth-century-B.C. Greek philosophers, the Stoics, who believed that men should be free from passions, unmoved by grief or joy, and passively receptive in enduring setbacks to health, happiness, and prosperity. Stoicism is reflected in the work of Epictetus, a first-century Greek philosopher, and that of Marcus Aurelius, a second-century Roman emperor and writer. The *stock character of the "strong, silent man" exhibits stoicism, and to a degree, so do some of the characters in some of the *novels and *short stories of Rudyard Kipling, Jack London, and Ernest Hemingway.

story

A narrative, either true or *fictitious, in *prose or *verse, designed to interest, amuse, or inform hearers or readers. (See BALLAD, EPIC, FICTION, NOVEL, PLOT, SHORT STORY, TALE. Also, see ACTION, ANECDOTE, CHRONICLE, FABLE, NOVELLA, ROMANCE.) This statement by Robert Louis Stevenson, himself a noted teller of stories, is informative:

> There are only three ways of writing a story: you may take a plot and fit *characters to it; or you may take a character and choose *incidents and *situations to develop it, or you may take a certain *atmosphere and get action and persons to express and realize it.

Also useful is this comment by Guy de Maupassant about the purpose and effect of a story, and indeed of all *fiction:

> The public is composed of numerous groups who cry to us [writers]: "Console me, amuse me, make me sad, make me sympathetic, make me dream, make me laugh, make me shudder, make me weep, make me think."

story-within-a-story

A narrative enclosed within another. Examples are the lengthy *incidents scattered through the adventures of Dickens's Mr. Pickwick and his friends (*The Pickwick Papers*) that create as much interest as the major narrative. Other examples appear in the form of *anecdotes and incidents related by Huck and Jim in Twain's *The Adventures of Huckleberry Finn.* See FRAME STORY.

stream of consciousness

A manner of writing in which a character's perceptions and thoughts are presented as occurring in *random form. In this *technique, ideas and sensations are revealed without regard for logical sequences, distinctions between various levels of reality (sleep, waking, etc.), or *syntax. Stream of consciousness, a phrase coined by William James in his *Principles of Psychology* (1890), attempts to set forth the inner thoughts of a *character in the seemingly haphazard fashion of everyday thinking. This method of writing has been used by many authors, among them James Joyce, Virginia Woolf, Dorothy Richardson, and William Faulkner. See INTERIOR MONOLOGUE, SOLILOQUY.

stress

(1) Importance, significance; (2) physical, mental, or emotional tension or strain; (3) *accent or *emphasis on *syllables in a metrical pattern, or in words alone (see ARSIS, ICTUS.) Thus, (1) Stendhal, in *The Red and the Black,* places stress (significance) upon the conflicting elements in Julien Sorel's personality that brought about his downfall; (2) Martin Arrowsmith, in Sinclair Lewis's *Arrowsmith,* undergoes stress when he is deciding between professional, financial success and pure science; and (3) stress falls upon the first syllable of *gunner.*

strophe

The part of an ancient Greek choral *ode sung by the chorus when moving from right to left. (See ANTISTROPHE, EPODE.) In a *Pindaric ode, the strophe is the first of the three series of lines forming the divisions of each section. In modern poetry, *strophe* may refer to any separate section of a *poem that is not a true *stanza because it does not follow a regularly repeated *pattern.

structure

The planned framework of a literary selection. (See ORGANIZATION, OUTLINE.) For instance, the structure of a *play is based upon its divisions into acts and scenes; the structure of an essay depends upon a list of topics and the *order of their presentation; the structure of a *Spenserian stanza is determined by its use of eight iambic pentameter lines followed by an *alexandrine, etc. In *New Criticism, *structure* is used to refer to that part of a poem subject to *paraphrase, that is, the *explicit statement of a selection as opposed to its *texture (*images, *sound *pattern, etc.)

Sturm und Drang

A German expression meaning "storm and stress." The phrase is now used to refer to a time of trouble, difficulty, and *stress in the life of an individual or nation. Historically, Sturm und Drang applied to an eighteenth-century revolutionary literary movement in Germany characterized by opposition to established forms of society, extreme nationalism, and impetuosity in *style and *diction. Goethe's *Faust* reveals the influence of this movement.

style

(1) The manner of putting thoughts into words; (2) a characteristic mode of construction and expression in writing and speaking; (3) the characteristics of a literary selection that concern form of expression rather than the thought conveyed.

Style, derived from a Latin word meaning "writing instrument," cannot be satisfactorily defined, but hundreds of experts have tried. Lord Chesterfield defined *style* as "the dress of thought." Alfred North Whitehead, a philosopher and mathematician, said, "Style is the ultimate morality of mind." Cardinal Newman wrote, "Style is a thinking out into language." Jonathan Swift suggested "Proper words in proper places make the true definition of style." Buffon, an eighteenth-century French writer and naturalist, said, "The style is the man himself."

If style is thought to consist of the mannerisms and methods of an individual writer, then one can refer to the *pompous* style of Dr. Johnson, the *whimsical* style of Charles Lamb, the *allusive* style of T. S. Eliot, the *clipped* style of Hemingway, etc. Most critics agree, however, that "what one says" and "how he says that something" are basic elements in style. Therefore, style may be thought of as the impress (influence) of a writer's personality upon his subject matter.

style sheet

A listing of rules of *usage in *style as employed by a newspaper, magazine, or book publisher. A style sheet, or style book, contains directions covering punctuation, spelling, typography, etc., employed by printers, editors, and writers. An example of such a work is the *Style Manual* of the United States Government Printing Office.

suavity

Agreeable politeness, *urbanity, *courtesy. *Suavity* is often used as a *synonym for *sophistication, *savoir faire,* and *worldliness.* A suave person, polished in his manners and speech, may or may not be genuine and sincere. Compared with all others in Aldous Huxley's *Brave New World,* Bernard Marx, a "citizen of the world," is the *essence of suavity.

subconscious

As a noun, *subconscious* refers to a person's own mental processes of which he is not fully aware, that is, "unreportable" activities of the mind. As an adjective, *subconscious* means "existing or operating in the mind beneath or beyond consciousness." The subconscious minds of literally thousands of *characters in literature have been portrayed or plundered during the past century. See COLLECTIVE UNCONSCIOUS, EGO, FREUDIANISM, ID, INTERIOR MONOLOGUE, JUNGIAN, STREAM OF CONSCIOUSNESS.

subjectivity

Concentration upon self; the personal, reflective involvement of a person with himself or of a writer with his material. (See OBJECTIVITY.) *Subjectivity* refers to writing in which the expression of personal feeling and experience is primary. Samuel Butler's *The Way of All Flesh,* Somerset Maugham's *Of Human Bondage,* and Thomas Wolfe's *You Can't Go Home Again* are representative of many semiautobiographical works. (See BILDUNGSROMAN.) *Autobiography is almost wholly subjective, as many *personal essays are. Many of the essays and *poems of Dylan Thomas are centered upon the author's experiences and individualized reactions.

Subjectivity also refers to the thoughts and feelings of literary characters. In *My Last Duchess,* for instance, the central element is the speaker's revelation of himself. In *biography and the *psychograph, emphasis on the personality of the subject being examined is almost constant. In critical writing, the personal *taste and individual literary standards of the critic are fully involved. (See CRITICISM.) In the sense of "privacy of thought" and individualism, subjectivity is a pervasive element in literature.

sublimity

Nobility, impressiveness, grandeur. *Sublimity* refers to qualities in a literary work that transport a reader, carry him out of himself, and set his thoughts on a loftier plane. Presumably all purposeful writers seek to attain "the sublime" in their work, but sublimity is commonly considered to have been reached only by such masterpieces as Dante's *Divine Comedy,* Shakespeare's plays, Milton's *Paradise Lost,* Goethe's *Faust,* and perhaps another score or so of literary monuments.

subordination

Position in a lower order, or rank; dependency. *Subordination* is a grammatical term, such as the use of *subordinate* for a dependent clause or phrase. In writing, an author subordinates (places under, reduces), for example, attention to one *character in order to play up another or emphasizes, say, *plot, while subordinating *characterization, *setting, and *theme. In *Les misérables,* Victor Hugo subordinated every element of this novel of adventure to the character, exploits, and inner feelings of Jean Valjean.

subplot

A secondary, or minor, *plot in a play or other literary work which may contrast with the principal plot, highlight it, or be unrelated. See COUNTERPLOT.

sub rosa

A Latin *term meaning "under the rose." The phrase is used to mean "confidentially," "secretly," "privately." It came to have these meanings because, in ancient times, a rose was used as a *symbol of the sworn confidence of participants in a secret meeting.

subsidiary rights.

A publishing term used to refer to rights and privileges that are secondary, supplementary, or subordinate to a principal or primary grant. For example, the contract for publication of a *manuscript would grant the publisher the right to publish the work in book form but might reserve to the author such subsidiary rights as those involving dramatic presentation, television, motion pictures, etc.

substantive

A word of several meanings, *substantive* is used in grammar to refer to a noun, pronoun, or other construction that can act as a subject or object in a sentence. In more general use, *substantive* means (1) real or actual; (2) of considerable amount, quantity, or stature; (3) essential. In legal *jargon, *substantive* applies to "rules of right" as distinguished from "rules of procedure" (that is, a matter of principle or substance rather than method).

subsumption

Consideration or treatment of something (idea, topic, term, *proposition) as part of something more comprehensive; the act of bringing a case, instance, etc., under a more general heading or rule. For example, treating the *ballad under the classification of narrative *poetry is an act of subsumption.

subtlety

In literature, *subtlety* refers to the delicacy, refinement, perceptiveness, and nicety with which an author develops an idea or unfolds a narrative. A subtle writer is clever and ingenious in *characterization, for example, always careful to make finely drawn distinctions and to be delicate in discriminating among personality traits, etc. Lambert Strether, the *protagonist in Henry James's *The Ambassadors,* is portrayed with subtlety; Clyde Griffiths, the protagonist of Theodore Dreiser's *An American Tragedy,* is portrayed forcefully and bluntly, *not* subtly.

succès d'estime

A French term that refers to success (favorable or prosperous outcome) won by merit and respect rather than by popularity. Many of the world's greatest literary *classics are more respected than read; many esteemed authors of the past and present have been revered more than they have been rewarded with popularity and financial success.

succubus

Any demon or evil spirit; a prostitute. In *medieval times, *succubus* referred to a female spirit of evil, thought to have sexual intercourse with men in their sleep. See INCUBUS.

suffix

Something added to the end of something else. In language, a suffix is an affix that *follows* the element to which it is added. See AFFIX, COMBINING FORM, PREFIX, STEM (ROOT).

The exact meaning of suffixes is sometimes difficult to determine, but knowledge of the general sense of common suffixes is invaluable in reading. For instance, the suffix *-age* has a loose meaning of "belonging to," "pertaining to." *Postage,* a combination of *post* and *age,* obviously "has to do" with a series of stations along a route that receive and dispatch mail. With the sense of *-age* in mind, such words as *bondage, coinage,* and *fruitage* become immediately clear.

Some common suffixes (a few of which are also combining forms) are shown in the following list:

-al	denial, refusal
-ana	Americana, collegiana
-ance	connivance, nonchalance
-dom	kingdom, freedom
-er	loiterer, embezzler
-est	highest, sayest
-fold	manifold, twofold
-ful	beautiful, harmful
-graph	monograph, lithograph
-hood	childhood, priesthood
-ice	apprentice, novice
-ish	British, girlish
-ism	barbarism, plagiarism
-ist	dramatist, antagonist

-ity	civility, nobility
-less	peerless, homeless
-let	bracelet, ringlet
-like	lifelike, childlike
-logy	trilogy, theology
-ly	saintly, beastly
-ment	abridgment, ornament
-ness	kindness, preparedness
-phone	telephone, megaphone
-polis	metropolis, megalopolis
-ship	friendship, statesmanship
-some	twosome, quarrelsome
-ward	toward, afterward
-ways	always, sideways
-wise	clockwise, sidewise
-y	dreamy, infamy

suggestio falsi

A Latin term for "false suggestion," used infrequently in *criticism to refer to a misleading comment or to an obvious attempt at deception. The remark by Lady Macbeth under the entry DOUBLE ENTENDRE is a suggestio falsi.

summary

A brief but *comprehensive statement or recapitulation of previously noted facts or ideas; a statement or restatement of main points. See ABRIDGMENT, BRIEF, DIGEST, EPITOME, SYNOPSIS.

superego

A term largely used in *psychoanalysis to refer to man's *psyche, or psychic apparatus. Man's superego is that mental and emotional force which reconciles his *ego drives and his social and ethical ideas and ideals. Illness results when the superego fails to mediate between man's drives and his responsibilities to *society. In literary, and less scientific, circles than *psychiatry, *superego* is an approximate *synonym for "conscience," "ethics," or "acceptance of moral law." Macbeth and Iago acted as they did because their superegos failed them. In Dickens's *A Tale of Two Cities,* Sydney Carton's superego enabled him to perform a deed which gave real meaning to his life. See EGO, EGOISM; ID.

supernaturalism

That which is above and beyond what is natural; events not explainable by known laws and observations. (See PRETERNATURAL.) Speculating about the unknown and inexplicable has been a preoccupation of mankind through all recorded history; the development of *myths, *legends, and *epics is an indication of this obsession. Explorations of the *occult and of *infinity, *mysticism, and *numerology are other manifestations of the consuming desire of man to know what lies beyond the finite mind. Imaginative and inventive *fiction and *poetry have built upon this appeal and have fostered it since the beginnings of literature.

supramundane

A learned word meaning "spiritual," "celestial," "above and beyond earthly, worldly consideration." *Supramundane,* derived from Latin words meaning "above the world," is usually applied to speculations about *infinity.

surprise ending

A sudden and unexpected turn in the action occurring at the end of a work, especially a *short story. Such a conclusion is a *trick ending if it has not been previously hinted at or prepared for. See CLUE (CLEW), FORESHADOWING.

surrealism

A *style in *literature and painting that stresses the *subconscious or the nonrational aspects of man's existence. *Surrealism,* which means "above, beneath, or beyond reality," was first applied to a movement which sprang up in France at the end of World War I. Influenced by *Freudianism and horrified by the brutality of war, some painters and writers presented *imagery by stressing chance effects in disorderly array, much like the *random sequence of events or recollections experienced in dreams. Surrealism, which has been largely confined to French writers and artists, was a development from *dadaism. Much of the work of Salvador Dali, a Spanish painter, has been surrealistic; parts of Joyce's *Finnegans Wake* illustrate some qualities of surrealism.

survey

A general or comprehensive view of a *situation, topic, area of study, etc. A survey is an overview of a subject, an attempt to provide coverage of all significant items and elements in the topic or area being examined. See COMPENDIUM, OUTLINE.

suspense

A state of mental uncertainty, excitement, or indecision. *Suspense,* which involves awaiting an outcome or decision, is derived from Latin words meaning "hanging up" and therefore left undecided. In literature, *suspense* refers to the anticipation of readers (or of an audience) concerning the outcome of events in a *novel, *story, or *play. Suspense is a quality of *tension in a *plot which sustains interest and makes readers ask "what happens next?" Suspense may vary from the introduction of a *clue in a *formula *detective story to that employed in Sophocles's *Oedipus Rex* (withholding of the knowledge that Oedipus has killed his real father). In this drama, the suspense involved is not a writer's trick: readers or spectators, fully aware that Oedipus will eventually understand, share his doubts, fears, and uncertainties throughout the play.

suspension of disbelief

Denial of doubt; withholding questions about truth and actuality. The phrase was first used by Coleridge in *Biographia Literaria:* "that willing suspension of disbelief for the moment, which constitutes poetic faith." Earlier, Ben Jonson had written, "To many things a man should owe but a temporary belief, and suspension of his own judgment." The willingness of readers to suspend doubt about the real truth or *verisimilitude of a *character or happening in literature makes possible the acceptance of imaginative creations in prose and verse. See BELIEF.

switchback

A *shoptalk term used by some writers, editors, and film producers as a *synonym for flashback. One may either "switch" or "flash" to a scene depicting *action that occurred prior to what is taking place at the time of insertion. See FLASHBACK.

sycophant

A servile flatterer; a self-seeking, fawning parasite; a sponger. *Sycophant* is derived from Greek words meaning "to show figs," presumably implying an informer against persons who robbed the sacred fig trees, and thus a "toady" or "stool pigeon." Uriah Heep, in Dickens's *David Copperfield,* is a sycophant.

syllabic verse

*Doggerel or *poetry, the lines of which are measured by number of syllables rather than by *accent. Syllabic verse is rare in English, but Milton and Pope experimented with it, and so has Marianne Moore. The *haiku is a form of syllabic verse.

syllable

A segment of speech (that is, a word or part of a word) produced with a single pulse of air pressure (one vocal impulse) from the lungs: *boy, love, strength.* In writing, a syllable is a character or set of characters representing such an element of speech. As an *archaism, *syllable* also meant "to speak," as in Milton's line in *Comus:* "And airy tongues that syllable men's names." That *syllable* implies both *sound and time is suggested by Shakespeare's phrase in *Macbeth:* "To the last syllable of recorded time."

syllabus

An *abstract or *outline of the main points of a speech, article, series of lectures, course of study, etc. *Syllabus* is used in law to refer to a short *summary of the legal basis of a court's decision.

syllepsis

The use of a word or expression to perform two grammatical functions. Syllepsis, a form of *zeugma, is illustrated under that entry.

syllogism

A *formula or *pattern for the logical presentation of an argument. In a syllogism, an argument is presented in three divisions: a major *premise, a minor premise, and a conclusion. A typical syllogism is

Major premise: All men are mortal.
Minor premise: My friend is a man.
Conclusion: My friend is mortal.
or
All X is $Y;$ all Y is $Z;$ therefore, all X is Z.

See ARGUMENTATION, DEDUCTION, ENTHYMEME, INDUCTION, LOGIC, SORITES.

symbol

Something used for, or regarded as, representing something else. More specifically, a symbol is a word, phrase, or other expression having a complex of associated meanings; in this sense, a symbol is viewed as having values different from those of whatever is being symbolized. Thus, a flag is a piece of cloth which stands for (is a symbol of) a nation; the cross is a symbol of Christianity; the swastika was a symbol of Nazi Germany; the hammer and sickle is a symbol of communism. Many poets have used the rose as a symbol of youth or beauty; the "hollow men" of T. S. Eliot are a symbol of *decadence; Moby Dick is a symbol of evil; the *allegory and the *parable make use of symbols. See GENERAL SEMANTICS, SEMANTICS, WORD.

symbolism

The practice of representing objects or ideas by *symbols or of giving things a symbolic (associated) character and meaning. John Bunyan built all of his *The Pilgrim's Progress* on symbolism: the story of man's progress through life to heaven or hell as told through the adventures of Christian, Faithful, Mr. Worldly Wiseman, and others who symbolize man in his various guises. Coleridge's *The Rime of the Ancient Mariner* is symbolism throughout: mankind's universal journey into despair and wickedness and then back to repentance, punishment, and stability and wholesomeness of spirit.

Symbolism is also applied to a nineteenth-century movement in the literature and art of France, a revolt against *realism. Symbolists of this era tried to suggest life through the use of symbols and *images. Among leaders of this movement were Baudelaire, Rimbaud, and Verlaine, who influenced the movements of *impressionism and *imagism.

symmetry

Correspondence in size, form, and arrangement of parts; regularity of corresponding segments or units of a whole. In literature, *symmetry* has the basic meaning of *proportion—the *order and *organization of parts of a literary selection so that they harmonize and also complement each other. A symmetrical novel, for example, is regular in form, well proportioned, and equally developed in each of its parts as to length and emphasis.

sympathy

Fellow feeling, compassion. *Sympathy* applies to a feeling of harmony between persons of like opinions or tastes, persons who share a sense of congeniality. When a reader experiences concern, admiration, or pity for a literary character, he is feeling sympathy; if he actually feels with such a character on a personally and deeply involved basis, he is experiencing and expressing *empathy. An author's sympathetic (understanding, perceptive) treatment of a character induces in readers such feelings as sorrow, compassion, love, approval, and commiseration. See CATHARSIS.

symposium

A meeting, or conference, for the discussion of a particular subject. *Symposium,* from Greek words meaning "drinking together," usually refers to a friendly discussion of a philosophical or political idea or principle, but the term may refer to a *panel discussion. *Symposium* applies also to a collection of opinions or *articles contributed by various authors on a selected topic. (See ANTHOLOGY, CHRESTOMATHY.) One of Plato's best-known dialogues is the *Symposium.*

syncopation

In music, *syncopation,* a basic characteristic of *jazz, refers to a shifting of normal *accent, usually by stressing regularly unaccented beats. In *prosody, syncopation involves shifting *stresses in the established *meter of a line to achieve a different effect. For instance, in the normal rhythm of speech, stress would fall on *three* and *sons* in the expression "that her three sons were gone." In *The Wife of Usher's Well,* a popular ballad, the line would be scanned as regular iambic *trimeter: "That her / three sons / were gone." Tennyson's line "Than nev/er to / have loved / at all" is iambic *tetrameter, as shown. In ordinary speech, stress would fall on *nev-, loved,* and *all.*

syncope

The contraction, or abbreviation, of a word by omitting syllables or letters. *Syncope* is illustrated in *ne'er* (from *never*) and *o'er* (from *over*). See SYNERESIS.

syndrome

A group of related or coincident events, actions, or situations; a *pattern of circumstances, signs, or indications which characterize a particular social, economic, or political condition. *Syndrome* is a term borrowed from medicine (pathology, psychiatry), where it refers to a group of symptoms that together are characteristic of a specific disease or condition.

synecdoche

A figure of speech in which a part is used for the whole or the whole for a part, the special for the general or the general for the special. Synecdoche, a kind of *metaphor, is illustrated by the use of *five sail* for *five ships;* "Give us this day our daily bread," with *bread* representing not only *food* but general sustenance; *motor* for *automobile; the fleet* for *a group of sailors; a Jezebel* for *a wicked woman,* etc. In a sonnet, Shakespeare uses the word *rhyme* to refer to the entire poem:

> Not marble, nor the gilded monuments
> Of princes, shall outlive this powerful rhyme.

syneresis

The contraction of two vowels or two syllables into one. Syneresis occurs often in poetry, where it is employed to meet metrical requirements: *mould'ring, 'tis, flow'r, am'rous, wat'ry.* See SYNCOPE.

synesis

A grammatical construction in which agreement in form is replaced by agreement in meaning. Synesis, which in Greek meant "understanding," is illustrated by the expression "the group *are*" rather than "the group *is.*" Where synesis occurs, a collective noun (such as *group, committee, crowd, jury, clergy)* is considered to be composed of individuals rather than thought of as a unit.

synesthesia

The close association of an *image or sensation perceived by one of the senses with that received by another. In synesthesia a certain *sound, for example, induces the sight of a certain color. *Blue note* (sight, sound) and *cool green* (touch, sight) are synesthetic expressions. The French poet Baudelaire described certain scents as being "soft as oboes, green as meadows" (smell, touch, sight, sound).

synonym

A word having the same, or nearly the same, meaning as another in the same language. Rarely are two words identical in meaning, but many do share a similar "denotative" sense. (See CONNOTATION, DENOTATION.) For example, synonyms for *sad* are *depressed, dejected, despondent, disconsolate, discouraged, downcast, downhearted, gloomy, melancholic, mournful,* and *unhappy.* Synonyms for *glad* include *cheerful, cheery, elated, happy, joyous,* and *merry.* Words roughly synonymous with *habitation* or *dwelling* include *abode, domicile, home, house, residence.*

synopsis

A condensed statement providing a general view of a topic or subject. A synopsis is a form of *abridgment and is closely related in meaning to *compendium, *conspectus, *résumé, and *summary. The term is more often used with *fiction than with *nonfiction.

synoptic

An adjective describing the act of "taking a general view of the principal parts of a subject." *Synoptic* is widely used in the phrase *synoptic Gospels,* a reference to the first three books of the New Testament: Matthew, Mark, and Luke. Accounts of the birth, life, ministry, and death of Jesus Christ given in these books possess a similarity that constitutes "a general view" of the subject.

syntax

The arrangement and grammatical relations of words in a sentence. *Syntax* may be more fully defined as a study of the rules for forming grammatical sentences in a language, the arrangement of morphemes, *words, and phrases in meaningful utterances. In general usage, *syntax* is employed as a *synonym for *grammar.

Grammar, however, is a *comprehensive term. It consists of three parts: syntax, morphology, and phonology. (See MORPHEME, PHONEME.) Syntax refers to the *structure of *sentences. Morphology shows how *stems (roots), *inflections, *prefixes, and *suffixes are put together to form the shapes of words. Phonology deals with the sound system of a language and may be referred to as "the grammar of speech."

synthesis

The combining of elements into a single, unified whole; an entity (or whole) formed by a combination of items. (See ANALYSIS.) All literature results from synthesis because it is shaped from miscellaneous materials and is molded into composite form by the hands, hearts, and minds of literary craftsmen.

T

tableau

A picturesque grouping of persons or objects. *Tableau,* a French word meaning "board" or "picture," refers to the representation of living persons suitably dressed and posed in a silent, static grouping. Tableaux are used in *musical comedy, in *pageants, and in theatrical performances of various kinds. In several of the plays of Eugene O'Neill and Thornton Wilder, characters on stage are "frozen" in position for a brief time to reinforce the dramatic implications of a situation. Such a brief scene is sometimes called a *tableau vivant* ("living picture").

table of contents

A listing of the chapters or other formal divisions of a *book or *document. A table of contents, if used at all, invariably appears in the *front matter of books in English. See INDEX.

taboo

Forbidden or excluded from use by custom, order, or *taste. *Taboo* is a term that originated among peoples of the South Pacific, where it was used to refer to acts and objects set apart and thus forbidden for general use or sight. In literature, certain subjects have usually been considered taboo, but some writers of *naturalism and *realism have considered no subject forbidden to their use. See CENSORSHIP, OBSCENITY, PORNOGRAPHY, PROFANITY.

tabula rasa

A Latin phrase meaning "scraped tablet" or "clean slate." The term is applied to (1) a mind not yet affected by experiences and impressions of life and (2) an existing *situation in which past events and circumstances have been cleared up or forgotten in preparation for a fresh start. See ATAVISM, CATHARSIS, COLLECTIVE UNCONSCIOUS.

tags

(1) *Hackneyed phrases or quotations; (2) often-repeated words or labels, especially prevalent in *characterization and *description, that refer to physical features, etc.; (3) additions or afterthoughts; (4) word groups used in *dialogue to keep track of speakers: *he said, she replied,* etc.

tale

A narrative relating the details of some real or imaginary event or *incident. From an *Old English word for *speech, tale* is often applied to simple, loosely plotted stories told in the first person. Examples of tales are those in Chaucer's *The Canterbury Tales,* Jonathan Swift's *A Tale of a Tub* (a comedy in verse), and Sir Walter Scott's *Wandering Willie's Tale* (from *Redgauntlet*). The term may also refer to a *novel: *A Tale of Two Cities* (Dickens), *The Old Wives' Tale* (Arnold Bennett). See FICTION, NARRATION, SHORT STORY.

talisman

A stone, ring, or other object supposed to possess *occult powers; anything worn as a charm because of its influence on human feelings or actions. The sash (girdle) which Gawain accepts to protect himself from injury *(Sir Gawain and the Green Knight)* is a talisman.

tall tale

A narrative which relates bizarre, exaggerated, hard-to-believe events or occurrences. The exploits of Davy Crockett, Mike Fink, and Paul Bunyan are tall tales. Mark Twain's *The Celebrated Jumping Frog of Calaveras County* is an excellent example of the tall (exaggerated, incredible) tale.

tanka

A *form of Japanese poetry similar to the haiku. A tanka consists of thirty-one syllables arranged in five lines. See HAIKU, IMAGISM.

taste

A sense of what is harmonious, fitting, or beautiful; the perception and enjoyment of what constitutes excellence in literature (or other arts). *Taste* is a term often used in *criticism to designate the basis for approval or rejection of a work of art. Joseph Addison, the English essayist, remarked that "taste discerns the beauties of an author with pleasure and the imperfections with dislike." Wide experience in reading can alter one's taste; in fact, T. S. Eliot suggested that a primary function of criticism should be "the correction of taste." Basically, however, taste is a matter of *subjectivity.

tautology

Needless repetition of an idea without the addition of meaning, forcefulness, or clearness. From a Greek word meaning "saying the same," tautology is illustrated by such an expression as "He wrote his own autobiography." See CIRCUMLOCUTION, CONCISENESS, DEADWOOD, PERIPHRASIS, PLEONASM, VERBIAGE.

technique

The manner and ability with which a writer (or other artist) employs the skills of his craft; the body of specialized methods and procedures used in a specific field. The technique of a novelist, for instance, involves *characterization, the building of *conflict, the development of *suspense, the writing of *dialogue, etc. The technical performance of a poet is judged by his knowledge of *diction, *meter, *rhythm, etc. See STYLE.

telegraphic style

A style of writing, also called *telegraphese,* distinguished by omissions, abbreviations, and combinations that "save" words. Example: "Expect leave six evening arrive motel ten."

telepathy

Communication between minds by some means other than sensory perception. From two Greek words meaning "transmission of feelings over a distance," telepathy appears often in situations where one character senses or feels what another is thinking or becomes aware of some happening at a remote distance. Several examples of telepathy occur, for example, among the brother, the sister, and the narrator in Poe's *The Fall of the House of Usher.* See ATAVISM, COLLECTIVE UNCONSCIOUS, EMPATHY, SYMPATHY.

telestich

A poem in which the last letters of successive lines form a word, phrase, or consecutive letters of the alphabet. See ABECEDARIUS, ACROSTIC, MESOSTICH.

television

The broadcasting (transmission and reproduction) of a view, scene, or *image by means of radio waves to receivers that project it on a picture tube. The process involved is the conversion of light rays into electrical impulses in such a manner that they can be transmitted (sent) and then reconverted by a receiver into visible light rays forming an image (picture). *Tele-* is a learned borrowing from Greek meaning "distant," especially transmission over a distance, as in *telegraph, telephone,* and *television.*

tempo

The characteristic rate, *rhythm, *pace, or *pattern of a literary selection. A well-constructed *detective story moves at a rapid tempo, a *double-decker novel at a slow tempo. (See MOVE-MENT.) The tempo of Browning's *How They Brought the Good News from Ghent to Aix* is rapid, the rhythm echoing the flying hoofbeats of horses. The tempo of Keats's *Ode on Melancholy* is slow, in keeping with the somber mood of the subject.

temporal

(1) Worldly; concerned with the present life of this world; (2) temporary, enduring for a limited time only. *Temporal* has a basic meaning of "time," but it has been extended to represent a contrast to *spiritual* and *eternal.* Both meanings of *temporal* are expressed in this quotation from the Bible (2 Corinthians 3): "The things which are seen are temporal; but the things which are not seen are eternal." In *The Merchant of Venice,* Shakespeare uses *temporal* in his comment on mercy:

> The quality of mercy is not strained,
> It droppeth as the gentle rain from heaven
> Upon the place beneath . . .
>   . . . it becomes
> The throned monarch better than his crown;
> His sceptre shows the force of temporal power,
> The attribute to awe and majesty,
> Wherein doth sit the dread and fear of kings;
> But mercy is above this sceptred sway,
> It is enthroned in the hearts of kings,
> It is an attribute to God himself.

tenor

The course of thought and meaning that runs through a *composition; the drift or *purpose of anything written or spoken. As a term in *rhetoric, *tenor* is referred to as the subject of a *metaphor: in "She is an angel," *she* is the tenor of the *figure of speech. When Macbeth refers to life as "a tale told by an idiot," *life* is the tenor of this figurative phrase.

tensile

An adjective referring to *tension,* the act of stretching or straining or the condition of being stretched or strained. The tensile strength of a literary selection is the degree of emotional strain, *suspense, and anxiety which is created for a reader as he awaits the outcome of a *plot, as he hurries along to discover "how it turns out."

tension

In *New Criticism, tension is thought of as the quality that provides *form and *unity for an artistic work. Presumably, this concept has grown from the ancient Greek notion that the universe is a conflict of opposites regulated by a Supreme Mind, or external justice. Certain critics maintain that tension exists between the *literal and metaphorical meanings of a work of art, between what is written and its implications.

tercet

A *stanza of three lines rhyming together or connected by *rhyme with an adjacent group of three lines, a *triplet. (See TERZA RIMA.)

> When as in silks my Julia goes,
> Then, then, methinks, how sweetly flows
> That liquefaction of her clothes.
>
> Next, when I cast mine eyes, and see
> That brave vibration, each way free,
> O, how that glittering taketh me!
>
> Robert Herrick, *Upon Julia's Clothes*

tergiversation

Changing one's attitudes or opinions about a cause or subject. Robert Browning, in *The Lost Leader,* accused Wordsworth of tergiversation when the latter "defected" from liberalism to conservatism. Actually, many writers of the past and present have altered their attitudes from time to time, because, as John Milton wrote in *Areopagitica:*

> Where there is much desire to learn, there of necessity will be much arguing, much writing, many opinions; for opinion in good men is but knowledge in the making.

terminal rhyme

Identity of *sound occurring at the ends of lines of poetry. See END RHYME.

terra incognita

A Latin term meaning "an unknown earth." The phrase is used to refer to an unexplored region, subject of inquiry, or topic of any kind.

terza rima

Originally, an Italian form of iambic verse consisting of eleven-syllable lines arranged in *tercets, the middle line of each tercet rhyming with the first and last lines of the following *stanza: *aba, bcb, cdc, ded,* etc. (See RHYME SCHEME.) Terza rima, meaning "third rhyme," is the metrical form of many of the best-known poetic works in world literature, Dante's *The Divine Comedy* being the most famous of all. Here are two stanzas in terza rima from Shelley's *Ode to the West Wind:*

> Make me thy lyre, even as the forest is:
> What if my leaves are falling like its own!

The tumult of thy mighty harmonies
Will take from both a deep, autumnal tone,
Sweet though in sadness. Be thou, Spirit fierce,
My spirit! Be thou me, impetuous one!

testament

An agreement, or covenant. *Testament* is most often applied
to the two major portions of the *Bible, the Old and New Testaments, but the term also means "last will," "bequest," and "dis-
pensation of property." A recent example of the use of
testament in the sense of "witness" and "affirmation" is Robert
Bridges's *The Testament of Beauty,* a *compendium of the
experience and wisdom of an artistic spirit.

tetralogy

Four works which make up a set; a series of four related *novels,
*operas, or *plays. *Tetralogy,* from Latin terms meaning
"four" and "words," applies to two groupings of Shakespearean
*history plays: (1) the three parts of *Henry VI* and *Richard
III;* (2) *Richard II,* the two parts of *Henry IV,* and *Henry V.*
A tetralogy in music is the four parts comprised in Wagner's
Ring of the Nibelungs. See TRILOGY.

tetrameter

A line of four metrical feet. See METER.

tetrastich

A *stanza or complete *poem consisting of four lines. *Tetrastich*
and quatrain are *synonyms.

textbook

A volume used by students as a standard work for a particular
branch of study. (See TRADE BOOK.) A text edition is a special
*edition of a book for distribution to schools or colleges, subject
to a special rate of discount to sellers.

textual

An adjective applying to the text (actual wording) of anything
written or spoken. In literature, it is often used in the phrase
textual criticism, an activity which tries to reconstruct the
original *manuscript or authoritative text of a literary work. See
EXPLICATION.

texture

The interwoven or intertwined threads and strands which
make up a fabric. Thus, the phrase *fabric of fiction* refers to
the framework and *structure of *novels and *short stories. In
*New Criticism, however, *texture* is a term applied to all the
elements of a literary work, especially a poem, after its essential,
or basic, meaning has been abstracted or paraphrased. Such
elements include *meter, *imagery, *metaphor, *rhyme, and
*tone. By this *criterion, *structure consists of the "statement"

or "argument" of a selection, and texture includes everything else: sequence of *images, connotative meanings of words, phonetic *patterns, etc. Combined, texture and structure provide what some New Critics refer to as the *ontology of a poem.

theater

(1) A building, part of a building, or outdoor area for the housing and staging of dramatic presentations; (2) dramatic works collectively, such as the theater of Ibsen or the theater of France; (3) the quality and effectiveness of dramatic presentation, as "good theater," "dull theater," etc. *Theater,* from Greek words meaning "seeing place," has been variously interpreted and applied since the expression was first used to refer to outdoor spaces such as the Theater of Dionysus on the sloped side of the Acropolis in Athens. But the term has been a living part of literature for thousands of years and still involves a basic meaning of the presentation in *dialogue or *pantomime of *action involving *conflict between *characters.

theater-in-the-round

A current *synonym for arena theater, a viewing place with seats surrounding, or nearly surrounding, a central platform. Entrances and exits are usually made through the aisles. See ARENA THEATER.

Theater of the Absurd

An *avant-garde style of playwriting and presentation in which *conventions of *structure, *plot, and *characterization are ignored or distorted. In this contemporary form of drama, an irrational quality of nature is stressed, and man's isolation and aloneness are made central elements of *conflict. In Theater of the Absurd (*absurd* means "senseless," "illogical," "contrary to common sense"), *characters may appear in different forms and identities and may change sex, age, and personality; the presentation may have no fixed or determinable *setting; the sequence of time is fluid and indefinite. (See SURREALISM.) Among playwrights of this *genre may be included Edward Albee, Samuel Beckett, Jean Genet, Eugène Ionesco, and Harold Pinter. See EXISTENTIALISM.

theatricality

A quality of those actions and scenes that are artificial, spectacular, or extravagantly affected and pompous. Theatricality, an approximate *synonym for *exhibitionism* and *display,* is apparent in lavish *spectacles characteristic of elaborate *musical comedies and costly *pageants.

theme

(1) The central and dominating idea in a literary work; (2) a short *essay, such as a school or college *composition; (3) the message or moral implicit in any work of art. Thus, the theme (central idea) of Keats's *Ode on a Grecian Urn* is the permanence of art and the shortness of human life; the theme of Euripides's *The Trojan Women* is anguish over the seeming necessity for war. For further comment, see CARPE DIEM, UBI SUNT THEME.

theory (theoretical)

A conception, or view, of something; an explanation accounting for conjectured or known facts and conditions. (See HYPOTHESIS.) *Theory* is often used to mean "belief," "notion," or "opinion." *Theoretical* means "existing only in theory," "hypothetical," "speculative," and "not practical." Thus, *existentialism, for example, is a theoretical approach to *literature; one may express the theory that literature reflects life, or that it influences life, or that it *is* life.

thesaurus

A *dictionary, *encyclopedia, or other reference work, especially a treatment of *synonyms and *antonyms. *Thesaurus,* from a Greek word for "treasure," also means a storehouse, a repository of information. The best-known such work in English is Peter Mark Roget's *Thesaurus of the English Language.*

thesis

A *proposition for consideration, especially one to be discussed and proved or disproved; a *dissertation involving research on a particular subject. Thesis, from a Greek term meaning both "a setting down" and "something set down," differs from *theme in that the former deals with specific subject matter, whereas the latter refers to a general, pervasive, and dominating idea.

A thesis novel (or play), sometimes referred to as a novel (or drama) of ideas, illustrates, develops, and reinforces an *attitude or *point of view of its author. See PROBLEM NOVEL, PLAY; PROPAGANDA; ROMAN À THÈSE; SOCIOLOGICAL NOVEL, PLAY.

thespian

An actor or actress. Derived from the name of a sixth-century-B.C. Greek poet, *thespian* is usually applied in a derogatory sense to a self-important, "theatrical" stage person.

three unities

Classical principles of dramatic construction. See UNITIES, THREE; UNITY.

threnody

A *poem, *song, or speech of sorrow and lamentation. A threnody is a *dirge, a funeral song, a *lament. See MONODY.

thumb index

A series of labeled notches cut along the fore edge of a book to indicate divisions or sections. See INDEX.

timbre

The quality of a *sound, independent of *pitch and loudness, from which its manner of production can be inferred. *Timbre,* primarily a term in *phonetics, in music refers to the sound made by a particular instrument or voice. In both music and *prosody, *timbre* applies to the *tone (tone color) of sound.

tirade

An outburst of bitter words. *Tirade,* derived from Italian meaning "to shoot" or "a volley," may also refer to a long, uninterrupted speech on stage. (See CURSE, HARANGUE, INVECTIVE, MALEDICTION, SOLILOQUY.) The long speech in Dickens's *David Copperfield* in which Wilkins Micawber contemptuously unmasks Uriah Heep as a "transcendent and immortal hypocrite and perjurer" is a tirade.

title page

The page at the beginning of a book which indicates the name of the book, the author's or editor's name, and publication information (identity of publisher, place and date of publication). See BASTARD TITLE, HALF TITLE.

tmesis

The separation of a compound word by inserting another word or words between its parts. Tmesis, from Greek for "a cutting," is illustrated by "what things soever" for "whatsoever things" and "South, make no mistake, Carolina."

toast

A salutation; words of greeting, congratulation, or good wishes uttered before drinking. Presumably, this meaning of *toast* is figurative; the person being toasted adds flavor to the drink comparable to that added to bread by browning. In Sheridan's *School for Scandal,* this toast is offered:

> ... here's to the housewife that's thrifty!
> Let the toast pass;
> Drink to the lass;
> I'll warrant she'll prove an excuse for a glass.

tome

A large, heavy, or learned book. *Tome* may also refer to a volume forming part of a larger work: the word is derived from a Greek term meaning "a cut-off section."

tone

(1) An author's *attitude or *point of view toward his subject; in this sense, the tone of Flaubert's *Madame Bovary* is realistic, somber, and depressing; the tone of *The Swiss Family Robinson* is romantic and adventurous. (2) The devices used to create the *mood and *atmosphere of a literary work; in this sense, the tone of a poem consists of its *alliteration, *assonance, *consonance, *diction, *imagery, *meter, *rhyme, *symbolism, etc. (3) The musical quality in language. In *The Science of English Verse,* Sidney Lanier, an American poet and critic, suggested that the *sounds of words exhibit the qualities of timbre in music. The coordination of a series of sounds (rhyme to rhyme, vowel to vowel, etc.) he called tone color. See TIMBRE.

tongue twister

A word, or series of words, difficult to pronounce. Tongue twisters usually result from *alliteration ("Peter Piper picked a peck . . . ") or a change in consonant sounds ("the least police"; "the next best bet"). See SPOONERISM.

topical

An adjective referring to matters and concerns of current interest. *For Whom the Bell Tolls,* a 1940 novel by Ernest Hemingway, is topical: at that time, the problems of fascism and Nazism were receiving worldwide attention. *Topical* also has a meaning of "subject" or "topic"; a topical essay such as Milton's *Areopagitica* deals with one item: freedom of the press.

toponymy

The study of place-names. Toponymy, from Greek terms meaning "name of place," is the subject of George R. Stewart's *American Place-Names,* a dictionary giving the linguistic meaning and derivation of 12,000 names throughout the continental United States. See ONOMASTICS.

totem

An emblem of a family, group, or clan. From a North American Indian phrase meaning "brother-sister kin," *totem* usually refers to an object, animal, or bird which serves as a distinctive mark for those who adopt it or to which a group considers itself related. See SYMBOL.

touchstone

A test, *criterion, or standard, meanings derived from the use of this stone in detecting the purity of gold and silver. (See CONTROL, PROTOTYPE, SHIBBOLETH.) Matthew Arnold wrote:

> . . . there can be no more useful help for discovering what poetry belongs to the class of the truly excellent, and can therefore do us most good, than to have always in one's mind lines and expressions

of the great masters and to apply them as a touchstone to other poetry.

tour de force

A French phrase meaning "feat of strength or skill." The phrase applies to an exceptional achievement by an author, a stroke of genius unlikely to be equaled. (See CHEF D'OEUVRE.) André Malraux's *Man's Fate* was a tour de force. The phrase also refers to an adroit maneuver or skillful *technique in handling a difficult *situation. In *The Glass Key,* a hard-boiled *detective story, Dashiell Hammett has his fictional sleuth not only track down a murderer but, by a tour de force, also break up a bootlegging gang. The technique by which the *meter mirrors and echoes the pounding of hoofbeats in Browning's *How They Brought the Good News from Ghent to Aix* is a tour de force.

tract

A *pamphlet, *leaflet, or brief *treatise, usually dealing with a political or religious topic. *Tract* is derived from a Latin word meaning "to handle," "to treat."

trade book

A volume published in a form suitable for the general public and ordinarily available from a bookdealer (retailer). A trade book (one designed for the general trade, or general public) is distinguished from a *limited edition and text edition. (See TEXTBOOK.) A trade edition, designed for the general reader, is distinguished from a text (or textbook) edition. See EDITION.

tradition

A body of customs, beliefs, skills, or *sayings handed down from generation to generation or age to age. Thus, *popular ballads, *folktales, and *proverbs have been passed down through the centuries by oral tradition, or *oral transmission. Tradition, from Latin words meaning "given through," may be thought of as a body of literary *conventions inherited from the past: the tradition of *pastoral literature has lived for more than 2,000 years. Repairing stone walls was, and remains, a New England tradition, as is indicated in Robert Frost's *Mending Wall.* Nearly all the acts, customs, and beliefs of rustic natives in Hardy's *The Return of the Native* are traditional.

tragedy

A calamity, disaster, or fatal event. In literature, *tragedy* refers to any *composition with a somber *theme carried to a disastrous conclusion. From a Greek term meaning "goat song," tragedy involves death just as the sacrifice of *goats, *totems of primitive peoples, did in ancient rituals.

Specifically, *tragedy* is applied to a dramatic work, in prose or verse, that traces the career of a noble person whose character is flawed by some defect (jealousy, excessive ambition, pride, etc.) and whose actions cause him to break some moral precept or divine law, with ensuing downfall and destruction.

In the eighteenth century, writers of tragedy began to consider men and women of the middle classes as *protagonists. In today's theater, tragedy is often concerned with *proletarian themes; in such plays, the cause of downfall is the evils of society rather than flaws in character or the intervention of fate. See ACT, AGON, CATHARSIS, COMEDY, CONFLICT, DRAMA, HAMARTIA, HUBRIS.

tragic flaw

The principal defect (weakness in character) which leads to destruction. *Tragic flaw* and *hamartia are *synonyms.

tragicomedy

Any literary *composition, especially a *drama, combining elements of *tragedy and *comedy; an *incident or *episode of mixed tragic and comic action. *Tragicomedy* is usually applied to *plays in which events are apparently leading to a *catastrophe but in which happy endings are brought about by changes in circumstances or the intervention of a *deus ex machina. Shakespeare's *The Merchant of Venice* is a romantic comedy, but it is also a tragicomedy. Another example of the type is Corneille's *Le Cid.*

tranche de vie

A French term meaning "slice of life." See SLICE OF LIFE for discussion of this *technique of presenting a segment of actual and direct human experience.

transcendentalism

A form of philosophical *romanticism which places reliance on man's intuition and conscience. From Latin words meaning "climbing beyond," transcendentalism held that man's inner consciousness is divine, that in nature is revealed the whole of God's moral law, and that ultimate truth can be discovered by man's inmost feelings and a *morality guided by conscience.

Transcendentalism was based on doctrines of various European philosophers, especially the German Immanuel Kant (1724–1804), and was advanced by Goethe, Carlyle, and Coleridge. It took on special significance in New England, where Emerson and Thoreau were its chief sponsors. The two *documents that best express transcendentalism are Emerson's *Nature* and Thoreau's *Walden.* These two authors and other transcendentalists believed in living close to nature, accepted the dignity of manual labor, sought intellectual companionship, and revered self-reliance. In essence, transcendentalism was a religious movement, a branch of *epistemology, a "way of knowing."

transition

A movement from one position (idea, condition, topic) to another. Skilled writers employ transitional devices (conjunctions and linking phrases, word repetition, etc.) to move from one scene to another, from one topic to the next. In a *television program, theatrical production, and the like, transition is accomplished by sound effects, changes in lighting, music, *panning, and similar devices. See DISSOLVE.

transitory

An adjective meaning "brief, short-lived, temporary." One of the enduring themes of literature, especially lyric *poetry, is the transitory nature of man's life, of love, of happiness. Thousands of writers have expressed in hundreds of ways the truth that nothing which is human is enduring, permanent, or eternal. See UBI SUNT THEME.

translation

(1) A change or conversion to another form or appearance, such as Dr. Jekyll's changing into Mr. Hyde in Stevenson's famous short story; (2) bearing, carrying, or moving from one place to another, such as the translation of an Old Testament prophet into Heaven; (3) the rendering of something written or spoken into another language. The best-known translation in English is the King James *Bible. (See AUTHORIZED.) Keats's sonnet *On First Looking into Chapman's Homer* was inspired by a translation from Greek by George Chapman (1559–1634), an English poet and translator.

transmogrification

A change in appearance or form, especially one that is bizarre or grotesque. Transmogrification occurs in some *fairy tales (people into toads, etc.) and in stories like Mary Shelley's *Frankenstein,* in which human and animal organs are transformed into a monster. See TRANSLATION.

travesty

A *burlesque of a serious literary work, marked by ludicrous, grotesque, and debased imitative style. Travesty, from a French word meaning "disguised" and Latin terms for "across" and "clothes," treats a dignified topic frivolously or absurdly, whereas a *mock epic treats an unimportant subject seriously. Cervantes' *Don Quixote* is a travesty on the medieval *romance.

treatise

A formal, systematic treatment of a topic, usually longer,

more detailed, and more thoroughly documented than an *essay. A treatise usually deals with the principles of an involved and difficult subject, such as David Hume's *Treatise of Human Nature.* See DISSERTATION.

triad

A group of three, especially of three closely related or associated persons, ideas, or objects. *Triad* is applied specifically to three lyric *stanzas of the *Pindaric ode: the *strophe, *antistrophe, and *epode.

tribrach

A metrical *foot of three short (unstressed) *syllables. The tribrach is uncommon in English verse. See FOOT, METER.

trick ending

A *synonym for *surprise ending. A trick ending, also called a twist ending, occurs when a totally unexpected and unprepared-for turn of events alters the outcome of action in a narrative work. The use of a *deus ex machina device usually results in such a conclusion. Many of the short stories of O. Henry have been judged to have trick endings, but some of them develop outcomes that are as imaginative and ingenious as they are tricky.

trilogy

A series of three novels, plays, or operas that, although individually complete, are related in *theme or sequence. (See SEQUEL.) The three parts of Shakespeare's *Henry VI* form a trilogy; so do John Dos Passos' *The 42nd Parallel, Nineteen-Nineteen,* and *The Big Money* (combined in *U.S.A.*) and Arnold Bennett's *Clayhanger* sequence: *Clayhanger, Hilda Lessways,* and *These Twain.* The term *trilogy* was originally applied to a group of three tragedies performed in *Dionysia, such as the *Oresteia* of Aeschylus that dramatized the Agamemnon-Orestes story. See TETRALOGY.

trimeter

A verse (line) of three feet. For examples of trimeter, see METER.

triolet

An eight-line *stanza employing only two *rhymes. *Triolet* means "little trio," a sense explained by the fact that the first line is repeated three times. This triolet is by Thomas Hardy:

> How great my grief, my joys how few,
> Since first it was my fate to know thee!
> Have the slow years not brought to view
> How great my grief, my joys how few,
> Nor memory shaped old times anew,
> Nor loving-kindness helped to show thee
> How great my grief, my joys how few,
> Since first it was my fate to know thee?

triplet

Three successive lines or verses, especially when rhyming and of the same length; a *stanza of three lines. (See TERCET, TERZA RIMA, TRISTICH.) This is a triplet by Archibald MacLeish:

> Graves in the wild earth: in the Godless sand:
> None know the place of their bones: as for mine
> Strangers will dig my grave in a stony land.

tristich

A *strophe, *stanza, or *poem consisting of three lines. A tristich, from Greek words meaning "three rows" or "three lines," is a synonym for TERCET, which see.

trisyllabic

Having three *syllables; a word such as *pen·du·lum*. *Trisyllabic* is sometimes used in the phrase *trisyllabic rhyme* (also called triple rhyme), as in *fortunate* and *importunate*. See FEMININE RHYME.

tritagonist

The third actor in ancient Greek tragedy. *Tritagonist* should be compared with *antagonist and *protagonist. See AGON.

triteness

A characteristic of writing or speech that lacks freshness and effectiveness because of constant overuse. *Triteness* (derived from a Latin verb meaning "to wear down") is a *synonym for *banality, *cliché, and *hackneyed language. See BROMIDE.

trivium

The three studies leading to a bachelor's degree in medieval universities: *grammar, *logic, and *rhetoric. The trivium was the lower division of the *seven liberal arts. See QUADRIVIUM.

trochee

A *foot of two syllables: a long (stressed) syllable followed by a short (unstressed) one as in the word *lucky*. For an example of the trochee, or trochaic verse, see METER.

trope

Any literary or rhetorical device (such as *metaphor, *metonymy, *simile, etc.) which consists of the use of words in other than their *literal sense. *Trope*, from a Greek word meaning "turn" or "turning," involves a turn or change of sense and is a *synonym for *figure of speech. *Trope* also refers to an addition to medieval liturgical *drama or to the *liturgy of religious services. One such amplification, the *quem quaeritis trope, was an important part of liturgical plays and *pageants.

tropism

A term from biology, tropism is the orientation (adjustment) of an organism through growth, rather than movement, in response to an external stimulus. In literature, a tropism is a compulsive reaction from external stimuli, the ideas and emotions within characters that are not spoken in *interior monologue and are not transmitted by sensations. Tropisms may also be defined as the things which are not said, the movements which cross the consciousness of characters fleetingly and vaguely. A tropism in *avant-garde writing is a form of "subconversation." See STREAM OF CONSCIOUSNESS.

troubadour

A *medieval lyric poet who wrote and sang *songs, chiefly on the theme of *courtly love. Troubadours were noted for inventiveness and experimentation in metrical forms. Troubadours were also known as trouvères, although the latter wrote songs of adventurous deeds as well as of chivalric love. See GLEEMAN, JONGLEUR, MINNESINGER.

truism

An obvious, self-evident truth. A truism, which may be a *maxim or *proverb, is always a *cliché and a *platitude.

Tudor

A reference to the reigns of Tudor monarchs in England, 1485–1603. Tudor was the name of the fifteenth-century Welshman, Owen Tudor, whose line became the ruling dynasty of England with the coronation of Henry VII in 1485 and ended with the death of Elizabeth I in 1603.

type

(1) A block, usually of metal, having on its upper surface a letter or character in relief; (2) a literary *genre, a *form of writing such as the novel, the essay, etc.; (3) a person with specific characteristics and qualities. In that type of *composition called the novel, Sinclair Lewis depicted a type of American businessman whose name has entered the language as Babbittry. See PROTOTYPE.

typescript

A typewritten copy of a *composition; typewritten matter as distinguished from handwritten or printed material. See COPY, MANUSCRIPT.

typography

The process, or art, of printing from type. *Typography* applies to the work of setting and arranging blocks of *type and also to the general character and appearance of printed material. See FORMAT.

typology

(1) A systematic study and classification of kinds of *type. (2) *Symbolism, the practice of representing things by objects; for instance, in the typology of American businessmen, Babbitt represents that *type which is smug and self-satisfied.

ubi sunt theme

This name is derived from the Latin words meaning "where are?" that began numerous *medieval poems. The full phrase, *Ubi sunt qui ante nos fuerunt* ("Where are those who were before us?"), suggests the impermanence of youth, beauty, and life itself. The ubi sunt theme (also referred to as a *formula and *motif) is memorably illustrated in the entry for BALLADE. See TRANSITORY.

ultima Thule

The highest degree attainable; the farthest point; the limit of any journey. Ultima Thule, a legendary island in "the Northern Ocean," has come to signify the *epitome of remoteness or any unattainable ideal or goal. These lines appear in Poe's *Dream-Land:*

> I have reached these lands but newly
> From an ultimate dim Thule—
> From a wild, weird clime that lieth, sublime,
> Out of Space—out of Time.

umlaut

A *diacritical mark used to indicate the *sound of a vowel, as in German *schön* ("beautiful") and *Tannhäuser* (the *opera by Richard Wagner).

unabridged

Not shortened. (See ABRIDGED.) *Unabridged* is an adjective often applied to a *dictionary which has not been reduced in size by a deliberate omission of terms and definitions and is therefore the most *comprehensive edition of a given work.

uncial

A descriptive name for capital letters with added curves, used chiefly in Greek and Latin *manuscripts of the third to the ninth century. *Uncial* also refers to manuscripts written in such letters.

understatement
A form of *humor or *irony in which something is intentionally represented less strongly or strikingly than facts would warrant. *Understatement,* remarks phrased in moderate, restrained terms, is an *antonym of *exaggeration and *hyperbole. See LITOTES, MEIOSIS.

unities, three
Principles of dramatic composition. According to *Aristotelian *aesthetics, a play was required to represent action as taking place in one day (unity of *time*), as occurring in one place (unity of *place*), and as having a single plot (unity of *action*). Plays in English have not usually observed these unities, which tend to restrict dramatic possibilities and limit *characterization. However, Shakespeare's *Comedy of Errors* and *The Tempest* do comply with these principles. A modern play which follows the unities of time, place, and action is Tennessee Williams's *Cat on a Hot Tin Roof.*

unity
Oneness; the state of being one. In literature, *unity* involves the concept that a work should exhibit some principle of *organization in which all parts are related in such a way that an organic whole is formed. Although a unified literary selection has a clear and logical relation of part to part, the source of unity varies from work to work. *Plot or *characterization or *mood or *theme may each be a unifying force. See CONTROLLING IMAGE, DOMINANT IMPRESSION, PURPOSE.

universality
The comprehensiveness of the universe; existence everywhere. Universality is a quality in literature which gives it a significance and appeal not limited to place or time. When writing presents emotions and actions common to all people of all civilizations in ways that remain meaningful indefinitely, that writing possesses universality. Longinus, a Greek philosopher of the third century, wrote, "We may regard those words as truly noble and sublime which please all and please always." For further comment on universality, see CLASSIC.

uppercase
A capital letter. (See LOWERCASE.) By extension, *uppercase* is sometimes used to describe persons, institutions, or events that are impressive, significant, or outstanding.

upstage

On or toward the back of the stage. (See DOWNSTAGE.) *Upstage* is also used as an adjective to mean haughty, aloof, or supercilious and as a verb to signify behaving snobbishly.

urbanity

Elegant politeness, courtesy; refinement; *suavity. *Urbanity,* derived from a Latin word meaning "city," may be contrasted with one meaning of *barbarism and with *Philistine but not necessarily with *pastoral. An urbane person is polished, elegant, and sophisticated.

usage

Custom, practice. In literature, *usage* applies to the *form and *structure of *types (*genres), to *conventions, to such diverse matters as spelling, punctuation, *format, *typography, *sentence structure, and dozens of related matters. In speech, usage is the standard which decrees what is "right" and "wrong" in oral communication. In general, usage refers to the customary manner in which a language is written or spoken.

utilitarianism

An eighteenth-century doctrine of ethics teaching that virtue and goodness are based on utility (usefulness) and that conduct should attempt to promote the greatest happiness for the greatest number of persons. *Utilitarianism* was considered synonymous with *pleasure* by its founder (Jeremy Bentham), but later writers, including John Stuart Mill, considered pleasure and happiness to be qualitative (matters of degree) rather than quantitative. See HEDONISM, HUMANISM.

utopian

Founded upon or involving ideal or imaginary perfection. *Utopian,* from a Greek word meaning "no place," "nowhere," is often applied to a *type of literature in which an ideal society is depicted. *Utopia,* which now means an ideal country or region, was a name (title) given in 1516 by Sir Thomas More to a book describing an imaginary island that enjoyed perfection in laws, politics, customs, etc. Among many earlier and later works dealing with a utopia as a visionary system of living are Plato's *Republic,* Francis Bacon's *New Atlantis,* Samuel Butler's *Erewhon,* Edward Bellamy's *Looking Backward,* H. G. Wells's *A Modern Utopia,* and Aldous Huxley's *Brave New World.* Numerous treatments of utopian subjects are obviously satiric. See SATIRE.

Utopian is also applied to persons considered idealistic and visionary and to ardent but impractical political or social reformers.

vade mecum

A Latin phrase meaning "go with me" and applied to any of several items a person might carry with him for frequent or regular use. *Vade mecum* is used most often for a manual, handbook, or other volume designed for ready reference and utilized as a "companion." The term is occasionally applied to one's controlling philosophy or fixed beliefs in life.

vanity publishing

The publication of books by a printing house that diverts all, or nearly all, costs and risks to an author. In this phrase, *vanity* has its most frequent meaning: "excessive pride" in one's accomplishments or self-styled accomplishments.

vaporous

Vaguely formed, unreliable, or fanciful. The term is applied to literary works that are airy and unsubstantial, as, for instance, *Cavalier poetry or some of the songs appearing more or less incidentally in Shakespeare's comedies.

vapors

Now an archaic term, *vapors* was used constantly in the eighteenth century to explain the eccentric behavior of people. Persons who acted strangely—in a mental depression, with low spirits—were said to be suffering from exhalations given off by the stomach or other organs. Heroines in novels of the era were especially subject to "attacks of the vapors," as is suggested in these lines by Edward Young:

> Sometimes, thro pride, the sexes change their airs:
> My lord has vapours, and my lady swears.

variorum

An adjective meaning "containing different versions of the text by various editors." A variorum edition of an author's work contains notes and comments by a number of scholars and critics. The term is an abbreviation of a Latin phrase, *cum notis variorum* ("with notes of various people"). Possibly the best-known variorum edition in English is the New Variorum Shakespeare.

vaudeville

A variety show, theatrical entertainment consisting of individual performances, acts, dances, dramatic sketches, acrobatic feats, and other unrelated stunts. The term is derived from Vau-de-Vire, a valley in France noted for satirical songs. Vaudeville has declined in popularity since the advent of talking films and, later, *television.

vehicle

A vehicle is a means of conveyance or transport. In literature, *vehicle* is extended to suggest the means by which one accomplishes his purpose. Thus it is said that an author used the vehicle of prose or poetry or that he chose the vehicle of *satire or *humor or whatnot. See GENRE, PURPOSE.

vellum

Lambskin, kidskin, or calfskin treated for use as a writing surface. *Parchment, made from the skin of sheep, was once widely used in the preparation of diplomas. Books bound in *vellum* are rare and costly. *Vellum,* derived from a French term for "of calf" and, more remotely, from a Latin word which, as a diminutive of *calf,* provides the word *veal,* is a form of rare and fine parchment.

venal, venial

These similar-appearing words occur constantly in literature and in comment on literary works. *Venal* means "corruptible," "open to bribery," and is derived from a Latin word equivalent in meaning to "for sale." *Venial* means "not seriously wrong," "able to be forgiven easily," "trifling," "minor." Its derivation is traced to a Latin word meaning "favor," "indulgence," or "love." Satan's revolt against God (as described in *Paradise Lost,* for example) was serious and therefore venal. When Mark Twain's Huck Finn ran away, his transgression was minor and therefore venial.

verbal, oral

These words are often confused in discussion of literary works. *Verbal* applies to words, oral or written, in which thought is expressed. *Oral* is properly applied only to what is uttered by word of mouth. A verbal agreement means an agreement *in words,* and an oral agreement means one that is only *spoken.*

verbatim

A term meaning "in exactly the same words," "corresponding word for word to the original source or text." During the *Middle Ages (before the advent of *printing), copyists spent long hours making verbatim copies of *manuscripts. An *anthology contains verbatim copies of the literary works it includes.

verbiage

Wordiness, an overabundance or superfluity of words. Certain *double-decker novels and other works notable more for excessive details and *atmosphere than for *theme or literary skills are said to be marked by verbiage.

verbid

A nonfinite verb form: an infinitive or participle. The term is a combination of *verb* and the suffix *-id* (meaning "membership").

verbosity

Long-windedness, wordiness, prolixity. Dr. Johnson's definition of *network* (a combination of filaments and lines) is an example of verbosity: "anything reticulated or decussated with interstices between the intersections."

verisimilitude

Likelihood, probability, the appearance or semblance of truth. A work in which action and characters seem to readers to be "acceptable" and to "make sense" as an adequate representation of reality is said to possess verisimilitude. This quality, whether the actuality and *realism of Steinbeck's *The Grapes of Wrath* or the imaginative power of Maugham's *Of Human Bondage,* is achieved by a skillful selection and presentation of what the reader is convinced is the stuff of life. The term can loosely be translated as "like truth."

verist

A term applied to those writers who maintain that rigid and total representation of truth and reality is essential to literature. Consequently, verists hold that everything that is real must be represented, not excluding the vulgar, the ugly, the sordid, and even the obscene. Such writers as D. H. Lawrence and Theodore Dreiser have been called verists by some critics. See REALISM.

vernacular

An adjective meaning "native" or originating in the place of its occurrence or use. A work written in the native idiom of a locality is said to be "in the vernacular." The language of rustics in many of Thomas Hardy's novels is vernacular as are many of their customs and beliefs. Robert Burns's choice of Scottish *locale and language resulted in the production of a body of vernacular literature.

vers de société

Humorous, light, and even sportive verse dealing with the follies and fashions of the era in which it is composed (see LIGHT VERSE). The term, French in origin and meaning "society verse," is applied to works that deal amusedly and amusingly with polite society and its often frivolous concerns. Vers de société is sometimes gently satiric and elaborately amorous, but it is always witty in intention if not in actuality. The Earl of Rochester wrote vers de société in this proposed *epitaph for Charles II of England:

> Here lies our sovereign lord, the King,
> Whose word no man relies on.
> He never says a foolish thing,
> Nor ever does a wise one.

verse

A term of several meanings, only one of which is basic and fully accurate: one line of a poem. *Verse* comes from a Latin word meaning "a turning" and is properly applied to the method by which one metrical line "turns" into a new line. A verse is also mistakenly called a *stanza, which is actually a succession of lines (verses) bound together by some scheme (usually *rhyme) and forming one of a series of similar groups that make up a *poem. *Verse* is also a name given to metrical composition in general. For a distinction between verse and a poem, see POETRY.

versification

Metrical *structure, the art and practice of composing verse in terms of related mechanical elements. Versification involves *accent, *foot, *meter, *rhyme, *rhythm, and *stanza form. For further discussion of versification, see METRICS, PROSODY, SCANSION. For a working definition, consider versification as a matter of the structural form of a *verse or a *stanza.

vers libre

A French term for *free verse. Vers libre, also known as *polyphonic prose, is distinguished from conventional verse by its irregular metrical pattern. Vers libre relies more upon *cadence than uniform metrical *feet and does not always follow the usual *rhythm of poetry. Vers libre (free verse) is an ancient form; the Psalms and the Song of Solomon from the Bible are in free verse. Much of the poetry of Walt Whitman and Carl Sandburg is vers libre, a form of experimentation that has contributed to freeing poetry from formal conventions of *structure and subject matter. An example of vers libre and a statement of its purpose appear in these lines by Ezra Pound:

> Go, little naked and impudent songs.

Go with a light foot!
(Or with two light feet, if it please you.)
Go and dance shamelessly!
Go with impertinent frolic.

verso

A left-hand page of a manuscript or book. *Verso* is an abbreviation of Latin *verso folio* ("with the page turned"). See RECTO.

viable

An adjective meaning "having the ability to live, grow, expand, or develop." *Viable* is applied in literature to ideas and concepts that are vivid and real, that are stimulating to the imagination, the intellect, or the senses. Writing which is not considered real, vivid, and stimulating is called nonviable.

Victorian

An adjective applied to the reign of Queen Victoria (1837–1901) and to the characteristic attitudes and qualities of that *era. Specifically, the term *Victorian* suggests complacency, hypocrisy, smugness, and moral earnestness. Features of the *epoch were self-satisfaction caused by greatly increased national wealth and prosperity; scientific and industrial advances; and strengthened standards of decency and morality. As applied to literature, *Victorian* usually connotes humorlessness, unquestioning acceptance of *orthodoxy and authority in religious and political matters, prudishness, and rigid adherence to moral and social *conventions. Actually, Victorian literature is complex and many-sided, but the word *Victorian* somewhat incorrectly carries labels of "empty respectability," "false modesty," and "callous unconcern."

videlicet

Usually abbreviated to *viz., videlicet* (a Latin term meaning "that is to say") is an expression in formal English for *namely.* It is common in eighteenth- and nineteenth-century prose but has rarely appeared in twentieth-century writing of any sort.

video

See AUDIO. *Video* in Latin means "I see."

viewpoint

An *attitude of mind, or the circumstances of an individual that contribute to an attitude. *Viewpoint* also means the place or position affording a view of any *action or *setting. See POINT OF VIEW.

vignette

A French term meaning "little vine" (from the vinelike

decorations in early *manuscripts and *books), *vignette* is now usually applied to a *sketch or other brief literary work notable for precision of phrasing and delicacy of feeling. It suggests "a pleasing picture" or "a brief impression" of a *scene, *character, or *situation.

villain

A character in a *play, *novel, *short story, or other work who constitutes an evil or unwholesome agency in the *plot. A villain acts in opposition to the *hero. (See AGON, ANTAGONIST.) In some works of literature, the villain is the center of interest: Satan in Milton's *Paradise Lost,* Macbeth in Shakespeare's *Macbeth,* Othello in Shakespeare's *Othello,* and Don Juan in works by Molière, Mozart, Dumas, Corneille, and Rostand.

villanelle

A short poem of fixed form, written in five three-line *stanzas (*tercets) and a concluding four-line stanza (*quatrain). Only two rhymes are employed in the entire length (nineteen lines) of a villanelle. Here are the first three stanzas of a villanelle by W. E. Henley:

A dainty thing's the Villanelle,
Sly, musical, a jewel in rhyme.
It serves its purpose passing well.

A double-clappered silver bell,
That must be made to clink in chime,
A dainty thing's the Villanelle.

And if you wish to flute a spell,
Or ask a meeting 'neath the lime,
It serves its purpose passing well.

virelay

An old French form for a short *poem. A virelay is composed of short lines using two *rhymes and having two opening lines recurring at intervals. Another form of virelay consists of *stanzas made up of shorter and longer lines, the lines of each kind rhyming within one stanza and with the rhymes of shorter lines within one stanza rhyming with longer lines in a succeeding stanza. Neither form appears in English literature of merit, possibly because of difficulties with the set rhyming of English words, to say nothing of monotony.

vis-à-vis

A French term meaning "face to face." The phrase also appears in literature with the meaning of one's "opposite number" (person of equal rank, position, etc.). As a preposition, *vis-à-vis* means "compared with," "in relation to."

viz.

Namely. See VIDELICET.

volta

An Italian word meaning "a turn," *volta* is used to refer to the change in thought and feeling which divides the *octave from the *sestet in some *sonnets. In many sonnets, the first eight lines (the octave) state a premise, ask a question, or suggest a theme; the concluding six lines (the sestet) resolve the problem suggested by providing a conclusion or giving some sort of answer. See ITALIAN SONNET.

voluptuary

A person who devotes his life to the pursuit and enjoyment of luxury and sensual pleasures. Those who participated in the orgiastic festivals of *Dionysia held in honor of Dionysus, the god of fertility and wine, were voluptuaries. Perhaps unfairly, Oscar Wilde has been called the greatest voluptuary in recent English literature because of sensual excesses. See HEDONISM.

vorticism

An artistic movement begun in the early twentieth century that relates art forms to the machine and to modern industrial civilization. *Vorticism,* stemming from *cubism and *futurism, insists on an imaginative reconstruction of nature in formal (mechanistic) designs, regarding lifelike representation as immaterial. The movement, once noisy and disturbing in literary circles, has lessened in shock value and activity during the past half century. Among writers caught up in the movement were Wyndham Lewis, Ezra Pound, and T. S. Eliot.

vowel rhyme

A form of *rhyme in which any vowel sound is permitted to agree with any other. Because the ear is accustomed to distinctions among the varied sounds of *a, e, i, o,* and *u,* vowel rhyme is infrequent in English verse, although Emily Dickinson occasionally used it. See NEAR RHYME.

vox populi

A Latin phrase meaning "voice of the people." It is used to refer to national sentiment, to majority opinion, and to grassroots feelings.

voyeurism

The practice of deriving sexual gratification from observing sexual acts or objects. The appeal of nudity and obscenity in certain modern plays and the graphic depiction of sexual acts in some modern novels and stories are traceable, at least in part, to voyeurism.

vulgarism

A word or phrase used in coarse, unrefined, and uneducated speech. (See BARBARISM.) A vulgarism is not necessarily indecent or obscene; the term derives its name from a Latin word meaning "the general public" and is applicable to all speech that is characterized by ignorance, lack of breeding, and tastelessness. See VERNACULAR.

vulgarity

The state or quality of being banal, lewd, or uncouth. The vulgarity attributed to some works of literature is due to their alleged lack of distinction, aesthetic value, and charm. See REALISM.

Vulgate

The Latin version of the Bible, prepared in the fourth century A.D. and used as an *authorized version in *liturgical services by the Roman Catholic Church. *Vulgate* has been extended to apply to any commonly recognized version or text of a work and further extended to mean "common" and "generally accepted."

W

Walpurgisnacht

The eve of May Day, when, according to legend, the witch world was supposed to revel in certain places. (The term is German for Walpurgis Night; Walpurgis was an eighth-century English nun involved in introducing Christianity to the Germans.) The word is used to suggest evil or bedlam.

Wanderjahr

A German term meaning "a year of wandering." The word is applied to a period in a person's life during which he is absent from his normal place of work or study and is engaged in travel, thought, and a search for new experiences or insight.

watermark

A design impressed into paper during manufacture, visible when held to light. Watermarks have been employed since the thirteenth century and have helped to establish the authenticity of certain *manuscripts, including some of James Boswell, the biographer of Johnson.

weak ending

A verse ending in which metrical *stress falls on a syllable or word which would not normally be stressed. In this excerpt from Shakespeare's *The Tempest,* stress falls on *and* at the end of the first line:

> Thy mother was a piece of virtue, and
> She said thou wast my daughter.

Weltanschauung

A German term for "manner of looking at the world." The term is sometimes applied to the philosophy of an individual or a group, sometimes to one's conception of world civilization and one's relation to it. A related word, also German, is *Weltansicht,* meaning "a world view," "an attitude toward life and reality."

welter

A confused mass; a jumble; a state of commotion or turmoil. During periods of political upheaval or opposing literary trends, writing and writers are in a welter of conflicting opinions, as during the latter half of the twentieth century.

Weltpolitik

A German word meaning "world politics"; it is applied to the policies that a nation follows in its international relations.

Weltschmerz

This German word meaning "world pain" may be defined as "sentimental pessimism." It expresses the sorrow, disillusionment, and discontent that one feels and reluctantly accepts as a part of life. Many writers of the past and present have exhibited Weltschmerz in their writings, actions, and attitude toward society, especially *avant-garde and *existentialist authors.

Western story

The traditional Western pits bad guys against good guys, depicts a long and dramatic chase or pursuit, and ends with the good guys bloody but victorious. The usual setting is a short main street in a frontier village. In recent years, some accomplished writers such as Walter Van Tilburg Clark, Conrad Richter, A. B. Guthrie, and H. L. Davis have written Western stories that avoid *hackneyed situations and *stereotyped characters, that treat the West as a dramatic *symbol, and that stay closer to real *history than *pulp writers and film serials do.

whimsy

Fanciful, capricious, or playful *humor dealing with odd or bizarre situations. Whimsical writing, such as the essays of Charles Lamb or the plays of Sir James M. Barrie, is inspired by fanciful or fantastic moods. *Whimsy* is formed from *whim* (freakish fancy, sudden desire) and *fantasy* (unrestrained imagination). Both *whimsy* and *whim* suggest a quaint, humorous inclination; *whim* emphasizes the idea of capriciousness, *whimsy* that of fancifulness. Peter Pan, the boy who never grew up, is a thoroughly whimsical character.

whodunit

An informal term for a narrative dealing with murder and detection of the criminal. See DETECTIVE STORY, ROMAN POLICIER.

widow

An incomplete line of type at the top of a page; a short last line of a paragraph.

wing

A flat (or platform) placed at the side of a stage, facing toward the auditorium, that conceals the area offstage. A series of wings, designed for quick and easy movement, is generally used on each side of the stage to provide scenes of varying depth, usually in conjunction with a backdrop (rear curtain). Wings are less important in theater design and staging than they were until a few decades ago because of increasing emphasis upon realistic settings.

wipe

A *technique in film editing by which the projected *image of a scene appears to be pushed off, or wiped off, the screen by the image that follows. See FADING.

wisecrack

An informal term for a clever, smart, or facetious remark. The plays of Oscar Wilde and Noel Coward, for instance, abound in wisecracks, although usually such scintillating remarks are classified as *bons mots or *wit.

wit

Acute perception and cleverly appropriate expression of ideas providing amusement and pleasure. *Wit* is derived from an Old English word (*witan*) meaning "to know"; hence comes the definition of *wit* as primarily a matter of sense and understanding. In comparison with *humor, wit is an intellectual display of cleverness and quickness of perception, whereas humor is less obviously mental in its approach to the weaknesses, foibles, and absurd ideas and actions of people generally. Wit is wholly dependent upon apt phrasing; humor rises from situations or incidents and does not rely on sharpness or felicity of expression. Humor involves a sympathetic recognition of humanity and its incongruities; wit plays with words, develops startling contrasts, and appears often in *epigrams and *paradoxes.

The ability to see, and to express recognition of, what is amusing and clever (the basic purpose of wit and humor) is clearly shown by that superb wit and humorist Falstaff in Shakespeare's *Henry IV*, Part 1. Falstaff's use of puns and his verbal fencing illustrate his wit. Falstaff's bluffing, his inward laughter at himself, and his and the reader's understanding of the ludicrousness of situations involved are elements of humor.

woodcut

A carved block of wood from which prints are made; an *impression or print from such a block. See BLOCK PRINTING.

word

A unit of language, a particular kind of sign called a *symbol.

A word has three relationships: with other words with which it is used; with persons who write, read, hear, or speak it; with the thing (object, idea) that it represents—its *referent. The relation of words with each other is a matter of *grammar. Relation between words and people is the concern of *general semantics. The relation of words to their referents is a matter of *semantics.

No word can ever really have a meaning as exact as, for instance, the measurements of a physical object. Words exist in people's minds and, since minds differ, no word can inevitably call up an identical meaning for everyone who uses or hears it. When Humpty Dumpty told Alice, "When I use a word, it means just what I choose it to mean—neither more nor less," he was far from speaking nonsense. Words are symbols whose arbitrary relation to what they represent must always be kept in mind.

writer's block

An inability to complete a work started or to begin a project that has been planned in the writer's mind but not set down. Many writers of the past and present have suffered from such blockages, apparently caused by mental and emotional disturbances more than by physical conditions.

writer's cramp

Spasmodic contractions of the muscles of thumb and forefinger, presumably caused by prolonged or excessive writing.

X

xenophobia

Unreasonable fear or hatred of foreigners or strangers or of customs and attitudes that appear foreign or strange. The attitude of Antonio and other characters to Shylock in Shakespeare's *Merchant of Venice* has been termed an example of xenophobia. The Moorish ancestry and background of Iago in *Othello* are considered by some readers an example of xenophobia as displayed in a *characterization containing elements of Satan, vice, malcontent, and envy.

xerography

A process for making copies of printed, pictorial, or written material from paper or film. Areas on a sheet of plain paper corresponding to areas on the original to be reproduced are sensitized with static electricity. The term derives its name from *xero,* a Greek combining element meaning "dry," and *graphy* ("drawing, writing"). See PRINTING.

Y

yahoo
A coarse, rough, uncouth person. The term was coined by Jonathan Swift, who applied it in *Gulliver's Travels* to a race of manlike brutes. Mark Twain and other writers have used *yahoo* to refer to yokels or louts (rustics, bumpkins).

Yahweh
A name for God that is commonly rendered as Jehovah. It is also spelled *Yahwe, Yahveh,* and *Yahve.*

yarn
An informal name for a *tale, especially a long, rambling story of adventure or bizarre events.

yearbook
A book published annually that contains information and statistics about the year just ended. College yearbooks and encyclopedia yearbooks are illustrative. See ALMANAC, ANNALS, ANNUALS.

yellow journalism
Sensational journalism which developed in the United States during the last two decades of the nineteenth century. It derives its name from an experiment in color printing designed to attract newspaper circulation.

Zeitgeist

A phrase from German meaning "the spirit of the time." It refers to the general trend of thought or feeling characteristic of a particular period of time. For example, during the *era immediately following World War I, many writers felt that, as a result of social upheaval, the world was in a Zeitgeist of cultural, political, and emotional instability. See LOST GENERATION.

zeugma

The use of a verb with two subjects or two objects or of an adjective with two nouns, although the verb or adjective is appropriate to only one noun: "to wage war and peace." This joining, or yoking, is called *syllepsis if the construction is grammatically correct. Strictly speaking, "with tearful eyes and hearts" is zeugma (an incorrect construction), and so is Dickens's statement in *The Pickwick Papers:* "Miss Bolo ... went straight home, in a flood of tears, and a sedan chair." "Neither John nor we are willing" is an example of syllepsis (the construction is correct, although the verb *are* does not agree in number with one of its subjects). See ENALLAGE.